PENGUIN BOOKS

COLOSSUS

'One of the world's 100 most influential people' *Time Magazine*

'A talented controversialist. He brings a wealth of historical knowledge to bear on big questions' *Independent*

'In *Colossus* he turns his formidable powers of analysis toward the "American Empire," offering a brief history as well as a provocative argument . . . it is sure to shake the assumptions of both fans and critics of the American Empire – including those who deny that such a thing even exists' Max Boot, author of *The Savage Wars of Peace: Small Wars and the Rise of American Power*

'Illuminating, entertaining and often contentious' *The Times*

'Niall Ferguson takes as a premise that an American empire exists and that the world at large benefits from it. Even those who disagree with his perspective will find *Colossus* an immensely learned and useful book written with great verve and historical breadth' William Roger Louis, author of *The British Empire in the Middle East, 1945–1951*

'Every page of *Colossus* is provocative. Niall Ferguson poses and puts tentative answers to every question that foreigners ask about America and that Americans ought to ask about themselves' Ernest May, author of *Strange Victory: Hitler's Conquest of France and Imperial Democracy*

'Challenging and provocative' *Mail on Sunday*

'Niall Ferguson combines a prodigious output with clear, fluent writing and the all-too-rare ability to blend economic analysis with that of politics' *Economist*

Niall Ferguson is Professor of International History at Harvard University, Senior Research Fellow of Jesus College, Oxford University, and a Senior Fellow of the Hoover Institution, Stanford University. He is the author of *Paper and Iron*, *The House of Rothschild* (two volumes), *The Pity of War*, *The Cash Nexus*, *Empire* and *Colossus*. He was also the editor of *Virtual History*. He lives in Oxfordshire with his wife and three children.

COLOSSUS

THE RISE AND FALL OF THE AMERICAN EMPIRE

NIALL FERGUSON

PENGUIN BOOKS

For John and Diana Herzog

PENGUIN BOOKS

Published by the Penguin Group
Penguin Books Ltd, 80 Strand, London WC2R 0RL, England
Penguin Group (USA), Inc., 375 Hudson Street, New York, New York 10014, USA
Penguin Group (Canada), 10 Alcorn Avenue, Toronto, Ontario, Canada M4V 3B2
(a division of Pearson Penguin Canada Inc.)
Penguin Ireland, 25 St Stephen's Green, Dublin 2, Ireland (a division of Penguin Books Ltd)
Penguin Group (Australia), 250 Camberwell Road, Camberwell, Victoria 3124, Australia
(a division of Pearson Australia Group Pty Ltd)
Penguin Books India Pvt Ltd, 11 Community Centre,
Panchsheel Park, New Delhi – 110 017, India
Penguin Group (NZ), cnr Airborne and Rosedale Roads, Albany
Auckland 1310, New Zealand (a division of Pearson New Zealand Ltd)
Penguin Books (South Africa) (Pty) Ltd, 24 Sturdee Avenue, Rosebank 2196, South Africa

Penguin Books Ltd, Registered Offices: 80 Strand, London WC2R 0RL, England

www.penguin.com

First published in the United States of America by The Penguin Press New York 2004
Published simultaneously in Great Britain by Allen Lane
Published with a new Preface in Penguin Books 2005

4

Copyright © Niall Ferguson, 2004, 2005

Printed in England by Clays Ltd, St Ives plc

CONTENTS

Old Europe will have to lean on our shoulders, and to hobble along by our side, under the monkish trammels of priests and kings, as she can. What a colossus shall we be.

THOMAS JEFFERSON, 1816

. . . to me strength is my bane,
And proves the source of all my miseries;
So many, and so huge, that each apart
Would ask a life to wail, but chief of all,
O loss of sight, of thee I most complain!
Blind among enemies, O worse than chains,
Dungeon, or beggary, or decrepit age!

MILTON, *Samson Agonistes*

PREFACE TO THE
PAPERBACK EDITION

The aide said that guys like me were "in what we call the reality-based community," which he defined as people who "believe that solutions emerge from your judicious study of discernible reality." I nodded and murmured something about enlightenment principles and empiricism. He cut me off. "That's not the way the world really works anymore," he continued. "We're an empire now, and when we act, we create our own reality. And while you're studying that reality—judiciously, as you will—we'll act again, creating other new realities, which you can study too, and that's how things will sort out. We're history's actors . . . and you, all of you, will be left to just study what we do."

RON SUSKIND, quoting a "senior advisor" to President Bush[1]

"History," he said, shrugging, taking his hands out of his pockets, extending his arms, and suggesting with his body language that it was so far off. "We won't know. We'll all be dead."

BOB WOODWARD, quoting President Bush[2]

I set out to write this book in the belief that the role of the United States in the world today could be better understood by comparing it with past empires. I understood well enough that most Americans feel uneasy about applying the word *empire* to their country, though an influential minority (as the first epigraph above confirms) are not so inhibited. But what I had not fully understood until the first edition of *Colossus* was published was the precise nature of "imperial denial" as a national condition. It is, I discovered, acceptable among American liberals to say that the United States is an empire—provided that you deplore the fact. It is also permitted to say, when among conservatives, that American power is potentially beneficent—provided that you do not describe it as imperial. What is not allowed is to say that the United States is an empire *and* that this might not be wholly bad. *Colossus* set out to do this, and thereby succeeded in antagonizing both conservative and liberal critics. Conservatives repudiated my contention that the United States is and, indeed, has always been an empire. Liberals were dismayed by my suggestion that the American empire might have positive as well as negative attributes.

As in Gilbert and Sullivan's *Iolanthe,* so in the United States today, it seems to be expected "That every boy and every gal / That's born into the world alive / Is either a little Liberal, / Or else a little Conservative!" But I am afraid this book is neither. Here, in a simplified form, is what it says:

1. that the United States has always been, functionally if not self-consciously, an empire;

2. that a self-conscious American imperialism might well be preferable to the available alternatives, but

3. that financial, human, and cultural constraints make such self-consciousness highly unlikely, and

4. that therefore the American empire, in so far as it continues to exist, will remain a somewhat dysfunctional entity.

The case for an American empire in *Colossus* is therefore twofold. First, there is the case for its functional existence; second, the case for the potential advantages of a self-conscious American imperialism. By self-conscious imperialism, please note, I have never meant that the United States should unabashedly proclaim itself an empire and its president an emperor; perish the thought. I merely mean that Americans need to recognize the imperial characteristics of their own power today and, if possible, to learn from the achievements and failures of past empires. It is no longer sensible to maintain the fiction that there is something wholly unique about the foreign relations of the United States. The dilemmas faced by America today have more in common with those faced by the later Caesars than with those faced by the Founding Fathers.[3]

At the same time, however, the book makes clear the grave perils of being an "empire in denial." Americans are not wholly oblivious to the imperial role their country plays in the world. But they dislike it. "I think we're trying to run the business of the world too much," a Kansas farmer told the British author Timothy Garton Ash in 2003, ". . . like the Romans used to."[4] To

such feelings of unease, American politicians respond with a categorical re-
assurance. "We're not an imperial power," declared President George W. Bush
on April 13, 2004, "We're a liberating power."[5]

Of all the misconceptions that need to be dispelled here, this is perhaps
the most obvious: That simply because Americans say they do not "do" empire, there cannot be such a thing as American imperialism. As I write,
American troops are engaged in defending governments forcibly installed by
the United States in two distant countries, Afghanistan and Iraq. They are
likely to be there for some time to come; even President Bush's Democratic
rival John Kerry implied in the first of last year's presidential debates that, if
he were elected, he would only "*begin* to draw the troops down in six
months."[6] Iraq, however, is only the front line of an American imperium
which, like all the great world empires of history, aspires to much more than
just military dominance along a vast and variegated strategic frontier.[7] Empire also means economic, cultural, and political predominance within (and
sometimes also without) that frontier. On November 6, 2003, in his speech
to mark the twentieth anniversary of the National Endowment for Democracy, President Bush set out a vision of American foreign policy that, for all
its Wilsonian language, strongly implied the kind of universal civilizing mission that has been a feature of all the great empires:

> The United States has adopted a new policy, a forward strategy of freedom
> in the Middle East. . . . The establishment of a free Iraq at the heart of the
> Middle East will be a watershed event in the global democratic revolu-
> tion. . . . The advance of freedom is the calling of our time; it is the calling
> of our country. . . . We believe that liberty is the design of nature; we be-
> lieve that liberty is the direction of history. We believe that human fulfill-
> ment and excellence come in the responsible exercise of liberty. And we
> believe that freedom—the freedom we prize—is not for us alone, it is the
> right and the capacity of all mankind.[8]

He restated this messianic credo in his speech to the Republican Party
convention last September [2004]:

> The story of America is the story of expanding liberty: an ever-widening
> circle constantly growing to reach further and include more. Our nation's

founding commitment is still our deepest commitment: In our world, and here at home, we will extend the frontiers of freedom. . . . We are working to advance liberty in the broader Middle East because freedom will bring a future of hope and the peace we all want. . . . Freedom is on the march. I believe in the transformational power of liberty: The wisest use of American strength is to advance freedom.[9]

Later that month, he used very similar words in the first presidential debate.[10]

To the majority of Americans, it would appear, there is no contradiction between the ends of global democratization and the means of American military power. As defined by their president, the democratizing mission of the United States is both altruistic and distinct from the ambitions of past empires, which (so it is generally assumed) aimed to impose their own rule on foreign peoples. The difficulty is that President Bush's ideal of freedom as a universal desideratum rather closely resembles the Victorian ideal of "civilization." "Freedom" means, on close inspection, the American model of democracy and capitalism; when Americans speak of "nation building" they actually mean "state replicating," in the sense that they want to build political and economic institutions that are fundamentally similar, though not identical, to their own.[11] They may not aspire to rule, but they do aspire to have others rule themselves in the American way.

Yet the very act of imposing "freedom" simultaneously subverts it. Just as the Victorians seemed hypocrites when they spread "civilization" with the Maxim gun, so there is something fishy about those who would democratize Fallujah with the Abrams tank. President Bush's distinction between conquest and liberation would have been entirely familiar to the liberal imperialists of the early 1900s, who likewise saw Britain's far-flung legions as agents of emancipation (not least in the Middle East during and after World War I). Equally familiar to that earlier generation would have been the impatience of American officials to hand over sovereignty to an Iraqi government sooner rather than later. Indirect rule—which installed nominally independent native rulers while leaving British civilian administrators and military forces in practical control of financial matters and military security—was the preferred model for British colonial expansion in many parts of Asia, Africa, and the Middle East. Iraq itself was an example of indirect rule after the Hashemite dynasty was established there in the 1920s. The crucial question today is whether or not the United States has the capabilities, both material and moral, to make a success of its version of indirect rule. The danger lies in the inclination of American politicians, eager to live up to their own emancipatory rhetoric as well as to "bring the boys back home," to unwind their overseas commitments prematurely—in short, to opt for premature decolonization rather than sustained indirect rule. Unfortunately, history shows that the most violent time in the history of an empire often comes at the moment of its dissolution, precisely because—as soon as it has been announced—the withdrawl of imperial troops unleashes a struggle between rival local elites for control of the indigenous armed forces.

But is the very concept of empire itself an anachronism? A number of critics have objected that imperialism was a discreet historical phenomenon which reached its apogee in the late nineteenth century and has been defunct since the 1950s. "The Age of Empire is passed," declared the *New York Times* as L. Paul Bremer III left Baghdad in June 2004:

> The experience of Iraq has demonstrated . . . that when America does not disguise its imperial force, when a proconsul leads an "occupying power," it is liable to find itself in an untenable position quickly enough. There are three reasons: the people being governed do not accept such a form of rule, the rest of the world does not accept it, and Americans themselves do not accept it.[12]

As one reviewer of *Colossus* put it, "nationalism is a much more powerful force now than it was during the heyday of the Victorian era."[13] According to another, the book failed "to come to terms with the tectonic changes wrought by independence movements and ethnic and religious politics in the years since the end of World War II."[14] A favorite argument of journalists is—perhaps not surprisingly—that the power of the modern media makes it impossible for empires to operate as they did in the past, because their misdeeds are so quickly broadcast to an indignant world.

Such arguments betray a touching naïveté about both the past and the

present. First, as I try to argue in the introduction, empire was no temporary condition of the Victorian age. Empires, by contrast, can be traced
back as far as recorded history goes; indeed, most history is in fact the
history of empires, precisely because empires are so good at recording,
replicating, and transmitting their own words and deeds. It is the nation
state—an essentially nineteenth-century ideal type—which is the historical novelty, and which may yet prove to be the more ephemeral entity.
Given the ethnic heterogeneity and restless mobility of mankind, that is
scarcely surprising. In fact, many of the most successful nation states of the
present started life as empires; what is the modern United Kingdom of
Great Britain and Northern Ireland if not the legatee of an earlier English
imperialism? Secondly, it is a Rooseveltian fantasy that in 1945 the age of
empire came to an end amid a global springtime of the peoples. On the
contrary, the Second World War merely saw the defeat of three would-be
empires—German, Japanese, and Italian—by an alliance between the old
West European empires (principally the British, since the others were so
swiftly beaten) and two newer empires—that of the Soviet Union and that
of the United States. The Cold War also had the character of a clash of
empires. Although the United States ran, for the most part, an "empire by
invitation" where its troops were deployed and was elsewhere more of a
hegemon (in the sense of an alliance leader) than an empire, the Soviet
Union was and remained, until its precipitous decline and fall, a true empire. Moreover, the other great Communist power to emerge from the
1940s, the People's Republic of China, remains in many respects an empire
to this day. Its three most extensive provinces—Inner Mongolia, Xinjiang,
and Tibet—were all acquired as a result of Chinese imperial expansion,
and China continues to lay claim to Taiwan as well as numerous smaller
islands, to say nothing of some territories in Russian Siberia and Kazakhstan.

Empires, in short, are always with us. Nor is it immediately obvious
why the modern media should reduce the capacity of an empire to sustain
itself. The growth of the popular press did nothing to weaken the British
Empire in the late nineteenth and early twentieth century; on the contrary,
the mass-circulation newspapers tended to enhance the popular legitimacy
of the empire. Anyone who watched how American television networks
covered the invasion of Iraq ought to understand that the mass media are

not necessarily solvents of imperial power. As for nationalism, it is something of a myth that this was what brought down the old empires of Western Europe. Far more lethal to their longevity were the costs of fighting
rival empires—empires that were still more contemptuous of the principle
of self-determination.[15]

Another common misconception is that there will always be less violence in the absence of an empire than in its presence, and that the United
States would therefore make the world a safer place if it brought its troops
home from the Middle East. One way to test such arguments is to ask the
counterfactual question: Would American foreign policy have been more
effective in the past four years—or, if you prefer, would the world be a
safer place today—if Afghanistan and Iraq had not been invaded? In the
case of Afghanistan, there is little question that what Joseph Nye has called
"soft power" would not have sufficed to oust the sponsors of al Qa'eda
from their stronghold in Kabul. There would have been no elections in
Afghanistan in 2004 had it not been for the hard power of the U.S. military. In the case of Iraq, it is surely better that Saddam Hussein is the prisoner of an interim Iraqi government than still reigning in Baghdad.
Open-ended "containment"—which was effectively what the French
government argued for in 2003—would, on balance, have been a worse
policy. Policing Iraq from the air while periodically firing missiles at sus-
pect installations was costing money without solving the problem posed by
Saddam. Keeping U.S. troops in Saudi Arabia indefinitely was not an option. Sanctions may have disarmed Saddam (at the time, of course, we
could not be sure) but they were also depriving ordinary Iraqis. In any case,
the sanctions regime was on the point of collapse thanks to a systematic
campaign by Saddam's regime to buy votes in the United Nations Security
Council—a campaign of systematic corruption that was made easy by the
United Nations' oil-for-food program. In short, the policy of regime
change was right; arguably, the principal defect of American policy toward
Iraq was that the task had been left undone for twelve years. Those who
fret about the doctrine of pre-emption enunciated in President Bush's National Security Strategy should bear in mind that the overthrow of Saddam
was as much post-emption as pre-emption, since Saddam had done nearly
all the mischief of which he was capable some time before March 2003.

Yet it would be absurd to deny that much of what has happened in the past year—to say nothing of what has been revealed about earlier events—has tended to undermine the legitimacy of the Bush administration's policy. To put it bluntly: What went wrong? And have failures of execution fatally discredited the very notion of an American imperial strategy?

The first seed of future troubles was the administration's decision to treat suspected al Qa'eda personnel captured in Afghanistan and elsewhere as "unlawful enemy combatants," beyond both American and international law. Prisoners were held incommunicado and indefinitely at Guantánamo Bay in Cuba. As the rules governing interrogation were chopped and changed, many of these prisoners were subjected to forms of mental and physical intimidation that in some cases amounted to torture.[16] Indeed, Justice Department memoranda were written to rationalize the use of torture as a matter for presidential discretion in time of war. Evidently, some members of the administration felt that extreme measures were at once justified by the shadowy nature of the foe they faced, and at the same time legitimized by the public appetite for retribution after the terrorist attacks of September 11, 2001. All of this the Supreme Court rightly denounced in its stinging judgment, delivered in June of last year [2004]. As the justices put it, not even the imperatives of resisting "an assault by the forces of tyranny" could justify the use by an American president of "the tools of tyrants." Yet power corrupts, and even small amounts of power can corrupt a very great deal. It may not have been official policy to flout the Geneva Conventions in Iraq, but not enough was done by senior officers to protect prisoners held at Abu Ghraib from gratuitous abuse—what the inquiry chaired by James Schlesinger called "freelance activities on the part of the night shift."[17] The photographic evidence of these "activities" has done more than anything else to discredit the claim of the United States and its allies to stand not merely for an abstract liberty but also for the effective rule of law.

Second, it was more than mere exaggeration on the part of Vice President Cheney, the former CIA chief George Tenet, and, ultimately, President Bush himself—to say nothing of Prime Minister Tony Blair—to claim they knew *for certain* that Saddam Hussein possessed weapons of mass destruction. This was, we now know, a downright lie that went far beyond what the available intelligence indicated. What they could legitimately have said was this: "After all his evasions, we simply can't be sure whether or not Saddam Hussein has any weapons of mass destruction. So, on the precautionary principle, we just can't leave him in power indefinitely. Better safe than sorry." But that was not enough for Dick Cheney, who felt compelled to make the bald assertion: "Saddam Hussein possesses weapons of mass destruction." Bush himself had his doubts, but was reassured by Tenet that it was a "slam-dunk case."[18] Other doubters soon fell into line. Still more misleading was the administration's allegation that Saddam was "teaming up with al Qa'eda." Sketchy evidence of contacts between the two was used to insinuate Iraqi complicity in the 9/11 attacks, for which not a shred of proof has been found.

Third, it was a near disaster that responsibility for the postwar occupation of Iraq was seized by the Defense Department, intoxicated as its principals became in the heat of their *blitzkrieg*. The State Department had spent long hours preparing a plan for the aftermath of a successful invasion. That plan was simply junked by Secretary Rumsfeld and his close advisors, who were convinced that once Saddam had gone, Iraq would magically reconstruct itself (after a period of suitably ecstatic celebration at the advent of freedom). As one official told the *Financial Times* last year, Undersecretary Douglas Feith led

> a group in the Pentagon who all along felt that this was going to be not just a cakewalk, it was going to be 60–90 days, a flip-over and hand-off, a lateral or whatever to . . . the INC [Iraqi National Congress]. The DoD [Department of Defense] could then wash its hands of the whole affair and depart quickly, smoothly and swiftly. And there would be a democratic Iraq that was amendable to our wishes and desires left in its wake. And that's all there was to it.[19]

When General Eric Shinseki, the army chief of staff, stated in late February 2003 that "something of the order of several hundred thousand soldiers" would be required to stabilize postwar Iraq, he was brusquely put down by Deputy Secretary Wolfowitz as "wildly off the mark." Wolfowitz professed himself "reasonably certain" that the Iraqi people would "greet us as liberators." Such illusions were not, it should be remembered, confined to neoconservatives in the Pentagon. Even General Tommy Franks was under the impression that it would be possible to reduce troop levels to just 50,000 after eighteen months. It was left to Colin Powell to point out to the president that "regime change" had serious—not to say imperial—implications. The "Pottery Barn rule," he suggested to Bush, was bound to be applicable to Iraq: "You break it, you own it."[20]

Fourth: American diplomacy in 2003 was like the two-headed Pushmepullyou in Dr. Doolittle—it faced in opposite directions. On one side was Cheney, dismissing the United Nations as a negligible factor. On the other was Powell, insisting that any action would require some form of UN authorization to be legitimate. It is possible that one of these approaches might have worked. It was, however, a mistake to try both at once. Europe was in fact coming around as a consequence of some fairly successful diplomatic browbeating. No fewer than eighteen European governments signed letters expressing support of the impending war against Saddam. Yet the decision to seek a second UN resolution—on the grounds that the language of Resolution 1441 was not strong enough to justify all-out war—was a blunder that allowed the French government, by virtue of its permanent seat on the UN Security Council, to regain the diplomatic initiative. Despite the fact that more than forty countries declared their support for the invasion of Iraq and three (Britain, Australia, and Poland) sent significant numbers of troops, the threat of a French veto, delivered with a Gallic flourish, created the indelible impression that the United States was acting unilaterally—perhaps even illegally.[21]

All of these mistakes had one thing in common. They sprang from a failure to learn from history. For among the most obvious lessons of history is that an empire cannot rule by coercion alone. It needs above all legitimacy—in the eyes of the subject people, in the eyes of the other great powers and, above all, in the eyes of the people back home. Did those concerned know no history? We are told that President Bush was reading Edward Morris's *Theodore Rex* as the war in Iraq was being planned; presumably he had not reached the part when the American occupation sparked off a Filipino insurrection. Before the invasion of Iraq, Deputy National Security Advisor Stephen Hadley was heard to refer to a purely unilateral American invasion as "the imperial option." Did no one else grasp that occupying and trying to transform Iraq (with or without allies) was a quintessentially imperial undertaking—and one that would not only cost money but would also take many years to succeed?

Had policy makers troubled to consider what befell the last Anglophone occupation of Iraq, they might have been less surprised by the persistent resistance they encountered in certain parts of the country during 2004. For in May 1920 there was a major anti-British revolt there. This happened six months after a referendum (in practice, a round of consultation with tribal leaders) on the country's future, and just after the announcement that Iraq would become a League of Nations "mandate" under British trusteeship rather than continue under colonial rule. Strikingly, neither consultation with Iraqis nor the promise of internationalization sufficed to avert an uprising.

In 1920, as in 2004, the insurrection had religious origins and leaders, but it soon transcended the country's ancient ethnic and sectarian divisions. The first anti-British demonstrations were in the mosques of Baghdad, but the violence quickly spread to the Shiite holy city of Karbala, where British rule was denounced by Ayatollah Muhammad Taqi al-Shirazi, the historical counterpart of today's Shiite firebrand, Moktada al-Sadr. At its height, the revolt stretched as far north as the Kurdish city of Kirkuk and as far south as Samarra. Then, as in 2004, much of the violence was more symbolic than strategically significant—British bodies were mutilated, much as American bodies were at Fallujah. Still, there was a real threat to the British position. The rebels systematically sought to disrupt the occupiers' infrastructure, attacking railways and telegraph lines. In some places, British troops and civilians were cut off and besieged. By August 1920 the situation in Iraq was so desperate that the general in charge appealed to London not only for reinforcements but also for chemical weapons (mustard gas bombs or shells), though, contrary to historical legend, these turned out to be unavailable and so were never used.[22]

This brings us to the second lesson the United States might have learned from the British experience. Reestablishing order is no easy task. In 1920 the British eventually ended the rebellion through a combination of aerial bombardment and punitive village-burning expeditions. Even Winston Churchill, then the minister responsible for the Royal Air Force, was shocked by the actions of some trigger-happy pilots and vengeful ground troops. And despite their overwhelming technological superiority, British forces still suffered more than 2,000 dead and wounded. Moreover, the British had to keep troops in Iraq long after the country was granted "full sovereignty." Although Iraq was declared formally independent in 1932, British troops remained there until the 1950s (see chapter six).

Is history repeating itself? For all of the talk in 2004 of restoring "full sovereignty" to an interim Iraqi government, President Bush made it clear that he intended to "maintain our troop level . . . as long as necessary" and that U.S. troops would continue to operate "under American command." This in itself implied something significantly less than full sovereignty. For if the new interim Iraqi government did not have control over a well-armed foreign army in its own territory, than it lacked one of the defining characteristics of a sovereign state: a monopoly over the legitimate use of violence. That was precisely the point made in April of 2004 by Marc Grossman, undersecretary of state for political affairs, during Congressional hearings on the future of Iraq. In Grossman's words: "The arrangement would be, I think as we are doing today, that we would do our very best to consult with that interim government and take their views into account." But American commandes would still "have the right, and the power, and the obligation" to decide on the appropriate role for their troops.[23]

There is, in principle, nothing inherently wrong with "limited sovereignty"; in both West Germany and Japan, as chapter two shows, sovereignty was limited for some years after 1945. Sovereignty is not an absolute but a relative concept. Indeed, it is a common characteristic of empires that they consist of multiple tiers of sovereignty. In what Charles Maier has called the "fractal geometry of empire," the imperial hierarchy of power contains within it multiple scaled-down versions of itself, none fully sovereign. Again, however, there is a need for American policy makers and voters to understand the imperial business they are now in. For this business can have costly overheads.

The problem is that for indirect rule—or "limited sovereignty"—to be successful in Iraq, Americans must be willing to foot a substantial bill for the occupation and reconstruction of the country. Unfortunately, in the absence of a radical change in the direction of the U.S. fiscal policy, their ability to do so is set to diminish, if not to disappear—the bottom line of chapter eight.

Since President Bush's election in 2000, total federal outlays have risen by an estimated $530 billion, an increase of nearly a third. This increase can only be partly attributed to the wars the administration has fought; higher defense expenditures account for just 30 percent of the total increment, whereas increased spending on health care accounts for 17 percent, that on Social Security and that on income security for 16 percent apiece, and that on Medicare for 14 percent.[24] The reality is that the Bush administration has increased spending on welfare by rather more than spending on warfare. Meanwhile, even as expenditure has risen, there has been a steep reduction in the federal government's revenues, which slumped from 21 percent of gross domestic product in 2000 to less than 16 percent in 2004.[25] The recession of 2001 played only a minor role in creating this shortfall of receipts. More important were the three successive tax cuts enacted by the administration with the support of the Republican-led Congress, beginning with the initial $1.35 trillion tax cut over ten years and the $38 billion tax rebate of the Economic Growth and Tax Reform Reconciliation Act in 2001, continuing with the Job Creation and Worker Assistance Act in 2002, and concluding with the reform of the double taxation of dividend income in 2003. With a combined value of $188 billion—equivalent to around 2 percent of the 2003 national income—these tax cuts were significantly larger than those passed in Ronald Reagan's Economic Recovery Tax Act of 1981.[26] The effect of this combination of increased spending and reduced revenue has been a dramatic growth in the federal deficit. President Bush inherited a surplus of around $236 billion from the fiscal year 2000. At the time of writing, the projected deficit for 2004 was $413 billion, representing a swing from the black into the red of two-thirds of a trillion dollars.[27]

Government spokesmen have sometimes defended this borrowing spree as a stimulus to economic activity. There are good reasons to be skeptical about this, however, not least because the principal beneficiaries of these tax cuts have, notoriously, been the very wealthy. (Vice President Cheney belied the macroeconomic argument when he justified the third tax cut in the following candid terms: "We won the midterms. This is our due."[28]) Another Cheney aphorism that is bound to be quoted by future historians was his assertion that "Reagan proved deficits don't matter."[29] But Reagan did nothing of the kind. The need to raise taxes to bring the deficit back under control was one of the key factors in George H. W. Bush's defeat in 1992; in turn, the systematic reduction of the deficit under Bill Clinton was one of the reasons long-term interest rates declined and the economy boomed in the later 1990s. The only reason that, under Bush junior, deficits have not seemed to matter is the persistence of low interest rates over the past four years, which has allowed Bush—in common with many American households—to borrow more while paying less in debt service. Net interest payments on the federal debt amounted to just 1.4 percent of the GDP last year, whereas the figure was 2.3 percent in 2000 and 3.2 percent in 1995.[30]

Yet this persistence of low long-term rates is not a result of ingenuity on the part of the U.S. Treasury. It is in part a consequence of the willingness of the Asian central banks to buy vast quantities of dollar-denominated securities such as ten-year Treasury bonds, with the primary motivation of keeping their currencies pegged to the dollar, and the secondary consequence of funding the Bush deficits.[31] It is no coincidence that just under half the publicly held federal debt is now in foreign hands, more than double the proportion ten years ago.[32] Not since the days of tsarist Russia has a great empire relied so heavily on lending from abroad. The trouble is that these flows of foreign capital into the United States cannot be relied on to last indefinitely, especially if there is a likelihood of rising deficits in the future. And that is why the Bush administration's failure to address the fundamental question of fiscal reform is so important. The reality is that the official figures for both the deficit and the accumulated federal debt understate the magnitude of the country's impending fiscal problems because they leave out of account the huge and unfunded liabilities of the Medicare and Social Security systems.[33] The United States derives a significant benefit from the status of the dollar as the world's principal reserve currency; it is one reason why foreign investors are prepared to hold such large volumes of dollar-denominated assets. But reserve-currency status is not divinely ordained. It could be undermined if international markets took fright at the magnitude of America's still latent fiscal crisis.[34] A decline in the dollar would certainly hurt foreign holders of U.S. currency more than it would hurt Americans. But a shift in international expectations about U.S. finances might also bring about a sharp increase in long-term interest rates, which would have immediate and negative feedback effects on the federal deficit by pushing up the cost of debt service.[35] It would also hurt highly geared American households, especially the rising proportion of them with adjustable-rate mortgages.[36]

Empires need not be a burden on the taxpayers of the metropolis; indeed, many empires have arisen precisely in order to shift tax burdens from the center to the periphery. Yet there is little sign that the United States will be able to achieve even a modest amount of "burden sharing" in the foreseeable future. During the Cold War, American allies contributed at least some money and considerable manpower to the maintenance of the West's collective security. But those days are gone. At the Democratic Party convention in Boston in July 2004, and again in the presidential debate on foreign policy two months later, John Kerry pledged to "bring our allies to our side and share the burden, reduce the cost to American taxpayers, and reduce the risk to American soldiers," in order to "get the job done and bring our troops home." "We don't have to go it alone in the world," he declared. "And we need to rebuild our alliances."[37] Yet it is far from clear that any American president would be able to persuade Europeans today to commit additional troops to Iraq, or even to subsidize the American presence there. In accepting his party's nomination, Kerry recalled how, as a boy, he watched "British, French, and American troops" working together in postwar Berlin. In those days, however, there was much bigger incentive— symbolized by the Red Army units that surrounded West Berlin—for European states to support American foreign policy. It is not that the French or the Germans (or for that matter the British) were passionately pro-American during the Cold War; on the contrary, U.S. diplomats constantly fretted about anti-Americanism in Europe, on both the left and the right. Nevertheless, as long as there was a Soviet Union to the East, there was one overwhelming argument for the unity of "the West." That ceased to be the case fifteen years ago, when the reforms of Mikhail Gorbachev caused the Russian empire to crumble. And ever since then, the incentives for transatlantic harmony have grown steadily weaker. For whatever reason, Europeans do not regard the threat posed by Islamist terrorism as sufficiently serious to justify unconditional solidarity with the United States. On the contrary, since the Spanish general election, they have acted as if the optimal response to the growing threat of Islamist terrorism is to distance themselves from the United States. An astonishingly large number of Europeans see the United

States as itself a threat to international stability. In a recent Gallup pole, 61 percent of Europeans said they thought the European Union plays "a positive role with regard to peace in the world"; just 8 percent said its role was negative. No fewer than 50 percent of those polled took the view that the United States now plays a negative role.[38]

So the United States is what it would rather not be: a Colossus to some, a Goliath to others—an empire that dare not speak its name.[39] Yet what is the alternative to American empire? If, as so many people seem to wish, the United States were to scale back its military commitments overseas, then what?

We tend to assume that power, like nature, abhors a vacuum. In the history of world politics, it seems, someone is always the hegemon, or is bidding to play that role. Today, it is the United States; a century ago, it was the United Kingdom. Before that, it was France, Spain, and so on. The great nineteenth-century German historian Leopold von Ranke portrayed modern European history as an incessant struggle for mastery, in which a balance of power was possible only through recurrent conflict. More recent historians have inferred that as the superpowers of the Cold War era succumb to "overstretch," their place will be taken by new powers. Once it was supposed to be Germany and Japan. These days, wary realists warn of the ascent of China and Europe. Power, in other words, is not a natural monopoly; the struggle for mastery is both perennial and universal. The "unipolarity" identified by some commentators following the Soviet collapse cannot last much longer, for the simple reason that history hates a hyperpower. Sooner or later, challengers will emerge, and back we must go to a multipolar, multipower world. In other words, if the United States were to conclude from its experience in Iraq that the time has come to abandon its imperial pretensions, some other power or powers would soon seize the opportunity to bid for hegemony.

But what if no successor were to emerge? What if, instead of a balance of power, there were an absence of power? Such a situation is not unknown in history. Unfortunately, the world's experience with power vacuums (or eras of "apolarity," if you will) is hardly encouraging. Anyone who looks forward eagerly to an American retreat from hegemony should bear in mind that, rather than a multipolar world of competing great powers, a world with no hegemon may be the real alternative to U.S. primacy. Apolarity could turn out to mean not the pacifist utopia envisaged in John Lennon's dirge "Imagine," but an anarchic new Dark Age.

Why might a power vacuum arise early in the twenty-first century? The reasons are not especially hard to imagine. Consider the three principal contenders for the succession if the United States were to succumb to imperial decline. Impressive though the European Union's recent enlargement has been—not to mention the achievement of a twelve-country monetary union—the reality is that demographic trends almost certainly condemn Europe to decline (see chapter seven). With fertility rates dropping and life expectancies rising, West European societies are projected to have median ages in the upper forties by the middle of this century. Indeed, "Old Europe" will soon be truly old. By 2050, one in every three Italians, Spaniards, and Greeks is expected to be sixty-five or older, even allowing for ongoing immigration.[40] Europeans therefore face an agonizing choice between Americanizing their economies, i.e., opening their borders to much more immigration, with all the cultural changes that would entail, or transforming their union into a kind of fortified retirement community, in which a dwindling proportion of employees shoulder the rising cost of outmoded welfare systems. These problems are compounded by the Euro area's sluggish growth, a consequence of labor market rigidities, high marginal tax rates, and relatively low labor inputs (notably in terms of working hours).[41] Meanwhile, the EU's still incomplete constitutional reforms mean that individual European nation states continue to enjoy considerable autonomy outside the economic sphere, particularly in foreign and security policy. Eastward enlargement may look like a solution to the EU's creeping senescence, but each additional member makes the task of managing the Union's confederal institutions more difficult.

Optimistic observers of China insist the economic miracle of the past decade will endure, with growth continuing at such a pace that within thirty or forty years China's gross domestic product will surpass that of the United States.[42] Yet it is far from clear that the normal rules for emerging markets have been suspended for Beijing's benefit. First, a fundamental incompatibility exists between the free-market economy, based inevitably on private property and the rule of law, and the Communist monopoly on power, which breeds corruption and impedes the creation of transparent fiscal, monetary, and regulatory institutions. As is common in "Asian tiger" economies, production is running far ahead of domestic consumption—thus making the economy heavily dependent on exports—and even further ahead of domestic financial development. Indeed, no one knows the full extent of the problems in the Chinese domestic banking sector.[43] Those Western banks that are buying up bad debts to establish themselves in China must remember that this strategy was tried once before: a century ago, in the era of the "Open Door" policy, when American and European firms rushed into China only to see their investments vanish amid the turmoil of war and revolution. Then, as now, hopes for China's development ran euphorically high, especially in the United States. But those hopes were dashed, and could be disappointed again. A Chinese currency or banking crisis could have immense ramifications, especially when Western investors realize the difficulty of repatriating assets held in China. When foreigners invest directly in factories rather than through intermediaries such as bond markets, there is no need for domestic capital controls. It is no easy thing to repatriate a steel mill.

With birthrates in Muslim societies more than double the European average, the Islamic countries of Northern Africa and the Middle East are bound to put some kind of pressure on Europe and the United States in the years ahead. If, for example, the population of Yemen could exceed that of Germany by 2050 (as the United Nations forecasts), there must either be dramatic improvements in the Middle East's economic performance or substantial emigration from the Arab world to aging Europe. Yet the subtle Muslim colonization of Europe's cities—most striking in France, where North Africans populate whole suburbs of cities like Marseille and Paris—may not necessarily portend the advent of a new and menacing "Eurabia."[44] In fact, the Muslim world is as divided as ever, and not merely along the traditional fissure between Sunnis and Shiites. It is also split between those Muslims seeking a peaceful *modus vivendi* with the West (an impulse embodied in the Turkish government's desire to join the EU) and those drawn to the revolutionary "Islamism" of renegades like Osama bin Laden. Opinion polls from Morocco to Pakistan suggest high levels of anti-American sentiment, but not unanimity. In Europe, only a minority expresses overt sympathy for terrorist organizations; most young Muslims in England clearly prefer assimilation to jihad. We are still a long way from a bipolar clash of civilizations, much less the rise of a new caliphate that might pose a geopolitical threat to the United States and its allies.

In short, each of the obvious potential successors to the United States— the European Union and China—seems to contain within it the seeds of future decline; while Islam remains a diffuse force in world politics, lacking the resources of a superpower.

Let us now imagine that American neo-conservative hubris meets its nemesis in Iraq and that the Bush administration's project to democratize the Middle East at gunpoint ends in ignominious withdrawal. Suppose also that no aspiring rival power steps in to fill the resulting vacuums—not only in Iraq but conceivably also Afghanistan, the Balkans, to say nothing of Haiti. What would an apolar future look like? The answer is not easy, as there have been very few periods in world history with no contenders for the role of global, or at least regional, hegemon. The nearest approximation in modern times might be the 1920s, when the United States walked away from President Woodrow Wilson's project of global democracy and collective security centered on the League of Nations. There was certainly a power vacuum in Central and Eastern Europe after the collapse of the Romanov, Habsburg, Hohenzollern, and Ottoman empires, but it did not last long. The old West European empires were quick to snap up the choice leftovers of Ottoman rule in the Middle East. The Bolsheviks had reassembled the czarist empire by 1922. And by 1936 German revanche was already well advanced.

One must go back much further in history to find a period of true and enduring apolarity; as far back, in fact, as the ninth and tenth centuries. In this era, the two sundered halves of the Roman Empire—Rome and Byzantium—had passed the height of their power. The leadership of the Western half was divided between the pope, who led Christendom, and the heirs of Charlemagne, who split up his short-lived empire under the Treaty of Verdun in 843. No credible claimant to the title of emperor emerged until Otto was crowned in 962, and even he was merely a German prince with pretensions (never realized) to rule Italy. Byzantium, meanwhile, was grappling with the Bulgar rebellion to the north, while the Abbasid caliphate initially established by Abu al-Abbas in 750 was in steep decline by the middle of the tenth century. In China, too, imperial power was in a dip between the T'ang and Sung dynasties.

The weakness of the older empires allowed new and smaller entities to flourish. When the Khazar tribe converted to Judaism in 740, their khanate occupied a Eurasian power vacuum between the Black Sea and the Caspian Sea. In Kiev, far from the reach of Byzantium, the regent Olga laid the foundation for the future Russian Empire in 957 when she embraced the Orthodox Church. The Seljuks—forebears of the Ottoman Turks—carved out the Sultanate of Rum as the Abbasid caliphate lost its grip over Asia Minor. Africa had its mini-empire in Ghana; Central America had its Mayan civilization. Connections between all these entities were minimal or nonexistent. This condition was the antithesis of globalization. The world was broken up into disconnected, introverted civilizations.

One distinctive feature of the era was that, in the absence of strong secular polities, religious questions often produced serious convulsions. Indeed, it was religious institutions that often set the political agenda. In the eighth and ninth centuries, Byzantium was racked by controversy over the proper role of icons in worship. By the eleventh century, the pope felt confident enough to humble Holy Roman Emperor Henry IV during the battle over which of them should have the right to appoint bishops. The new monastic orders amassed considerable power in Christendom, particularly the Cluniacs, the first order to centralize monastic authority. In the Muslim world, it was the *ulema* (clerics) who truly ruled. This ascendancy of the clergy helps to explain why the period ended with the extraordinary holy wars known as the Crusades, the first of which was launched by European Christians in 1095. Yet this apparent clash of civilizations was in many ways just another example of the apolar world's susceptibility to long-distance military raids directed at urban centers by more backward peoples. The Vikings repeatedly attacked West European towns in the ninth century—Nantes in 842, Seville in 844, to name just two. Small wonder that the future seemed to lie in creating small, defensible, political units: the Venetian republic—the quintessential city-state, which was conducting its own foreign policy by 840—or Alfred the Great's England, arguably the first thing resembling a nation state in European history, created in 886.

Could an apolar world today produce an era reminiscent of the age of

Alfred? It could, though with some important and troubling differences. Certainly, one can imagine the world's established powers retreating into their own regional spheres of influence. But what of the growing pretensions to autonomy of the supranational bodies created under U.S. leadership after the Second World War? The United Nations, the International Monetary Fund, the World Bank, and the World Trade Organization each considers itself in some way representative of the "international community." Surely their aspirations to global governance point to the true alternative to American empire—a new Light Age of collective security and international law, the very antithesis of the Dark Ages?[45] Yet universal claims were also an integral part of the rhetoric of that distant era. All the empires maintained that they ruled the world; some, unaware of the existence of other civilizations, may even have believed that they did. The reality, however, was not a global Christendom, nor an all-embracing Empire of Heaven, but political fragmentation. And that is also true today. For the defining characteristic of our age is not a shift of power upward to supranational institutions, but downward. With the end of states' monopoly on the means of violence and the collapse of their control over channels of communication, humanity has entered an era characterized as much by disintegration as integration. If free flows of information and of the means of production empower multinational corporations and nongovernmental organizations (as well as evangelistic religious cults of all denominations), the free flow of destructive technology empowers both criminal organizations and terrorist cells. These groups can operate, it seems, wherever they choose, from New York to Najaf, from Madrid to Moscow. By contrast, the writ of the international community is not global at all. It is, in fact, increasingly confined to a few strategic outposts such as Kabul and Baghdad. In short, it is the non-state actors who truly wield global power—including both the monks and the Vikings of our time.

Waning empires, religious revivals, incipient anarchy, a retreat into fortified cities: These are the Dark Age experiences that a post-imperial world could conceivably find itself reliving. The symptoms are already not far to seek. The trouble is, of course, that this Dark Age would be an altogether more dangerous one than the Dark Age of the ninth and tenth centuries. The world is much more populous—roughly twenty times more. Technology has transformed production, of course; now human societies depend not merely on fresh water, livestock, and the harvest but also on machines that have vastly increased our productivity. Unfortunately, the principal fuels on which our machines run are known to be finite in supply; they also pollute the earth's atmosphere, altering its climate, even as they are used. Technology has upgraded deliberate destruction, too. It is now possible not just to sack a city but to obliterate it. For all these reasons, the prospect of an apolar world should perturb us today a great deal more than it perturbed the heirs of Charlemagne. If the United States is to retreat from global hegemony—its fragile self-image dented by minor setbacks on the imperial frontier—its critics at home and abroad must not pretend that they are ushering in a new era of multipolar harmony, or even a return to the good old balance of power. For the alternative to unipolarity may not be multipolarity at all. It could be apolarity—a global vacuum of power. And far more dangerous forces than rival great powers would benefit from such a not-so-new world disorder.

The best case for empire is always the case for order. Liberty is, of course, a loftier goal. But only those who have never known disorder fail to grasp that it is the necessary precondition for liberty. In that sense, the case for American empire is simultaneously a case against international anarchy— or, to be precise, of a proliferation of regional vacuums of power. None of this is to pretend that the United States is a perfect empire. Empires are by their very nature compromised by the power that they wield; they inexorably engender their own dissolution at home even as they impose order abroad. That is why our expectations should not be pitched too high. If it is hard enough to be an empire when you believe you have a mandate from heaven, how much harder is it for the United States, which believes that heaven intended it to free the world, not rule it.

Sadly, there are still a few places in the world that must be ruled before they can be freed. Sadly, the act of ruling them will sorely try Americans, who instinctively begrudge such places the blood, treasure, and time that they consume. Yet, saddest of all, there seems to be no better alternative for the United States and the world—and that is this book's bottom line. Once, one hundred and sixty years ago, America's imperial destiny seemed manifest. It has since become obscure. But it is America's destiny just the same. The only question that remains is: How much longer will this self-denying empire endure? The answer *Colossus* offers is: Not long, in the absence of fundamental reappraisal of America's role in the world. If this book contributes anything to bring that reappraisal about, then it will have served its intended purpose.

INTRODUCTION

AL JAZEERA: Would it worry you if you go by force into Iraq that this might create the impression that the United States is becoming an imperial, colonial power?

RUMSFELD: Well I'm sure that some people would say that, but it can't be true because we're not a colonial power. We've never been a colonial power. We don't take our force and go around the world and try to take other people's real estate or other people's resources, their oil. That's just not what the United States does. We never have and we never will. That's not how democracies behave. That's how an empire-building Soviet Union behaved but that's not how the United States behaves.[1]

They played a lot of Risk, the board game where color-coded armies vied to conquer the world. It took hours, so it was great for killing time. Private First Class Jeff Young . . . was so good at it that the other guys formed coalitions to knock him out first.

MARK BOWDEN, *Black Hawk Down*[2]

AGE OF EMPIRES

One of the most popular of computer games in the world is called Age of Empires. For several months my own ten-year-old son was all but addicted to it. Its organizing premise is that the history of the world is the history of imperial conflict. Rival political entities vie with one another to control finite resources: people, fertile land, forests, gold mines and waterways. In their endless struggles the competing empires must strike a balance between the need for economic development and the exigencies of warfare. The player who is too aggressive soon runs out of resources if he has not taken the trouble to cultivate his existing territory, to expand its population and to accumulate gold. The player who focuses too much on getting rich may find himself vulnerable to invasion if he meanwhile neglects his defenses.

Many Americans doubtless play Age of Empires, just as the Rangers in Mogadishu played its board game predecessor, Risk. But remarkably few Americans—or, for that matter, American soldiers—would be willing to admit that their own government is currently playing the game for real.

This book argues not merely that the United States is an empire but that it always has been an empire. Unlike most of the previous authors who have remarked on this, I have no objection in principle to an American empire. Indeed, a part of my argument is that many parts of the world would benefit from a period of American rule. But what the world needs today is not just any kind of empire. What is required is a *liberal* empire— that is to say, one that not only underwrites the free international exchange of commodities, labor and capital but also creates and upholds the conditions without which markets cannot function—peace and order, the rule of law, noncorrupt administration, stable fiscal and monetary policies—as well as provides public goods, such as transport infrastructure, hospitals and schools, which would not otherwise exist. One important question this book asks is whether or not the United States is capable of being a successful liberal empire. Although the United States seems in many ways ideally endowed—economically, militarily and politically—to run such an "empire of liberty" (in Thomas Jefferson's phrase), in practice it has been a surprisingly inept empire builder. I therefore attempt to explain why the United States finds being an empire so difficult; why, indeed, its imperial undertakings are so often short-lived and their results ephemeral.

Part of my intention is simply to interpret American history as in many ways unexceptional—as the history of just another empire, rather than (as many Americans still like to regard it) as something quite unique. However, I also want to delineate the peculiarities of American imperialism, both its awesome strengths and its debilitating weaknesses. The book sets recent events—in particular, the terrorist attacks of September 11 and the invasions of Afghanistan and Iraq—in their long-run historical context, suggesting that they represent less of a break with the past than is commonly believed. Thus, although this is partly a work of contemporary political economy, inspired by my spending much of the past year in the United States, it is primarily a work of history. It is also, unavoidably, concerned with the future—or rather, with possible futures. The later chapters of the book ask how enduring the American empire is likely to prove.

Is the American empire mightier than any other in history, bestriding the globe as the Colossus was said to tower over the harbor of Rhodes? Or is this giant a Goliath, vast but vulnerable to a single slingshot from a diminutive, elusive foe? Might the United States in fact be more like Samson, eyeless in Gaza, chained by irreconcilable commitments in the Middle East and ultimately capable only of blind destruction? Like all historical questions, these can only be answered by comparisons and counterfactuals, juxtaposing America's empire with those that have gone before and considering other imaginable pasts, as well as possible futures.

IMPERIAL DENIAL

It used to be that only critics of American foreign policy referred to the "American Empire." During the cold war, of course, both the Soviet Union and the People's Republic of China harped incessantly on the old Leninist theme of Yankee imperialism, as did many Western European, Middle Eastern and Asian writers, not all of them Marxists.[3] But their claim that overseas expansion was inspired by sinister corporate interests was not so very different from the indigenous American critiques of late-nineteenth and early-twentieth-century overseas expansion, whether populist, progressive or socialist.[4] In the 1960s these critiques fused to produce a new and influential historiography of American foreign policy usually referred to as revisionism.[5] Historians like Gabriel and Joyce Kolko argued that the cold war was the result not of Russian but of American aggression after 1945, an argument made all the more attractive to a generation of students by the contemporaneous war in Vietnam—proof, as it seemed, of the neocolonial thrust of American foreign policy.[6] The reassertion of American military power under Ronald Reagan prompted fresh warnings against the "imperial temptation."[7]

This tradition of radical criticism of American foreign policy shows no sign of fading away. Its distinctive, anguished tone continues to emanate from writers like Chalmers Johnson, William Blum and Michael Hudson,[8] echoing the strictures of an earlier generation of anti-imperialists (some of whom are themselves still faintly audible).[9] Yet criticism of American empire was never the exclusive preserve of the political Left. In the eyes of Gore Vidal, the tragedy of the Roman Republic is repeating itself as farce, with the "national-security state" relentlessly encroaching on the prerogatives of the patrician elite to which Vidal himself belongs.[10] Meanwhile, far to the Right, Pat Buchanan continues to fulminate in the archaic isolationist idiom against East Coast internationalists intent on entangling the United States—against the express wishes of the Founding Fathers—in the quarrels and conflicts of the Old World. In Buchanan's eyes, America is following not the example of Rome but that of Britain, whose empire it once repudiated but now imitates.[11] Other, more mainstream conservatives—notably Clyde Prestowitz—have also heaped scorn on "the imperial project of the so-called neoconservatives."[12]

In the past three or four years, however, a growing number of commentators have begun to use the term *American empire* less pejoratively, if still ambivalently,[13] and in some cases with genuine enthusiasm. Speaking at a conference in Atlanta in November 2000, Richard Haass, who went on to serve in the Bush administration as director of policy planning in the State Department, argued that Americans needed to "re-conceive their global role from one of traditional nation-state to an imperial power," calling openly for an "informal" American empire.[14] This was, at the time, bold language; it is easy to forget that during the 2000 presidential election campaign it was George W. Bush who accused the Clinton-Gore administration of undertaking too many "open-ended deployments and unclear military missions."[15] As Thomas Donnelly, deputy executive director of the Project for the New American Century, told the *Washington Post* in August 2001, "There's not all that many people who will talk about it [empire] openly. It's discomforting to a lot of Americans. So they use code phrases like 'America is the sole superpower.'"[16]

Such inhibitions seemed to fall away in the aftermath of the terrorist attacks of September 11, 2001. In a trenchant article for the *Weekly Standard,* published just a month after the destruction of the World Trade Center, Max Boot explicitly made "The Case for an American Empire." "Afghanistan and other troubled lands today," Boot declared, "cry out for the sort of enlightened foreign administration once provided by self-confident Englishmen in jodhpurs and pith helmets."[17] When his history of

America's "small wars" appeared the following year, its title was taken from Rudyard Kipling's notorious poem "The White Man's Burden," written in 1899 as an exhortation to the United States to turn the Philippines into an American colony.[18] The journalist Robert Kaplan also took up the imperial theme in his book *Warrior Politics,* arguing that "future historians will look back on 21st-century United States as an empire as well as a republic."[19] "There's a positive side to empire," Kaplan argued in an interview. "It's in some ways the most benign form of order."[20] Charles Krauthammer, another conservative columnist, detected the change of mood. "People," he told the *New York Times,* were "now coming out of the closet on the word 'empire.'"[21] "America has become an empire," agreed Dinesh D'Souza in the *Christian Science Monitor,* but happily it is "the most magnanimous imperial power ever." His conclusion: "Let us have more of it."[22] Writing in *Foreign Affairs* in 2002, the journalist Sebastian Mallaby proposed American "neo-imperialism" as the best remedy for the "chaos" engendered by "failed states" around the world.[23] One reading of Michael Ignatieff's recent critique of American "nation building" efforts in Bosnia, Kosovo and Afghanistan is that these have not been *sufficiently* imperialistic to be effective.[24]

While Mallaby and Ignatieff are perhaps best described as liberal interventionists—proponents of what Eric Hobsbawm has sneeringly dismissed as "the imperialism of human rights"—the majority of the new imperialists are neoconservatives, and it was their views that came to the fore during and after the invasion of Iraq in 2003. "Today there is only one empire," wrote James Kurth in a special "Empire" issue of the *National Interest,* "the global empire of the United States. The U.S. military . . . are the true heirs of the legendary civil officials, and not just the dedicated military officers, of the British Empire."[25] Speaking on Fox News in April 2003, the editor of the *Weekly Standard,* William Kristol, declared: "We need to err on the side of being strong. And if people want to say we're an imperial power, fine."[26] That same month the *Wall Street Journal* suggested that the British naval campaign against the slave trade in the mid-nineteenth century might provide a model for American policy against nuclear proliferation.[27] Max Boot even called for the United States to establish a Colonial Office, the better to administer its new possessions in the Middle East and Asia.[28]

Within the Pentagon the figure most frequently associated with the "new imperialism" is Deputy Secretary Paul Wolfowitz, who first won notoriety, as undersecretary of defense under the current president's father, by arguing that the aim of U.S. policy should be to "convince potential competitors that they need not aspire to a greater role or pursue a more aggressive posture to protect their legitimate interests."[29] That line, so controversial when it was written back in 1992, now seems remarkably tame. Nine years later the Office of the Secretary of Defense organized a Summer Study at the Naval War College, Newport, to "explore strategic approaches to sustain [U.S. predominance] for the long term (~50 years)," which explicitly drew comparisons between the U.S. and the Roman, Chinese, Ottoman and British empires.[30] Such parallels clearly do not seem outlandish to senior American military personnel. In 2000 General Anthony Zinni, then commander in chief of the U.S. Central Command, told the journalist Dana Priest that he "had become a modern-day proconsul, descendant of the warrior-statesman who ruled the Roman Empire's outlying territory, bringing order and ideals from a legalistic Rome."[31] It is hard to be certain that this was irony.

Officially, to be sure, the United States remains an empire in denial.[32] Most politicians would agree with the distinction drawn by the historian Charles Beard back in 1939: "America is not to be Rome or Britain. It is to be America."[33] Richard Nixon insisted in his memoirs that the United States is "the only great power without a history of imperialistic claims on neighboring countries,"[34] a view echoed by policy makers throughout the past decade. In the words of Samuel R. "Sandy" Berger, President Clinton's national security adviser, "We are the first global power in history that is not an imperial power."[35] A year later, while campaigning to succeed Clinton, George W. Bush echoed both Nixon and Berger: "America has never been an empire. We may be the only great power in history that had the chance, and refused—preferring greatness to power, and justice to glory."[36] He has reverted to this theme on several occasions since entering the White House. In a speech he made at the American Enterprise Institute shortly before the invasion of Iraq, Bush stated: "The US has no intention of determining the precise form of Iraq's new government. That choice belongs to the Iraqi people. . . . We will remain in Iraq as long as necessary and not a day more. America has made and kept this kind of commitment before in the peace that followed a world war. After defeating enemies, we did not leave behind occupying armies, we left constitutions and parliaments."[37] He reiterated this lack of imperial intent in a television address to the Iraqi people on April 10, when he declared: "We will help you build a peaceful and representative government that protects the rights of all citizens. And then our military forces will leave. Iraq will go forward as a unified, independent and sovereign nation."[38] Speaking on board the *Abraham Lincoln* aircraft carrier on May 1, the president rammed the point home: "Other nations in history have fought in foreign lands and remained to occupy and exploit. Americans, following a battle, want nothing more than to return home."[39] The same line is taken by Defense Secretary Donald Rumsfeld, as the epigraph to this introduction makes clear. Indeed, it appears to be one of the few issues about which all the principal figures in the Bush administration are agreed. Speaking at the George Washington University in September last year, Secretary of State Colin Powell insisted: "The United States does not seek a territorial empire. We have never been imperialists. We seek a world in which liberty, prosperity and peace can become the heritage of all peoples, and not just the exclusive privilege of a few."[40]

Few Americans would dissent from this. Revealingly, four out of five Americans polled by the Pew Global Attitudes survey last year agreed that it was "good that American ideas and customs were spreading around the world."[41] But were the same people to be asked if they considered this a consequence of American imperialism, hardly any would concur.

Freud defined *denial* as a primitive psychological defense mechanism against trauma. Perhaps it was therefore inevitable that in the aftermath of the September 11 attacks, Americans would deny their country's imperial character more vehemently than ever. Yet as U.S. foreign policy has moved from the defense to the offense, the need for denial would seem to have diminished. It may thus be therapeutic to determine the precise nature of this empire—since empire it is, in all but name.

HEGEMONY AND EMPIRE

Julius Caesar called himself *imperator* but never king. His adopted heir Augustus preferred *princeps*. Emperors can call themselves what they like, and so can empires. The kingdom of England was proclaimed an empire—by Henry VIII—before it became one.[42] The United States by contrast has long been an empire, but eschews the appellation.

Define the term *empire* narrowly enough, of course, and the United States can easily be excluded from the category. Here is a typical example: "Real imperial power . . . means a *direct* monopoly control over the organization and use of armed might. It means *direct* control over the administration of justice and the definition thereof. It means control over what is bought and sold, the terms of trade and the permission to trade. . . . Let us stop talking of an American empire, for there is and there will be no such thing."[43] For a generation of "realist" writers, eager to rebut Soviet charges of American imperialism, it became conventional to argue that the United States had only briefly flirted with this kind of formal empire, beginning with the annexation of the Philippines in 1898 and ending by the 1930s.[44] What the United States did after the end of the Second World War was, however, fundamentally different in character. According to one recent formulation, it was "not an imperial state with a predatory intent"; it was "more concerned with enhancing regional stability and security and protecting international trade than enlarging its power at the expense of others."[45]

If the United States was not an empire, then what was it? And what is it now that the empire it was avowedly striving to "contain" is no more? "The only superpower"—existing in a "unipolar" world—is one way of describing it. *Hyperpuissance* was the (certainly ironical) coinage of the former French foreign minister Hubert Védrine. Some writers favor more anemic terms like global *leadership*,[46] while Philip Bobbitt simply regards the United States as a particularly successful form of nation-state.[47] A recent series of seminars at Harvard's Kennedy School opted for the inoffensive term *primacy*.[48] But by far the most popular term among writers on international relations remains *hegemon*.[49]

What is this thing called hegemony? Is it merely a euphemism for *empire*, or does it describe the role of the *primus inter pares*, the leader of an alliance, rather than a ruler over subject peoples? And what are the hegemon's motives? Does it exert power beyond its borders for its own self-interested purposes? Or is it engaged altruistically in the provision of international public goods?

The word was used originally to describe the relationship of Athens to the other Greek city-states when they leagued together to defend themselves against the Persian Empire; Athens led but did not rule over the others.[50] In so-called world-system theory, by contrast, hegemony means more than mere leadership, but less than outright empire.[51] In yet another, narrower definition, the hegemon's principal function in the twentieth century was to underwrite a liberal international commercial and financial system.[52] In what became known, somewhat inelegantly, as hegemonic stability theory, the fundamental question of the postwar period was how far and for how long the United States would remain committed to free trade once other economies, benefiting from precisely the liberal economic order made possible by U.S. hegemony, began to catch up. Would Americans revert to protectionist policies in an effort to perpetuate their hegemony or stick with free trade at the risk of experiencing relative decline? This has been called the hegemon's dilemma, and it appeared to many writers to be essentially the same dilemma that Britain had faced before 1914.[53]

Yet if the British Empire was America's precursor as the global hegemon, might not the United States equally well be Britain's successor as an Anglophone empire? Most historians would agree that, if anything, American economic power after 1945 exceeded that of Britain after 1815, a comparable watershed of power following the final defeat of Napoleonic France. First, the extraordinary growth in productivity achieved between around 1890 and 1950 eclipsed anything previously achieved by Britain, even in the first flush of the Industrial Revolution. Secondly, the United States very deliberately used its power to advance multilateral and mutually balanced tariff reductions under the General Agreement on Tariffs and Trade (later the World Trade Organization). Thus the reductions of tariffs achieved in the Kennedy Round (1967) and in subsequent "rounds" of negotiation owed much to American pressures such as the "conditionality" attached to loans from the Washington-based International Monetary Fund. By contrast, the nineteenth-century spread of free trade and free navigation—the "public goods" most commonly attributed to the British Empire—were as much spontaneous phenomena as they were direct consequences of British power. Thirdly, successive U.S. governments allegedly took advantage of the dollar's role as a key currency before and after the breakdown of Bretton Woods. The U.S. government had access to a "gold mine of paper" and could therefore collect a subsidy from foreigners in the form of seigniorage (by selling foreigners dollars and dollar-denominated assets that then depreciated in value).[54] The gold standard offered Britain no such advantages, and perhaps even some disadvantages. Finally, the Pax Britannica depended mainly on the Royal Navy and was less "penetrative" than the "full-spectrum dominance" aimed for today by the American military. For a century, with the sole exception of the Crimean War, Britain felt unable to undertake military interventions in Europe, the theater most vital to its own survival, and when it was forced to do so in 1914 and in 1939, it struggled to prevail.[55] We arrive at the somewhat paradoxical conclusion that a hegemon can be more powerful than an empire.

The distinction between hegemony and empire would be legitimate if the term *empire* did simply mean, as so many American commentators seem to assume, direct rule over foreign territories without any political representation of their inhabitants. But students of imperial history have a more sophisticated conceptual framework than that. At the time, British colonial administrators like Frederick Lugard clearly understood the distinction between "direct" and "indirect" rule; large parts of the British Empire in Asia and Africa were ruled indirectly—that is, through the agency of local potentates rather than British governors. A further distinction was introduced by John Gallagher and Ronald Robinson in their seminal 1953 article on "the imperialism of free trade." This encapsulated the way the Victorians used their naval and financial power to open the markets of countries outside their colonial ambit.[56] Equally illuminating is the now widely accepted distinction between "formal" and "informal empire." The British did not formally govern Argentina, for example, but the merchant banks of the City of London exerted such a powerful influence on its fiscal and monetary policy that Argentina's independence was heavily qualified.[57] In the words of one of the few modern historians to attempt a genuinely comparative study of the subject, an empire is "first and foremost, a very great power that has left its mark on the international relations of an era . . . a polity that rules over wide territories and many peoples, since the management of space and multi-ethnicity is one of the great perennial dilemmas of empire. . . . An empire is by definition . . . not a polity ruled with the explicit consent of its peoples. [But] by a process of assimilation of peoples of democratization of institutions empires can transform themselves into multinational federations or even nation states."[58] It is possible to be still more precise than this. In table 1 below I have attempted a simple typology intended to capture the diversity of forms that can be subsumed under the category "empires." Note that the table should be read as a menu rather than as a grid. For example, an empire could be an oligarchy at home, aiming to acquire raw materials from abroad, thereby increasing international trade, using mainly military methods, imposing a market economy, in the interests of its ruling elite, with a hierarchical social character. Another empire might be a democracy at home, mainly interested in security, providing peace as a public good, ruling mainly through firms and NGOs, promoting a mixed economy, in the interests of all inhabitants, with an assimilative social character.

The first column reminds us that imperial power can be acquired by more than one type of political system. The self-interested objectives of imperial expansion (column two) range from the fundamental need to ensure the security of the metropolis by imposing order on enemies at its (initial) borders to the collection of rents and taxation from subject peoples, to say nothing of the perhaps more obvious prizes of new land for settlement, raw materials, treasure and manpower, all of which, it should be emphasized, would need to be available at lower prices than they would cost in free exchange with independent peoples if the cost of conquest and colonization were to be justified.[59] At the same time, an empire may

TABLE 1

Metropolitan System	Self-interested Objectives	Public Goods	Methods of Rule	Economic System	Cui Bono?	Social Character
Tyranny	Security	Peace	Military	Plantation	Ruling elite	Genocidal
Aristocracy	Communications	Trade	Bureaucracy	Feudal	Metropolitan populace	Hierarchical
Oligarchy	Land	Investment	Settlement	Mercantilist	Settlers	Converting
Democracy	Raw materials	Law	NGOs	Market	Local elites	Assimilative
	Treasure	Governance	Firms	Mixed	All inhabitants	
	Manpower	Education	Delegation to local elites	Planned		
	Rents	Conversion				
	Taxation	Health				

provide "public goods"—that is, intended or unintended benefits of imperial rule flowing not to the rulers but to the ruled and indeed beyond to
third parties: less conflict, increased trade or investment, improved justice
or governance, better education (which may or may not be associated with
religious conversion, something we would not nowadays regard as a public good) or improved material conditions. The fourth column tells us that
imperial rule can be implemented by more than one kind of functionary:
soldiers, civil servants, settlers, voluntary associations, firms and local elites
all can in different ways impose the will of the center on the periphery.
There are almost as many varieties of imperial economic system, ranging
from slavery to laissez-faire, from one form of serfdom (feudalism) to another (the planned economy). Nor is it by any means a given that the benefits of empire should flow simply to the metropolitan society. It may only
be the elite of that society that reaps the benefits of empire (as Lance E.
Davis and R. A. Huttenback claimed in the case of the British Empire);[60]
it may be colonists drawn from lower-income groups in the metropole; it
may in some cases be subject peoples or the elites within subject societies.
Finally, the social character of an empire—to be precise, the attitudes of
the rulers toward the ruled—may vary. At one extreme lies the genocidal
empire of National Socialist Germany, intent on the annihilation of specific ethnic groups and the deliberate degradation of others. At the other
extreme lies the Roman model of empire, in which citizenship was ob-
tainable under certain conditions regardless of ethnicity (a model with obvious applicability to the case of the United States). In the middle lies the
Victorian model of complex racial and social hierarchy, in which inequalities of wealth and status were mitigated by a general (though certainly not
unqualified) principle of equality before the law. The precise combination
of all these variables determines, among other things, the geographical
extent—and of course the duration—of an empire.

With a broader and more sophisticated definition of empire, it seems
possible to dispense altogether with the term *hegemony*. Instead, it can be argued with some plausibility that the American empire has up until now,
with a few exceptions, preferred indirect rule to direct rule and informal
empire to formal empire. Indeed, its cold war–era hegemony might better
be understood as an "empire by invitation."[61] The question is whether or
not the recent, conspicuously uninvited invasions of Afghanistan and Iraq

presage a transition to more direct and formal imperial structures. Adapting the terminology of table 1, the American empire can therefore be summed up as follows. It goes without saying that it is a liberal democracy and market economy, though its polity has some illiberal characteristics[62] and its economy a surprisingly high level of state intervention ("mixed" might be more accurate than "market"). It is primarily concerned with its own security and maintaining international communications and, secondarily, with ensuring access to raw materials (principally, though not exclusively, oil). It is also in the business of providing a limited number of public goods: peace, by intervening against some bellicose regimes and in some civil wars; freedom of the seas and skies for trade; and a distinctive form of "conversion" usually called Americanization, which is carried out less by old-style Christian missionaries than by the exporters of American consumer goods and entertainment. Its methods of formal rule are primarily military in character; its methods of informal rule rely heavily on nongovernmental organizations and corporations and, in some cases, local elites.

Who benefits from this empire? Some would argue, with the economist Paul Krugman, that only its wealthy elite does—specifically, that part of its wealthy elite associated with the Republican Party and the oil industry.[63] The conventional wisdom on the Left is that the United States uses its power to impoverish people in the developing world. Others would claim that many millions of people around the world have benefited in some way or another from the existence of America's empire—not least the West Europeans, Japanese and South Koreans who were able to prosper during the cold war under the protection of the American nuclear "umbrella"—and that the economic losers of the post–cold war era, particularly in sub-Saharan Africa, are victims not of American power but of its absence. For the American empire is limited in its extent. It conspicuously lacks the voracious appetite for territorial expansion overseas that characterized the empires of the West European seaboard. It prefers the idea that foreigners will Americanize themselves without the need for formal rule. Even when it conquers, it resists annexation—one reason why the duration of its offshore imperial undertakings has tended to be, and will in all probability continue to be, relatively short. Indeed, a peculiarity of American imperialism—perhaps its principal shortcoming—is its excessively short time horizon.

ANGLOPHONE EMPIRES

All told, there have been no more than seventy empires in history. If the *Times Atlas of World History* is to be believed, the American is, by my count, the sixty-eighth. (Communist China is the sixty-ninth; some would claim that the European Union is the seventieth.) How different is the American empire from previous empires? Like the ancient Egyptian, it erects towering edifices in its heartland, though these house the living rather than the dead. Like the Athenian Empire, it has proved itself adept at leading alliances against a rival power. Like the empire of Alexander, it has a staggering geographical range. Like the Chinese Empire that arose in the Ch'in era and reached its zenith under the Ming dynasty, it has united the lands and peoples of a vast territory and forged them into a true nation-state. Like the Roman Empire, it has a system of citizenship that is remarkably open: Purple Hearts and U.S. citizenship were conferred simultaneously on a number of the soldiers serving in Iraq last year, just as service in the legions was once a route to becoming a *civis romanus*. Indeed, with the classical architecture of its capital and the republican structure of its constitution, the United States is perhaps more like a "new Rome" than any previous empire—albeit a Rome in which the Senate has thus far retained its grip on would-be emperors. In its relationship with Western Europe too, the United States can sometimes seem like a second Rome, though it seems premature to hail Brussels as the new Byzantium.[64]

The Roman parallel is in danger of becoming something of a cliché.[65] Yet in its capacity for spreading its own language and culture—at once monotheistic and mathematical—the United States also shares features of the Abbasid caliphate erected by the heirs of Muhammad. Though it is often portrayed as the heir—as well as the rebellious product—of the western European empires that arose in the sixteenth century and persisted until the twentieth, in truth the United States has as much, if not more, in common with the great land empires of central and eastern Europe. In the nineteenth century the westward sweep of American settlers across the prairies had its mirror image in the eastward sweep of Russian settlers across the steppe. In practice, its political structures are sometimes more reminiscent of Vienna or Berlin than they are of The Hague, capital of the last great imperial republic, or London, hub of the first Anglophone empire. To those who would still insist on American "exceptionalism," the historian of empires can only retort: as exceptional as all the other sixty-nine empires.

Let us consider more precisely the similarities and differences between this American empire and the British Empire, against which the United States at first defined itself, but which it increasingly resembles, as rebellious sons grow to resemble the fathers they once despised. The relationship between the two Anglophone empires is one of the leitmotifs of this book for the simple reason that no other empire in history has come so close to achieving the things that the United States wishes to achieve today. Britain's era of "liberal empire"—from around the 1850s until the 1930s—stands out as a time when the leading imperial power successfully underwrote economic globalization by exporting not just its goods, its people and its capital but also its social and political institutions. The two Anglophone empires have much in common. But they are also profoundly different.

As we have seen, the United States is considered by some historians to be a more effective "hegemon" than Great Britain. Yet in strictly territorial terms, the latter was far the more impressive empire. At its maximum extent between the world wars the British Empire covered more than 13 million square miles, approximately 23 percent of the world's land surface. Only a tiny fraction of that was accounted for by the United Kingdom itself: a mere 0.2 percent. Today, by contrast, the United States accounts for around 6.5 percent of the world's surface, whereas its fourteen formal dependencies[66]—mostly Pacific islands acquired before the Second World War— amount to a mere 4,140 square miles of territory. Even if the United States had never relinquished the countries it at one time or another occupied in the Caribbean and Latin America between the Spanish-American War and the Second World War, the American empire today would amount to barely one-half of 1 percent of the world's land surface. In demographic terms, the formal American empire is even more minuscule. Today the United States and its dependencies together account for barely 5 percent of the world's population, whereas the British ruled between a fifth and a quarter of humanity at the zenith of their empire.

On the other hand, the United States possesses a great many small areas of territory within notionally sovereign states that serve as bases for its armed services. Before the deployment of troops for the invasion of Iraq, the U.S. military had around 752 military installations in more than 130 countries.[67] Significant numbers of American troops were stationed in 65 of these.[68] Their locations significantly qualify President Bush's assertion in his speech of February 26, 2003, that "after defeating enemies [in 1945], we did not leave behind occupying armies."[69] In the first year of his presidency, around 70,000 U.S. troops were stationed in Germany, and 40,000 in Japan. American troops have been in those countries continuously since 1945. Almost as many (36,500) were in South Korea, where the American presence has been uninterrupted since 1950. Moreover, new wars have meant new bases, like Camp Bondsteel in Kosovo, acquired during the 1999 war against Yugoslavia, or the Bishkek air base in Kyrgyzstan, an "asset" picked up during the war against the Taliban regime in Afghanistan. At the time of writing, about 10,000 American troops are still based in Afghanistan, and it seems certain that a substantial force of 100,000 will have to remain in Iraq for at least the next few years.[70]

Nor should it be forgotten what formidable military technology can be unleashed from these bases. Commentators like to point out that "the Pentagon's budget is equal to the combined military budgets of the next 12 or 15 nations" and that "the US accounts for 40–45 per cent of all the defense spending of the world's 189 states."[71] Such fiscal measures, impressive though they sound, nevertheless understate the lead currently enjoyed by American armed forces. On land the United States has 9,000 M1 Abrams tanks. The rest of the world has nothing that can compete. At sea the United States possesses nine "supercarrier" battle groups. The rest of the world has none. And in the air the United States has three different kinds of undetectable stealth aircraft. The rest of the world has none. The United States is also far ahead in the production of "smart" missiles and pilotless high-altitude "drones."[72] The British Empire never enjoyed this kind of military lead over the competition. Granted, there was a time when its network of naval and military bases bore a superficial resemblance to America's today.[73] The number of troops stationed abroad was also roughly the same.[74] The British too relished their technological superiority, whether it took the form of the Maxim gun or the *Dreadnought*. But their empire never dominated the full spectrum of military capabilities the way the United States does today. Though the Royal Navy ruled the waves, the

French and later the Germans—to say nothing of the Americans—were able to build fleets that posed credible threats to that maritime dominance, while the British army was generally much smaller and more widely dispersed than the armies of the continental empires.

If military power is the *sine qua non* of an empire, then it is hard to imagine how anyone could deny the imperial character of the United States today. Conventional maps of U.S. military deployments understate the extent of America's military reach.[75] A Defense Department map of the world, which shows the areas of responsibility of the five major regional commands, suggests that America's sphere of military influence is now literally global.[76] The regional combatant commanders—the "proconsuls" of this *imperium*—have responsibility for swaths of territory beyond the wildest imaginings of their Roman predecessors. USEUCOM extends from the westernmost shore of Greenland to the Bering Strait, from the Arctic Ocean to the Cape of Good Hope, from Iceland to Israel.[77]

It is of course a truth universally acknowledged that large overseas military commitments cannot be sustained without even larger economic resources. Is America rich enough to play the part of Atlas, bearing the weight of the whole world on its shoulders? This was a question posed so frequently in the 1970s and 1980s that it became possible to speak of "declinism" as a school of thought. According to Paul Kennedy, military and fiscal "overstretch" doomed the United States—like all "great powers"[78] before it—to lose its position of economic dominance.[79] For a brief time after the fall of the Berlin Wall it was possible to rejoice that the Soviet Union had succumbed to overstretch first.[80] The economic travails of Japan, once touted as a future geopolitical contender, added to the sense of national recuperation. While America savored a period of "relative ascent" unlike any since the 1920s, when an earlier peace dividend had fueled an earlier stock market bubble, declinism itself declined. By the end of the 1990s, however, commentators had found new rivals about which to worry. Some feared the European Union.[81] Others looked with apprehension toward China.[82] Samuel Huntington too saw "unipolarity" as only a transient phenomenon: as Europe united and China grew richer, so the world would revert to a "multipolarity" not seen since before the Second World War.[83] In Emmanuel Todd's eyes, French fears about American "hyperpower" ignored the reality of an impending decline and fall.[84]

If recent rates of growth of population and output were to continue for another twenty years, America could conceivably be overtaken as the largest economy in the world by China as early as 2018.[85] Yet it is highly unlikely that growth rates in either country will be the same in the next two decades as in the previous two. All we can say with certainty is that in 2002 American gross domestic product, calculated in international dollars and adjusted on the basis of purchasing power parity, was nearly twice that of China and accounted for just over a fifth (21.4 percent) of total world output—more than the Japanese, German and British shares put together. That exceeds the highest share of global output ever achieved by Great Britain by a factor of more than two.[86] Indeed, calculated in current U.S. dollars, the American share of the world's gross output was closer to a third (32.3 percent), double the size of the Chinese and Japanese economies combined.[87] In terms of both production and consumption, the United States is already a vastly wealthier empire than Britain ever was.[88]

Nor are these the only measures of American economic dominance. In Britain's imperial heyday, only a handful of corporations could really be described as "multinational," in the sense of having substantial proportions of their assets and workforce in overseas markets. Today the world economy is dominated by such firms, a substantial number of which—ranging from Exxon Mobil to General Motors, from McDonald's to Coca-Cola, from Microsoft to Time Warner—are American in origin and continue to have their headquarters in the United States. The recent history of McDonald's provides a vivid example of the way American corporations have expanded overseas in search of new markets, much as the old Hobson-Lenin theory of imperialism would have led one to expect. In 1967 McDonald's opened its first foreign outlets in Canada and Puerto Rico. Twenty years later it had nearly 10,000 restaurants in 47 countries and territories, and by 1997 no fewer than 23,000 restaurants in over 100 countries. In 1999, for the first time, the company's foreign sales exceeded its American sales. Today there are more than 30,000 McDonald's restaurants in over 120 countries; fewer than half, 12,800, are in the United States.[89] Like Donald Rumsfeld, Ronald McDonald needs his map of the world, and it presents a striking alternative geography of American empire. In the words of the company's chief operating officer, "There are 6½ billion people on the Earth and only 270 million live in the US. . . . Who else is positioned around the globe to deal with that opportunity?"[90] *Coca-colonization* is a hackneyed catchphrase of the antiglobalization "movement," but it conveys a certain truth when one considers the geographical range of the soft drink company's sales: 30 percent to North America, 24 percent to Latin America, 22 percent to Europe and the Middle East, 18 percent to Asia and 6 percent to Africa. Significantly, the Real Thing's fastest-growing market is the People's Republic of China.[91]

The relatively rapid growth of the American economy in the 1980s and 1990s—at a time when the economy of its principal cold war rival was imploding—explains how the United States has managed to achieve a unique revolution in military affairs while at the same time substantially reducing the share of defense expenditures as a proportion of gross domestic product. The Defense Department Green Paper published in March 2003 forecast total expenditure on national defense to remain constant at 3.5 percent of GDP for at least three years.[92] That should be compared with an average figure during the cold war of 7 percent. Given Paul Kennedy's "formula" that "if a particular nation is allocating *over the long term* more than 10 per cent . . . of GNP to armaments, that is likely to limit its growth rate," there seems little danger of imminent imperial overstretch.[93] In short, in terms of economic resources as well as of military capability the United States not only resembles but in some respects exceeds the last great Anglophone empire.

GOING SOFT

One argument sometimes advanced to distinguish American hegemony from British empire is qualitative. American power, it is argued, consists not just of military and economic power but also of "soft" power. According to Joseph Nye, the dean of Harvard's Kennedy School, "A country may obtain the outcomes it wants in world politics because other countries want to follow it, admiring its values, emulating its example, aspiring to its level of prosperity and openness." Soft power, in other words, is getting what you want without "force or inducement," sticks or carrots: "It is the ability to entice and attract. Soft power arises in large part from our values."[94] In America's case, "it comes from being a shining 'city upon a hill'"—an enticing new Jerusalem of economic and political liberty.[95] Nye is not so naïve as to assume that the American way is inherently attractive to everyone, everywhere. But he does believe that making it attractive matters more than in the past because of the global spread of information technology.[96] To put it simply, soft power—or what other writers have called Americanization—can reach the parts that hard power cannot reach.[97]

But does this make American power so very different from imperial power? On the contrary. If anything, it illustrates how very like the last Anglophone empire the United States has become. The British Empire too sought to make its values attractive to others, though initially—before the advent of modern communications technology—the job had to be done by "men on the spot." British missionaries, intent on spreading their islands' various brands of Christianity, fanned out across the globe. British businessmen too introduced their distinctive styles of accounting and management. British administrators applied their notions of law and order. And British schoolmasters drummed reading, writing and arithmetic into colonial elites. Together all of them contrived to spread British leisure pursuits like cricket and afternoon tea. The aim was without question to "entice and attract" people toward British values. Moreover, these footslogging efforts were eventually reinforced by new technology. After the advent of transoceanic telegraphs, London-based press agencies could supply newspapers around the world with Anglocentric content, but it was the advent of wireless radio—and specifically the creation of the British Broadcasting Corporation—that really ushered in the age of soft power in Nye's sense of the term. On Christmas Day 1932 King George V was able to broadcast to the entire British Empire. Within six years the BBC had launched its first foreign-language service—in Arabic—and by the end of 1938 it was broadcasting in all the major languages of continental Europe. There is no question that the BBC played an important part in encouraging dissent in Axis-occupied territories during the war; why else did Joseph Goebbels so obsessively prosecute Germans caught listening to it? In some ways, the soft power that Britain could exert in the 1930s was greater than the soft power of the United States today. In a world of newspapers, radio receivers and cinemas, in which the number of content-supplying corporations (often national monopolies) was relatively small, the overseas broadcasts of the BBC could hope to reach a relatively large number of foreign ears. Yet whatever soft power Britain thereby wielded did little to halt the precipitous decline of British power after the 1930s.

This raises the question of how much America's soft power really matters today. If the term is to denote anything more than cultural background music to more traditional forms of dominance, it surely needs to be demonstrated that the United States can secure what it wants from other countries without coercing them or suborning them, but purely because its cultural exports are seductive. One reason for skepticism about the extent of American soft power today is the geographical reach of these cultural exports. True, thirty-nine of the world's eighty-one largest telecommunications corporations are American, and around half of all the world's countries rely principally on the United States to supply their cinemas with films. But a very large proportion of Hollywood's exports go to longstanding American allies within the Organization of Economic Cooperation and Development. Apart from Japan, Asian countries—particularly India—import very few American productions. Likewise, most translations of American books and foreign users of American Internet sites are to be found in Europe and Japan. The only other region where a major channel of communication may be said to be dominated by American culture is Latin America, where 75 percent of television programs are U.S.-made.[98] It would be too much to conclude that American soft power is therefore abundant where it is least needed. It may well be that a high level of exposure to American cinema and television is one of the reasons why people in Western Europe, Japan and Latin America are still, on the whole, less hostile to the United States than their counterparts elsewhere. Still, the fact remains that the range of American soft power is more limited than is generally assumed. The Middle East, where the BBC began its foreign-language broadcasting, is now much more resistant to the charms of "Anglobalization" than it was then. The advent of Al Jazeera shows that the entry barrier into the soft power game is now quite low. Even in war-torn Somalia, American forces found their foes able to dominate the local airwaves with anti-American propaganda. Soft power could not avert genocide in Rwanda: when the United Nations Secretary-General Boutros Boutros-Ghali asked the Clinton administration to jam the murderous broadcasts of Radio Mille Collines, he was informed that such a step would be too expensive.[99]

There is one exception, and that exception provides another example of what the British Empire and today's American empire have in common. Missionaries are as important a channel for cultural dissemination in the developing world today as they were a century and a half ago. Because of the multiplicity of Christian sects involved, it is not easy to find reliable figures for the total number of American missionaries working outside the United States today. Estimates (for Protestant missionaries only) suggest that there are between 40,000 and 64,000, a relatively small number compared with the 300,000 or so American missionaries working within the United States.[100] Nevertheless, even small numbers of evangelical missionaries can achieve a good deal, furnished as they are with substantial funds from congregations at home. In April 1994 the Churches of Christ had a total of 223 missionaries in Latin America, with the largest number (81) in Brazil. Seven years later, although the number of missionaries in the region had fallen by nearly half, the total membership of Churches of Christ congregations had increased by 60 percent.[101] One estimate (published in 1990) puts the proportion of Latin Americans who are now Protestant as high as 20 percent.[102] The extraordinary display of evangelical faith by the victorious Brazilian team after the last soccer World Cup final lends credibility to that estimate. More recently, encouraged by evangelists like Luis Bush (himself born in Argentina), missionaries have turned their attention to the "unevangelized" millions who inhabit a so-called window of opportunity between the tenth and fortieth latitudes. According to the Center for the Study of Global Christianity at Gordon-Conwell Theological Seminary in South Hamilton, Massachusetts, the number of Christian missionaries to Islamic countries has almost doubled since 1982, from around 15,000 to 27,000; half of them are Americans.[103]

But what of America's official, secular values and altruistic goals? Are these not fundamentally different from those of past empires, which were selfish and exploitative in their intentions? It is often argued that American policy makers since Woodrow Wilson have renounced imperialism, seeking instead to encourage the spread of Wilsonian principles: international law, democracy and the free market.[104] Somehow—presumably because they are so self-evidently good—these ideas have "come to dominate international affairs." The most that the United States therefore

needs to do is "act as the chief of the constabulary" to prevent any unen-
lightened forces from challenging this benign world order.[105]

There is certainly no shortage of vintage Wilsonian rhetoric in President Bush's "National Security Strategy" published in September 2002,
which explicitly states that it is a goal of American foreign policy "to extend the benefits of freedom across the globe." "We will actively work,"
the document declares, "to bring the hope of democracy, development,
free markets, and free trade to every corner of the world . . . America
must stand firmly for the nonnegotiable demands of human dignity: the
rule of law; limits on the absolute power of the state; free speech; freedom
of worship; equal justice; respect for women; religious and ethnic tolerance; and respect for private property."[106] Yet this "strategy of openness" is
not without its imperial precursors.[107] From the second half of the nineteenth century until the Great Depression, the British Empire shared many
of the same aspirations.[108] The young Winston Churchill once defined the
goals of British imperialism as being "[to reclaim] from barbarism fertile
regions and large populations . . . to give peace to warring tribes, to administer justice where all was violence, to strike the chains off the slave, to
draw the richness from the soil, to plant the earliest seeds of commerce
and learning, to increase in whole peoples their capacities for pleasure and
diminish their chances of pain. . . ."[109] Is this so very different from the
language of American idealism? As Senator J. William Fulbright observed
in 1968, "The British called it the 'white man's burden.' The French called
it their 'civilizing mission.' Nineteenth-century Americans called it 'manifest
destiny.' It is now being called the 'responsibilities of power.'"[110] The "promotion of freedom" or the "strategy of openness" is merely its latest incarnation.[111] The fact is that liberal empires nearly always proclaim their own
altruism. When he spoke of the United States as an "empire of liberty,"
Thomas Jefferson was merely purloining a hoary trope of British imperialism. Edmund Burke had identified "freedom" as a defining characteristic of the British Empire as early as 1766.[112]

Like the British Empire, in any case, the United States reserves the
right to use military force, as and when it sees its interests threatened—not
merely reactively but on occasion preemptively. Thus President Bush's
"National Security Strategy" asserts that the United States reserves the

right to "act preemptively . . . to forestall or prevent . . . hostile acts by our adversaries . . . even if uncertainty remains as to the time and place of the enemy's attack."[113] Soft power is merely the velvet glove concealing an iron hand.

A BRITISH MODEL?

Unlike the majority of European writers who have written on this subject, I am fundamentally in favor of empire. Indeed, I believe that empire is more necessary in the twenty-first century than ever before. The threats we face are not in themselves new ones. But advances in technology make them more dangerous than ever before. Thanks to the speed and regularity of modern air travel, infectious diseases can be transmitted to us with terrifying swiftness. And thanks to the relative cheapness and destructiveness of modern weaponry, tyrants and terrorists can realistically think of devastating our cities. The old, post-1945 system of sovereign states, bound loosely together by an evolving system of international law, cannot easily deal with these threats because there are too many nation-states where the writ of the "international community" simply does not run. What is required is an agency capable of intervening in the affairs of such states to contain epidemics, depose tyrants, end local wars and eradicate terrorist organizations. This is the self-interested argument for empire. But there is also a complementary altruistic argument. Even if they did not pose a direct threat to the security of the United States, the economic and social conditions in a number of countries in the world would justify some kind of intervention. The poverty of a country like Liberia is explicable not in terms of resource endowment; otherwise (for example) Botswana would be just as poor.[114] The problem in Liberia, as in so many sub-Saharan African states, is simply misgovernment: corrupt and lawless dictators whose conduct makes economic development impossible and encourages political opposition to take the form of civil war.[115] Countries in this condition will not correct themselves. They require the imposition of some kind of external authority.[116]

There are those who would insist that an empire is by definition incapable of playing such a role; in their eyes, all empires are exploitative in character. Yet there can be—and has been—such a thing as a liberal empire, one that enhances its own security and prosperity precisely by providing the rest of the world with generally beneficial public goods: not only economic freedom but also the institutions necessary for markets to flourish.[117] In this regard, Americans have more to learn than they are prepared to admit from their more self-confident British predecessors, who, after the mid-nineteenth-century calamities of the Irish Famine and the Indian Mutiny, recast their empire as an economically liberal project, concerned as much with the integration of global markets as with the security of the British Isles, predicated on the idea that British rule was conferring genuine benefits in the form of free trade, the rule of law, the safeguarding of private property rights and noncorrupt administration, as well as government-guaranteed investments in infrastructure, public health and (some) education.[118] Arnold Toynbee's injunction to his Oxford tutorial pupils destined for the Indian Civil Service was clear: "If they went to India they were to go there for the good of her people on one of the noblest missions on which an Englishman could be engaged."[119]

Let me emphasize that it is not my intention to suggest that Americans should somehow adopt the Victorians as role models. The British Empire was very far from an *ideal* liberal empire, and there is almost as much to be learned from its failures as from its successes. But the resemblances between what the British were attempting to do in 1904 and what the United States is trying to do in 2004 are nevertheless instructive. Like the United States today, Great Britain was very ready to use its naval and military superiority to fight numerous small wars against what we might now call failed states and rogue regimes. No one who has studied the history of the British campaign against the Sudanese dervishes, the followers of the charismatic Wahhabist leader known as the Mahdi, can fail to be struck by its intimations of present-day conflicts. Yet like the United States today, the Victorian imperialists did not act purely in the name of national or imperial security. Just as American presidents of recent decades have consistently propounded the benefits of economic globalization—even when they have deviated from free trade in practice—British statesmen a century ago regarded the spread of free trade and the liberalization of commodity, labor and capital markets as desirable for the general good. And just as most Americans today regard global democratization on the American model as self-evidently good, so the British in those days aspired to export their own institutions—not just the common law but ultimately also parliamentary monarchy—to the rest of the world.

Americans easily forget that after the blunders of the late eighteenth century, British governments learned that it was perfectly easy to grant "responsible government" to colonies that were clearly well advanced along the road to economic modernity and social stability. Canada, New Zealand, Australia and (albeit with a restricted franchise) South Africa all had executives accountable to elected parliaments by the early 1900s. Nor was this benefit intended to be the exclusive preserve of the colonies of white settlement. On the question of whether India should ultimately be capable of British-style parliamentary government, Thomas Babington Macaulay was quite explicit, if characteristically condescending: "Never will I attempt to avert or to retard it [Indian self-government]. Whenever it comes it will be the proudest day in English history. To have found a great people sunk in the lowest depths of slavery and superstition, to have ruled them as to have made them desirous and capable of all the privileges of citizens, would indeed be a title to glory all our own."[120] Not dissimilar aspirations were being expressed in some quarters last year on the subject of democratizing the Arab world. Speaking at the United Nations in September of last year, President Bush himself made it clear that this was one of his objectives in invading Iraq.[121] As we shall see, however, the Americans were not the first Anglophone invaders to arrive in Baghdad proclaiming themselves to be "liberators" rather than conquerors.[122]

The structure of this book is straightforward. Chapter 1 considers the imperial origins of the United States and seeks to characterize the extent and limits of its empire up to the First World War. Chapter 2 asks why, despite its vast economic and military capabilities, the United States had such difficulties in imposing its will on so many of the countries where it intervened during the twentieth century. It also offers some explanations for the exceptional successes of American "nation building" in West Germany, Japan and South Korea.

Chapter 3 argues that the events of September 11, 2001, though they struck Americans like a bolt from the blue, represented the culmination of well-established historical trends: the contradictions of American policy in the Middle East, the growing dependence of Western economies on oil from the Persian Gulf and the adoption and development of terrorism as a tactic by Arabs hostile to the United States and its allies. Perhaps the biggest change the terrorists wrought was in American attitudes; this was not the kind of change that they intended. It was 9/11 that converted an instinctively introverted, if not isolationist, administration and electorate to the idea of waging a war against real, suspected or even potential sponsors of terrorism. Yet here too there were important continuities. The real historical turning point—the moment when the twenty-first century may be said to have begun—was not 9/11 but 11/9. The fall of the Berlin Wall on November 9, 1989, changed the context of American power far more profoundly than the fall of the World Trade Center. Malignant though it is, Islamic fundamentalist terrorism remains a far less potent threat to the United States than the Soviet Union once was.

Chapter 4 asks if American policy in Iraq since 1990 can be understood as a descent from "multilateralism" to "unilateralism." I suggest that, on the contrary, it has been the United Nations that has performed a shifting role in the last decade and a half, and American policy has been in large measure improvised in response to the failures of the UN and, in particular, to the failures of the European powers represented on the UN Security Council. It was during the 1990s that the United States learned, through bitter experience, the value of credible military interventions in countries where state terror was being used against ethnic minorities. It also learned that these did not require explicit authorization in the form of UNSC resolutions. "Coalitions of the willing" could suffice.

Chapter 5 makes the case for contemporary empire in the aftermath of the wars in Iraq and Afghanistan by considering the costs and benefits of the last great Anglophone empire. The suggestion here is that liberal empire makes sense today in terms of both American self-interest and altruism. For many former colonies, the experiment with political independence has been a failure in economic and in political terms. Sub-Saharan Africa, in particular, has been impoverished not by the oft-denounced legacies of colonialism but by decades of misrule since independence. By contrast, a liberal imperial model offers the best prospects for economic growth by guaranteeing not just economic openness but, more important, the institutional foundations for successful development. Chapter 6 attempts a provisional cost-benefit analysis of the American occupation of Iraq, asking if the liberal imperial model can work in that unfortunate country. The chapter suggests that American objectives in 2003—to ensure the disarmament of Iraq, to overthrow a vicious tyrant and to transform fundamentally the politics of the Middle East—were both laudable and attainable. However, it is far from clear as I write that the United States is capable of committing either the manpower or the time needed to make a success of its "nation building" in Iraq, much less in Afghanistan. This is primarily because the American electorate is averse to the kind of long-term commitment that history strongly suggests is necessary to achieve a successful transition to a market economy and representative government. Though I fervently hope to be proved wrong, I therefore question whether America has the capacity to build effective civilian institutions in Iraq, given its historic preference for short-term, primarily military interventions and its reluctance to learn that these seldom, if ever, work.

Chapter 7 compares American and European versions of empire and asks if today's European leaders, and some American scholars, are correct to foresee a time when the European Union will act as an effective counterweight to American power. At times during 2003 this already appeared to be happening. Yet in reality the European Union is almost the antithesis of an empire; its institutions are designed not to harness and wield power but to disperse it between the member states and the regions within its borders.

Finally, chapter 8 challenges the thesis that growing overseas military commitments may drag the United States toward economic overstretch. There is no question that the United States is an unusual empire in its dependence on foreign capital to finance both private consumption and government borrowing. Yet its twin deficits are not the result of too many foreign military interventions. In fact, it is the domestic fiscal commitments of the federal government that seem likely to overstretch it in the years ahead. The true feet of clay of the American Colossus are the impending fiscal crises of the systems of Medicare and Social Security.

My conclusion (for those readers who like an indication of their ultimate destination) is that the global power of the United States today— impressive though it is to behold—rests on much weaker foundations than is commonly supposed. The United States has acquired an empire, but Americans themselves lack the imperial cast of mind. They would rather consume than conquer. They would rather build shopping malls than nations. They crave for themselves protracted old age and dread, even for other Americans who have volunteered for military service, untimely death in battle. It is not just that, like their British predecessors, they gained their empire in "a fit of absence of mind." The problem is that despite occasional flashes of self-knowledge, they have remained absentminded—or rather, in denial—about their imperial power all along. Consequently, and very regrettably, it is quite conceivable that their empire could unravel as swiftly as the equally "anti-imperial" empire that was the Soviet Union.

Those who wish to perpetuate American primacy by achieving and maintaining full-spectrum dominance are, in short, facing the wrong way. For the threat to America's empire does not come from embryonic rival empires to the west or to the east. I regret to say that it may come from the vacuum of power—the absence of a will to power—within.

PART I

RISE

CHAPTER 1

THE LIMITS OF THE AMERICAN EMPIRE

What to that redoubted harpooneer, John Bull, is poor Ireland, but a Fast-Fish? What to that apostolic lancer, Brother Jonathan, is Texas but a Fast-Fish? And concerning all these, is not Possession the whole of the law?

But if the doctrine of Fast-Fish be pretty generally applicable, the kindred doctrine of Loose-Fish is still more widely so. That is internationally and universally applicable.

What are the Rights of Man and the Liberties of the World but Loose-Fish? . . . What is the great globe itself but a Loose-Fish? . . . What was America in 1492 but a Loose-Fish, in which Columbus struck the Spanish standard by way of waifing it for his royal master and mistress? What was Poland to the Czar? What Greece to the Turk? What India to England? What at last will Mexico be to the United States? All Loose-Fish.

HERMAN MELVILLE, *Moby Dick*, chapter 89

INTIMATIONS OF EMPIRE

It is commonplace to assume that having been forged in a war of independence against imperial rule, the United States could never become an empire in its own right. Many Americans today would accept the verdict of the historian Rupert Emerson, writing in 1942: "With the exception of the brief period of imperialist activity at the time of the Spanish-American war, the American people have shown a deep repugnance to both the conquest of distant lands and the assumption of rule over alien peoples."[1] The irony is that there were no more self-confident imperialists than the Founding Fathers themselves.

The empire they envisaged was, to be sure, very different in character from the empire from which they had seceded. It was not intended to resemble the maritime empires of Western Europe. But it did have much in common with the great land empires of the past. Like Rome, it began with a relatively small core—the founding states' combined area today is just 8 percent of the total extent of the United States—which expanded to dominate half a continent. Like Rome, it was an inclusive empire, relatively (though not wholly) promiscuous in the way that it conferred citizenship.[2] Like Rome, it had, at least for a time, its disenfranchised slaves.[3] But unlike Rome, its republican constitution has withstood the ambitions of any would-be Caesars—so far. (It is of course early days. The United States is 228 years old. When Caesar crossed the Rubicon in 49 B.C., the Roman Republic was 460 years old.)

That the United States would expand was decided almost from its very inception. When, in the draft Articles of Confederation of July 1776, John Dickinson proposed setting western boundaries of the states, the idea was thrown out at the committee stage. To George Washington the United States was a "nascent empire," later an "infant empire."[4] Thomas Jefferson told James Madison he was "persuaded no constitution was ever before as well calculated as ours for extending extensive empire and self-government." The initial "confederacy" of thirteen would be "the nest from which all America, North and South [would] be peopled."[5] Indeed, Jefferson observed in a letter of 1801 that the short history of the United States had already furnished "a new proof for the falsehood of Montesquieu's doctrine, that a republic can be preserved only in a small territory. The reverse is the truth."[6] Madison agreed; in the tenth of the *Federalist Papers,* he forcefully argued for "extend[ing] the sphere" to create a larger republic.[7] Alexander Hamilton too referred to the United States—in the opening paragraph of the first of the *Federalist Papers*—as "in many respects the most interesting . . . empire . . . in the world."[8] He looked forward eagerly to the emergence of a "great American system, superior to the control of all trans-Atlantic force of influence, and able to dictate the terms of connection between the Old and the New World."[9]

Such intimations of grandeur were widespread. William Henry Drayton, chief justice of South Carolina, declared in 1776: "Empires have their zenith—and their descension [*sic*] to a dissolution. . . . The British Period is from the Year 1758, when they victoriously pursued their Enemies into every Quarter of the Globe. . . . The Almighty . . . has made choice of the present generation to erect the American Empire. . . . And thus has suddenly arisen in the World, a new Empire, stiled [sic] the United States of America. An Empire that as soon as started into Existence, attracts the Attention of the Rest of the Universe; and bids fair, by the blessing of God, to be the most glorious of any upon Record."[10] Thirteen years later a Congregational minister named Jedidiah Morse published his *American Geography*, predicting that the "last and broadest seat" of empire would be in America, "the largest empire that ever existed": "We cannot but anticipate the period, as not far distant, when the American Empire will comprehend millions of souls, west of the Mississippi. . . . Europe begins to look forward with anxiety to her West Indian Islands, which are the natural legacy of this continent, and will doubtless be claimed as such when America shall have arrived at an age which will enable her to maintain her right."[11]

In the space of less than a century the vision of a continental empire was largely realized. Yet Morse's prediction that America's expansion would go beyond the continent's two ocean shores was only very feebly fulfilled. Why?

FRONTIER FOR SALE

The overland expansion was easy; this is often forgotten. For one thing, the Native American populations were too small and technologically backward to offer more than sporadic and ineffectual resistance to the hordes of white settlers swarming westward, enticed by the prospect of virgin land. Around 6 million immigrants came to the United States between 1820 and 1869, and nearly 16 million in the years to 1913. Already in 1820 the indigenous population had numbered just 325,000 (a mere 3 percent of population), their numbers having been roughly halved in the previous century by disease and small wars.[12] The new Republic simply continued the old British practice of treating traditional native hunting grounds as *terra nullius*, free, ownerless land. Jefferson talked of an expansion based "not on conquest, but [on] principles of compact and equality."[13] Like so much that he wrote on the subject of equality, however, this was an implicitly qualified statement. Just as the "rights of man" did not apply to his or any other plantation owner's slaves, so territorial expansion would not be based on the consent of the indigenous peoples of North America. As early as 1817 the secretary of war, John C. Calhoun, inaugurated the policy of removing "Indians" beyond the ninety-fifth line of longitude, a policy that became law in 1825.[14] President Andrew Jackson's professions of humanitarian intent scarcely disguised the ruthlessness of what was being done: "[This] just and humane policy recommended . . . [the Indians] to quit their possessions . . . and go to a country to the west where there is every probability that they will always be free from the mercenary influence of white men. . . . Under such circumstances the General Government can exercise a paternal control over their interests and possibly perpetuate their race."[15] In sum, the Native American tribes were to be coerced into exchanging "their possessions" for the "possibility" of perpetuating their race under their expropriators' "paternal control." In his seminal study, *The Significance of the Frontier in American History* (1893), Frederick Jackson Turner later sought to portray continental expansion as the source of America's alleged democratic vigor. In reality, expansion was achieved by a combination of land hunger, religious zeal and military force—in that order.[16] The number of settlers and sectarians was always vastly greater than the number of soldiers concerned. Between 1816 and 1860 the American army numbered on average less than 20,000 men, little more than one-tenth of 1 percent of the population—a tiny ratio of military participation by European standards.[17] The Indian Wars were doubtless cruel, but they were small wars. The Shawnees and the Seminoles needed a European ally to stand any chance of victory. After 1815 the prospect of such support disappeared, and the Indians were on their own.

Matters were also made easy for the growing Republic by the fact that none of the other European (or Europeanized) powers with territorial claims in North America posed a potentially fatal threat to the United States after 1783. In one respect, Jefferson was right. When it came to securing territory from them, this would not be an empire based on conquest. Rather, it would be an empire purchased for cash—or, to be precise, for government bonds. When the United States offered these in exchange for territory, the owners seldom hesitated to sell. The territory acquired in 1803 roughly doubled the size of the United States, including as it did all or at least a part of thirteen future states. "Louisiana," as this vast area was then known, was bought, not fought for, because neither of its previous owners, the French and the Spanish, saw any strategic benefit in retaining it. Ironically, it was in part the British navy that made the Louisiana Purchase possible; had it not been for its dominance of the Atlantic sea-lanes, which had effectively confined Napoleon's power to the European continent, Jefferson's offer might not have been so readily accepted. To exchange real estate covering roughly eight hundred thousand square miles for $11.2 million in freshly printed U.S. federal government bonds was, for the French, a financial expedient. For the United States the deal was, in effect, the mother of all mortgages—and, it should be added, one brokered by the London bank Barings.[18] By contrast, when the United States went to war against Britain between 1812 and 1815, it only succeeded in gaining a trifling amount of additional territory to the south; after Spanish authority in Florida disintegrated and residents around Baton Rouge proclaimed the Republic of West Florida, Madison ordered its annexation.[19] Dreams of annexing Canada were dispelled—despite a fleeting occupation of Toronto—by effective British resistance. The treaties of 1818 and 1819, with Britain and Spain respectively, were successes more for diplomacy than for arms. Britain agreed to a northern boundary along the forty-ninth parallel, giving up any claim to much of what became North Dakota, while Spain relinquished Florida and recognized a new western boundary along the border of what was to become Oklahoma.

Even the acquisition of Texas owed as much to cash and peaceful colonization as to conquest. From 1821 until 1834 Stephen Austin established and ran his colony with the consent of the Mexican authorities, which were in fact more generous than the United States toward would-be settlers. In 1829 Austin wrote enthusiastically to his sister and brother-in-law, urging them to come to Texas and describing the Mexican government as "the most liberal and munificent Govt. on earth to emigra[n]ts." "After being here one year," he added, "you will oppose a change even to Uncle Sam." As late as 1832 his "standing motto" was still "Fidelity to Mexico."[20] Two years before, a decree had prohibited Americans from settling in Texas. But although this prompted the settlers to summon their own convention, they resolved merely to send Austin to petition the government in Mexico City.[21] Only in 1835, after Austin had spent the better part of a

year in jail, and after repeated harassment by Mexican troops, did the settlers take up arms.[22]

Yet when the Texans, fresh from victory over General Antonio de Santa
Anna's army, voted all but unanimously for annexation by the United
States, they were rebuffed.[23] Despite the fact that Andrew Jackson had previously offered to buy Texas from the Mexicans for five million dollars, he
was unable to overcome resistance to annexation within Congress. In effect,
the Texans had independence thrust back upon them.[24] Only by flirting
with Great Britain—raising the prospect of a British satellite to the south of
the United States as well as to the north—was the Texan president Sam
Houston able to resuscitate his country's bid to join the Union; even then,
a second proposal for accession was rejected by the Senate in June 1844. It
was the emergence of Texas as an election issue that tipped the balance.
Martin Van Buren lost the Democratic nomination to James K. Polk because he refused to endorse annexation, while Polk went on to defeat the
Whig Henry Clay, who wanted to delay Texan accession.[25] When Texas
became the twenty-eighth state of the Union in December 1845, John
O'Sullivan, editor of the *Democratic Review*, portrayed it as "the fulfillment
of our manifest destiny to overspread the continent."[26] Yet the possibility of
annexation had presented itself at least a decade earlier. The fact that it took
so long to happen suggests that there were, after all, less manifest limits to
U.S. expansion. The crucial obstacle in this case had been that in Texas slavery was permitted. Northern abolitionists detected in the campaign to acquire new states in the South and West a stratagem to increase the number
of slave states in the Union. The fateful question posed by the South's peculiar institution would hamper the expansion of the United States until it
was finally settled by the bloodiest war Americans have ever fought—the
one they fought against each other.

War with Mexico came after, rather than before, the annexation of
Texas; it was a war fought in part because the buyer and the vendor could
not agree on the price of the Texan purchase. American citizens had claims
against the Mexican government amounting to $6.5 million; these the
Mexicans declined to recognize.[27] In March 1846 Polk ordered General
Zachary Taylor to march from the Nueces River to the Rio Grande. The
Mexicans declared a "defensive war"; the Polk administration replied by ac-
cusing them of spilling "American blood on American soil." Neither side

anticipated how one-sided the ensuing conflict would be; indeed, General Ulysses S. Grant later repented of what he called "one of the most unjust [wars] ever waged by a stronger against a weaker nation."[28] In less than a year the U.S. Army won a succession of engagements decisively, smashing Santa Anna's significantly larger force at Buena Vista in February 1847. Another army under General Winfield Scott landed at Veracruz and marched on Mexico City, capturing the capital that September.[29] Yet force of arms alone did not decide the fate of Texas, or the fates of its western neighbors. Under the Treaty of Guadalupe Hidalgo of February 1848, the Americans once again exchanged dollars for land. To be precise, by assuming up to $5 million of the claims of its citizens against Mexico, the United States acquired the territory down to the Rio Grande, and for a further $15 million, it added to its shopping basket the provinces of New Mexico and Upper California, territory that now comprises most of New Mexico, Arizona, California, Colorado, Utah and Nevada.[30] These were vast acquisitions. They were also an investment that paid an immediate return since gold had been discovered in California just months before. Moreover, because little of the new land was suitable for plantation agriculture, annexation was less controversial than it had been in the case of Texas.

In a speech to the Senate in 1850, William Henry Seward had hailed California's accession to the Union, declaring: "The world contains no seat of empire so magnificent as this, which . . . offers supplies on the Atlantic shores to the overcrowded nations of Europe, while on the Pacific coast it intercepts the commerce of the Indies. The nation thus situated must command . . . the empire of the seas, which alone is real empire.[31] But events seemed to suggest that the real empire was the empire of diplomacy and the dollar. A year after Seward's speech the United States had secured the territory of Oregon by agreeing that the existing border between British and American territory—the forty-ninth parallel—should be extended to the Pacific. Those bellicose voices who called for war and the pushing of the border to the fifty-fourth parallel (beyond Prince Rupert) went unheeded.[32] In 1853 the American ambassador to Mexico, James Gadsden, acquired a further strip of territory from Mexico (the area south of the Gila River, which today straddles southwestern New Mexico and southern Arizona). This time the price was $10 million, the highest price per acre ever paid by the United States for territory (see table 2). And fifteen years later, at the initiative of Secretary of State William Seward, the United States acquired a further 570,000 square miles of what appeared largely to be tundra by buying Alaska from the Russian tsar for $7.2 million.

Nothing illustrates more clearly the limits of American expansion than the failure of the United States to acquire any other territory north of the forty-ninth parallel. We should not forget that the Founding Fathers had originally intended to unite "the inhabitants of all the territory from Cape Breton to the Mississippi."[33] Yet as we have seen, bids to seize Canada by force had failed, first during the War of Independence and again in the War of 1812. Moreover, when it came to continental expansion, Canada proved every bit as dynamic as did the United States. It was the American purchase of Alaska that precipitated the creation of the federal Dominion of Canada (1867), which by 1871 extended from the Atlantic to the Pacific (and the economic success of which demonstrated conclusively that a repudiation of British political institutions was not a prerequisite for success on the North American continent). There was and is nothing much that is natural about

TABLE 2. BUYING AN EMPIRE:
MAJOR AMERICAN TERRITORIAL ACQUISITIONS, 1803–1898

Date	Treaty or Act	Property	Acquired from	Total Area (Acres)	Price ($)	Price per Acre (Cents)
1803	Louisiana Purchase	Louisiana	France	559,513,600	15,000,000	3
1819	Adams–Onís Treaty	East Florida	Spain	46,144,640	15,000,000	33
1846	Oregon Treaty	Pacific Northwest south of 49th parallel	Great Britain	192,000,000	–	0
1848	Guadalupe-Hidalgo	Texas, California, New Mexico etc.	Mexico	338,680,960	15,000,000 +5,000,000	6
1850	Texas Cession	New Mexico	Texas	78,926,720	10,000,000	13
1853	Gadsden Purchase	Southern Arizona, New Mexican border	Mexico	18,988,800	10,000,000	53
1867	Alaska Purchase	Alaska	Russia	375,296,000	7,200,000	2
1898	Treaty of Paris	Philippines	Spain	74,112,000	20,000,000	27

Source: Richard B. Morris (ed.), *Encyclopedia of American History*, p. 599; Charles Arnold-Baker, *The Companion to British History*.

the northern frontier of the United States, which follows a degree of latitude for most of its length and then effectively bisects the Great Lakes; it does not even stick to the course of the St. Lawrence River. This arbitrary two-and-a-half-thousand-mile line perfectly illustrates the limits of nineteenth-century American power. The stark reality is that in the first century of their existence under an independent republic, Americans spilled far more blood fighting one another (in what was, in effect, their war of unification) than they had to spill fighting for continental *lebensraum*. By the 1860s the question for which Americans were prepared to fight and die was not how big their republic should be but how free it should be.

EMPIRE AT SEA

The United States had already mounted a number of small-scale naval expeditions in the period before the Civil War, little forays like the wars of 1801–06 against the Barbary pirates (to be precise, the pasha of Tripoli).[34] But actual annexation of territory beyond the shores of the continent was another matter. Was it even constitutional? Chief Justice Roger Brooke Tancy's opinion in the notorious *Dred Scott* decision (1857)[35] stated that there was "certainly no power given by the Constitution to the Federal Government to establish or maintain colonies bordering on the United States or at a distance, to be ruled and governed at its own pleasure; nor to enlarge its territorial limits in any way, except by admission of new States."[36] This seemed to make it plain that there could be no colonies or other forms of dependent territories, only new states. Partly for that reason, when Santo Domingo (the future Dominican Republic) effectively offered itself up for annexation in 1869, the proposal was defeated in Congress.[37] Thirty years later, however, A. Lawrence Lowell could argue quite differently. "Possessions may also be so acquired," he wrote in the *Harvard Law Review,* "as not to form part of the United States, and in that case constitutional limitations, such as those requiring uniformity of taxation and trial by jury, do not apply."[38] The timing of Lowell's article was significant, for by 1899 the United States had acquired a clutch of new territorial possessions, few, if any, of which seemed suitable candidates for statehood.

Late-nineteenth-century American imperialism was in many ways similar in character to the imperialisms of Europe in the same era. Whereas the first phase of American expansion had been driven by mass migration and the colonization of very thinly populated land, this phase was motivated by a combination of strategic, commercial and ideological impulses. The *fons et origo* of American grand strategy was a heroic negative, the "doctrine" proclaimed by President James Monroe in 1823, which asserted "as a principle . . . that the American continents, by the free and independent condition which they have assumed and maintain, are henceforth not to be considered as subjects for future colonization by any European powers."[39] For decades this was little more than Yankee bluff.[40] The British established the colony of British Guiana (now Guyana) out of three formerly Dutch possessions in 1831 and continued blithely to colonize north of the forty-ninth parallel as if oblivious of Monroe's great declaration. In 1839 they seized the island of Ruatán off the coast of Honduras; in the 1850s they briefly occupied the nearby Bay Islands; in 1862 they turned Belize into the colony of British Honduras.[41] The French too ignored the Monroe Doctrine, attempting to transform Mexico into a satellite under the ill-starred emperor Maximilian in the 1860s; the failure of this scheme was only partly due to American sabre-rattling. European powers made multiple interventions in Latin America, often on debt-collecting missions, before, during and after the American Civil War.[42] It was only toward the end of the nineteenth century that (as Secretary of State Richard Olney put it) the United States could be regarded as "practically sovereign on this continent"—"not because of the pure friendship or good will felt for it . . . not simply by reason of its high character as a civilized state, nor because wisdom and justice and equity are the invariable characteristics of the dealings of the United States . . . [but] because in addition to all other grounds, its infinite resources combined with its isolated position render it master of the situation and practically invulnerable."[43]

Even that analysis left something out; until such times as the United States had a world-class navy, it could not really enforce its claim to what amounted to a hemispheric exclusion zone. In the 1880s the American fleet was still an insignificant entity, smaller even than the Swedish.[44] However, inspired by Captain Alfred Thayer Mahan's hugely influential book *The Influence of Sea Power upon History,* the United States embarked on a navy-building program more ambitious even than Germany's. The achievement was astonishing: by 1907 the American fleet was second only to the Royal Navy.[45] With this, the Monroe Doctrine belatedly acquired credibility.[46] When Britain and Germany blockaded Venezuela in 1902, in response to attacks on European ships and defaults on European debts, it was Theodore Roosevelt's threat to send fifty-four American warships from Puerto Rico that persuaded them to accept international arbitration.[47] By the early 1900s Great Britain recognized the United States as one of those rival empires serious enough to be worthy of appeasement.[48]

As in the case of the European battleship mania, maritime power was justified in terms of overseas commercial interests. Before the 1880s few American businessmen had any thought for opportunities beyond the borders of the United States; there was patently more than enough money to be made at home. True, in the 1850s some southerners had dreamed of striking beyond even Texas to establish new slave states in Central America; with some such scheme in mind, the Tennessee adventurer William Walker had managed to seize control of Nicaragua in the mid-1850s.[49] In 1859 a bill even went before Congress for the annexation of Cuba.[50] But with the outbreak—and, more important, the outcome—of the Civil War, all such notions went into abeyance for a generation. Not until the 1880s could James G. Blaine, leader of the Republican Party and secretary of state, give voice to the idea that there might also be "openings of assured and profitable enterprise" for northern industry "in the mines of South America and the railroads of Mexico . . . even in mid-ocean."[51] "While the great powers of Europe are steadily enlarging their colonial domination in Asia and Africa," he declared, it was "the especial province of this country to improve and expand its trade with the nations of America."[52] Albert J. Beveridge, senator for Indiana in the early 1890s, went further still:

> American factories are making more than the American people can use; American soil is producing more than they can consume. Fate has written our policy for us; the trade of the world must and shall be ours. . . . We will establish trading posts throughout the world as distributing points for American products. . . . Great colonies governing themselves, flying our flag and trading with us, will grow about our posts of trade. . . . And American law, American order, American civilization, and the American

flag will plant themselves on shores hitherto bloody and benighted, but by those agencies of God henceforth to be made beautiful and bright.[53]

It was a commercial megalomania personified by Joseph Conrad's character Holroyd, the bumptious East Coast plutocrat who appears in *Nostromo:*

Now, what is Costaguana? It is the bottomless pit of 10 per cent loans and other fool investments. European capital has been flung into it with both hands for years. Not ours, though. We in this country know just about enough to keep indoors when it rains. We can sit and watch. Of course, some day we shall step in. We are bound to. But there's no hurry. Time itself has got to wait on the greatest country in the whole of God's Universe. We shall be giving the word for everything: industry, trade, law, journalism, art, politics, and religion, from Cape Horn clear over to Smith's Sound, and beyond, too, if anything worth taking hold of turns up at the North Pole. And then we shall have the leisure to take in hand the outlying islands and continents of the earth. We shall run the world's business whether the world likes it or not. The world can't help it—and neither can we, I guess.[54]

Yet such talk, though perhaps in a slightly less brash idiom, might equally well have been overheard in one of the London clubs. The components of economic imperialism were essentially the same on both sides of the Atlantic: a desire to reduce other people's tariffs (hence the "Open Door"),[55] a confidence that overseas investment would beget new export markets (especially important in the depression of 1893–97), but also a readiness to use political and military leverage to outwit the competition.[56] Equally familiar to students of European imperialism are the ideological currents that were at work: the social Darwinism expounded by Josiah Strong, author of *Expansion Under New World-Conditions* (1900);[57] the shrill chauvinism of the Hearst and Pulitzer papers.[58]

In the eyes of many British observers—from Kipling to Buchan, from Chamberlain to Churchill—America's bid for overseas markets thus had much in common with Britain's *fin de siècle* "scramble" for more colonies. This, after all, was the era when the *New York Times* could declare: "We are a part, and a great part, of the Greater Britain which seems so plainly destined to dominate this planet."[59] Yet two related things made the American experiment with empire different from its transatlantic counterpart. First, the political base for imperialism was narrower; empire appealed much more to the elites of the industrialized North than to the rest of the country. Secondly, the economic rationale of acquiring colonies was more open to doubt. Britain had embraced free trade as early as the 1840s. Nothing had subsequently been done to protect British farmers from the influx of cheaper foodstuffs, as steamships, railways and refrigerators integrated the world's corn and meat markets. Britain seemed self-evidently to need a global *imperium,* if only to secure the flow to its domestic emporium of goods it could not grow itself. Moreover, the bankers of the City of London, whose business it was to direct British capital overseas, had a vested interest in a continuation of both free trade and empire. How could the debtor countries of the New World be expected to honor their obligations if their exports of primary products did not have free access to the British market? And if they did threaten to default, what better way to prevent them from doing so than to occupy their countries and govern them according to sound economic principles?[60] In the United States there were men who made similar arguments, but there were powerful protectionist lobbies pushing in the opposite direction. Their argument was that the United States had no need of British-style colonies if their function was simply to inundate the American market with goods that Americans could just as well produce for themselves (albeit less cheaply). Other opponents, dismayed at the changing complexion of the immigrants coming to the United States, saw colonies as just a further source of inferior racial stock.[61] Though they shared some of its underlying prejudices, protectionism and nativism proved to be false friends to imperialism; *pace* Kipling, their proponents had no real interest in shouldering "the white man's burden."

The first American overseas possessions were islands desirable only as naval bases or sources of guano. The atoll of Midway, formally annexed in 1867 by Captain William Reynolds of the USS *Lackawanna,* was among the first of these maritime filling stations. A decade later the United States secured the right to use the harbor of Pago Pago on the Samoan island of Tutuila, though it was not until 1899, following a civil war in Samoa, that the entire island became an American possession.[62] A year before, Guam had also been acquired, along with Wake Island. Besides being small—even the largest, Guam, is barely two hundred square miles in size—all these new outposts were exceedingly far away. The nearest, Midway, was literally midway between Los Angeles and Shanghai. The most remote, Guam, lay between Japan and New Guinea, nearly fifty-eight hundred miles west of San Francisco. The first true American colony was also in the Pacific: Hawaii.

That an eight-island archipelago located over two thousand miles from the American mainland should have ended up being the fiftieth state of the Union is a true historical puzzle, particularly as other, more obvious candidates for integration into the United States were passed over. Three groups combined to Americanize Hawaii: missionaries, sugar planters and navalists. To the last group, Hawaii offered, in the words of Secretary of State Hamilton Fish, an attractive "resting spot in the mid-ocean, between the Pacific coast and the vast domains of Asia, which are now opening to commerce and Christian civilization," not to mention a way of "curbing" the already discernible rise of Japan.[63] To the sugar producers of the islands themselves, the United States represented a potentially vast market, if tariff-free trade could be achieved. The mission schools meanwhile prepared the Hawaiians for subjugation. The steps toward this fate were swiftly taken: in 1875 a free trade treaty was signed,[64] in 1887 a naval coaling station was established at Pearl Harbor, and in 1893 Queen Liliuokalani was overthrown in a *coup d'état* orchestrated by the American minister to the islands, John L. Stevens. Yet—just as had happened in the case of Texas—Congress drew back. Despite Stevens's warnings that Hawaii would otherwise become "a Singapore, or a Hong Kong, which could be governed as a British colony,"[65] his plan for annexation was rejected.[66] Sugar producers feared competition,[67] and racialists feared "bad blood and bad customs" (since Americans made up just 2 percent of the islands' population), while liberals suspected that the American minority had less than democratic intentions. When, in 1897, a draft treaty for annexation ran into bipartisan opposition once again, Theodore Roosevelt was moved to lament "the queer lack of imperial instinct that our people show."[68] It was only after the news of the American victory over Spanish forces in the Philippines that a resolution for annexation could be passed.[69]

The Hawaiians resisted—but they resisted peacefully. In the election to the first territorial legislature, a Home Rule Party won a majority of seats by mobilizing native voters, who defied the clause in the Organic Act that all debate should be in English.[70] Only by co-opting Jonah Kuhio Kalanianaole, a royal prince who had initially resisted the American takeover, was the local Republican Party able to compete. Little more than a front man for the interests of the Honolulu Chamber of Commerce and the Hawaiian Sugar Planters' Association, Prince Kuhio could only bewail impotently the decline and fall of his people.[71] While the five big sugar companies tightened their grip on the islands' most fertile areas, the original inhabitants were "rehabilitated": in effect, shunted onto marginal land.[72] This not unfamiliar colonization process did not quite go according to plan, however. The natives had been sidelined in classic fashion, but their places were not taken by American settlers. Instead, as had already been the case before annexation, it was Japanese and later Filipino migrants who came to populate Hawaii. Despite measures to exclude newcomers, the Japanese community grew rapidly. In the early 1920s three in every hundred voters were Japanese, but by 1936 the proportion was one in four.[73] Hawaii might be strategically valuable to the United States, but it offered enterprising Americans few economic opportunities to equal those available at home.

Why did Hawaii ultimately become a state, but not Puerto Rico, ceded to the United States by Spain in 1898? It was certainly not a matter of distance, since the latter is a good deal nearer to the American mainland (just over a thousand miles from Miami). Nor, in economic terms, did one sugar plantation have more to offer than the other. The answer is in fact a legal technicality, revealed when Puerto Rican producers sought to challenge the imposition of tariffs on their exports to the United States. In two simultaneous judgments in 1901, the Supreme Court concluded that Puerto Rico was not a foreign country, but that it was not domestic territory either, and that therefore a tariff on its products was constitutional. Of particular importance was the distinction drawn by Justice Edward Douglass White between annexation and incorporation (which required congressional authority). In his opinion, "Puerto Rico had not been incorporated into the United States, but was merely appurtenant thereto as a possession." As such, only certain "fundamental" provisions of the Constitution applied to it. The significance of this ruling, which defined that strange limbo between independence and American statehood occupied by Puerto Rico ever since, was that decisions could now be taken retrospectively about the status of other possessions. Since, under the terms of their acquisition, "formal" as well as "fundamental" provisions of the Constitution had been extended to both Alaska and Hawaii, they must by definition have been incorporated and therefore entitled to full statehood, which they eventually attained in 1959.[74]

The judgments of 1901 appeared to clear the way legally for the annexation of new and larger colonies that could be treated like Puerto Rico as "organized but unincorporated" and therefore outside the domain of the Constitution. Why, then, has the United States not got more Puerto Ricos? The answer can be expressed in two words: the Philippines.

What happened in the Philippines has unfortunately proved to be far more typical of American overseas experience than what happened in Hawaii and Puerto Rico. To be precise, seven characteristic phases of American engagement can be discerned:

1. Impressive initial military success
2. A flawed assessment of indigenous sentiment
3. A strategy of limited war and gradual escalation of forces
4. Domestic disillusionment in the face of protracted and nasty conflict
5. Premature democratization
6. The ascendancy of domestic economic considerations
7. Ultimate withdrawal

The speed of the American victory over Spain in 1898 was certainly striking. Within just three months of the American declaration of war—the trumped-up pretext for which was the accidental explosion of the battleship *Maine* in Havana Bay, supposedly the fault of Spain—the Spanish forces in both the Caribbean and the Philippines were defeated. However, the Americans refused to recognize that the Filipinos who had sided with them against Spain had been fighting for their independence, not for a change of colonial master.[75] McKinley's reported justification for annexing the islands was a masterpiece of presidential sanctimony, perfectly pitched for his audience of Methodist clergymen:

> I walked the floor of the White House night after night until midnight; and I am not ashamed to tell you . . . that I went down on my knees and prayed Almighty God for light and guidance more than one night. And one night late it came to me this way—I don't know how it was but it came. . . . (1) That we could not give them back to Spain. . . . (2) That we could not turn them over to France and Germany—our commercial rivals in the Orient . . . (3) that we could not leave them to themselves—they were unfit for government . . . (4) that there was nothing left for us to do but to take them all, and educate the Filipinos, and uplift and civilize and Christianize them, and by God's grace do the very best we could by them as our fellow-men for whom Christ also died.[76]

As McKinley portrayed it, annexation was an onerous duty, thrust upon the United States by the will of Providence.[77] Such religious appeals doubtless had considerable public resonance.[78] The decisive arguments for the occupation within the American political elite were nevertheless more military and mercenary than missionary.[79]

The rebellion against American annexation, led by Emilio Aguinaldo, began soon after the publication of the terms of the Treaty of Paris, which ceded the Philippines to the United States in return for twenty million dollars (roughly the same price that had been paid for Texas, California and the other Mexican cessions fifty years before, and therefore a good deal less land per dollar). The islands turned out to cost the United States even more than that. In the space of three years the number of American troops committed to the Philippines rose from just 12,000 to 126,000.[80] Although Aguinaldo was captured in March 1901, and the war declared officially over in July 1902, resistance continued on some islands for years afterward. It was not a pleasant war; nor was it to be the American military's last taste of jungle warfare against guerrillas indistinguishable from civilians.[81] Senior officers swiftly resorted to harsh measures: Brigadier General Jacob H. Smith ordered his men on the island of Samar to take no prisoners—a breach of the laws of war—adding: "I wish you to kill and burn, the more you kill and the more you burn the better you will please me . . . I want all persons killed who are capable of bearing arms."[82] By the time the fighting was over, more than 4,000 American servicemen had lost their lives, over 1,000 more than had been killed in the war against Spain. Approximately four times as many Filipinos were killed in action, to say nothing of civilians who died because of war-related hunger and disease.[83] Meanwhile, William Howard Taft, a judge from Ohio, was put in charge of a five-man civilian commission that sought to win Filipinos over by building schools and improving sanitation, proving, as one of the commissioners ingenuously put it, that "American sovereignty was . . . another name for the liberty of the Filipinos."[84] The war alone had cost six hundred million dollars. How much would postwar reconstruction add to the bill?

It was not, however, its cost that aroused the initial domestic opposition to the war in the Philippines so much as the principle of the thing. We should not imagine, of course, that the Anti-Imperialist League spoke for a majority of voters.[85] But its membership included two former presidents, Grover Cleveland and Benjamin Harrison, a dozen senators from both parties, eight former members of Cleveland's cabinet, to say nothing of the millionaire industrialist Andrew Carnegie. The league had enough leverage to make Filipino independence a part of the 1900 Democratic Party platform.[86] And in Mark Twain it had on its side the most influential American man of letters of the day.

Twain's attitudes anticipate those of future generations of American antiwar intellectuals. He had begun by welcoming the "liberation" of the Philippines from Spain, writing to a friend in June 1898: "It is a worthy thing to fight for one's freedom. It is another sight finer to fight for another man's. And I think this is the first time it has been done." But by October 1900 he had "read carefully" the Treaty of Paris and concluded "that we do not intend to free but to subjugate the people of the Philippines. . . . And so I am an anti-imperialist. I am opposed to having the eagle put its talons in any other land." Twain's voice was muffled. *Harper's Bazaar* rejected his short story "The War Prayer," in which an aged stranger utters the following prayer before a congregation: "O Lord our Father, our young patriots, idols of our hearts, go forth to battle—be Thou near them! . . . O Lord our God, help us to tear their soldiers to bloody shreds with our shells; help us to cover their smiling fields with the pale forms of their patriotic dead; . . . help us to wring the hearts of their unoffending widows with unavailing grief; help us to turn them out roofless with their little children wandering and unfriended in the wastes of their desolated land." Privately, but not publicly, Twain described McKinley as the man who had sent U.S. troops "to fight with a disgraced musket under a polluted flag" and suggested that the flag in question should have "the white stripes painted black and the stars replaced by the skull and crossbones."[87] His disapprobation carried weight. Opponents of a war do not need to command majority support to undermine a war effort. Although the Democrats failed to thwart annexation in Congress,[88] and although their candidate was defeated by McKinley, the extent of opposition to annexation in the Democratic press was impressive.[89] The revelation that General Smith and Colonel Littleton W. T. Waller had ordered the summary execution of Filipino prisoners gave the antiwar campaign a glaring opportunity to embarrass the government.[90] McKinley could be sure of victory in 1900 only by distancing himself from full-blown imperialism.[91]

Theodore Roosevelt had once likened the Filipinos to the Apaches and Aguinaldo to Sitting Bull.[92] Thrust into the presidency by McKinley's assassination, he nevertheless hastened to create at least the semblance of democracy in the Philippines, privately admitting that he would "only be too glad to withdraw" from what seemed to be America's Boer War.[93] The first elections to the national legislature called into being by the Organic Act saw fifty-eight out of the Assembly's eighty seats go to nationalists who had campaigned for immediate independence. Within less than a decade the so-called Jones Act (1916) confirmed that the islands would be granted independence "as soon as a stable government can be established." Yet it was not nationalist pressure that determined when that day would come. Nor did the decision to grant the Philippines their independence reflect a wholly sincere repudiation of the original annexation on the part of the United States. The decisive campaign for Filipino independence was in fact waged by a coalition of sectional lobbies within the U.S. Congress, motivated almost solely by their own self-interests: sugar, dairy and cotton producers who wanted to exclude Philippine cane sugar and coconut oil from the U.S. market, hand in glove with trade unionists pressing for immigration restrictions against Filipino workers. Indeed, so harsh were the provisions of the original American independence offer of 1933 that the islands' legislature refused to accept it. Although the Tydings–McDuffie Act of 1934 was somewhat less punitive—it left the future of the American military bases on the islands open to negotiation—its economic provisions remained essentially the same. Independence would mean a phased imposition of American tariffs on Philippine products, a heavy blow to an economy that by this time relied on the American market to buy more than three-quarters of its exports.[94] There was much less for Filipinos to celebrate when independence finally came in 1946 than is generally appreciated.

It is perhaps too harsh to dismiss American rule over the Philippines as a failure. But it was certainly far from the success that Franklin Roosevelt later made out.[95] Quite apart from the economic plight of the islanders as they were squeezed out of the American market, the strategic gains of American rule proved to be negligible. First, the grandiose American plans for the economic penetration of Asia—which were, after all, the whole point of establishing bases across the Pacific—were no more than half realized. Secondly, when the Japanese launched their military challenge against the United States in December 1941, the American bases from Pearl Harbor to Subic Bay proved to be easy targets.

DICTATING DEMOCRACY

There was, however, an alternative to formal European-style imperialism; indeed, the decision to grant the Philippines political (if not commercial) freedom was part of that alternative. Instead of occupying and running fully fledged colonies, the United States could instead use its economic and military power to foster the emergence of "good government" in strategically important countries. Initially, that meant not just pro-American government but also American-style government. The development of this new approach to empire, which had something in common with the British notion of indirect rule, owed much to the presidency of Woodrow Wilson. But the underlying idea can be traced back to his predecessor Theodore Roosevelt's Corollary to the Monroe Doctrine (December 1904), which declared: "Chronic wrongdoing, or an impotence which results in a general loosening of the ties of civilized society, may in America, as elsewhere, ultimately require intervention by some civilized nation, and in the Western Hemisphere, the adherence of the United States to the Monroe Doctrine may force the United States, however reluctantly, in flagrant cases of wrongdoing or impotence, to the exercise of an international police power."[96] Wilson, however, went further. Just a week after entering the White House, the new president declared to the press that, in future, cooperation with Latin American countries would be possible "only when supported at every turn by the orderly processes of just government based on law, not upon arbitrary or irregular force. . . . We can have no sympathy with those who seek to seize the power of government to advance their own personal interests and ambition." The implicit Wilson Corollary was that only certain types of government would be tolerated by the United States in Latin America. Military dictators were out, but so too were revolutionaries. "The agitators in certain countries wanted revolutions," he remarked, "and were inclined to try it on with the new administration . . . he was not going to let them have one [a revolution] if he could prevent it."[97] The future would therefore lie with governments that had the good sense to position themselves between the abhorrent extremes of "arbitrary . . . force" and "revolution." Against unacceptable regimes the United States reserved the right to use force.[98]

Just where such a policy might lead became suddenly clear to the British foreign secretary Sir Edward Grey in 1913, when Wilson declared his intention not to recognize the government of General Victoriano Huerta, who had seized power in Mexico following the assassination of the liberal premier Francisco Madero. After Walter Page, the American ambassador in London, had explained his government's position to Grey, the following conversation ensued:

GREY: Suppose you have to intervene, what then?
PAGE: Make 'em vote and live by their decisions.
GREY: But suppose they will not so live?
PAGE: We'll go in and make 'em vote again.
GREY: And keep this up 200 years?
PAGE: Yes. The United States will be here for two hundred years and it can continue to shoot men for that little space till they learn to vote and to rule themselves.[99]

Thus was born the paradox that was to be a characteristic feature of American foreign policy for a century: the paradox of dictating democracy, of enforcing freedom, of extorting emancipation.

It should be said at once that, alongside this "new principle," the older imperialist impulses continued to work. Economic and strategic considerations, plus the usual assumptions of racial superiority—all these played their part in U.S.–Latin American relations. Indeed, the Wilsonian approach was in many ways simply grafted onto preexisting policies in the region.

The strategic crux of American policy was the Central American isthmus and the long crescent of islands—stretching from the Straits of Florida to the island of Trinidad—that separate the Caribbean from the Atlantic, what Henry Cabot Lodge called the "outwork essential to the defense" of the continental "citadel."[100] The countries that therefore mattered most in the region were Nicaragua and Panama as well as the islands of Cuba and Hispaniola, divided since 1844 between Haiti and the Dominican Republic.[101]

What seemed the vital question of control over the projected canal across the isthmus was resolved by military means in 1903. The U.S. Marines had in fact been sent to Colombia on two previous occasions (in 1885 and 1895), but it was their third intervention, this time in support of Panamanian separatists, that proved to be decisive. In essence, Roosevelt used the U.S. Navy to establish Panama as an independent state after the Colombian Senate refused to ratify an agreement leasing land for the construction of the canal.[102] Within ninety minutes of the secessionists' coup, the United States formally recognized the Republic of Panama, which obligingly granted Washington a ten-mile-wide strip of territory through which the canal would be built.[103] This was achieved with an almost laughably small show of force. The sole reported casualties were "a Chinaman in Salsipuedes Street and . . . an ass."[104]

The Panama Canal was opened in 1914 and remained under direct American control until 1979. But plans had also existed to build a canal farther north through Nicaragua; indeed, before volcanic eruptions there in 1902 caused consternation in the U.S. Senate, that country had seemed to offer the more likely route (via Lake Nicaragua).[105] American business interests in the country were scarcely enormous: total U.S. investment there amounted to no more than $2.5 million in 1912, compared with $1.7 billion for Latin America as a whole.[106] However, when the Nicaraguan dictator José Santos Zelaya appeared to be flirting with an Anglo-French syndicate—and when two Americans were executed for their part in a rebel attack—the United States broke off diplomatic relations. Zelaya was forced to resign, and a new government was installed, with American backing, under Adolfo Díaz, former treasurer of the La Luz and Los Angeles Mining Company.[107] In 1912, at his request, three thousand marines were sent to quell a revolt against him; a small detachment of a hundred remained there for thirteen years, propping up his regime.[108] The fruit of this intervention was the 1916 Bryan-Chamorro Treaty, which, in return for $3 million, gave the United States exclusive rights to build a canal through Nicaragua as well as a naval base on the Gulf of Fonseca.[109]

In Cuba too business interests and strategic calculation pointed to recurrent intervention rather than annexation—dependence but not occupation. Though the defeat of Spain in 1898 had offered the opportunity to take over the island, American troops were there only briefly. McKinley had talked merely of "ties of singular intimacy and strength" between Cuba and the United States.[110] The form these would take was specified in Senator Orville H. Platt's Amendment, incorporated in the Cuban Constitution in 1902, which gave the United States the right to intervene if necessary "for the preservation of Cuban independence, the maintenance of a government adequate for the protection of life, property and individual liberty."[111] The amendment precluded any bilateral strategic arrangement between Cuba and a rival foreign power, thus giving the United States an effective veto power over the island's foreign policy. It circumscribed the country's future borrowing. And it entitled the United States to establish naval bases on the Cuban coast; the first to be leased was Guantánamo Bay on the eastern tip of the island.[112] It was not long before the right of intervention in Cuban political life was exercised. When a revolt threatened to topple a newly elected president in September 1906, a force of marines was deployed and a provisional government established under an American governor-general. But even the once-bullish Roosevelt now professed to "loathe the thought of assuming any control over the island such as we have over Puerto Rico and the Philippines." By now he had largely lost his faith in the idea that "thickly peopled tropical regions" like Cuba could be run "by self-governing northern democracies."[113] Two and a half years later the American troops left, having installed a new president.[114] They returned briefly to the island in 1912, to quell a revolt by former slaves, and again from 1917 until 1922, when the losing side refused to accept the election of President Mario Menocal. It was no coincidence that Menocal was the managing director of the Cuban-American Sugar Company.[115]

The Dominican Republic was placed in a comparable condition of political and economic dependence, just short of outright conquest. "I have," declared Roosevelt, "about the same desire to annex it as a gorged boa-constrictor might have to swallow a porcupine wrong-end-to."[116] Instead the tried-and-tested imperial method was adopted of controlling the collection of customs, the government's principal source of revenue. Under the *modus vivendi* of 1905, the United States was empowered to retain up to 55 percent of customs receipts for the purpose of debt service. What Lord Cromer was to late-nineteenth-century Cairo, Professor Jacob H. Hollander of Johns Hopkins University became to Santo Domingo, determining the size of its debt and the allocation of its customs revenues.[117] As in Cuba and Nicaragua, however, finding suitable puppets proved problematic. The assassination of President Ramón Cáceres in 1911 plunged the country's government into confusion, prompting the United States to oust one would-be successor and install another.[118] In 1914 a new Dominican president defied American demands for yet more stringent fiscal controls; when a revolution broke out, there seemed no alternative but once again to send in the marines. Finally, in November 1916, the country was placed under American military government, and it remained in that condition for six years. It was, said Wilson solemnly, "the least of the evils in sight in this very perplexing situation."[119]

To the west, in neighboring Haiti, the story was similar. Between 1900 and 1913 the United States dispatched small detachments of troops no fewer than sixteen times, but still the island's politics lurched from crisis to crisis; there were no fewer than six presidents in the four years from 1912 to 1915. When President Guillaume Sam was murdered in the latter year, Wilson once again dispatched the marines, who established order after considerable bloodshed.[120] That September a new president was installed on condition that he accept a treaty similar to the Platt Amendment. In this case Haiti's finances, police, press and public works were put under

American supervision. The American naval commander in charge of the operation imposed *de facto* military rule in coastal towns.[121]

Thus began a history of spasmodic intervention in Central America and the Caribbean that has continued to the present day. As a policy it has been, to put it mildly, disappointing. Indeed, when one compares the two territories in the region that the United States formally annexed—Puerto Rico and the Virgin Islands (purchased from Denmark in 1916)—with the countries it sought to control by indirect means, it is difficult to avoid the conclusion that annexation might have been better for all these places. Between the wars American enthusiasm for the Roosevelt Corollary faded; the Wilsonian belief that the people of the region could somehow be "taught . . . to elect good men" lost credibility. In 1924 the marines pulled out of the Dominican Republic.[122] Any pretense of interest in democratic government in Honduras was abandoned in the course of the 1920s; by 1932 the United Fruit Company, which dominated the country's banana production, was content to coexist peacefully and profitably with the authoritarian Tiburcio Carías Andino, who ruled the country until 1948.[123] "Intervention," Herbert Hoover told reporters shortly after being elected president, "is not now, never was, and never will be a set policy of the United States."[124] In fact, his successor, Franklin Roosevelt, lost little time in intervening in Cuba; the upshot, however, was another military dictatorship under a young sergeant named Fulgencio Batista. In 1934 the Platt Amendment was effectively torn up; all that survived of American control over Cuba was the Guantánamo Bay base. That same year Roosevelt pulled the American troops out of Haiti too.

Perhaps the most dispiriting case of all was Nicaragua, which by the mid-1920s was in the grip of civil war between rival Liberal and Conservative factions. In went the marines once more, this time to thwart a coup attempt by Emiliano Chamorro, back went Díaz to the presidential palace and along came Henry L. Stimson to broker some kind of settlement. In the summer of 1927 he might have succeeded, but for the obstinate resistance of one Liberal commander, Augusto César Sandino.[125] Elections were held in 1928, and again in 1932, but the marines found themselves embroiled in a grueling guerrilla war against the Sandinistas, whom not even the precocious use of airpower could dislodge from their mountain fastnesses. By 1932 the question being asked by many Americans was:

"Why are we in Nicaragua and what the hell are we doing there?"[126] One correspondent to the *New York Times* sounded a note that has proved especially resonant: "We ought to go down there and clean up that situation or get out of there and stay out. There's no use us sending a handful of our boys down there to be butchered."[127] (In fact, total U.S. fatalities were 136.) In January 1933 the last marines were withdrawn. Thirteen months later Sandino was executed by the first Nicaraguan-born commander of the U.S. trained National Guard, Anastasio Somoza García, who two years later installed himself as president. The Somoza dictatorship was to endure for two generations, until 1979.

This was not the way Wilson had planned it. The dream of using American military force to underwrite American-style governments in Central America had failed miserably. There was only one true democracy in the entire region by 1939, and that was Costa Rica, where the United States had never intervened. In some respects, to be sure, the United States had succeeded in establishing itself as the hemispheric hegemon it had for so long claimed to be. As an investor it grew in importance, gaining on (though not quite surpassing) the previously dominant British. As a diplomatic arbiter between the quarrelsome republics of the south it also played an influential role, particularly in the 1920s.[128] But as a liberal empire, seeking to export its own political institutions to Latin America, it had achieved precious little. All that Franklin Roosevelt could do was to dress up failure as "good neighborly" tolerance. Somoza might, alas, be a "son of a bitch," but as Roosevelt's secretary of state is said to have pointed out, he was nevertheless "our son of a bitch."[129] The most damning verdict of all on American policy came from General Smedley D. Butler, the most decorated marine of his generation, in an article he wrote for the magazine *Common Sense* in 1935:

> I helped make Haiti and Cuba a decent place for the National City Bank boys to collect revenues in. I helped in the raping of half a dozen Central American republics for the benefit of Wall Street. The record of racketeering is long. I helped purify Nicaragua for the international banking house of Brown Brothers in 1909–1912. I brought light to the Dominican Republic for American sugar interests in 1916. I helped make Hon-

duras "right" for American fruit companies in 1903. . . . Looking back on it, I feel I might have given Al Capone a few hints. The best *he* could do was to operate his racket in three city districts. We Marines operated on three *continents*.[130]

This would always be the most damaging allegation against American imperialism: that for all its high-minded statements of intent, it boiled down to a Wall Street racket.

And what of Mexico, which had inspired Wilson's doctrine of democratic intervention? In 1914 American patience with the Huerta regime ran out, and a small force of marines was sent to seize control of the key port and oil terminal of Veracruz and prevent the importation of German arms. Doubly beset by U.S.-backed rebel forces and a tax strike by the U.S. oil companies, Huerta resigned, surrendering power to the rebel leader Venustiano Carranza.[131] The Carranza regime was nothing if not a product of American policy. Yet within two years the United States acted in a way that seemed calculated to undermine Carranza's authority, by sending American troops across the Mexican border in pursuit of Pancho Villa, a former Carranza ally turned renegade.[132] Before long General John J. Pershing's "punitive expedition" was deep inside Mexican territory, failing to find Villa, but skirmishing with the regular Mexican Army.[133] Alarmed at the prospect of a full-scale American-Mexican war, Wilson drew back, and Pershing was forced to "sneak home under cover like a whipped cur with his tail between his legs."[134] Not for the last time in its history, the United States had embarked on a manhunt, had failed to catch the man and had ended up alienating an erstwhile ally.[135] The endemic violence of Mexican politics meanwhile continued unabated.[136] And before long a new and portentous word began to be applied to the heirs of the Mexican Revolution: American observers began to detect symptoms of the "Bolshevik virus" (though at this stage the influence of nationalists like Carlos Calvo was unquestionably greater than that of Lenin).[137] Article 27 of the new Mexican Constitution of 1917 asserted that all subterranean mineral rights belonged to the Mexican nation, posing an implicit threat of nationalization to American oil companies.[138] It was bad enough that Smedley Butler had tried to "make Mexico . . . safe for American oil interests in 1914." What was perhaps worse was the possibility that he might have failed.

"We Americans are the peculiar, chosen people," Herman Melville wrote in *White Jacket*, "the Israel of our time; we bear the ark of liberties of the world."[139] In the course of the twentieth century American leaders were to resort ever more frequently to such biblical language in their efforts to dignify, if not to sanctify, U.S. foreign policy. In doing so, they were following the example of earlier empire builders, not least McKinley. The extension of American values, both economic and political, beyond the frontiers of the United States seemed as much a matter of "manifest destiny" as the expansion of the frontier itself. Yet there was a chronic problem of execution. The farther into the tropics the United States sought to reach, the weaker its grip proved to be. The "empire of liberty" plainly had much to offer places like Cuba, Nicaragua and Mexico, to say nothing of the Dominican Republic and Haiti. But the will to make them permanent components of a greater American Republic turned out to be lacking; Hawaii and Puerto Rico alone were retained, not least because they were the most docile of the candidates for colonial status. The rest were offered a combination of sermons about political and fiscal rectitude and occasional military raids. The discrepancy between high-minded ends and means—"shoot[ing] men . . . till they learn to vote and to rule themselves"—was perfectly encapsulated in Mexico. The antics of General Pershing, as he galloped around Mexico in an obsessive pursuit of Pancho Villa, resembled nothing more than a burlesque of Melville's *Moby Dick*—without the final, climactic confrontation.

Perhaps Pershing was right. Given another expedition, he might, like Ahab, have finally caught up with his "loose fish." But it was not to be. On May 28, 1917, the general sailed for Europe as the commander of the American Expeditionary Force, with instructions to harpoon a bigger fish. The United States had struggled to make good its claim to hemispheric hegemony. The paradox is that its imperial grip proved more firm when it was confronted with the bigger challenge of global power.

CHAPTER 2

THE IMPERIALISM OF
ANTI-IMPERIALISM

American planes, full of holes and wounded men and corpses[,] took off
backwards from an airfield in England. . . .

The formation flew backwards over a German city that was in flames.
The bombers opened their bomb bay doors, exerted a miraculous magnet-
ism which shrunk the fires, gathered them into cylindrical steel containers,
and lifted the containers into the bellies of the planes. . . .

When the bombers got back to their base, the steel cylinders were
taken from the racks and shipped back to the United States of America,
where factories were operating night and day, dismantling the cylinders,
separating the dangerous contents into minerals.

KURT VONNEGUT, *Slaughterhouse 5*[1]

America's primary weapons . . . are stockings, cigarettes, and other mer-
chandise. They want to subjugate the world, yet they cannot subdue little
Korea.

JOSEF STALIN[2]

WORLD WAR

It might be said that two calamitous events helped turn the United States
from hesitant dominance of the Americas to what has sometimes been
called globalism.[3] The first was the sinking of the Cunard liner *Lusitania*
by the German submarine *U-20* on May 7, 1915, off the Old Head of
Kinsale on the south coast of Ireland. Nearly 1,200 people lost their lives;
among the drowned were 128 American passengers.[4] The second was the
Japanese attack on Pearl Harbor on December 7, 1941, which sank or
wrecked three cruisers, three destroyers and eight battleships and killed

2,403 Americans, most of them sailors. It was these two acts of maritime aggression that forced Americans to answer what has been called the oldest question in American foreign policy: whether to safeguard American security "by defense on this side of the water or by active participation in the lands across the oceans."[5] The analogy with a later calamity, that of September 11, 2001, scarcely needs to be pointed out.

In reality, of course, "active participation in the lands across the oceans" had been going on almost from the moment of the Republic's inception and was already far advanced long before 1915, to say nothing of 1941. Why did any Americans want to sail to Europe in the middle of a war and with a well-known risk of submarine attack? They certainly were not all tourists. As for Pearl Harbor, what more tangible evidence could be found for their country's earlier transoceanic activism than a fifty-year-old naval base two thousand miles from the American mainland? In any case, it was not the sinking of the *Lusitania* that brought the United States into the First World War—or even the Germans' final, desperate resort to unrestricted submarine warfare in February 1917—but the exposure of a spectacularly clumsy attempt by the German Foreign Ministry to enlist both Japan and Mexico on the side of the Central Powers in the event of an American decision for war. The inducement the Germans offered President Carranza was "an understanding . . . that Mexico is to re-conquer the lost territories in Texas, New Mexico and Arizona."[6]

The issue for the United States was no longer a choice between globalism and isolation, whatever that might mean in practice; the decision for world power had already been taken long before the world wars. The real issue, as Walter Lippmann astutely observed in an article for the *New York World* in 1926, was simply one of self-knowledge: "We continue to think of ourselves as a kind of great, peaceful Switzerland, whereas we are in fact a great, expanding world power. . . . Our imperialism is more or less unconscious."[7] There is nothing new, as Lippmann's observation indicates, about the idea that the United States is an "empire in denial." The extraordinary thing is that it was able to remain in denial even after some twenty years of global conflict. As the German economist Moritz Julius Bonn put it perceptively, "The United States have been the cradle of modern Anti-Imperialism, and at the same time the founding of a mighty Empire."[8] He wrote those words two years after the end of the *Second* World War.

The defining characteristic of American foreign policy in the three decades prior to 1947 was the insistence of successive presidents that the United States could somehow be a great power without behaving like any previous great power. German miscalculation presented Woodrow Wilson with an opportunity to do so, an opportunity not unlike that which presented itself to the Younger Pitt's successors in the closing years of the Napoleonic Wars. With the European powers exhausted by years of slaughter, it was possible for an American expeditionary force to decide the outcome of a global struggle, much as Wellington's army had struck the mortal blow against Bonaparte in 1814–15.[9] Yet Wilson could not be content with the traditional fruits of victory: imposing reparations, new borders and even a new regime on the losing side. Stung, perhaps, by the charges that the United States had intervened only "at the command of gold"[10]—to underwrite Wall Street's loans to Britain and France—his overwrought mind craved nothing less than a reconstruction of the entire international system. As early as December 1914 he had proposed that any peace settlement "should be for the advantage of the European nations regarded as Peoples and not for any nation imposing its governmental will upon alien people."[11] The following May he informed the members of the League to Enforce Peace that "every people has a right to choose the sovereignty under which they shall live."[12] "Every people," he declared categorically in January 1917, "should be left free to determine its own polity,"[13] spelling out a year later what that would mean in practice in points five to thirteen of his famous Fourteen Points.[14] As envisaged by Wilson, the new "League of Nations" would not merely guarantee the territorial integrity of its member states but might consider making future territorial adjustments "pursuant to the principle of self-determination."[15] To Europeans this might seem revolutionary; to Americans, Wilson insisted, it was as self-evident as the opening lines of the Declaration of Independence: "These are American principles, American policies. We could stand for no other. And they are also the principles and policies of forward looking men and women everywhere, of every modern nation, of every enlightened community. They are the principles of mankind and must prevail."[16]

There were three difficulties with all this. The first was that it was richly hypocritical. In 1916 Wilson had drafted a speech that included the characteristically sententious line "It shall not lie with the American people to dictate to another what their government shall be. . . ." His secretary of state, Robert Lansing, wrote succinctly in the margin: "Haiti, S Domingo, Nicaragua, Panama."[17] The second problem, which a better knowledge of Central Europe's ethnic geography might have helped him avoid, was that the application of self-determination would produce a significantly enlarged German Reich, an outcome unlikely to be congenial to those powers that had fought Germany for three years without American military assistance. But the fatal flaw of the Wilsonian design was that it simply could not be sold to a skeptical Senate. There was a vast gulf between the bold assertion of the Roosevelt Corollary, which simply authorized the United States to do what it liked in Latin America, and the airy commitments of the League Covenant, which would have obliged the United States to "respect and preserve against external aggression the territorial integrity and existing independence of all Members of the League." When Henry Cabot Lodge proposed to make ratification of the peace treaty conditional on certain "reservations"—reservations that the British and French were prepared to live with—Wilson refused to compromise. He instructed Democratic senators to vote against any such qualified version of the treaty, pinning his hopes on the presidential election that a stroke then prevented him from fighting.

The Europeans wanted the Americans to bind themselves to the new postwar order. The Americans preferred to retain their freedom of action. So insuperable did this division of opinion appear in the 1920s that a further question needs to be addressed. Why was it possible after 1945 to overcome it? What changed between Wilson and Truman? Two answers suggest themselves. One is obvious. In the aftermath of the First World War the United States was comparatively sanguine about the threat posed by the Bolshevik regime that had established itself in Russia after the October 1917 Revolution. Although the United States, along with Britain, committed troops to support the White side in the civil war that ensued, it was a halfhearted effort—surprisingly so in the American case, since the greater part of the immense army assembled to fight the Germans had arrived in Europe too late to see action. The United States was not war-weary, as the Europeans were. It merely underestimated the monster that had been born in Moscow. In February 1919 Wilson's adviser Colonel Edward M. House sent William C. Bullitt to Russia, ostensibly to report on "conditions political and economic therein," in fact to sound out peace terms with Lenin's government. Bullitt (a youthful champagne socialist) saw what he wanted to see; after their three-week junket he and the journalist who accompanied him concluded that they had seen the future and "it works!" True, the economy was in dire straits, but this was a temporary inconvenience, like the "red terror," which (so Bullitt confidently reported) was in any case already "over." Wilson did not need much persuading. Even before Bullitt left for Moscow, he had concluded that American troops were doing "no sort of good in Russia."[18] American attitudes were very different in the 1940s.

The second change related to the American economy. The stimulus of the First World War to U.S. growth was substantially less than the stimulus of the Second. As figure 1 shows, the Second World War had in every respect a bigger impact. The years before the war were dominated by the most severe and persistent depression in American history, the war more than doubled gross national product in real terms and the end of the war led to a severe slump. By contrast, economic performance before, during and after the First World War was subject to markedly less severe fluctuations. The recession of 1907–09 was minor compared with what happened in the 1930s, American entry into the First World War had a relatively muted impact on output and although there was a sharp downturn in 1921–22, the recession of 1946–48 was in fact more severe. Nor is it without significance that the recovery in the latter case was in large measure due to rearmament, which did not play a major role in the 1920s boom.

THE IMPERIALISM OF ANTI-IMPERIALISM

Imperial denial manifested itself time and again in the 1940s. Even before the United States entered the war, Henry Luce, the proprietor of *Time* and *Life* magazines, had urged Americans "to seek and to bring forth a vision of America as a world power, which is authentically American. . . . America as the dynamic center of ever-widening spheres of enterprise, America as the training center of the skilled servants of mankind, America as the Good Samaritan, really believing again that it is more blessed to give than

FIGURE 1

U.S. GNP in Constant Prices, 1900–22 and 1930–52

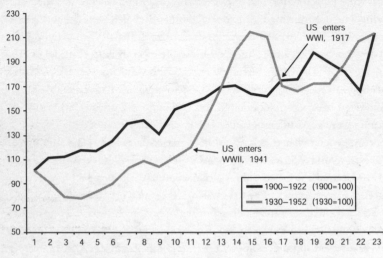

Source: B. R. Mitchell, *International Historical Statistics: The Americas,* pp. 761–74.

to receive, and America as the powerhouse of the ideals of Freedom and Justice—out of these elements surely can be fashioned a vision of the Twentieth Century . . . the first great American Century."[19] The contrast between these grandiloquent injunctions and the panic-stricken reactions when Japan attacked Pearl Harbor could not have been more complete.[20] In the words of one reporter, "No American who lived through that Sunday will ever forget it. It seared deeply into the national consciousness, shearing away illusions that had been fostered for generations. And with the first shock came a sort of panic. This struck at our deepest pride. It tore at the myth of our invulnerability. Striking at the precious legend of our might, it seemed to leave us naked and defenseless."[21] Writing in the *Washington Post,* Lippmann spoke of Americans as an "awakened people." Yet even as the roused giant struck back, growing ever more assured of its share in an Allied victory after the battle of Midway, there remained a reluctance to acknowledge the irrevocable nature of the global commitment.

Franklin Roosevelt's anti-imperialism was to be especially influential, not least because of his leading role among the architects of the postwar international order. "The colonial system means war," he had told his son in 1943. "Exploit the resources of an India, a Burma, a Java; take all the wealth out of those countries, but never put anything back into them, things like education, decent standards of living, minimum health requirements—all you're doing is storing up the kind of trouble that leads to war." When Roosevelt briefly visited Gambia en route to the Casablanca Conference, it struck him as a "hell-hole"—"the most horrible thing I have ever seen in my life." Colonialism seemed to him synonymous with "Dirt. Disease. [And a] very high mortality rate."[22] It was largely on the basis of such assumptions that the president envisaged the postwar world as also a postimperial world. "When we've won the war," he declared, "I will work with all my might and main to see to it that the United States is not wheedled into the position of accepting any plan that will further France's imperialistic ambitions, or that will aid or abet the British Empire in its imperial ambitions."[23] In Roosevelt's eyes, article III of the Atlantic Charter of August 1941, which asserted "the rights of all peoples to choose the form of government under which they will live," applied as much to the peoples living under British rule as to those whose territory had been invaded by the Germans and Japanese. "You have four hundred years of acquisitive instinct in your blood," he told his ally Churchill, "and you just don't understand how a country might not want to acquire land somewhere else if they can get it." "The British would take land anywhere in the world," he complained, "even if it were only rock or a sand bar."[24]

Churchill habitually saw Roosevelt's anti-imperialism as the legacy of America's origins in the War of Independence. As he put it in *The Hinge of Fate,* "The President's mind was back in the American War of Independence, and he thought of the Indian problem in terms of the thirteen colonies fighting George III. . . ."[25] But this was no idiosyncrasy; most Americans shared Roosevelt's views. An opinion poll conducted in 1942 revealed that six out of ten regarded the British as colonial oppressors.[26] *Life* magazine declared bluntly in October of the same year: "One thing we are sure we are *not* fighting for is to hold the British Empire together."[27]

Yet even as Americans pledged themselves to make war against the empires of their allies and enemies alike, all unacknowledged, their own empire grew apace. By November 1943 the Joint Chiefs of Staff had drawn up an extensive shopping list of postwar bases to be leased or held under international authority. In the Atlantic the new lines of defense would run through Iceland, the Azores, Madeira, the west coast of Africa and Ascension Island; in the Pacific, from Alaska through Attu, Paramushir, the Bonin (Ogasawara) Islands, the Philippines, New Britain, the Solomons, Fiji, Samoa, Tahiti, and not forgetting Clipperton and the Galápagos. Roosevelt personally asked the Joint Chiefs to include the Marquesas and the Tuamotu Archipelago in the U.S. sphere of influence.[28] In places like Micronesia, postwar "trusteeship" turned out to mean American control.[29] The secretary of the navy, Frank Knox, told Congress that, as far as he was concerned, all the islands occupied by the Japanese during the war "had become Japanese territory and as we capture them they are ours."[30] To British observers, the imperial character of American postwar planning was quite unmistakable. Alan Watt, of the Australian Legation in Washington, detected as early as January 1944 "signs in this country of the development of a somewhat ruthless Imperialist attitude."[31] The historian Arnold Toynbee, tutor and mentor to a generation of British imperial administrators, recognized "the first phase of a coming American world empire."[32] In the words of Harold Laski, America would soon "bestride the world like a colossus; neither Rome at the height of its power nor Great Britain in the period of its economic supremacy enjoyed an influence so direct, so profound, or so pervasive."[33] Meanwhile Roosevelt piously pressed Churchill to relinquish not just Gambia, one of the few British possessions the president ever visited, but even India and Hong Kong.

Unlike so many later critics of U.S. foreign policy, Toynbee had little difficulty reconciling himself to American imperialism. As he observed, "Her hand will be a great deal lighter than Russia's, Germany's or Japan's, and I suppose these are the alternatives. If we do get an American empire instead, we shall be lucky."[34] Given the seeming inevitability of their own bankrupt empire's decline, the British regarded a transfer of global power to the United States as the best available outcome of the war. In two countries the Americans lived up to such British expectations: Japan and the western zone of occupied Germany. Indeed, these stand out as the two most successful cases of American imperial rule at any time. It is not surprising that these were the precedents President Bush most frequently cited in arguing for a policy of nation building in Iraq last year. "America

has done this kind of work before," he told the American people in a television address on September 7, 2003. "Following World War II, we lifted
up the defeated nations of Japan and Germany, and stood with them as
they built representative governments. We committed years and resources
to this cause. And that effort has been repaid many times over in three generations of friendship and peace."[35] Yet the occupations of West Germany
and Japan were not quite as Americans today like to recall them. Indeed,
until as late as 1947 it was very far from certain that the United States
would commit so much time and money to these former "rogue states."
Under different circumstances, the usual incoherent and halfhearted pattern
of American intervention, seen before in the Philippines, the Caribbean
and Central America, might very well have repeated itself.

When General Douglas MacArthur landed at Atsugi Airfield, near Yoko-
hama, on August 30, 1945, there was indeed an element of *déjà vu* about
the scene. MacArthur's father, Arthur, had been the American commander
in the Philippines at the height of the fighting from early 1900 until mid-
1901. In 1914 Douglas MacArthur had been among the junior officers
sent to occupy Veracruz. MacArthur had been in command of U.S. forces
in the Philippines when the Japanese attacked the islands in 1941 (narrowly escaping capture). Small wonder MacArthur's approach to the occupation of Japan bore the stamp of an earlier generation of American
empire builders.

As supreme commander for the Allied powers (SCAP), MacArthur
was omnipotent. "I had," he later recalled, "not only the normal executive
authorities such as our own President has in this country, but I had legislative authority. I could by fiat issue directives."[36] From his general headquarters in the Dai-ichi Building in downtown Tokyo, MacArthur and his
staff, which initially numbered fifteen hundred, but which more than
tripled in size in the space of three years, set out to achieve a "revolution"
from above, to impose American "civilization" on a people most of them
regarded as racially inferior.[37]

The trouble was that the aims of American policy were from the outset
contradictory. On the one hand, by a combination of war crimes trials and
purges, the Japanese elites were supposed to be cured of their militaristic,

undemocratic ways. On the other, MacArthur could not govern Japan without the assistance of the existing Japanese bureaucracy. On the one hand, the Japanese were to be "reeducated" and their political system democratized. On the other, this was to be achieved by an absolute monarch in the person of MacArthur. On the one hand, Japan's economy was to be deprived of its war-making potential. On the other, living standards had to be improved in order to avoid an excessively costly occupation.

The compromises that emerged undeniably worked, in the sense that Japan emerged from MacArthur's rule as a democracy, albeit one dominated by a single party, and a dynamic market economy, albeit one based on a great deal more state intervention and a great deal more cartellike business collusion than existed in the United States. Yet this success was in many ways a triumph for the law of unintended consequences. The Americans set out to "get at the individual Japanese and remold his ways of thinking and feeling."[38] They achieved nothing of the sort; attempts at Christianization, with which MacArthur certainly sympathized, came to naught.[39] Nor were Japan's institutions more than partially transformed. The principal achievement of the occupation was to persuade the Japanese simply (in John Dower's phrase) to "embrace defeat"; to renounce the pursuit of military power in what had proved an unwinnable competition against the United States in favor of the pursuit of economic riches as the Americans' junior partners.

Superficially, the changes were impressive. The war crimes trials led to the conviction of all Japan's war leaders, barring the emperor Hirohito himself, as well as around four thousand smaller fry, of whom more than nine hundred were executed. In addition, more than two hundred thousand senior figures were forced out of their positions in the country's armed services, political parties and major corporations. The education system was overhauled, liberalized and decentralized; so was the police force. Civil, political and religious liberties were enshrined: women enfranchised, trade unions legalized, the press gradually freed.[40] Though (on MacArthur's recommendation)[41] the emperor remained under the new constitution of May 1947, he was henceforth no more than a figurehead; power was vested in a government responsible to a bicameral legislature. Japan was constitutionally bound to resort to armed force only in self-defense.[42]

Yet barely 1 percent of senior Japanese civil servants lost their jobs, and it was through the civil service that the Americans governed.[43] How, otherwise, could the American occupation have functioned? Japan's postwar masters were almost completely ignorant of the language and culture of their new subjects. Colonel Charles Kades, who played a pivotal role in the drafting of the constitution of 1947, later admitted: "I had no knowledge whatsoever about Japan's history or culture or myths. . . . I was blank on Japan. . . ."[44] Moreover, the Americans generally confined themselves to their own "Little America" in Tokyo. As one of MacArthur's senior staff put it, "For more than five years, with the rarest of exceptions, the only thing MacArthur saw of Japan physically was on the automobile route between the Dai-ichi Building and his quarters at the American Embassy, a distance of about a mile."[45] According to another insider, "only sixteen Japanese ever spoke with him [MacArthur] more than twice."[46] The wife of an American colonel later recalled being able to "walk from one end to the other [of Little America] . . . without ever being out of sight of an American face. . . ."[47]

The achievement of the American occupations of Japan and West Germany most often emphasized today was the extraordinary economic recovery both countries enjoyed. In neither case was this an outcome the occupiers originally intended. On the contrary, the initial plan was to *weaken* their economies and impoverish their peoples. The mood among many Americans as the war drew to a close was retributive, not regenerative. One adviser to the State-War-Navy Coordinating Committee (SWNCC) proposed "almost [the] annihilation of the Japanese as a race."[48] The more restrained report of the Pauley Commission of late 1945 recommended the reduction of Japanese shipbuilding, chemicals and steel production, as well as the payment of reparations through the transfer of industrial plants to countries the Japanese had occupied during the war. In January 1946 the statistician and management expert W. Edwards Deming proposed the dismantling of monopoly companies; this was adopted by the SWNCC, which passed it on to the SCAP; as late as May 1947 it was still the centerpiece of economic policy when it was adopted by the Far Eastern Commission as directive FEC-230. The same concept underlay the Anti-Monopoly Law (April 1947) and the Deconcentration Law (December 1947), which designated over three hundred companies for dissolution.[49] The targets of these measures were the notorious *zaibatsu*, in whose hands the ownership of Japanese industry had indeed been quite closely concentrated before 1945.[50] Yet there was a problem—one that has been a characteristic of nearly all American occupations.

In theory—and in most of history—empires acquire foreign territory in order to collect rents of some sort, whether by taxing their inhabitants or by extracting natural resources. In practice, American occupations tend to cost American taxpayers money, at least to begin with. The army that occupied Japan was large: four hundred thousand strong at first, and although that number soon halved, it did not fall below one hundred thousand until 1957.[51] Though the soldiers' pay and the costs of their food continued to be covered by the U.S. Treasury, it was intended that the housing, office space, heating, light and transportation that the occupiers required would be paid for by the Japanese under the heading "war termination costs." Yet in the immediate postwar period the Japanese were in no condition to shoulder such a burden. In June 1946 the inhabitants of war-ravaged Tokyo were surviving on just 150 calories per day, a tenth of the recommended intake.[52] In the first budgets of the new Japanese government, the occupation costs accounted for a third of total government spending.[53] Aid to Japan, primarily to pay for imported food and fertilizer, amounted to $194 million between August 1945 and December 1946. Despite all their schemes to "downsize" the Japanese economy, the Americans plainly had an interest in its rapid recovery.

The story was not wholly dissimilar in the American zone of occupation in western Germany, with one important difference. MacArthur relished his role as viceroy. His counterpart in Germany, a military engineer named General Lucius D. Clay, who succeeded Eisenhower as military governor of the U.S.-occupied zone, could scarcely have felt less enthused about his post. "Nobody talked to me about what our policies were in Germany," Clay later recalled. "They just sent me over there. I did not want the job. After all, we were still fighting a war, and to be the occupying deputy military governor in a defeated area while the war was still going on in the Pacific was about as dead-looking an end for a soldier as you could find."[54] The Joint Chiefs of Staff, in their April 1945 directive (JCS 1067), envisaged that the American commander in Germany would wield "supreme legislative, executive and judicial authority" and instructed him to exercise his power in a manner that was "just but firm and aloof."[55] Clay could not wait to get rid of this unlooked-for responsibility. From the outset he planned that the military government would be short-lived; he aimed to cut his staff from twelve thousand to six thousand by February 1, 1946, and set July 1 as the target date for handing power over to a completely civilian government.[56] Like Eisenhower, he believed that "the Government of Germany should, at the very earliest practicable moment, pass to a civilian organization."[57] But until this was possible, he argued, it was the job of the State Department, not the U.S. Army, to run the occupation.

After a reverse power struggle between the State and War departments, in which each side sought to pass the buck to the other, Truman fudged the issue by entrusting policy making to the former but leaving the administrative work to the latter.[58] The argument nevertheless dragged on throughout 1947, with the State Department at length agreeing in principle to take over, only to dither over the practicalities; finally, in March 1948, Truman decided to leave Clay in charge. Throughout this period Clay struggled to retain good-quality officers in Germany, a task that was far from easy given the uncertain duration of army control.[59] As he later reflected, "It was hard work, and it was not fun. . . . If we had not had our army officers to call on originally, and then to persuade them to stay as civilians, I do not think that we could ever have staffed the occupation."[60] The more expert Americans like George Shuster and George Kennan remarked on their colleagues' ignorance of Germany's culture, which often went hand in hand with the arrogance of the conqueror.[61] Though more recent scholarship has been less harsh in its verdicts, the picture that emerges is, once again, scarcely that of an ideal occupation.[62] What was planned did not happen. What happened was not planned. This was not so much an empire by invitation as an empire by improvisation.

A case in point was the policy of denazification. After four early stabs at the problem, the directive of July 7, 1945, alighted on the notion of "guilt by officeholding," creating 136 mandatory removal categories; supplementary to this was Clay's Law No. 8 of September 26, which decreed that former Nazis thus defined should be reemployed only in menial jobs. Yet as in Japan, so in Germany: to get rid of all the senior administrative personnel of the previous regime was a recipe for chaos. As early as the winter of 1945–46, the disruption caused by so many internments and demotions convinced Clay of the need to change tack.[63] As he put it in

March 1946, "With 10,000 people I couldn't do the job of denazification. It's got to be done by the Germans."[64] What this meant was an inundation of questionnaires, designed to get the Germans to rank themselves on a precisely calibrated scale of malfeasance: major offenders, offenders, lesser offenders, followers, fellow travelers and (as the Germans joked) the "Persil white." Clay later called denazification his "biggest mistake," a "hopelessly ambigious procedure" that created a "pathetic 'community of fate' between small and big Nazis."[65] Comparably ambitious and ineffectual were the plans envisaged in JCS 1067 to establish "a coordinated system of control over German education and an affirmative program of reorientation . . . designed completely to eliminate Nazi and militaristic doctrines. . . ."[66] In fact, academic life swiftly reverted to its old, accustomed pattern. The professors who had once embraced nazism now embraced Nato-ism; most kept their jobs. The first important evidence of cultural change was the emergence of a liberal press, but that was as much the work of the occupied as the occupiers, whose role was essentially permissive.

The democratization of Western Germany was, without question, one of the great successes of American postwar policy. But it is important to recognize that it was driven forward in large measure by Clay's desire to hand over power to a civilian authority as soon as possible. If the State Department refused to do the job, then once again it would have to be the Germans themselves. Although JCS 1067 had envisaged "the preparation for an eventual reconstruction of German political life on a democratic basis," its bottom line was that, for the foreseeable future, "no political activities of any kind [would] be countenanced unless authorized."[67] The Americans in Germany, however, were positively impatient for German political activities to begin. In the first working session of the Allied Control Council (ACC) on August 10, 1945, they proposed the immediate creation of German central administrative institutions, headed by German state secretaries, to implement the general directives of the ACC.[68] Fritz Schäffer, who had belonged to the conservative Bavarian People's Party before 1933, was appointed prime minister of Bavaria within four weeks of V-E Day (though he was dismissed after just a few months). Parties were allowed to organize in the American zone almost at once, and as early as October 1945 Clay created a Council of Minister Presidents (*Länderrat*) in Stuttgart, to which he delegated a rapidly increasing number of administrative responsibilities. By the end of 1945 all the new or reconstituted states (*Länder*) throughout the U.S. zone had German governments and "pre-parliaments." In the first half of the following year, local governments were formed, and elections held, first locally and then, successively, at the level of *Landkreis* (district), city and finally state. By October all the American-controlled states had their own constitutions, which were approved by the military government and then by referenda; simultaneously, elections to the new state parliaments were held.[69]

In September 1946 Secretary of State James F. Byrnes made a speech in Stuttgart in which he stressed the American commitment to a rapid democratization of Germany:

> It never was the intention of the American Government to deny to the German people the right to manage their own internal affairs as soon as they were able to do so in a democratic way, with genuine respect for human rights and fundamental freedoms. . . . It is the view of the American Government that the German people . . . under proper safeguards, should now be given the primary responsibility for the running of their own affairs. . . . It is our view that the German people should now be permitted and helped to make the necessary preparations for setting up a democratic German government. . . . While we shall insist that Germany observe the principles of peace, good-neighborliness, and humanity . . . the American people hope to see peaceful, democratic Germans become and remain free and independent. . . . The American people who fought for freedom have no desire to enslave the German people. The freedom Americans believe in and fought for is a freedom which must be shared with all willing to respect the freedom of others. . . . The American people want to return the government of Germany to the German people. The American people want to help the German people to win their way back to an honorable place among the free and peace-loving nations of the world.[70]

With those words he expressed a recurrent aspiration of American occupations before and since: the hope for a rapid transition from military rule to democratic self-government. Yet this hope could be fulfilled in Germany only because the Germans themselves could still recollect how democratic institutions functioned. After all, they had been shut down for just twelve years. Certainly, if the Germans had needed detailed instructions from Clay and his colleagues, they would have been disappointed. As Clay later admitted, "I did not have very much experience in the field [of democracy] myself, never having voted at that time. I came from a state where soldiers were not allowed to vote." On one occasion, he, John Foster Dulles and a group of State Department officials "spent a whole day disagreeing on a definition of democracy. This was entirely within the American delegation. We could not agree on any common definition for democracy."[71] During discussions with the future German chancellor Konrad Adenauer, Clay sought guidance from Washington on the subject of federalism but found he "could never get a strict definition for what they really intended to do to create a federal government." He ruefully concluded: "I think we have a peculiar idea of our government being perfect without knowing really and truly how it works."[72]

The leading historian of the American occupation of Germany has concluded that "the newborn West German government of 1949 . . . was conceived and delivered by the American Army," but this was more out of expediency than democratizing expertise.[73] In any case, it is important not to overstate the extent to which West Germany truly was democratized. Although the first elected West German government took over from the military government in the spring of 1949, the Occupation Statute enacted that year severely circumscribed the German politicians' control over their own foreign and defense policy. It also reserved to the occupying forces the right "to resume . . . the exercise of full authority if they consider that to do so is essential to security or to preserve democratic government in Germany."[74]

By contrast, the economic recovery of Germany happened with painful slowness. As in the case of Japan, this was largely because the initial thrust of postwar policy was either directly or indirectly to inhibit rather than stimulate growth—insofar as there was a coherent thrust at all. There was in fact a tension from the outset between the harshly retributive ideas for deindustrialization of Henry Morgenthau's 1944 plan and the more pragmatic aims of the army reflected in its *Handbook for the Military Government of Germany;* nor was there any consensus among the departments of State, War and Treasury, to say nothing of the Joint Chiefs of Staff.[75] JCS 1067 was a compromise document, but it still retained elements of the Morgenthau Plan. Thus it formally instructed the military government to "take no steps (a) looking toward the economic rehabilitation of Germany, or (b) designed to maintain or strengthen the German economy."[76] Instead Clay should aim to "decentralize the structure and administration of the German economy to the maximum possible extent" and to "require the Germans to use all means at their disposal to maximize agricultural output." At the same time, he was told "to ensure the production and maintenance of goods and services required to prevent starvation or such disease and unrest as would endanger occupying forces."[77] The result was a zone-wide SNAFU, as the testimony of numerous insiders like Harold Zink, Lewis Brown, and Carl Friedrich revealed in the later 1940s, when many of them returned to American universities to turn their experiences into dissertations.

There were, in fact, numerous attempts to change the direction of economic policy in the American zone. From the very outset, Lewis Douglas, Clay's financial adviser, dismissed JCS 1067 as the work of "economic idiots" who would "forbid the most skilled workers in Europe from producing as much as they can for a continent that is desperately short of everything."[78] As early as September 1945 a report drawn up by Calvin Hoover for the military government acknowledged the "conflict between an extreme degree of industrial disarmament spread over a number of key industries and the goal of maintaining a minimum German standard of living . . . while providing for the costs of the occupying forces."[79] In November, at Truman's instigation, Byron Price, the wartime director of U.S. censorship, toured Germany; he recommended a complete revision of policy.[80] By December 1945 Washington had done a complete volte-face. Now there was no intention "to eliminate or weaken German industries of a peaceful character." The sole American "desire [was] to see Germany's economy geared to a world system."[81] In his Stuttgart speech the following September, Byrnes admitted what Douglas had recognized from the beginning: "Recovery in Europe . . . will be slow indeed if Germany with her great resources of iron and coal is turned into a poorhouse."[82] With the merging of the American and British zones in January 1947, the aim became "the expansion of German exports . . . as rapidly as world conditions permit."[83] Yet progress at the time seemed desperately slow, something we tend today to forget. At the end of 1945 Clay had described the German economy as "practically at a standstill."[84] More than eighteen months later he had to threaten resignation to get the State Department to agree to a target for German industrial output of 75 percent of its prewar level, a target that was not in fact attained in the U.S.-U.K. bizone until the last quarter of 1948.[85] As in the Japanese case, a policy intended to achieve economic stagnation simply raised the effective costs of occupation. As late as 1948 one German economist calculated that occupation costs would consume nearly half the total tax take for the year; even in 1950 they still accounted for more than a third of the federal government's budget.[86] Yet Germany was simultaneously receiving substantial aid from the United States.[87] This was neither popular nor profitable. In both economies, fiscal chaos was matched by rampant inflation, which in Germany seemed reminiscent of the hyperinflation of 1923. And had not Hitler been the "foster-child of the inflation"?[88]

It was not in fact an irenic desire to make a success of nation building that resolved the economic problems of occupied Japan and Germany. On the contrary—and this would prove crucial throughout the cold war period—it was the fear of a rival empire. For an empire in denial, there is really only one way to act imperially with a clear conscience, and that is to combat someone else's imperialism. In the doctrine of containment, born in 1947, the United States hit on the perfect ideology for its own peculiar kind of empire: the imperialism of anti-imperialism.

The new rationale for American empire was sketched out in George F. Kennan's top secret "long telegram" sent to Washington from Moscow in February 1946, in which he warned that "Nothing short of complete disarmament, delivery of our air and naval forces to Russia and resigning of powers of government to American Communists" would allay Stalin's "baleful misgivings."[89] Truman drew his own conclusions from Kennan's warning in his address to a joint session of both houses of Congress on March 12, 1947. "It must be the policy of the United States," he declared, "to support free peoples who are resisting attempted subjugation by armed minorities or by outside pressures."[90] Just which outside pressures the Americans had in mind was spelled out by Kennan four months later in an anonymous and epoch-making article for *Foreign Affairs,* entitled "The Sources of Soviet Conduct," which warned of "Soviet pressure against the free institutions of the Western world" and Moscow's aim to "encroach . . . upon the interests of a peaceful and stable world." "It is clear," Kennan argued, "that the main element of any United States policy toward the Soviet Union must be that of long-term, patient but firm and vigilant containment of Russian expansive tendencies." In this analysis, Russian imperialism was a given. Kennan's point was that it was "something that can be contained by the adroit and vigilant application of counter-force at a series of constantly shifting geographical and political points, corresponding to the shifts and maneuvers of Soviet policy [and] . . . designed to confront the Russians with an unalterable counterforce at every point. . . ."[91] By 1950 official U.S. policy had outstripped even Kennan. In NSC 68 the National Security Council spelled out in alarming language the threat the United States now faced:

> The Soviet Union, unlike previous aspirants to hegemony, is animated by a new fanatic faith, antithetical to our own, and seeks to impose its absolute authority over the rest of the world. . . . The issues that face us are momentous, involving the fulfillment or destruction not only of this Republic but of civilization itself. . . . The fundamental design of those who control the Soviet Union and the international communist movement is to retain and solidify their absolute power, first in the Soviet Union and second in the areas now under their control. In the mind of the Soviet leaders, however, achievement of this design requires the dynamic extension of their authority and the ultimate elimination of any effective opposition to their authority. . . . The design, therefore, calls for the complete subversion or forcible destruction of the machinery of government and structure of society in the countries of the non-Soviet world and their replacement by an apparatus and structure subservient to and controlled from the Kremlin. . . . The United States, as the . . . center of power in the non-Soviet world and the bulwark of opposition to Soviet

expansion, is the principal enemy whose integrity and vitality must be
subverted or destroyed. . . .[92]

What made all this so persuasive, though in many ways it was coincidental, was the catastrophic failure in any way to "contain" communism in
China, for by this time the Nationalist armies of Chiang Kai-shek had
been driven right off the Chinese mainland by the Marxist Mao Zedong
and his peasant army—the revolutionary heirs of postwar chaos, just as
Lenin and the Bolsheviks had been thirty years before. Yet for all its defensive connotations, the American notion of containment, predicated
though it was on the threat from another, malignant empire, was itself implicitly an imperial undertaking, as Truman himself let slip when he pronounced America's responsibility to be even greater than those that had
once faced "Darius I's Persia, Alexander's Greece, Hadrian's Rome [and]
Victoria's Britain." The only way to "save the world from totalitarian-
ism,"[93] Truman argued, was for "the whole world [to] adopt the American
system," for "the American system" could survive only by becoming "a
world system."[94]

For a self-consciously anti-imperial political culture, containment offered the resolution of all the earlier tensions between republican virtue
and the exercise of global power. It had one immediate and profoundly
important consequence: in three distinct ways, it dramatically accelerated
the pace of economic recovery in Japan and West Germany. First, both
economies received a massive cash infusion in the form of direct American aid. Secondly, plans to change the structures of ownership and organization were shelved in favor of plans to maximize growth. Thirdly,
rearmament, not only in the United States but in the former enemy countries themselves, provided a stimulus in its own right. The results deserved
to be called a *Wirtschaftswunder.* What was truly wondrous, however, was
that for the first time the American empire began to pay for itself.

The recovery of Germany tends to get more attention than the recovery of Japan because it was a part of Secretary of State George Marshall's
celebrated plan for European reconstruction. But what went on in Asia was
just as important, maybe even more so. Aid to Japan more than doubled:
from January to December 1947 it amounted to $404 million, compared
with less than $200 million for all of the previous year and a half. In 1948

American aid rose again, to $461 million. In 1949 it peaked at $534 million.[95] The total amount, more than $1.5 billion, provided a helpful economic boost. At the same time, the campaign to dissolve the *zaibatsu* was abandoned. Many, notably Mitsui and Mitsubishi, were never dissolved; the eighty or so that were wound up quickly reconstituted themselves. In 1951 just three firms accounted for 96 percent of pig iron output.[96] The new macroeconomic approach was outlined in December 1948 in a nine-point "Line" drawn up by the Detroit banker Joseph Dodge. It was far from being a policy of liberalization: wage and price controls were imposed to counter inflation, and imports were also rationed, with priority given to the export industries.[97] As for the purging of the Right, that was now forgotten.[98] In John Dower's words, power was firmly entrusted to the prime minister Yoshida Shigeru's "ruling tripod of big business, bureaucracy and conservative party."[99]

In West Germany the story was broadly the same. Plans to dismantle the big industrial and financial concerns were largely shelved; the political position of Adenauer's Christian Democrats remained dominant until the 1960s. The ensuing "economic miracle" was in fact less spectacular than Japan's, but it was still more impressive than the recoveries seen nearly everywhere else in Europe.[100] Prior to 1948, industrial output was still running at less than half its 1936 level, by March 1949 it had leaped to 89 percent. Annual exports nearly doubled in the same period.[101] How much of this can be attributed to direct American aid and how much to changes of policy—particularly the currency reform of June 1948—is debatable. Unveiled by Marshall at Harvard in June 1947 and enacted the following April, the four-year European Recovery Program is sometimes discussed as if it had bought Western Europe for the United States the way dollars had once bought Alaska. But the amounts concerned should be kept in perspective. The total outlay averaged not much more than 1 percent of U.S. GNP. In any case, West Germany was not its principal beneficiary. In all, sixteen countries received Marshall aid, to the tune of $11.8 billion; there was a further $1.5 billion in the form of loans. Germany got just over 10 percent of the total, roughly half the amounts that went to France and—the single biggest recipient—Britain.[102] Marshall aid in itself did not guarantee economic recovery; had it done so, Britain would have had the economic miracle, whereas it actually had the reverse. It seems more plausible to attribute the West German miracle to the surge of confidence generated by the new deutschmark, accompanied as it was by a lifting of price controls.[103]

It has often been said that American aid boosted growth by instilling confidence. This may be true. But equally important may have been the confidence instilled by the continuing presence of American troops and the integration of the two countries into the new American structure of security treaties. The combination of dollars and deutschmarks might have achieved much less had not Clay decided to break the Soviet siege of West Berlin with an unprecedented eleven-month airlift between June 1948 and May 1949. Although the formal occupations of Japan and West Germany ended in, respectively, 1952 and 1955, substantial numbers of American troops remained there for another fifty years; indeed, remain there to this day.[104] This was another unintended outcome. Before the chill of cold war had descended, the Americans had proposed a treaty to enforce demilitarization of Germany for twenty-five or even forty years, but it had been turned down by the other powers.[105] By 1953 six American divisions were deployed in West Germany, along with nine other divisions from other members of the new North Atlantic Treaty Organization, including West Germany itself. Rearmament—not just of the United States but of the other NATO members—contributed a further stimulus to the industries of all concerned.

The new policies inspired by containment did more than prime the pump of the occupied countries' economies, thereby reducing the share of the costs of occupation the Americans themselves had to pay. By boosting Japanese and German growth under conditions of increasingly liberal trade, they created new and dynamic markets for American exports. As early as 1948 and 1949, goods sold to West Germany already accounted for close to 7 percent of total U.S. exports. By 1957 Germany and Japan had for the first time overtaken Great Britain in their importance for American trade (see figure 2). There was, in short, a self-interested rationale for stimulating the recovery of America's erstwhile foes. In notes he prepared for Marshall before the announcement of the aid program, Kennan had argued that the money was needed "so that they [the Europeans] can buy from us" and so "that they will have enough self-confidence to withstand outside pressures." Now the calculation was vindicated: the United States

FIGURE 2

Percentage Shares of American Exports, 1946–61

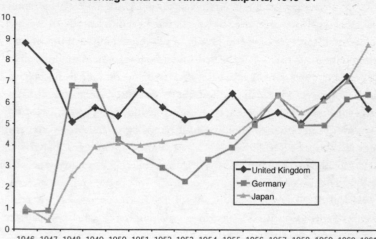

Source: *Historical Statistics of the United States,* p. 903.

had "a very real economic interest in Europe" stemming "from Europe's role . . . as a market and as a major source of supply for a variety of products and services."[106]

At last, it seemed, the elusive virtuous circle had been established. American idealism could be assuaged because an imperial policy was being pursued in the name of anti-imperialism. But American self-interest could also be satisfied because the occupation of foreign countries turned out— after a remarkably short time—to pay a dividend. On this basis, it was possible to transform West Germany and Japan successfully from rogue regimes of the very worst type into paragons of capitalist economics and democratic politics.

Only one puzzle remains. Why, if the combination of long-term occupation and mutual economic benefit proved so successful in these two cases, was it so seldom repeated elsewhere?

MACARTHUR'S RUBICON

In 1948, as the era of containment began, the United States was at the zenith of its relative economic power. In the preceding decade the output of the American economy had grown in real terms by two-thirds. It now accounted for roughly a third of total world output, three times the share of its rival empire, the Soviet Union.[107] Despite accounting for just 6 percent of the world's population, the United States produced nearly half the world's total electrical power and held roughly the same proportion of the world's monetary gold and gold-equivalent bank reserves. American firms controlled nearly three-fifths of the world's total oil reserves. They dominated the international production of automobiles.[108] Truman spoke with pardonable exaggeration when he declared: "We are the giant of the economic world. Whether we like it or not, the future pattern of economic relations depends on us. The world is watching to see what we shall do. The choice is ours."[109]

That choice took a distinctive and novel form. The United States embarked on a sustained push to reduce international trade barriers through multilateral negotiations under the General Agreement on Tariffs and Trade. Barriers to international capital movements were given less priority; it was thought preferable to revert to the pre-Depression system of fixed exchange rates, though with the dollar rather than gold bullion as the anchor. Two new international institutions were brought into being to manage the world's financial system: the World Bank and the International Monetary Fund. But the essence of American "hegemony" was the preferential treatment of American allies when it came to the allocation of loans and grants of aid (whether for development or military purposes).[110] Given the size of the American economy relative to those of even its wealthiest allies, sums that were, from an American viewpoint, relatively modest (see figure 3) could appear very large to the recipients. Total economic aid for the period 1946 to 1952 amounted to nearly 2 percent of U.S. GNP, half of it accounted for by the Marshall Plan. Over the ensuing decade—including the heady years when John F. Kennedy pledged to "pay any price, bear any burden [and] meet any hardship . . . to assure the survival and the success of liberty"—it dropped to below 1 percent.

FIGURE 3

United States Foreign Aid as a Percentage of GNP, 1946–73

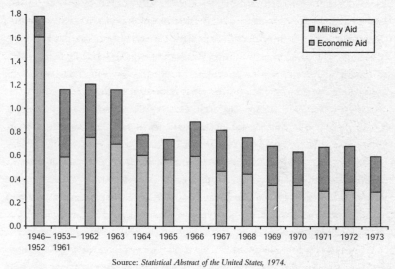

Source: *Statistical Abstract of the United States, 1974.*

Far more important were American military expenditures. Having been slashed in the immediate aftermath of victory over Germany and Japan, these began to climb steeply after 1948, from under 4 percent of GDP to a peak of 14 percent in 1953, more than a fivefold increase in cash terms.[111] Part of what this purchased of course was increased stocks of atomic bombs: in 1947 the United States had possessed just fourteen, but by the end of 1950 the number had risen to nearly three hundred and by 1952 to more than eight hundred.[112] There was a smaller but still substantial increase in the country's conventional forces. Between 1948 and 1952 American military manpower rose by a factor of two and a half, reaching what was to prove the postwar peak of 3.4 million. Even after the Korean War, military readiness remained well above the level of the late 1940s. As late as 1973 the defense budget was still close to 6 percent of GDP, and the armed forces numbered 2.2 million.[113] A substantial minority of these troops were stationed abroad in a network of old and new bases, some in territory directly controlled by the United States but most in politically independent countries that were American allies. By 1967 American service personnel were stationed in sixty-four countries: nineteen of them in Latin America, thirteen in Europe, eleven in Africa, eleven in the Near East and South Asia and ten in East Asia.[114] The United States had treaties of alliance with no fewer than forty-eight different countries, ranging from Britain and West Germany to Australia and New Zealand, from Turkey and Iran to Pakistan and Saudi Arabia, from South Vietnam and South Korea to Taiwan and Japan.[115] This has justly been called an empire by invitation. But what is striking is that the United States accepted so many of the invitations it received. According to one estimate, there were 168 separate instances of American armed intervention overseas between 1946 and 1965.[116]

Yet there is a puzzle. Mighty though the United States was in economic, in military and indeed in diplomatic terms, its interventions had very mixed results. According to one assessment of nine post-1945 interventions that could be characterized retrospectively as attempts at nation building, only four can be judged successful, in the sense of establishing stable democratic systems. Two of these have already been discussed; the other two—Grenada in 1983 and Panama in 1989—came only in the closing stages of the cold war, after much more serious failures. It has been suggested that American interventions were more likely to be successful when they were undertaken multilaterally (that is, in partnership with allies) and supported democratic forces in the country in question, rather than military elites.[117] This argument, however, applies anachronistic criteria to a period when the containment of Communist expansion, rather than democratic nation building, was the objective of policy. A more pertinent question might be why the United States failed to achieve containment in so many of the countries the Soviets or the Chinese sought forcibly to penetrate. To be precise, why was it that the vastly richer Americans had to settle for such a high proportion of "ties" (notably Korea) and outright defeats (notably Cuba and Vietnam) in a contest they might have been expected nearly always to win?

There are four answers to this question. The first is geographical: the United States had to reach much farther than the Soviet Union in all the major theaters of strategic competition except Latin America and the Caribbean. The second is a matter of military technology: once the Soviets acquired just a single atomic bomb they could pose a more serious threat to the United States than had ever before been conceivable. It then transpired that they were prepared to build an even bigger arsenal than the Americans, so that the balance of nuclear advantage—as well as the balance in conventional forces—swung against the United States. Thirdly, as an empire based on consent, the United States had much less power over its allies than the Soviet Union did over its satellites, most obviously in Europe, where the Russians did not shrink from putting tanks in the streets to enforce their will, at a time when West European leaders expected to be treated as near equals by Washington.[118] Finally, and perhaps most important, American policy makers had to take much more notice of their own citizens' views than did their Soviet counterparts. Unfortunately, when put to the test of electoral popularity, containment fared disappointingly. Much as they abhorred and feared the "Red menace," Americans were not prepared to wage prolonged conventional wars to defeat it. Once this was apparent, the credibility of American pledges "to support any friend [and] oppose any foe" rapidly waned.

There is an important inference to be drawn from all this. Arguably, the United States might have been able to win a "hot" war against communism had it made full use of its economic and military capabilities in the early 1950s. But this would have been possible only if there had been a decisive shift in the nature of American domestic politics, one that might have tipped the constitutional balance from republic to empire proper. In 1951, as we shall see, this possibility momentarily presented itself. Americans spurned it. An empire by invitation overseas was one thing. Nobody, it turned out, wanted to invite an emperor home.

The Korean War was a direct consequence of Communist aggression. First, the Russians refused to allow free, UN-supervised elections to go ahead in their zone of occupation.[119] Then, in April 1950, Stalin authorized the North Korean leader Kim Il Sung to invade the Republic of Korea and overthrow its democratically elected (though not very liberal) government.[120] It is easy to see why Stalin decided to gamble on war by proxy. The United States had previously indicated that it was content to acquiesce in a division of the peninsula analogous to the division of Germany; indeed, since 1948 it had been withdrawing American troops from the country. In January 1950 Secretary of State Dean Acheson had indicated that he did not regard South Korea as vital to American security. That same month the House of Representatives actually rejected the administration's Korean aid bill, though this decision was later overturned.[121] Even so, Truman had every right to call the invasion an act of "unprovoked aggression," and in the absence of Russian representation on the UN Security Council he had no difficulty in obtaining a resolution calling on member states to "furnish such assistance to the Republic of Korea as may be necessary to repel the armed attack and to restore peace and security in the area." With fifteen other nations contributing troops to the ensuing war effort, the United States appeared to have might as well as right on its side.[122] Moreover, American public opinion was at first overwhelmingly in favor of intervention. Three-quarters of voters polled in July 1950 approved of Truman's action; significantly, more than half of those in favor regarded it as necessary "to stop Russia."[123] MacArthur's decision to attack the North Koreans from the rear by landing forces at Inchon gave the public a taste of victory. There was strong popular support for his decision to chase the invaders back across the thirty-eighth parallel, raising the possibility of a regime change in the North and the unification of Korea.[124] Shortly before the first American troops crossed the parallel, public support for the war reached 81 percent.

It was not the Chinese counterattack in November 1950 in itself that prevented the destruction of North Korea. Though the initial impact of the Chinese intervention was dramatic, briefly turning the U.S.-led coalition temporarily into "a leaderless horde,"[125] the Americans unquestionably had the capability to defeat Mao's fledgling People's Republic. Three things stopped this from happening. The first was the noisy opposition of America's allies to the possibility of an atomic strike against China.[126] The second was the Truman government's own anxiety that such a strike would precipitate a Soviet counterstrike against Western Europe.[127] Although the United States had roughly seventeen times the number of atomic bombs the Russians had, American policy was to do nothing that might increase the risk of "World War Three."[128] The third and most important reason, however, was that the man who might have overcome both these obstacles was politically outmaneuvered.

The year 1951 was perhaps the only moment in its history that the

American Republic came close to meeting the fate of the Roman Republic. The man who would play the part of Caesar was the architect of the new Japan, now commander in chief of the UN forces in Korea, General Douglas MacArthur. Convinced that Truman's chosen strategy of "limited war" was fatally mistaken, MacArthur effectively crossed the Rubicon by publicly saying so. In defying Truman, he had not only popular support but also the backing of the Republican leadership in Congress and of a substantial proportion of the conservative press. When Truman dismissed him and MacArthur returned home to a hero's welcome, the Constitution itself seemed in peril. It has sometimes been argued that MacArthur was defeated because he was wrong about American strategy. This is debatable. MacArthur was certainly wrong in thinking he could ignore or subvert the orders of his commander in chief. But Caesar too had been in the wrong when he defied the Roman Senate; it had not stopped him from prevailing. The real reason MacArthur did not follow in Caesar's footsteps was that he was outwitted by a more politically skilled opponent.

Truman had long detested MacArthur—"Mr. Prima Donna, Brass Hat, Five Star MacArthur," he privately dubbed him. As far as the president was concerned, "Dugout Doug" was a "speechmaker" and a "showman," who regarded himself as "God's righthand man"—a "proconsul for the government of the United States [who] could do as he damned [well] pleased."[129] As early as January 1948 he predicted that MacArthur might seek to oust him by "mak[ing] a grand march across the country about a month before the Republican convention."[130] There is no question that MacArthur was guilty of what Truman called "insubordination." The first transgression was the general's letter to the national convention of the Veterans of Foreign Wars, intended to be read publicly on August 28, 1950, which denounced "those who advocate appeasement and defeatism in Asia." This he withdrew at Truman's request, but not before its contents had leaked to the press. The second offense came on March 24, 1951, when MacArthur knowingly preempted, and thereby stymied, Truman's carefully laid plans to open negotiations with the Chinese, about which he had been notified four days previously. To some European observers, this was little short of a *pronunciamento*.[131] The third came on April 5, when the Republican leader in the House of Representatives read out a letter from MacArthur that argued for the employment of "maximum counterforce" against China and concluded: "There is no substitute for victory." This was clearly in breach of a White House directive of the previous December, requiring State Department authorization for all public statements by MacArthur.[132] Technically Truman's case was cast-iron. But politically it was insufficient. It was vital that MacArthur's strategic arguments also be discredited. To this end Truman worked assiduously—and in the end successfully—to win over MacArthur's military superiors on the Joint Chiefs of Staff.

When MacArthur was informed of his dismissal on April 11—not from a presidential emissary, as had been intended, but from an aide who had heard the news on the radio after an extraordinary nocturnal press conference at the White House—he resolved to return to the United States and "raise hell."[133] He had little difficulty. When the news of his dismissal broke, there was outrage. Senior Republicans talked wildly of multiple impeachments, sentiments echoed by the *Chicago Tribune*. MacArthur was hailed as "one of the greatest military leaders since long before the days of Genghis Khan," a "giant" and a "deserving idol of the American people"; Truman was nothing more than a drunk and a pygmy, the leader of a "popular-front Communist-dominated Government."[134] There were pro-MacArthur demonstrations from New York to San Gabriel, California, from Baltimore to Houston. Four state legislatures passed resolutions condemning the president's decision. Telegrams poured in from all over the country, overwhelmingly against Truman. The president's approval rating crashed to 26 percent; a Gallup poll put support for MacArthur at 69 percent. Those in the White House who joked that MacArthur would "wade ashore" and burn the Constitution amid a "21-atomic bomb salute" were doing their best to make light of a grave political crisis.[135] MacArthur's return was no laughing matter. His address to Congress was a bravura performance, running the gamut of mawkish sentiments from the pious to the patriotic. It was watched on television by thirty million people and punctuated by thirty eruptions of applause from the people's elected representatives. "We heard God speak here today, God in the flesh, the voice of God!" exclaimed a delirious congressman. One senator "felt that if the speech had gone on much longer there might have been a march on the White House."[136] MacArthur himself strutted through the streets of New York in an impromptu parade that is said to have drawn a crowd of up to seven million. It was a triumph worthy of a Caesar.

Yet Truman prevailed—not through any public appeal, but by quietly and methodically securing the support of MacArthur's fellow soldiers. MacArthur's argument was, first, that "limited war" was undermining the morale of the American forces in Korea; secondly, that the United States should escalate its operations against China, attacking the Chinese airfields in Manchuria and blockading the Chinese coast; thirdly, that the Chinese Nationalist forces in Formosa (now Taiwan) should be mobilized on the side of the United States; and finally, that up to fifty atomic bombs should be dropped on Chinese cities.[137] The alternative to "victory" was "appeasement," which would merely "beget new and bloodier war." Truman's retort was that the war in Korea was "a Russian maneuver," designed to distract the United States from the much more important question of Western Europe, which an all-out attack on China might prompt the Russians to invade.[138] Fatally for MacArthur, Truman convinced the Joint Chiefs of Staff to back him. It helped that MacArthur's successor, General Matthew B. Ridgway, so quickly stiffened the resolve of the American forces in Korea.[139] But the key was the testimony of the chairman of the Joint Chiefs of Staff, General Omar Bradley, at the hearings held jointly by the Senate's Foreign Relations and Armed Services committees. Memorably, Bradley argued that an all-out war against China would have left Western Europe at the mercy of the Soviets; it would have been "the wrong war at the wrong place at the wrong time and with the wrong enemy."[140] MacArthur had no answer to this. As "theater commander" he did not "know all of the details" about the European position, nor had he "gone into" the "global problem."[141] These were fatal admissions. By the time the Senate hearings ended, MacArthur's credibility had evaporated. A poll in late May revealed that public support for him had fallen to 30 percent, his speaking tour through Texas flopped and a campaign to "draft MacArthur for president" was a damp squib.[142] Liberals like Walter Lippmann, who had recognized the threat to the Republic, breathed sighs of relief.[143]

MacArthur had tried to cross the Rubicon only to sink before reaching the other side. Politically he had miscalculated. But had he been wrong on the strategic question of how to win in Korea? It is at least arguable that he had a case.[144] For a start, limited war did not deliver the swift agreement with China that Truman had hoped for. Armistice talks began in July 1951; they did not reach a conclusion for another two years. This was not just because of the official stumbling block, the question of whether or not the Chinese and North Korean prisoners of war should be forcibly repatriated.[145] It was also because limited war waged simultaneously with peace talks gave the Chinese no reason to fear an escalation by the United States. For precisely that reason, the strategy MacArthur had advocated ended up being seriously discussed again just months after his departure. In January 1952 Truman himself advocated issuing an ultimatum, informing the Soviet Union that the United States would blockade the Chinese coast and destroy Chinese bases in Manchuria if there were no change of policy within ten days. This would mean "all out war. It means that Moscow, St. Petersburg, Mukden, Vladivostock, Pekin[g], Shanghai, Port Arthur, Dairen, Odessa, Stalingrad, and every manufacturing plant in China and the Soviet Union will be eliminated." Three months later the JCS recommended the "tactical use of atomic weapons."[146] When negotiations broke down yet again in the autumn, Ridgway's successor, General Mark Clark, sent a plan to Washington "designed to obtain military victory and achieve an armistice on our terms"; it explicitly raised the possibility of atomic strikes "against appropriate targets."[147] Truman's successor, Eisenhower, also contemplated using atomic warheads "on a sufficiently large scale" to bring the conflict to an end.[148] This had been MacArthur's position all along. It was also the public's position. Asked if they favored "using atomic artillery shells against communist forces . . . if truce talks break down," 56 percent of those polled said yes.[149]

It may have been precisely this belated threat that persuaded the Chinese finally to back down on the issue of voluntary repatriation of prisoners. If so, then MacArthur was at least partly vindicated. Limited war had not succeeded in securing an end to the war; only the threat of an atomic escalation had. By overruling MacArthur, Truman and the Joint Chiefs of Staff had unwittingly prolonged the war for more than two years. By the time the armistice was signed (on July 27, 1953), more than thirty thousand American servicemen had lost their lives (though it is worth remembering that casualty rates declined sharply after 1951).[150] Many more had been wounded, and more than seven thousand had endured the miseries of captivity, which more than a third did not survive. Nearly four thousand troops from other countries who participated on the UN side were also killed. South Korean losses were vastly higher, over four hundred thousand.[151] Worse, the outcome was no better than a tie. Korea was divided in two, leaving the armed forces of the North poised, where they remain to this day, just thirty-five miles from Seoul.

In some ways what the Korean War revealed was the remarkable self-limiting character of the American Republic. The United States in 1951 had both the military capability and the public support to strike a decisive military blow against Maoist China. Many another imperial power would have been unable to resist the window of opportunity afforded by America's huge lead in the atomic arms race. Yet Truman drew back, and the general who defied him was thwarted. Why? The lesson Henry Kissinger and others drew from Korea was that America's allies were as much a hindrance as a help. As Kissinger argued in 1956, "Either the alliances add little to our effective strength or they do not reflect a common purpose, or both. . . . We have to face the fact that only the United States is strong enough domestically and economically to assume worldwide responsibilities and that the attempt to obtain the prior approval by all our allies of our every step will lead not to common action but inaction. . . . We must reserve the right to act alone, or with a regional grouping of powers, if our strategic interest so dictates."[152] It was undeniable that the multilateral nature of the Korean intervention created some difficulties. MacArthur's strategy was clearly not one that America's European or Commonwealth allies wanted. Yet it seems clear that Truman would have opted for limited warfare even if the United States had been acting alone. The irony was that in acting as he did—in upholding the authority of the president and the republican Constitution in the face of MacArthur's challenge—Truman was acting against the popular will. In the month of MacArthur's dismissal, support for the war had stood at around 63 percent. By October 1952 less than half that proportion of those polled believed the war in Korea had been "worth fighting" (see figure 4). The trouble with limited war turned out to be that public patience with it was even more limited. It would take the United States another long war to learn that lesson, and this war would

FIGURE 4

Support for the Korean War, 1950–53

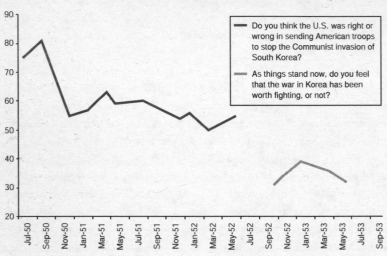

Source: John E. Mueller, *War, Presidents and Public Opinion*, Table 3.3, p. 54.

end not in a tie but in a humiliating defeat. The paradox of the imperial Republic was that it was the civilian political elite—along with sections of the military—that favored limited war, much more than the wider electorate.

THE EMPIRE STRIKES OUT

The real "lesson of Vietnam" had already been evident in Korea. But American policy makers chose to learn the wrong lessons. Not only did they resolve in future to act without the supposed encumbrance of allies and the United Nations, but they also resolved to act through proxies rather than on their own account. This made matters worse, not better. At least a Korean-style approach to the problem of Vietnam might have achieved a draw in the form of partition between North and South. An even more limited approach to imperialism was foredoomed to total failure.

There is no need here for the wisdom of hindsight. In Graham Greene's prophetic novel *The Quiet American*, written when the United States was still propping up the doomed French colonial regime, American attitudes toward Indochina are personified by Pyle, who fails to see that he is as much of a "colonialist" as the cynical British narrator whom he befriends (and, symbolically, cuckolds):

> [Pyle] was talking about the old colonial powers—England and France, and how you couldn't expect to win the confidence of Asiatics. That was where America came in now with clean hands.
>
> "Hawaii, Puerto Rico," I said. "New Mexico."
>
> . . . He said . . . there was always a Third Force to be found free from Communism and the taint of colonialism—national democracy he called it; you only had to find a leader and keep him safe from the old colonial powers.[153]

Pyle fails to grasp that this search for indigenous collaborators is quintessentially imperial. Nor does he see that to install such a Third Force without a long-term commitment to the country is bound to end in disaster. In an attempt to convince him of this, Greene's narrator draws an explicit parallel with the British in India and Burma: "'I've been in India, Pyle, and I know the harm liberals do. We haven't a liberal party any more—liberalism's infected all the other parties. We are all either liberal conservatives or liberal socialists: we all have a good conscience. . . . We go and invade the country: the local tribes support us: we are victorious: but . . . [in Burma] we made peace . . . and left our allies to be crucified and sawn in two. They were innocent. They thought we'd stay. But we were liberals and we didn't want a bad conscience.'"[154]

Those South Vietnamese who acted on the assumption that the Americans would stay—would at least defend a partition on the Korean model—underestimated the growing power of liberalism and a bad conscience within the American elite. Even a young American officer like Philip Caputo, who openly averred that he was "battling . . . the new barbarians who menaced the far-flung interests of the new Rome," did so with a strangely apologetic air:[155] "Maybe it was the effect of my grammar-school civics lessons, but I felt uneasy [searching a Vietnamese village], like a burglar or one of those bullying Redcoats who used to barge into American homes during our Revolution. . . . I smiled stupidly and made a great show of tidying up the mess before we left. See, lady, we're not like the French. We're all-American good-guy GI Joes. You should learn to like us. We're Yanks, and Yanks like to be liked. We'll tear this place apart if we have to, but we'll put everything back in its place."[156] The effects of such imperial denial were ultimately crippling to American strategy. Within a short time, the reality—that imperialists are seldom loved—began to sink in, as one disillusioned veteran put it: "We're supposed to be saving these people and obviously we are not looked upon as the saviors here. They can't like us a whole lot. If we came into a village, there was no flag waving, nobody running out to throw flowers at us, no pretty young girls coming out to give us kisses as we march through victorious. 'Oh, here come the fuckng Americans again. Jesus, when are they going to learn?'"[157]

American military planners defined military success in terms of the ratio of enemy losses to their own losses; hence such grisly measures as the "net body count" and the "kill ratio." As figure 5 shows, even by their own criteria the high point of American military success was in 1967 or 1968; by 1971 the war was clearly being lost. Of course there was an ingenuousness as well a callousness about such calculations. The reality of military success is that it is also determined by how big a proportion of each side's manpower is being lost and, more important, by the morale of each side's combatants and civilians. In the end, it is more important to get the other side to surrender or flee than to inflict death and wounds.[158] Over the entire period of the conflict the United States certainly inflicted higher absolute numbers of casualties on North Vietnam and the Vietcong than were suffered by American forces and the South Vietnamese. But as the American presence was scaled down in Vietnam, and as the willingness of Americans to sacrifice soldiers' lives there diminished, so the odds tipped in favor of their more committed enemy.

Could the Vietnam War have been won if it had been fought more ruthlessly? In the eyes of many American military analysts, Vietnam exposed the flaws in the concept of limited war. General William Westmoreland, who commanded U.S. combat forces until 1968, blamed the "ill-considered" policy of "graduated response," which he believed had prevented a swift and decisive resolution of the conflict.[159] General Bruce Palmer argued that "the graduated, piecemeal employment of airpower against North Vietnam violated many principles of war."[160] Colonel Harry G. Summers blamed U.S. military planners for pursuing Vietcong guerrillas who were deployed to harass the U.S. Army until larger divisions from the North could be sent

FIGURE 5

The "Net Body Count" and the "Kill Ratio," Vietnam, 1966–72

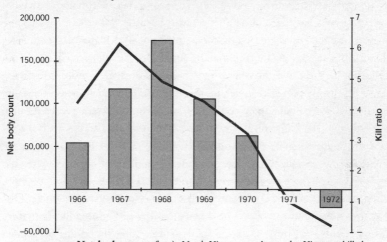

DEFINITIONS: **Net body count** (bars): North Vietnamese Army plus Vietcong killed, missing or captured in action, less American forces plus South Vietnamese Army killed, missing or captured in action. **Kill ratio** (line): North Vietnamese Army plus Vietcong killed, missing or captured in action, divided by American forces plus South Vietnamese Army killed, missing or captured in action.
Source:http://www.vietnamwall.org/pdf/casualty.pdf

down. The Americans exhausted themselves in this "counterinsurgency" effort; instead they should have driven into Laos to seal off the enemy infiltration routes running south, leaving the fight against the Vietcong to South Vietnamese troops.[161] This was a view echoed by Secretary of Defense James Schlesinger. "One of the lessons of the Vietnamese conflict," he later wrote, "is that rather than simply counter your opponent's thrusts, it is necessary to go for the heart of the opponent's power; destroy his military forces rather than simply being involved endlessly in ancillary military operations."[162] According to Admiral Thomas H. Moorer, the United States "should have fought in the north, where everyone was the enemy, where you don't have to worry whether or not you were shooting friendly civilians. . . . The only reason to go to war is to overthrow a government you don't like."[163]

At the level of tactics too the war could have been fought more effectively. American troops who had been trained to fight the Red Army in

Central Europe took time to adjust to the jungle-covered mountains and paddy fields of Vietnam, took time to learn the dark arts of war against guerrillas.[164] This process was not made easier by the demoralizing system of one-year tours of duty, which undermined unit cohesion and flattened the collective learning curve.[165] Yet ultimately the Americans did show signs of having solved the operational and tactical challenges of the war. The North Vietnamese sneered that the Americans' "sophisticated weapons, electronic devices and the rest were to no avail" against a mobilized populace.[166] But in the final stages of the war the Americans were making devastating use of helicopter gunships, "smart" bombs and intensive bombardment by B-52s. It was this new style of air war that all but obliterated a North Vietnamese invading force at Easter 1972.[167]

There were other ways the war effort could have been improved. There was not a clear chain of command: CINCPAC (commander in chief, Pacific) ran the air war on North Vietnam from Hawaii, while CO-MUSMACV (commander, U.S. Military Assistance Command, Vietnam) ran operations in South Vietnam. Intelligence gathering could have been better.[168] Given the importance of liaison between the United States and the South Vietnamese government it was propping up, there could have been better coordination between American military leadership and American diplomatic representation.[169] Yet even if the strategic, operational and tactical conduct of the war had been twice as effective, there was a fundamental political impediment to success: the war's declining popularity. As early as October 1967—just two and a half years after the first marines arrived to defend Da Nang Airport[170]—more voters disapproved of the war than approved of it (see figure 6). The orthodox interpretation of this decline in public belligerence is that it was caused by rising American casualties. There is certainly a superficial—and indeed a statistical—correlation between the two variables.[171] Yet the determinants of popular support for war are more complex than such calculations assume. Casualties in Vietnam were not exceptionally high by comparison with other foreign wars fought by the United States. The total number of American servicemen killed in action in 1967—9,378—was less than 2.5 percent of total U.S. forces in Vietnam. In all, just 1.4 percent of the 8.7 million American military personnel who served in Southeast Asia were killed; 2.2 percent were severely disabled. The world wars were significantly more lethal. The real

FIGURE 6

The Vietnam War: Casualties and Popularity

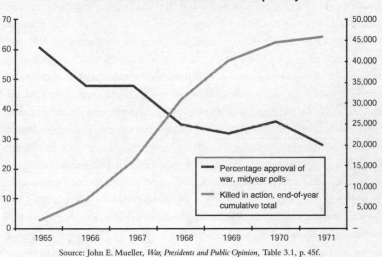

Source: John E. Mueller, *War, Presidents and Public Opinion,* Table 3.1, p. 45f.

problem was that by 1967 a rising proportion of Americans was doubtful that even these numbers were justified by the war's objectives. Lack of clarity about America's aims in Vietnam, lack of confidence that these could be achieved quickly and lack of conviction that the stated aims were worth prolonged sacrifice: these were what caused public support for the war to slide as the body count rose inexorably toward its cumulative total, which was not far short of 60,000 (of whom 47,000 were killed in action).

It is hard to say which was cause and which was effect. Was it the declining popularity of the war that persuaded Lyndon Johnson to seek a negotiated peace, or was it the other way around? There are those who would argue that American society by the 1960s was simply incapable of pursuing such a war to a successful conclusion.[172] But there is a strong case to be made for a lack of effective political leadership. Johnson simply failed to make the case for war either to the public or to Congress.[173] Worse, as early as Christmas 1965 he embarked on a strategy of seeking peace negotiations by suspensions of the air war against Hanoi. This gambit, repeated in September 1967, proved disastrous. By indicating an American readiness to accept a compromise peace, it encouraged the North Vietnamese to keep fighting, while creating an expectation in the United States that an end to the war was in sight. It is no coincidence that public disapproval of the war overtook public approval the following month. Yet even in early 1968 it was still not too late. More than 40 percent of voters still believed that if the United States gave up the struggle, "the Communists will take over Vietnam and then move on to other parts of the world."[174] Lance Corporal Jack S. Swender was very far from the only American who believed it was better to "fight to stop communism in South Vietnam than in Kincaid, Humboldt, Blue Mound, or Kansas City."[175] Westmoreland was inflicting heavy losses on the enemy as the Tet offensive foundered. The fatal mistakes were the new defense secretary Clark Clifford's refusal to send more troops and Johnson's decision to announce another partial bombing halt in the hope of starting talks. From this point onward American policy became a search for an honorable exit—latterly any kind of exit.

This was a goal which Nixon and Kissinger pursued with great ruthlessness. Secretly bombing Cambodia while secretly parleying with Le Duc Tho in Paris was doubly Machiavellian. But the position they had inherited from Johnson was beyond salvage. The cease-fire eventually signed in January 1973 was a death sentence for the South Vietnamese regime, which the Americans had originally intervened to save, while the "collateral damage" caused in Cambodia did nothing to stop that country from falling under the most brutal of all the Communist regimes in Asia. The fall of Phnom Penh to the Khmer Rouge and the flight of the last Americans from Saigon happened within days of one another in April 1975. The humiliation of American "imperialism"—a term of abuse now heard as often in the American as in the Chinese press—seemed complete. What had once been called "the white man's burden," as Senator J. William Fulbright lamented in January 1968, had simply been relabeled the "responsibilities of power."[176] On balance, Americans preferred the irresponsibilities of weakness.

There were those who acknowledged what Greene had all along predicted: that the United States was the heir of European empire in Vietnam. "[If] this makes us the policemen of the world," wrote platoon leader Marion Lee Kempner just three months before his death in November 1966, "then so be it. Surely this is no more a burden than the British accepted from 1815 until 1915, and we have a good deal more reason to adopt it since at no time was Britain threatened during this period with total annihilation or subjection which, make no mistake about it, we are."[177] In many other minds, however, the condition of imperial denial nevertheless persisted. Louis J. Halle insisted that America was "not fighting in Indo-China for imperialistic reasons . . . we are not fighting there because we want to increase our territorial possessions or build an empire."[178] On the contrary, the Vietnam War was a simple case of mistaken identity. Kennedy and Johnson had made the tragic error of seeing the North Vietnamese regime as a mere instrument of world communism, the evil empire the United States had vowed to contain.[179] But it had turned out to be inspired more by a zealous nationalism; had not Ho Chi Minh himself approvingly cited the American Declaration of Independence?[180] The Saigon government, by contrast, had been unworthy of American support.[181] In any case, as such eminent analysts as George F. Kennan and Arthur J. Schlesinger Jr. now discerned, Indochina had been of marginal strategic significance.[182] The inference to be drawn was clear, and Nixon effectively drew it in the "doctrine" he enunciated at Guam. America should fight only when its national interests were at stake; imperiled regimes looking for U.S. sponsorship would henceforth have to do the dirty work themselves.

By the ignominious end of the American intervention in Indochina, such views were widely shared. In 1974 two-fifths of those polled agreed with the statement that "the U.S. should mind its own business internationally and let other countries get along as best they can on their own." Ten years before, just 18 percent had thought so.[183] The consensus that had emerged by 1978 was that the Vietnam War had been "more than a mistake; it was fundamentally wrong and immoral."[184] A succession of films rubbed this in. Though their budgets were large by Hollywood standards—in the case of *Apocalypse Now* fabulously so—these films proved conclusively that war films made better economic sense than actual wars. At even the most conservative estimate, the Vietnam War itself had cost over a hundred billion dollars, financed in large measure by borrowing; between 1964 and 1972 the gross federal debt had increased by roughly the same amount as had been spent on the conflict. Admittedly, that was not a huge increase in public indebtedness by comparison with what was to come in future decades. The biggest deficit of the Vietnam years was equivalent to just over 3 percent of American GDP, less than the deficit for 2003. In that sense, Vietnam was no more crippling in terms of dollars spent than it was in terms of blood spilled. Yet the fact that so many of the dollars had to be spent abroad proved to have serious implications for what was supposed to be the anchor currency of the international monetary system devised at Bretton Woods. On August 15, 1971, a year and a half before the last American troops left Vietnam, Richard Nixon appeared to acknowledge the end of U.S. economic supremacy with his decision to "close the gold window," ending the convertibility of the dollar and ushering a new era of floating exchange rates. Significantly, it had been European—and especially French—pressure on the dollar that had sounded the death knell for Bretton Woods, challenging (though not ending) the dollar's status as the world's predominant reserve currency. Failure in Vietnam did more than redefine American attitudes to the world, driving many Americans toward a repudiation of postwar globalism. It also changed the attitudes of the world toward the United States, unleashing a wave of anti-American feeling (not least within the West European intelligentsia) that was to endure for the rest of the cold war, no matter how egregious the repressiveness of Communist regimes around the world. The imperialism of anti-imperialism had come fatally unstuck if it was the United States that was cast in the role of the evil empire. Small wonder the most successful post-Vietnam movie of them all was in fact a science-fiction fable in which the audience was invited to identify with a ragtag collection of freedom fighters battling for an underdog Rebel Alliance against a sinister Galactic Empire. In *Star Wars* George Lucas perfectly expressed the American yearning not to be on the dark side of imperialism. It was not without significance that as his cinematic epic unfolded backward a generation later, the archvillain Darth Vader was revealed to have been an all-American Jedi Knight in his youth.

LITTLE CAESARS

Failure in Asia could of course be blamed on the sheer distance of Korea and Vietnam from the American mainland. Yet even in its own backyard—Latin America and the Caribbean—the United States found it surprisingly

TABLE 3. VIETNAM MOVIES—TOTAL BOX OFFICE RECEIPTS

Film	Release Date	Total Box Office Receipts
Coming Home	February 1978	$32,635,905
The Deer Hunter	December 1978	$48,979,328
Apocalypse Now	August 1979	$78,784,010
Platoon	December 1986	$138,530,565
Full Metal Jacket	June 1987	$46,357,676
Hamburger Hill	August 1987	$13,839,404
Good Morning Vietnam	December 1987	$123,922,370
Casualties of War	August 1989	$18,671,317
Born on the Fourth of July	December 1989	$70,001,698
Apocalypse Now Redux	August 2001	$4,626,290
We Were Soldiers	March 2002	$78,122,718
The Quiet American	November 2002	$12,988,801
Total		$667,460,082
Total Star Wars Series	May 1977	$1,802,544,288

Source: http://www.boxofficemojo.com

hard to make a success of the imperialism of anti-imperialism. There were plentiful interventions. But just as in the past, where Left-wing governments were overthrown with American assistance or approval, they were generally replaced by military dictatorships whose murderous conduct did nothing to endear the United States to Hispanic-Americans. This happened in Guatemala in 1954, in the Dominican Republic in 1965 and in Chile in 1973.[185] In justifying his decision to send troops to Santo Domingo, Johnson offered the classic rhetoric of imperial denial: "Over the years of our history our forces have gone forth into many lands, but always they returned when they were no longer needed. For the purpose of America is never to suppress liberty, but always to save it. The purpose of America is never to take freedom, but always to return it; never to break peace but to bolster it, and never to seize land but always to save lives."[186] The subsequent records of the wholly undemocratic regimes installed in each case made a mockery of these words. The most puzzling thing, however, was the failure of the United States to pull off a successful intervention in a country that was geographically nearer, economically more promising and strategically more valuable than all of these: Cuba. Not only was the United States powerless to prevent Fidel Castro's Communist Revolution from succeeding in 1959, but two years later it failed ignominiously to pull off a countercoup by anti-Castro exiles (the Bay of Pigs fiasco), and in

October 1962 it came to the brink of a third world war when the Soviet Union sent nuclear missiles to the island.[187] Only by secretly offering to withdraw American missiles from Turkey were the Kennedy brothers able to avoid what would indeed have been "one hell of a gamble"—namely, a U.S. invasion of Cuba—and secure the peaceful withdrawal of the Soviet weapons.[188] What the Cuban missile crisis revealed was that when the two superpowers confronted each another "eyeball to eyeball," they discovered that they had grown to resemble each other. We now know that both parties blinked in the confrontation; perhaps it was the surprise of recognition.[189] For in truth neither of the two anti-imperialist empires cared enough about Cuba to risk a thermonuclear duel. Not for the first or the last time, the principal beneficiary of this standoff was a petty dictator. So long as the superpowers could compete only through proxies, it was the little countries that got the Caesars—and, all too often, the Caligulas too.

CHAPTER 3

THE CIVILIZATION
OF CLASHES

If the sword falls on the United States after eighty years, hypocrisy raises its head lamenting the deaths of these killers who tampered with the blood, honor, and holy places of the Muslims. . . . When these defended their oppressed sons, brothers, and sisters in Palestine and in many Islamic countries, the world at large shouted. The infidels shouted, followed by the hypocrites. . . . They champion falsehood, support the butcher against the victim, the oppressor against the innocent child. . . . In the aftermath of this event . . . every Muslim should rush to defend his religion.

OSAMA BIN LADEN, October 7, 2001[1]

There is a human condition that we must worry about in times of war. There is a value system that cannot be compromised—God-given values. These aren't United States-created values. These are values of freedom and the human condition and mothers loving their children. What's very important as we articulate our foreign policy through our diplomacy and our military action, is that we never look like we are creating—[like] we are the author of these values.

GEORGE W. BUSH, 2002[2]

TO THE HOLY LAND

Empires throughout history have sought to control certain regions of the world for the sake of their mineral wealth. It was lead and silver that lured the Romans to Britain in the first century. It was gold that lured the conquistadors to Peru in the sixteenth century and the British to the Transvaal in the nineteenth. Empires have also traditionally sought to introduce their own cultures to the countries whose minerals they have extracted. England was Romanized just as much as the South African Rand was Anglicized. This model has suggested to many contemporary analysts that the American relationship with the Middle East has an imperial character. On the one hand, the United States has an obvious and long-standing interest in the immense oil reserves of the region. On the other, it is said, Americans aspire to transform its political culture, which has proved exceptionally resistant to democratization.

Yet if these have been the defining motivations of American policy toward the Middle East, then that policy has been very far from successful. U.S. control over Arabian oil fields declined steeply in the postwar era as a result of policies of nationalization, often adopted by overtly anti-American regimes. According to the scores awarded in the annual Freedom House survey, only Israel and Turkey—two out of the fifteen countries in the region—can be regarded as democracies today. That was also true in 1950, except that Egypt, Iran, Lebanon and Syria were all closer to political freedom then than they are today.

As the epigraphs above suggest, America's leaders do sometimes use language that seems to confirm the allegations of their most bitter opponents in the Arab world that they are bent on a new "crusade" against Islam. In a momentary lapse President George W. Bush even used the word *crusade* himself to characterize the war he wished to wage against terrorism following the attacks of September 11, 2001. Yet the notion of a "clash of civilizations" is as much of a caricature as the idea that the United States is interested solely in the Middle East's oil. It is rather more illuminating to conceive of the American role as that of a less than eager participant in the region's distinctive civilization of clashes, a dysfunctional culture in which rival religions and natural resources supply much of the content of political conflict, but the *form* is the really distinctive thing. That form is of course terrorism.

It is the conventional wisdom that September 11, 2001, was one of the turning points of modern history. It is not to diminish the magnitude of the suffering the terrorists inflicted on thousands of families—or of the shock to the American collective psyche—to suggest that it was nothing of the sort. Without a doubt, Osama bin Laden and his acolytes perpetrated ghastly crimes for which they must be held accountable. But that would be true regardless of their motives. The crucial point in the eyes of the historian is that those motives were the product of long-term historical forces, the origins of which lay decades earlier, and the direction of which was almost entirely unchanged afterward. On that bright late-summer's morning, the history of America's relations with the Middle East only seemed to reach a turning point. Like March 1848 in German history, September 2001 was in many ways the turning point at which that history failed to turn.

FIRST STEPS

It is often assumed that the greatest failure of American policy during the cold war was defeat in Vietnam. Yet the loss of much of Indochina to Communist regimes proved to be as strategically unimportant as it was politically embarrassing. The United States lost face. That was about all it lost. It was the people of Vietnam and Cambodia who paid the horrifically high price of American failure; Americans themselves were able to walk away from the wreckage of "containment." The reality, which dawned only slowly on policy makers in Washington, was that Vietnam did not really matter. Nor, on mature reflection, did Cuba, which was why the United States quietly abandoned the idea of toppling the Castro regime. Whether they were in Hanoi or Havana, Communists in developing countries proved to be relatively harmless from the point of view of American national security. In the latter case, they might make all kinds of mischief in other peripheral theaters: witness Castro's energetic participation in the Angolan and Ethiopian civil wars. But if the Caribbean mattered only slightly, then sub-Saharan African scarcely signified at all, by comparison with the one region of the world that, by the early 1970s, Americans could not possibly afford to "lose." This was the Middle East.

Many misconceptions exist about the attitude of the United States toward the region. One is that the United States is actuated by an unconditional, unquestioning "special relationship" with the state of Israel. Another is that the United States has been drawn to the Middle East mainly by the existence of vast oil reserves beneath its desert sands. Still a third is that the terrorist attacks of 9/11 were America's just deserts for her misdeeds in the region. Such notions are by no means confined to the membership of al Qa'eda. The fires had scarcely been quenched and the dust had barely begun to settle in Lower Manhattan when a succession of *bien-pensants* rushed to give vent to similar theories in the press.[3] The reality is a great deal more complicated. First, America's relationship with Israel has long been characterized by friction and ambivalence. It is anything but a marriage made in heaven. Secondly, the oil-rich United States is much less dependent on Middle Eastern oil than is Western Europe or Japan. "Control" of Arabian oil reserves is a goal the United States long ago renounced; if such control were really necessary to ensure the flow of oil to the Western world, it would be the oilless Germans and the Japanese who would be pressing for it with the greatest zeal. Thirdly, the phenomenon of terrorism in the Middle East—and indeed elsewhere—has until recently had relatively little to do with the United States. What was remarkable about 9/11 was simply that it had taken so long for a major terrorist outrage to happen on American soil. And what appears to have motivated the attackers could hardly be described as a misdeed, since American troops were stationed in Saudi Arabia primarily in order to defend that country and its neighbors from the aggression of another Arab state, Iraq.

So important has the Middle East been in American foreign policy during the past three decades that it is easy to forget how much less attention it used to be given.[4] Before the 1950s the American presence in the Middle East was as academic as it was strategic, taking the form of such notable institutions as the American universities in Cairo and Beirut, Roberts College in Istanbul and Alborz College in Iran. In September 1946 Loy W. Henderson, the director of the State Department's Office of Near Eastern and African Affairs, defined "the main objective" of American policy in the region as being "to prevent rivalries and conflicts of interest in that area from developing into open hostilities which eventually might lead to a third world war."[5] This cast the United States in the role of benign referee at most. More binding commitments were not much sought after. It was a British decision in effect to hand the Americans responsibility for Turkey (and, for that matter, Greece) in 1947. After that the British remained the dominant outside force in the region for at least another decade and even after the fiasco of the Suez crisis continued to consider the Persian Gulf a part of their sphere of influence.

The United States had long since acquired an economic interest in the region, it is true. From the 1920s onward, American oil companies had fought hard to establish a foothold there, forcing the reluctant British companies to grant them a stake in the Turkish (later Iraq) Petroleum Company a year after the British had struck oil at Baba Gurgur in 1927.[6] It was early days; even by 1940 Middle Eastern producers were still accounting for no more than 5 percent of world production. But the Americans had by now convinced themselves of the vast untapped potential there.[7] In the 1930s they worked assiduously, aided by the renegade British Arabist Harry St. John Philby, to turn the desert kingdom ruled by the Saudi family into an American satellite.[8] During the Second World War they took advantage of British weakness to propose a deal: the United States would take Saudi Arabia, leaving the British Persia; Iraq and Kuwait would be shared.[9] The pattern of U.S.-Saudi relations was already established: cash and arms for the Saudi royal family in return for oil concessions and military bases for the Americans.[10] The consortium of oil companies that formed the Arabian-American Oil Company (ARAMCO) became a channel for royal rents; soon they were paying as much as half of their revenues to the Saudis, payments that the U.S. Treasury treated as tax-deductible.[11] When John Foster Dulles became the first American secretary of state to visit the Middle East in 1953, he was impressed; the oil and other mineral resources of the region would, he declared, be "vital to our welfare."[12]

Yet if the United States had really believed that, it would surely have acted very differently in one fundamental respect. For nothing could have been better calculated to alienate the Arab peoples than consistent support for the state of Israel. The prompt recognition of the new state was in many ways Harry Truman's responsibility; he insisted on it in May 1948 against the advice of the State Department.[13] Truman's commitment has endured. By 1958 the paramount importance of the relationship to Israel had become an axiom of American foreign policy. In the words of a former American ambassador to Egypt, "Israel represents our oldest direct interest in the area. . . . The continuance of Israel as an independent state certainly represents a basic foreign policy commitment of the United States. . . ."[14]

Many analysts concentrate their attention on the reasons for this commitment: the political influence of the so-called Zionist lobby in the United States; feelings of guilt about the Holocaust among a wider public; the fact that Israel is a democratic oasis in the Middle East; the belief of evangelical Christians that the return of the Jews to the Holy Land is a sign of the imminence of Christ's Second Coming. What is less frequently noticed is how often Israel and the United States have disagreed. Truman's support for Israel did not extend to military assistance, for example. Dulles suspended aid to Israel on more than one occasion. The United States was hostile when Israel occupied Sinai and the Gaza Strip in 1956, insisting that the Israelis withdraw. It failed to ensure freedom of passage for Israeli shipping through the Strait of Tiran on the eve of the Six-Day War, despite having pledged to do so at the United Nations. Later the United States favored the internationalization of Jerusalem and expressed criticism of the Israeli policy of colonization in the territories captured from the Arabs in 1967.[15] Israel's occupation of Gaza and the West Bank has manifestly done little to serve American interests.

What really drew the United States into the Middle East in the 1950s was not Israel or oil but fear of the Soviet Union; to be precise, fear that the Russians would be able to capitalize on the crisis of the European empires as successfully in the Arab world as they had done in the Asian.[16] To begin with, as it turned out, the Russians were notably clumsy. Stalin's advances toward Tehran backfired;[17] by comparison, the British-inspired but CIA-executed overthrow of the Iranian premier Muhammad Mussadegh, who had rashly nationalized the Anglo-Iranian Oil Company, seemed to guarantee American dominance at minimal cost.[18] The American rationale for Operation Ajax was, in essence, preemptive containment. As one of the CIA operatives recalled, "It was about what the Soviets had done and what we knew about their future plans." Iran, in his view, had been "very high" on the Russian "priority list."[19]

Some Americans had doubts about the wisdom of backing the old colonialists against a popular leader who was manifestly no Marxist. In Egypt the initial American impulse was to back the nationalist demagogue—in this case Colonel Gamal Abdel Nasser—against the British; indeed, the State Department positively encouraged the Egyptian leader to demand the end of the British military presence in the Suez Canal Zone.

By 1956, however, Nasser's flirtations with the Russians and grandstanding appeals to the rest of the Arab world had irritated Eisenhower and Dulles so much that they resolved to call his (and Khrushchev's) bluff. The American refusal to finance Nasser's projected Aswan Dam prompted another spectacular nationalization, this time of the Suez Canal.[20] If, at this juncture, the United States had been able to control what were supposed to be two of its closest allies, Britain and Israel, things might have turned out quite differently, and not only in the Middle East. Instead the British prime minister Sir Anthony Eden agreed to a harebrained French scheme to reoccupy the Suez Canal Zone by force, on the pretext of stopping an Arab-Israeli War that the Israelis were happy to arrange. Not only did Eden fail to consult Eisenhower; he had been explicitly warned by the Americans that such a coup would not be endorsed by the United States, for the simple reason that it would look like an even more egregious neo-colonial adventure than the overthrow of Mussadegh and might drive the entire Middle East apart from Israel into Khrushchev's arms. Incredulously, Eisenhower asked: "How can we possibly support Britain and France if in doing so we lose the whole Arab world?"[21]

Unfortunately, Khrushchev's public threat to use nuclear weapons *appeared* to be the reason for the Anglo-French withdrawal,[22] whereas in reality it was the disastrous run on sterling and the American refusal to lend Britain a cent until Eden agreed to pull out. Worse, the disarray of the West gave the Russians a free hand to suppress with extreme brutality the reformist government of Imre Nagy in Hungary. Thus the United States got no credit in Cairo for pulling the plug on Eden[23] and just two years later found itself unable to do anything when, at Nasser's instigation, a group of Iraqi army officers staged a revolt in Baghdad that toppled and murdered the pro-British Hashemite monarch, Faisal II, and his prime minister, Nuri es-Said. The decision to send a force of fifteen thousand marines to Lebanon in the aftermath of this coup achieved nothing; indeed, it is hard to see what they could possibly have done there that would have influenced events in Baghdad or anywhere else. (Beirut at this time was still something of a cosmopolitan playground, very far from the war zone it later became.)[24] If American strategy was driven by a desire to control Middle Eastern oil, this was a serious setback. Not long after the coup the new Iraqi government revoked the Iraqi Petroleum Company's concession (thereby ending Britain's principal gain from its successful invasion of 1917); Iraq was among the first Arab countries to nationalize its oil industry.[25] Meanwhile the Saudis halted their arms purchases from the United States and declined to renew the lease on the Dhahran air base.[26] Unlike Castro in Cuba, Nasser had little interest in the Soviet economic model, but he too was happy to collect such bounty as Moscow had to offer and to jeer derisively at Washington.[27]

BETWEEN GAZA AND THE GULF

By the end of the 1950s three things were already painfully obvious about America's position in the Middle East. First, the Israelis regarded U.S. support as having, to all intents and purposes, no strings attached. They would do as they chose. Secondly, the American oil companies were as vulnerable as the British stake in the Suez Canal to nationalization by Arab governments that had no very obvious incentive to share the rents from their oil with foreigners. Thirdly, peaceful coexistence between Israel and its Arab neighbors was unlikely, if not impossible; somehow the United States had to minimize the damage caused by their conflict. The good news from an American standpoint was that Soviet penetration of the Middle East proved to be much less successful than might have been expected in 1958. The bad news was that there arose in the wake of the Arab-Israeli wars a more dangerous—or at least less predictable—threat than Soviet penetration. This was terrorism, the original sin of the modern Middle East. What Zionist extremists had once done to drive the British out of Palestine, Palestinian extremists now did to the Israelis, once their hopes of an Arab military victory had been dashed. The Arab states brought defeat upon themselves. A two-state solution to the conflict between Jews and Arabs in the former British mandate of Palestine was available at the outset, in the form of UN General Assembly resolution 181. The Arabs opted instead for war. Yet the combined forces of Lebanon, Syria, Iraq, Transjordan, and Egypt—supported by Saudi Arabia—failed miserably to strangle the infant state of Israel at birth. Suez was a humiliation for Britain and France, but for the Israelis it was a victory: the Gaza

Strip and Sharm el-Sheikh were seized, though afterward put under UN control; heavy losses were inflicted on Egyptian forces at relatively low cost to the Israeli Defense Forces. The Six-Day War of 1967 was a direct and legitimate response by Israel to transparent Egyptian-led preparations for a war; ten days before the first Israeli air strikes, Nasser had explicitly pledged to wipe Israel off the map. Once again the Arabs were easily beaten, once again the Israelis occupied Sinai and Gaza and now, in response to the Jordanian decision to join the Egyptian side, they also took Judea, including Jerusalem and Samaria (the West Bank), as well as the Golan Heights. Despite its initial successes, the Yom Kippur War of October 1973 ended up as another botched attack on Israel by Egypt and Syria. Even with Iraqi and then Soviet assistance, the Arab armies were driven back into their own territory. By 1982 the Israelis felt confident enough to invade Lebanon.

In their responses to these external threats, the Israelis felt under no obligation to consult the United States. The Americans were not warned about the Six-Day War; nor were they entirely jubilant at the successive Israeli victories. As Nixon commented in an interview in 1970, the Middle East had become "terribly dangerous. It is like the Balkans before World War I—where the two superpowers, the United States and the Soviet Union, could be drawn into a confrontation that neither of them wants because of the differences there."[28] As containment gave way to détente, neither superpower relished the prospect of another Arab-Israeli war. When it came in 1973, the Americans offered support to Israel only after it was clear that the Russians were helping the other side; in both cases assistance entitled the superpowers to press for a cease-fire. Yet brokering peace proved exceedingly difficult.[29] American and Israeli politicians continued to incant the now familiar lines about their "special relationship" and "deep friendship."[30] American aid to the country reached unprecedented heights: between 1976 and 1985 a quarter of all U.S. economic and military aid went to Israel—altogether some twenty-five billion dollars. This was equivalent to around 13 percent of Israeli gross national income (see figure 7). But the more the United States took on the role of honest broker between Israel and Egypt, the less such money seemed to buy.[31]

FIGURE 7

U.S. aid to Israel as a percentage of Israeli gross national income,
1966–2000

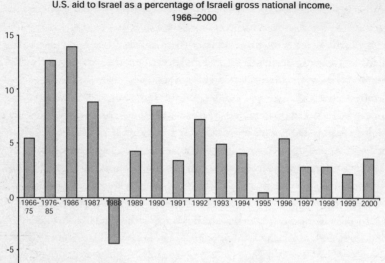

Note: In 1988 grant returns and principal repayments exceeded new grants and credits.

Source: Calculated from data in various issues of the *Statistical Abstract of the United States* and the
World Bank *World Development Indicators* database.

True, the Israeli prime minister Menachem Begin was persuaded by
President Jimmy Carter to relinquish Sinai for the sake of peace with
Egypt. That, however, was as far as he could go; talks about the future of
the occupied territories came to nothing. In December 1981, when Israel
decided to alter the status of the Golan Heights by bringing the area under
its own law, jurisdiction and administration, the United States supported a
UN resolution condemning this action.[32] When Israel invaded Lebanon
seven months later, the United States contributed to the peacekeeping
force that was deployed to prevent an escalation of the conflict. That same
year Ronald Reagan's attempt at a "fresh start" in the peace process was effectively vetoed by the Israelis. The Americans never contemplated a complete break with Israel. Indeed, the 1983 agreement between Reagan and
the Israeli prime minister Yitzhak Shamir was followed by a significant increase in military cooperation and economic assistance.[33] Yet the Israelis
tenaciously resisted American pressure to negotiate with the Palestinians. As

early as December 1988, Yasser Arafat accepted the American precondi-
tions for bilateral dialogue (renouncing terrorism, recognizing the state of
Israel and accepting UNSC Resolutions 242 and 338).[34] The Israelis, however, became less rather than more willing to contemplate a return to the
borders of 1967. With every passing year, as the settlement of the occupied
territories proceeded (by 1983 there were nearly thirty thousand Jewish settlers) and as Palestinians living there resorted to violence, a return to the *status quo ante* became harder to imagine. The Americans protested about the
policy of settlement and about the use of live ammunition against stone-
throwing Palestinians, but to no avail.[35]

The crucial difficulty for the Americans was that even as Israel established its military superiority over the Arab countries, forcing the Palestinians to resort to terrorism instead of conventional war, so the *economic*
importance of the Arab countries grew. In 1953 the United States still produced more than half of the total world oil production; by 1973 its share
had fallen to 21 percent. American imports of oil had once been insignificant; by 1977 they had risen to 46 percent of total consumption, and a
growing share of those imports came from the Middle East.[36] This had advantages as well as disadvantages for the United States. As the oil-export-
ing countries grew wealthy, they spent increasing amounts of money on
American goods and invested substantial amounts of their petrodollars in
the United States.[37] Between 1970 and 1972, for example, Saudi Arabia's
purchases of arms from American firms rose by a factor of twenty.[38] In the
years that followed, weapons worth eighty-three billion dollars were sold
to the Saudis.[39] In any case, a substantial part of the Middle Eastern oil industry was still in American hands, though this declined when the Saudis
finally nationalized ARAMCO.[40] Moreoever, it was not the United States
so much as its principal allies that had become truly dependent on Arab
oil.[41] In the cold war, this gave the future of the Middle East a strategic as
well as an economic dimension. As Eugene V. Rostow argued in 1975, "The
first and most basic [American interest] is the geopolitical importance of
the Middle East to the defense of Europe. Our alliance with western Europe is absolutely essential to the balance of world power on which the
primordial safety of the United States depends. . . . Hegemonial control of
the oil, the space and the mass of the region by the Soviet Union would
carry with it dominion over Western Europe as well. NATO would be dis-

mantled."[42] Up until this point, in fact, there seemed little cause for anxiety. The Soviets had more or less ceased to exert influence in Cairo since the expulsion of their military advisers in 1972. While they still had some leverage in Syria, that hardly represented "hegemonial control." The Americans, by contrast, had appeared to be taking over Britain's former position of predominance in the smaller gulf states that were among the best endowed with "black gold": Kuwait, the United Arab Emirates, Bahrain, Qatar and Oman.[43] Meanwhile, Kissinger's shuttle diplomacy not only persuaded Egypt and Israel to "disengage" in 1973–74 but also brought a swift end to the Saudi oil embargo.

However, there did not need to be a specifically *Soviet* control of Middle Eastern oil for both the United States and its allies to suffer acute economic pain. Arab control might suffice. The Libyan dictator Muammar al-Qaddafi had already demonstrated this after the 1967 Arab-Israeli war, when he had exploited increased Western demand for Libyan oil by raising prices and profit shares and finally nationalizing the oil companies' assets. Up until 1972 the United States had succeeded in squaring the circle of its support for Israel and its support for the Saudi king, who loathed Zionism as deeply as he loathed communism.[44] In 1973, however, the Saudis backed the Egyptian assault on Israel not with soldiers but with a 70 percent increase in oil prices and a rolling embargo that cut supplies of oil to supporters of Israel by 5 percent per month. When the Americans more than doubled their aid to Israel, the Saudis imposed a total embargo on exports to the United States. At a time when American and West European monetary authorities were still learning to live with floating exchange rates and when their fiscal authorities had largely embraced a vulgarized version of Keynesian demand management, the sharp spike in oil prices had dramatic consequences. Inflation surged, public finances lurched into the red, yet at the same time unemployment rose (see figure 8). Still worse "stagflation" was to follow in the aftermath of what was, in many ways, the most disastrous American foreign policy setback of all—the Iranian Revolution of 1979, which saw the American-backed shah, the once-vainglorious but now-ailing Mohammad Reza Pahlavi, supplanted not by a Soviet puppet but by something altogether unexpected: a radical, theocratic proponent of Islamic fundamentalism.

FIGURE 8

The Oil Price and the American "Misery" Index, 1970–2002

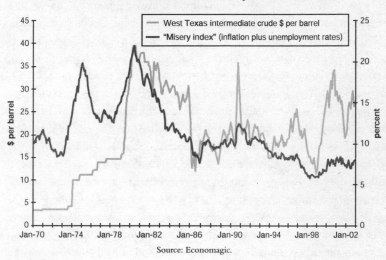

Source: Economagic.

The shah was not the worst of the despots installed and propped up by the United States during the cold war. True, the regime was very far from liberal, and the shah's penchant for conspicuous consumption was less than judicious. Compared with the dictators the United States cultivated in Nicaragua or Chile, however, he was an enlightened despot. The shah's Iran was a relatively unequal society, no doubt, by American or West European standards, but no more so than Turkey and less so than many Latin American countries. The extraordinary thing was the insouciance of its American architects as the regime slid toward the edge of a revolutionary abyss. To lose Vietnam to the heirs of Ho Chi Minh, as we have seen, had not really mattered in geopolitical terms. But to lose Iran to the ayatollah Ruhollah Khomeini, the Lenin of Islamic revolution, was a calamity whose ramifications were and remain incalculable. Iran was, after Turkey, the biggest of the Middle Eastern states, with a population three times that of Iraq. Crucially, it was second only to Saudi Arabia as an oil producer, accounting for over

10 percent of total world output in 1973, making it the third largest in the world (the United States was still the world's biggest at that time).[45]

In January 1980 President Carter, still reeling from the incarceration of fifty-two American hostages in the Tehran Embassy, anxiously attempted to redefine American strategy in the Middle East. Henceforth, he declared, "Any attempt by an outside force to gain control of the Persian Gulf region will be regarded as an assault on the vital interests of the United States . . . and such an assault will be repelled by any means necessary, including military force."[46] This was intended as a signal to the Soviet Union, which had just embarked on its own disastrously ill-conceived invasion of Afghanistan, not to exploit the Iranian crisis for its own ends. At the time it seemed a new nadir in the cold war; Carter himself described the Russian action as the greatest threat to world peace since 1945. In its aftermath, the arms race in Europe entered perhaps its most dangerous phase, with the deployment of intermediate-range nuclear missiles first by the Soviets and then—amid sometimes violent protests—by the Americans. Nor was it illogical to fear that Moscow would capitalize on the chaos in Tehran; it had long regarded Persia as a region of strategic importance and had indeed informally shared power there with Britain from the late nineteenth century until the 1940s. Yet the "outside force" Carter had in mind turned out not to be the problem in the Middle East. From now on it was forces *within* the region that would pose the most serious threats to American interests.

Like all revolutionary regimes, Khomeini's Iran was soon embroiled in a war with its neighbor. The Iraqi dictator, Saddam Hussein, fearing a pro-Iranian rising by his own country's Shiite population, decided to invade Iran in 1980. Kissinger's sardonic comment—"a pity they both can't lose"—reflected the dilemma the United States now confronted. A regime that regarded America as the "Great Satan" could scarcely be a tool of American policy, yet the Baathist tyranny of Saddam Hussein in Baghdad, though secular in the old Arab nationalist style, was only marginally more appealing. In a feat of *Realpolitik* that eclipsed even Kissinger's during the 1970s, the United States ended up giving assistance to both sides. Arms were secretly sold to Iran, first to buy the release of the embassy hostages, later to raise funds for American covert operations in Central America. Saddam meanwhile received substantial commodity credits, rising to more than one billion dollars in 1989, despite the fact that his forces not only used chemical weapons but on one occasion attacked an American warship.[47] If the outcome of the Gulf War was that neither side lost, it owed something at least to American Machiavellianism—the same deviousness that inspired the Reagan administration to channel cash and weapons to the mujahideen fighting the Red Army in Afghanistan.

The real difficulty the United States faced, however, was that exerting any direct influence in the gulf depended on being able to maintain some kind of military presence there. Yet one consequence of the Iranian Revolution was to make the Saudi regime distinctly unenthusiastic about giving American troops access to gulf bases. Although in the immediate aftermath of the revolution in Tehran, the Saudis welcomed the arrival of a squadron of American F-15s, which were followed in October 1980 by AWACS-equipped aircraft, they drew the line at Secretary of State Alexander Haig's "strategic consensus," which implied wider access to gulf bases for American troops. Significantly, the Rapid Deployment Joint Task Force set up to apply the Carter doctrine was at first based far away in Tampa, Florida. In May 1981 the Saudi-dominated Gulf Cooperation Council declared that the entire gulf region should be kept "free of international conflicts, particularly the presence of military fleets and foreign bases."[48] Only when it became clear that both Iran and Iraq were prepared to attack neutral shipping in the gulf did an American naval presence become acceptable. In 1987 Kuwaiti tankers were reflagged as American ships in order to justify U.S. naval protection.[49] Finally, in 1990, the Saudis relented and allowed American troops on their soil. It was to prove a decision fraught with danger for both parties. Unwittingly, the American empire had made a new and dangerous enemy.

THE LOGIC OF TERROR

Why did Osama bin Laden, himself a Saudi, order twenty-one of his followers, most of them also Saudis, to hijack four planes and fly them into the World Trade Center, the Pentagon and (in all likelihood) the White House? In their Declaration of the World Islamic Front for Jihad Against

the Jews and the Crusaders of February 23, 1998, he and his cosignatories
gave three reasons for issuing their notorious fatwa "to kill the Americans
and their allies":

> First, for over seven years the United States has been occupying the lands of
> Islam in the holiest of places, the Arabian Peninsula, plundering its riches,
> dictating to its rulers, humiliating its people, terrorizing its neighbors, and
> turning its bases in the Peninsula into a spearhead through which to fight
> the neighboring Muslim peoples.
>
> . . . Second, despite the great devastation inflicted on the Iraqi people
> by the crusader–Zionist alliance . . . the Americans are once again trying to
> repeat the horrific massacres . . .
>
> Third, if the Americans' aims behind these wars are religious and eco-
> nomic, the aim is also to serve the Jews' petty state and divert attention from
> its occupation of Jerusalem and murder of Muslims there. The best proof of
> this is their eagerness to destroy Iraq, the strongest neighboring Arab state,
> and their endeavor to fragment all the states of the region such as Iraq,
> Saudi Arabia, Egypt, and Sudan into paper statelets and through their dis-
> union and weakness to guarantee Israel's survival and the continuation of
> the brutal crusade occupation of the Peninsula.

The aim of killing Americans was therefore clear: it was in order "to
liberate the al-Aqsa Mosque and the holy mosque [Mecca] from their grip,
and in order for their armies to move out of all the lands of Islam, defeated
and unable to threaten any Muslim."[50] Bin Laden echoed these words in
his interview published in *Time* magazine eleven months later and just
eight months before the 9/11 attacks.[51] His goals, in short, were to get
American forces out of Saudi Arabia, to get them out of the Middle East
altogether, to overthrow Arab governments sympathetic to the United
States and to destroy the state of Israel. Subsequent statements attributed to
him are consistent on these points.[52]

Some Western commentators are deceived by bin Laden's rhetoric of
pan-Islamic, global jihad into imagining that he is a genuine harbinger of
a clash of civilizations.[53] It would be more accurate to say that bin Laden
is the offspring of the Middle East's distinctive civilization of clashes, a re-
tarded political culture in which terrorism has long been a substitute for
both peaceful politics and conventional warfare. No doubt it is gratifying
to imagine a collective Muslim sense of historical disenchantment, an old

superiority complex that centuries of historic decline have transformed into "a downward spiral of hate and spite, rage and self-pity, poverty and oppression."[54] Yet the ideology of al Qa'eda has relatively little in common with the belief systems of the majority of people in the largest Muslim countries, such as Indonesia and Turkey, to say nothing of the immigrant Muslim communities of the West. Even bin Laden's religious beliefs bear the idiosyncratic hallmarks of Wahhabism, which has historically been confined to the deserts of Arabia. Al Qa'eda is better understood as the extremist wing of a specifically Arab political religion, a term recently and illuminatingly used by the historian Michael Burleigh to capture the essential characteristics of nazism: its messianic leadership, its need to indoctrinate, its appetite for persecution.[55]

This is not, it should be noted, the same as saying that al Qa'eda is the product of "Islamo-fascism," though the two certainly have violence and anti-Semitism in common.[56] The Fascist movements of the 1920s and 1930s were never especially adept at terrorism, preferring to seize control of existing nation-states and to make war using traditional military forces. "Islamo-nihilism" would be nearer the mark, or perhaps "Islamo-bolshevism," for we should not forget that in their early years Lenin and Stalin were also terrorists. Indeed, there is more than a passing resemblance between "Hereditary Nobleman Ulyanov," as the young Lenin liked to style himself, hatching his plans for the overthrow of tsarism from dingy Swiss hotels, and the renegade Saudi millionaire, orchestrating the downfall of America from a secluded Afghan cave. That should also remind us that "Western civilization" (unless we take that to mean only the novel Protestant-Deist-Catholic-Jewish fusion that is today's American culture) has itself been capable in the past of producing political religions just as intolerant and bloodthirsty as today's Islamo-bolshevism.

Terrorism—meaning the sporadic use of violence by nonstate forces in pursuit of political goals—is nothing new, least of all in the Middle East and least of all against imperial powers. By the 1940s the British were all too familiar with it, since radical minorities among their Irish and Bengali subjects had long engaged in campaigns of assassination in pursuit of independence. Terrorism had already played a decisive role in bringing down the Habsburg and Romanov empires. Since the 1860s men like the Russian anarchist Sergei Nechaev had been preaching a doctrine of terrorism in which violence—notionally to further the "revolution"—came close to becoming an end in itself. It was Nechaev who wrote the *Revolutionary Catechism* (1868), which declared: "The revolutionary knows only a single science: the science of destruction . . . [His] purpose is only one: the quickest and most sure destruction of this filthy system."[57] Another European, the Italian Carlo Pisacane, coined the phrase "propaganda by deed."[58] Joseph Conrad too would have grasped at once the thinking behind bin Laden's choice of targets. Readers of his novel *The Secret Agent* will recall the words of Mr. Vladimir, the subversive mastermind who plots to bomb the Greenwich Observatory as one of a "series of outrages . . . executed here in this country." "These outrages," Vladimir explains, "must be sufficiently startling—effective. Let them be directed against buildings, for instance. . . . The attack must have all the shocking senselessness of gratuitous blasphemy . . . [and be] the most alarming display of ferocious imbecility." It must, in short, be a symbolic act that speaks for itself. "What is the fetish of the hour that all the bourgeoisie recognize—eh, Mr. Verloc?" Vladimir asks his intended bomber.[59] A hundred years ago the "fetish of the hour" was science; hence the attack on the observatory. In 2001 it was economics or, to be precise, economic globalization; hence, it might be argued, the attack on the World Trade Center.

Yet terrorism in the real world is about more than symbolism. It is the continuation of war by other means—by those who are too weak to wage proper war in pursuit of their political goals. The characteristic feature of terrorism is that its violence is sporadic. Its technology is primitive. Its operatives are, contrary to popular belief, highly vulnerable to countermeasures—especially when the terrorists have no bases on foreign soil from which to operate. The terrorist's resources are far inferior to those of the states against which he fights, so that most terrorist organizations depend on a combination of thieving and begging for their funds. It is possible for a terrorist organization to operate in a country without external sources of support, but it requires a secure locality where its members can prepare their attacks without fear of interdiction. When this is not available, the terrorists are bound to seek assistance from abroad. Countries that offer them support— or even mere sympathy—are unlikely to be targets for their violence. Conversely, foreign countries that assist the other side—the government against which the terrorists are fighting—may well find themselves drawn into the conflict.

Humiliated on the battlefield, the Arab states early on resorted to the sponsorship of terrorism by Palestinian exiles. Operating from bases in Egypt, Lebanon and Jordan, Palestinian fedayeen (literally "self-sacrifices") mounted numerous attacks on Israeli civilians after 1949. In the six years from 1951 to 1956, over four hundred Israelis were killed and nine hundred injured by these attacks. After the Six-Day War, the Palestine Liberation Organization operated with impunity from Jordanian territory until Israeli pressure forced its expulsion in 1970.[60] The PLO then moved to southern Lebanon, a country whose subsequent descent into civil war created an almost perfect seedbed for terrorist organizations (something the Syrian invasion in 1976 did nothing to alter). Terrorist attacks by PLO guerrillas based in Lebanon prompted the Israelis to invade that country in the wake of a particularly bloody hijacking in March 1978, though they subsequently agreed to hand over the border zone to a United Nations force. Four years later, in June 1982, Israel launched an all-out invasion of Lebanon, besieging the PLO's stronghold of West Beirut and once again driving their leaders out—this time to distant Tunisia. The Israeli defense minister Ariel Sharon was not content with this. His cynical decision to unleash the Israelis' Maronite Christian allies on Palestinian refugee camps at Sabra and Shatilla led directly to a horrific massacre that claimed between seven hundred and a thousand lives. Amid fierce international condemnation—in which the United States joined—UN peacekeepers were again deployed. Among them were several hundred U.S. marines.

The PLO and its associates had for many years waged their war on two fronts: not only directly against Israel but indirectly against Israelis or supposed Israeli sympathizers abroad. Terrorism is, however, a many-headed hydra. Though the PLO had been struck a severe blow by the Israeli invasion of Lebanon, the 1980s saw the emergence of new groups such as the Abu Nidal Organization, the Popular Front for the Liberation of Palestine, Hezbollah and Hamas. Whereas the PLO had owed more to nationalism and Marxism, this new generation of terrorists identified themselves primarily with Islam. What set their tactics apart from those of the 1960s and 1970s was their resort to suicide bombing and their much greater readiness to attack Americans. Less significance should probably be attached to the first of these traits. In most countries at most times, terrorists who have committed acts of murder have been in effect suicidal, since they have either died *in flagrante* or been executed subsequently for their crimes. Those experts who were momentarily baffled by the willingness of the 9/11 attackers to "kill themselves so as to kill others" were forgetting the many precedents for such behavior.[61] Far more important was the fact that the terrorists now considered Americans legitimate targets. The turning point in this regard came on April 18, 1983, when a suicide bomber attacked the American Embassy in Beirut, killing 63 people, including the CIA's entire Middle Eastern team.[62] Six months later, in another kamikaze mission, a truck packed with TNT was driven into a Lebanese barracks where American marines were billeted, killing 241 of them. The same tactic killed 4 people when it was used against the U.S. Embassy in Kuwait.

Such has been the impact of the attacks of September 2001 that it is easy to forget that the number of international terrorist incidents has in fact been declining since its peak in the mid-1980s (see figure 9). There were three times as many attacks in 1987 as there were in 2002. But at the same time (though with a dip in the years 1994–95), the proportion of attacks directed at Americans and American interests has been rising. As table 4 shows, more than one in ten of all the casualties of cross-border terrorism since 1991 has been an American. The World Trade Center was first attacked in 1993. This was followed by the bombings of the U.S. barracks in Saudi Arabia in 1996, the U.S. embassies in Nairobi and Dar-es-Salaam in August 1998 and the attack on the USS *Cole* at Aden in October 2000. It was hardly a wild prophecy when the Commission on National Security, chaired by Gary Hart and Warren B. Rudman, warned in its first September 1999 report: "Terrorists and other disaffected groups will acquire weapons of mass destruction and mass disruption, and some will use them. Americans will likely die on American soil, possibly in large numbers."[63] To repeat, the surprising thing about 9/11 was simply that it had not happened before. The United States had for years subsidized Israel. It had shored up the shah's regime in Iraq. It had deployed troops in Arabia.

FIGURE 9

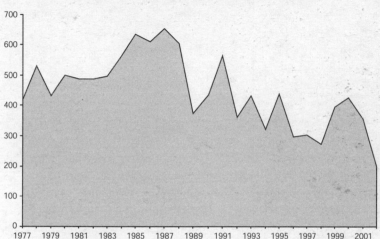

Total International Terrorist Incidents, 1977–2002

Source: Department of State, *Patterns of Global Terrorism*, various issues, http://www.usis.usemb.se/terror/.

There was no shortage of motivations for an attack by one or other of the Middle East's terrorist groups.

What was demonstrated to ordinary Americans on September 11, 2001, had been widely recognized by experts for many years. Not only were Americans a target, but they were also an easy target. Terrorism may not be new, but today's terrorists have astonishing advantages over their predecessors. Technology means that vast destruction can be inflicted at negligible cost; hence the rising number of casualties per attack.[64] A Kalashnikov assault rifle can be purchased for a few hundred dollars. The real cost of a nuclear warhead—and certainly the real cost of a kiloton of nuclear yield—are almost certainly lower today than at any time since the Manhattan Project achieved its goal. The first bomb cost around $2 billion in 1945 dollars. Converted into prices of 1993, that figure rises tenfold, enough to buy 400 Trident II missiles.[65] The fact that France could almost double its nuclear arsenal (from 222 warheads in 1985 to 436 in 1991) while increasing its defense budget by less than 7 percent in real terms speaks for itself.[66] Yet

TABLE 4

	Total Attacks	Total Casualties	Casualties per Attack	Attacks in North America	Casualties in North America	U.S. Citizen Casualties	U.S. Citizens as a Percentage of Casualties
1991	565	167	0.3	2	–	23	13.8
1992	363	729	2.0	2	1	3	0.4
1993	431	1,510	3.5	1	1,006	1,011	67.0
1994	322	988	3.1	0	–	12	1.2
1995	440	6,454	14.7	–	–	70	1.1
1996	296	3,225	10.9	–	–	274	8.5
1997	304	914	3.0	13	7	27	3.0
1998	274	6,059	22.1	–	–	23	0.4
1999	395	939	2.4	2	–	12	1.3
2000	426	1,196	2.8	–	–	70	5.9
2001	355	5,534	15.6	4	4,091	1,530	27.6
2002	199	2,738	13.8	–	–	61	2.2

Source: As for figure 9.

al Qa'eda needed nothing so sophisticated to destroy the tallest buildings in Manhattan: just flying lessons and box cutters. At the time of writing, it is possible to buy eighty hours of aircraft hire and instruction for less than $9,000. A box cutter with six blades costs $2.11. For a trifling outlay of cash, then, a handful of men were able to kill 3,173 people[67] and inflict immediate economic costs estimated at $27.2 billion, a tiny fraction of the estimated cumulative loss in national income, which was initially projected to be as high as 5 percent of GDP. For the insurance industry, the disaster's final costs were said to be between $30 billion and $58 billion; the American airlines were also hit hard, as was tourism. Taxpayers faced a bill not only for reconstruction but also for airline bailouts and substantially increased defense and "homeland security" expenditures.[68] The longer-term costs of the 9/11 attacks—in the form of increased uncertainty, market volatility, security costs and risk premiums—can still only be guessed at.[69]

The U.S. economy weathered this blow more easily than many feared at the time. Viewed in strictly economic terms, the attacks of September 11 were comparable with a very severe natural disaster: expensive but affordable, and of much less significance than the deflation of the stock market bubble that had begun a year and a half earlier.[70] Compared with the damage that might have been inflicted by the Soviet Union in the event that the cold war had turned hot, they were indeed trivial. Simply because World War III did not happen should not lead us to draw the wrong conclusion that al Qa'eda is more dangerous to the United States than was Soviet communism. As we have seen, the ideologies of the two entities bear certain resemblances to each other, but the military capabilities of Stalin, Khrushchev and Brezhnev exceeded those of bin Laden by numerous orders of magnitude. An attack by the Soviet Union would have left hundreds of thousands, if not millions, of Americans dead and would have obliterated not two towers but multiple cities. The problem with al Qa'eda is not that it is a big threat; it is that such a small and organizationally diffuse threat is exceedingly difficult to locate, whether to annihilate or to negotiate with. On one side, then, we have a powerful consensus that a man-made calamity like 9/11 must not be allowed to happen again. On the other we have the sneaking doubt that avoiding such a repetition may be all but impossible.

11/9

Just as it was a myth in the 1930s to believe that "the bomber will always get through," so it is a myth today that the terrorist will always get through. Domestic terrorism can be reduced, if not wholly eliminated, by a combination of policing and parleying. The problem of terrorism was a severe one in Western Europe during the 1970s as nationalist minorities (in Ireland and Spain) and extreme Marxists (in Italy, Germany and Greece) waged campaigns of assassination and destruction. Today, with the exception of the Basque separatist group Euskadi ta Askatasuna (ETA), the perpetrators of these crimes have been jailed, marginalized or induced to renounce violence. The number of terrorist incidents has fallen sharply.[71] The Provisional Irish Republican Army has effectively been split, its leadership ultimately forced to choose between the bullet and the ballot box, despite the fact that it is not even remotely close to attaining its goal of a united Ireland. The extreme Leftists of 1968 are dead, in jail or—their views miraculously moderated by the temptations of power—in government. No terrorist movement is immune from schism when confronted by both duress and dialogue.

Is such a defusion of terrorism conceivable in the Middle East? Not, it seems clear, so long as Israel seeks a purely military solution to the problem.[72] At the time of writing (the summer of 2003), violence between Israelis and Palestinians in both Israel and the occupied territories has claimed nearly three thousand lives since the beginning of the "al-Aqsa" intifada in September 2000: more than two thousand Palestinians and more than seven hundred Israelis.[73] That the government of Ariel Sharon has been driven to the construction of a wall around areas of Palestinian residence is a measure of its desperation; this is a policy that owes something to Ulbricht's East Germany and something to Verwoerd's South Africa—a Berlin Wall through the Holy Land to enforce a new apartheid.

Nor, however, will terrorism in the Middle East cease so long as there are states willing to sponsor it. Terrorist internationalism—or to be precise, the spread of international terror toward the United States—necessitated a cross-border response. It should have been obvious long before September 2001 that the support of terrorist groups by Afghanistan, Cuba, Iraq,[74] Iran, Libya, North Korea, Sudan and Syria could be stopped only by intervention in these countries' internal affairs. Such interventions were far from easy during the cold war, when any American action was certain to elicit a Soviet reaction. But even after the collapse of the Soviet Union had brought the United States an unexpected "hegemony by default,"[75] American policy makers found it hard to imagine doing more than meting out exemplary but largely symbolic punishments. In April 1986 President Reagan had ordered air strikes against five Libyan targets "to teach Qaddafi a lesson that the practice of state-sponsored terrorism carried a high cost," in the words of Defense Secretary Caspar Weinberger.[76] Twelve years later, in August 1998, President Clinton was still using the same tactic, launching missile strikes against alleged "terrorist-related facilities" in Afghanistan and Sudan in retaliation for the bombings of the American embassies in Kenya and Ethiopia.[77] These demonstrations achieved little. Indeed, the image of a cruise missile hitting an (empty) tent seemed to symbolize American impotence; in the words of Clinton's successor, such tactics were simply a "joke."[78]

Yet the United States began to grow more confident in its own military capability during the 1980s. After the nadir of April 1980, when an airborne attempt to rescue the American hostages in Tehran had failed ignominiously, there were important changes at the Pentagon. The United States continued to engage in covert anti-Communist operations in Central America, sponsoring the contras' war against the Sandinista regime that had come to power in Nicaragua in 1979, subsidizing the anti-Communist government in El Salvador and turning Honduras into little less than an American armed camp.[79] In many ways, this was the old "our son of a bitch" approach to the region, dressed up in cold war rhetoric that was only slightly fresher. Public interest was limited; one poll revealed that nearly a third of Americans thought the contras were fighting in Norway.[80] More novel were the overt interventions of the 1980s. In October 1983 President Reagan ordered a full-scale invasion of the tiny Caribbean island of Grenada to reverse a left-wing coup. The code name of the operation, Urgent Fury, conveyed something of the changing military mood.[81] Success in Grenada was followed in Panama six years later, when President George Bush Senior ordered the overthrow of the dictator General Manuel Noriega. Despite the fact that the United States had previously agreed to hand over the Panama Canal to Panama by January 1, 1990, Noriega's annulment of the elections of the previous May furnished the justification for a full-scale invasion by twenty-five thousand U.S. troops.[82] Operation Just Cause was a new departure: disproportionate force used unilaterally to overthrow, rather than install, a dictator.

This new self-confidence came partly from within. The Goldwater-Nichols Act (1986) had transformed the command structure of the American military, promoting the chairman of the Joint Chiefs of Staff to the role of principal military adviser to the president and, more important, creating a new elite of five "unified combatant commands," each with responsibility for all the armed services in a specific geographical area.[83] Of particular importance was the transformation of the Rapid Deployment Joint Task Force into a new Central Command, which was to be central in more than a geographical sense.[84] The redrawing of the atlas implicit in this new structure had important operational implications, since the United States patently did not have forces deployed equally in all five regions. CENTCOM in particular had relatively few available troops; the commander in charge of this strategically vital region, stretching from the Horn of Africa to Central Asia, was at first a chief with few Indians. One consequence of this was the growth in importance of the highly mobile

Special Operations forces.[85] Significantly, the substantial increases in the budgets of these new military entities coincided with sharp reductions in the funding of the State Department.[86] Above all, the process of rethinking the American way of war—to be precise, the process of learning the lessons of Vietnam—finally bore doctrinal fruit. As Bush Senior's chairman of the JCS, General Colin Powell spelled out what these lessons should be. Never again would the generation of officers who had led the war effort in Vietnam "quietly acquiesce in halfhearted warfare for half-baked reasons that the American people could not understand or support." Henceforth the United States "should not commit forces to combat overseas unless the particular engagement or occasion is deemed vital to our national interest and that of our allies"; when such cases arose, and only as a "last resort," troops should be committed "wholeheartedly, and with the clear intention of winning"; they should be given "clearly defined political and military objectives," but both the means and the ends "must be continually reassessed and adjusted if necessary," and there must be "some reasonable assurance we will have the support of the American people and their elected representatives in Congress." (It was partly to ensure that such support was forthcoming that Powell later added the important rider that all American interventions should have an "exit strategy.")[87]

Powell's emphasis on the need for clarity of purpose was sincere and salutary. Under his leadership, he explicitly stated, there would never be another fiasco like the Lebanon expedition of 1983. Yet it is important to remember that the new kind of intervention Powell had in mind was made possible only by a fundamental change in the global strategic context. The fact that the invasion of Panama happened little more than a month after the fall of the Berlin Wall was very far from coincidental.[88] Previously, the Soviet threat had inclined the United States to intervene covertly, often to preserve reliably anti-Communist Latin American dictators. Now, with the Soviet empire crumbling, intervention could be quite overt and, at least ostensibly, on behalf of democratic forces not just in Latin America but potentially anywhere. In that sense, the real historic turning point was not 9/11 but 11/9. After the East German revolution of November 9, 1989, it was suddenly apparent that the Soviet leader Mikhail Gorbachev would not or could not maintain the Russian empire by sending tanks into East European cities. Given the importance of Germany, a

Western-led reunification of which had been the stuff of previous Soviet leaders' darkest nightmares, it followed by implication that the United States now had a free hand more or less everywhere. On December 2 Bush and Gorbachev had formally declared the cold war over. On December 19 the invasion of Panama began.

When Saddam Hussein invaded Kuwait on August 2, 1990, he thus unwittingly created the opportunity for the United States to inflict on him the treatment it had just inflicted on Noriega. Or did he? For even with the Soviet Union in crisis, the Middle East was not quite Central America. A unilateral regime change in Panama had been implemented with barely a murmur of international protest. Yet for two crucial reasons Iraq proved to be different. The first was the belief (which was almost universal in 1990) that intervention in the Middle East required the sanction of the United Nations. The second was that such a sanction, even were it to be unanimous, would not be legitimate in the eyes of the stateless Islamo-Bolshevists. For America's victory in the cold war had—in the ruins of distant, half-forgotten Kabul—been their victory too.

The geographical focus of the American empire shifted repeatedly during the twentieth century. At the beginning of the century it had been a hemispheric empire, reaching eastward into the Caribbean, southward into Central America and westward into the Pacific. In the middle of the century it had reluctantly been forced to extend its reach to Europe, and for much of the cold war, the security of Western Europe seemed to matter more than Asia or, indeed, the Caribbean. Gradually, however, the Middle East came to be the hub around which American strategy turned: because of Israel, because of oil, because of terrorism. With the end of the cold war opportunities presented themselves to use America's reviving military power against one or more of those dangerous states that simultaneously threatened Israel, possessed oil and sponsored terrorism. The question was not whether the United States would act against these sworn enemies; it could not afford not to. The question was whether it would do so alone or in partnership with its traditional allies.

CHAPTER 4

SPLENDID MULTILATERALISM

A room without a view.

> VENEZUELAN DIPLOMAT DIEGO ARRIA, former president of the
> United Nations Security Council, describing the council's private
> meeting chamber, where the curtains are permanently drawn shut[1]

It's nice to say we can do it unilaterally, except you can't.

> SECRETARY OF STATE COLIN POWELL TO
> PRESIDENT GEORGE W. BUSH, August 5, 2002[2]

THE UNITED STATES
AND THE UNITED NATIONS

Does a true empire need allies, or can it achieve what it wants in the world single-handedly? In the eyes of many commentators, the threat posed by Saddam Hussein's Iraq exposed a simple dichotomy between "unilateralism" and "multilateralism." Throughout the 1990s the United States sought to deal with Saddam through the institutional structures of the "international community," a vague phrase usually intended to refer to the United Nations, but sometimes in reality flattering a few nations opposed to American policy. Critics of President George Bush Senior argued that he was too sensitive to the wishes of this international community when he failed to follow the UN-authorized expulsion of Iraq from Kuwait with an invasion of Iraq and a change of regime in Baghdad. Twelve years later critics of President George Bush Junior argued just the opposite: that he was too heedless of the wishes of the international community when he ordered—without explicit UN authorization—the invasion of Iraq and the overthrow of Saddam Hussein. In their view, the French government was consistently right in arguing for a multilateral approach to Iraq.

Yet this is in many ways a false dichotomy. The invasion of Iraq in 2003 was not without a legitimate basis in international law and was supported in various ways by around forty other states.[3] No country was so opposed to the regime change that it was willing to fight against it, other than with that least expensive and effective of weapons, rhetoric. On the other side, the French government can hardly be portrayed as an exemplar of "multilateral" virtue, any more than the United Nations Security Council can be regarded as the sole fount of legitimacy in international relations. The crisis in Iraq arose from deep ambiguities in the way the UN—and especially the Security Council—had behaved in the thirteen years prior to 2003. These were the years when, with the cold war over, a "new world order" was supposed to emerge, in which the UN, supported by the United States, would play a crucial role. Those who today exalt the United Nations and excoriate the United States have selective memories. For the cardinal sins of omission on the part of the former far outweigh the venal sins of commission on the part of the latter.

Victorian statesmen used to speak ironically about "splendid isolation," which in their view was no desirable situation for an empire.[4] Yet the 1990s revealed that an excessive obeisance to international institutions could also have disadvantages. Multilateralism too can be less than splendid.

The United Nations is in large measure a creation of the United States. The very name was suggested by Franklin Roosevelt when the twenty-six Allied states fighting the Axis powers were drawing up a joint declaration at the end of 1941. Three and a half years later the UN Charter was formally adopted by delegates from the original fifty member states in the San Francisco Opera House. Although it initially met in London, the Security Council and General Assembly have been housed since the 1950s on a site in New York donated by the Rockefeller family. And although the United States suspended the payment of its dues to the United Nations in 1996 at the instigation of the Republican-dominated Congress, those contributions were resumed and arrears partially paid in 1999.[5] At present, the

United States thus remains, as it has been since the inception of the UN, its biggest single contributor. More than a fifth (22 percent) of the regular two-year UN budget of $2.54 billion is paid for by the United States, only slightly less than the 25 percent quota prior to 1999. Moreover, American contributions also account for half the budget of World Food Program; a quarter of the budgets of UN peacekeeping operations, the International Atomic Energy Agency, the Office of the UN High Commissioner for Refugees and the International Civil Aviation Organization; and around a fifth of the budgets of the World Health Organization, the Children's Fund and the UN Development Program. Altogether, the United States claims that its assessed and voluntary contributions to the entire UN system of international organizations in 2002 were worth $3 billion.[6]

The point about the United Nations is not that it is an alternative to the United States. It is a creature of the United States. And its resources are so much smaller than those of the U.S. government that its functions can never be more than complementary to American power. To be precise, the annual budget of the United Nations is equivalent to around 0.07 percent of the U.S. federal budget, 0.4 percent of the U.S. defense budget and 17.6 percent of the U.S. international development and humanitarian assistance budget. In the words of the former secretary of state Madeleine K. Albright, who from 1993 to 1996 was the American permanent representative to the UN, the annual budget of the United Nations is "roughly what the Pentagon spends every thirty-two hours."[7] The UN could thus never hope to run counter to the United States and win; whenever there have been differences, as over the jurisdiction of the International Court of Justice, the United States has simply gone its own way.[8] Though America has done more of this kind of thing under President Bush, it is not a novelty.[9] The United States needs the United Nations, but it does not need to sign every international agreement the latter produces. The United Nations needs the United States even more, so it must be tolerant of its principal patron. Were an outright breach to occur between the United States and the United Nations, the latter would for all practical purposes be defunct.

Such checks on the power of the United States as exist today must therefore be sought behind the veil of "multilateralism." They will be found in the permanent overrepresentation on the UN Security Council of three former empires and one still existent empire: Britain, France, Russia and China. It is they, not the UN per se, that have the power to deny the foreign policy of the United States the sanction of the "international community" in the form of UNSC resolutions, and they can exercise this power singly as well as collectively. Thus, ironically, the seal of multilateral approval can be withheld by the unilateral action of just one other permanent member of the Security Council. That the United States tolerates this when it happens, as it did over Iraq last year, is a mark of its own self-restraint, but also of its own self-interest. The UNSC—rather like the regular conferences of the foreign ministers of the great powers during the nineteenth century—is a convenience, a clearinghouse for the interests of some (though not all) of the great powers of today. When it does legitimize American policy, it is positively useful. When it does not, on the other hand, it is no more than an irritant. And perhaps by providing a stage on which the former empires can indulge their own sense of self-importance, it renders them even less powerful than they might otherwise be—precisely because their presence is a subtle irritant to the ascendant economic powers of the present that are, for purely historical reasons, *not* permanent council members. Today the other four permanent members of the UNSC have economies with a combined gross domestic product of $4.5 trillion. This is slightly less than half the GDP of the United States. It is also less than three-quarters of the combined GDP of the three largest nonmembers of the Security Council: Japan, Germany and India.

GULF WAR I

When Saddam Hussein invaded Kuwait on August 2, 1990, he did so at one of the rare moments in history when the United Nations Security Council was in a position to give more or less unqualified support to an action the United States would certainly have carried out anyway. Within six days President George H. W. Bush announced that American troops would be deployed to Saudi Arabia to protect it from any further Iraqi aggression. In January the following year, with a huge armed force in place, the president ordered the expulsion of Iraqi forces from Kuwait. After a six-week air campaign Saddam's forces were routed in an overwhelming ground assault that lasted barely one hundred hours.

Five points are worth emphasizing. The first and most obvious is that with the Soviet Union in its death throes, the traditional obstacle to American policy on the Security Council vanished as surely as the Soviet boycott had removed it during the Korean crisis. Saddam's act of aggression had clearly violated the charter of the UN, but the pre-Gorbachev Kremlin would instinctively have opposed such a large-scale deployment of American forces as Operations Desert Shield and Desert Storm entailed. This time there was little difficulty in passing a series of resolutions that demanded that Iraq withdraw from Kuwait, embargoed Iraq's oil exports, authorized a blockade of the country's imports and finally authorized the United States and any other member states to use "all necessary means to liberate Iraq." Secondly, Saddam underestimated the American determination to "kick the Vietnam syndrome once and for all" (as President Bush put it) with a decisive military victory.[10] The combination of devastating bombardment and a four-day blitzkrieg annihilated the Iraqi Army with minimal American casualties, just 148 battle deaths out of a total deployment to the gulf region of over 1.1 million.[11] In the words of former CENTCOM Commander in Chief General Anthony Zinni: "Desert Storm worked . . . because we managed to go up against the only jerk on the planet who actually was stupid enough to confront us symmetrically, with less of everything, including the moral right to do what he did to Kuwait."[12]

The third point, however, was that precisely for fear of the Vietnam syndrome, the United States did not press home its advantage by invading Iraq itself. As chairman of the Joint Chiefs of Staff, Colin Powell urged Bush to stop the ground war, allowing at least half of Saddam's loyal Republican Guard to escape. Having incited rebellions against Saddam's regime by Kurds in the north and Shia Muslims in the south of the country, the United States stood aside as these were crushed.[13] The most that was done in the aftermath of victory was to impose, first, a security zone for the Kurds in northern Iraq and, later, two no-fly zones north of the thirty-sixth parallel and south of the thirty-second. These two operations (Operation Provide Comfort and Operation Southern Watch)[14] were once again multinational undertakings—French, British and Turkish aircrews were also involved—which had a UNSC resolution as their mandate. The United States continued to hope for Saddam's demise; in June 1993 President Clinton ordered a desultory cruise missile attack on Baghdad following an Iraqi-sponsored attempt to assassinate his predecessor with a car bomb when he visited Kuwait.[15] Nor did it cease to enforce the UN resolutions limiting Iraq's postwar military activities. There were further cruise missile strikes in 1996 to punish the Iraqis for violating the northern security zone, and again in December 1998 (Operation Desert Fox), prompted by Iraq's refusal to cooperate with UN Special Commission (UNSCOM) weapons inspectors.[16] But by the end of the 1990s it was abundantly clear that nothing short of a full-scale invasion would get rid of Saddam. There were also legitimate grounds for doubt that the system of weapons inspections would ever be wholly effective in eliminating the regime's efforts to acquire or accumulate "weapons of mass destruction," a shorthand term for nuclear, chemical and biological weapons.

In many ways, the first Gulf War had greater consequences outside Iraq than inside it. Even after the war had been won, U.S. forces were not wholly withdrawn from the Middle East. On the contrary, during the 1990s the number stationed there tended to increase, as table 5 shows, from just over six thousand in 1993 to sixteen thousand by 2000. As a proportion of American forces stationed abroad, this represented a tripling of the U.S. military commitment to the region. Especially remarkable was the rising number of American personnel stationed in Saudi Arabia, temporary "tenants" of the royal dynasty that happened to be accompanied by between one hundred and two hundred warplanes.[17] These figures understate the extent of the American presence because they do not take account of the number of U.S. naval vessels deployed in and around the gulf. Nor do they capture another aspect of the growing Saudi military dependency: between August 1990 and December 1992 the Saudi regime placed orders worth more than twenty-five billion dollars with U.S. armaments manufacturers. In effect, the Arabian political system, with its exceptionally low military participation rate, made Riyadh dependent for its security on American manpower and firepower.[18] As we have seen, however, this only served to fuel the resentment of the radical Islamist movement inside and outside Saudi Arabia. As early as 1991 Saudi clerics, including Safar al-Hawali, an authority often cited by Osama bin Laden, were denouncing "a larger Western design to dominate the whole Arab and Muslim world." Disgusted by the Saudi authorities' reliance on American protection (they had declined his offer to lead an Afghan-style guerrilla force against Saddam), bin Laden left Saudi Arabia in April 1991, traveling via Pakistan and Afghanistan to al Qa'eda's new base in Sudan.[19]

The fifth and final feature of the first Gulf War also had little to do with Iraq. This was what might be described as the marginalization of Israel. The Bush administration took the view that Israel should not serve as a center of military operations against Iraq—not even for supply, storage or medical purposes.[20] When Saddam fired Scud missiles at Tel Aviv, in an effort to cast himself as the archenemy of Zionism, the Americans worked energetically to prevent any Israeli retaliation. Moreover, in the wake of Desert Storm, Bush sought to apply pressure on Israel, in the hope of breaking the deadlock in the negotiations over the Palestinian question. In doing so, he reasserted the American conviction that any peace "must be grounded in the United Nations Security Council resolutions 242 and 338 and the principle of territory for peace."[21] Two months later Secretary of State James Baker remarked pointedly that he knew of no "bigger obstacle to peace than the settlement activity that continues not only unabated but at an enhanced pace." American loan guarantees worth ten billion dollars were allowed to lapse when the Israelis refused to accept conditions the United States attached to them.[22] After 1991 American aid to Israel was effectively frozen and in real terms declined. By 1999, as a proportion of Israeli gross national income, it was down to a third of its 1992 level.

TABLE 5. AMERICAN MILITARY PERSONNEL ON ACTIVE DUTY
IN THE MIDDLE EAST: 1993 AND 2000

	1993	2000
Total personnel in foreign countries	308,020	257,817
Bahrain	379	949
Egypt	605	499
Israel	42	36
Jordan	21	29
Kuwait	233	4,602
Oman	26	251
Qatar		52
Saudi Arabia	950	7,053
Syria	10	
Turkey	4,049	2,006
United Arab Emirates	25	402
Total	6,340	15,879
Percentage of all forces in foreign countries	2.1	6.2

Source: *Statistical Abstract of the United States, 1995* and *2002*.

NEVER SAY "NEVER AGAIN"

Bush the Elder could scarcely have been more rigorous in his commitment to the idea of a "new world order" under the aegis of the United Nations Security Council. Iraq was expelled and then contained according to the letter of its resolutions; Israel was to be forced to make peace with the Palestinians on the same basis. Yet events that were already unfolding by the time Bush left office in January 1993 were to force his successor to reexamine— albeit reluctantly and hesitantly—American attitudes toward the UN.

One of the time bombs Bush bequeathed to Clinton was the American involvement in the Somali civil war. At least five distinct military factions had been engaged in an escalating struggle for control of the country for most of the 1980s, but it was not until the end of 1992, with famine looming, that the United States became involved. Once again it did so with a mandate from the UN Security Council (resolution 794); a joint army, marine and navy task force was sent not to end the fighting but simply to facilitate the delivery of aid to the areas of greatest need. One of the new president's earliest foreign policy acts was to wind this force down, from twenty-six thousand men to just five thousand. However, when gunmen loyal to warlord Mohammed Farah Aidid, leader of the grandly named United Somali Congress, murdered twenty-four UN soldiers from Pakistan, the Security Council issued a new resolution (837) authorizing his arrest. Dutifully, the United States responded by sending a detachment of Army Rangers supported by the elite Delta Force.

Like all Americans, William Jefferson Clinton had learned his lesson from the Vietnam War. But it was a different lesson from Colin Powell's. Powell's, as we have seen, was that American forces should never fight other than from a position of overwhelming strength, with limited goals that could be swiftly attained while commanding public support. Clinton's was more simple. It was that presidents who presided over wars in which American soldiers died did not get reelected. The unspoken Clinton Doctrine was thus as simple and as radical as the Powell Doctrine: the United States should not engage in any military interventions that might endanger the lives of American service personnel. To this doctrine he was faithful throughout his eight years in office, as figure 10 shows: during the Clinton years, the chances of an American serviceman being killed by hostile action while on active duty were less than 1 in 160,000. He was six times more likely to be murdered by one of his comrades, nineteen times more likely to kill himself and fifty times more likely to die in an accident. Indeed, in 1999 a young American was almost as likely to be a victim of hostile fire if he stayed in high school than if he joined the army. Unfortunately for Clinton, almost the first military intervention he authorized resulted in a spectacular military debacle that left eighteen Americans dead. This was the now celebrated "Black Hawk Down" fiasco in Mogadishu.

According to Mark Bowden, it was not good luck but calculation that led the Somali forces to shoot down two of the American helicopters that had rashly been sent on a daylight mission to "snatch" Aidid and his lieutenants. "Every enemy advertises his weakness in the way he fights," Bowden has written: "To Aideed's fighters, the Rangers' weakness was apparent. They were not willing to die. . . . To kill Rangers, you had to make them stand and fight. The answer was to bring down a helicopter. Part of the Americans' false superiority, their unwillingness to die, meant they

FIGURE 10

Deaths of U.S. Service Personnel on Active Duty by Manner of Death, 1993–2000

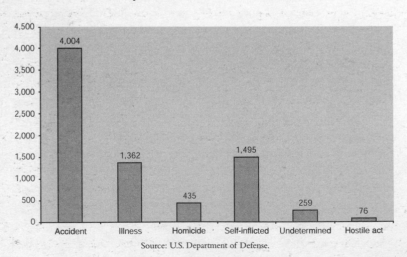

Source: U.S. Department of Defense.

would do anything to protect each other, things that were courageous but also sometimes foolhardy."[23] To read his account, based on interviews with survivors of the abortive raid, is to be impressed not only by the truth of this—indeed, by its understatement, since the Americans appear to have been willing to risk their lives to rescue even the bodies of their dead comrades[24]—but also by an unmentioned corollary, the Rangers' tremendous readiness to slaughter Somalis indiscriminately. The worst aspect of the Black Hawk Down episode was not that eighteen American soldiers died; it was that at least as many and probably more unarmed Somali men, women and children were indiscriminately mowed down by panicking Rangers.

Clinton's response took a form that has been characteristic of many American interventions before and since. He increased the number of troops, but at the same time he specified a date for their departure, just six months later. The plan to capture Aidid was quietly abandoned. Indeed, he was flown in a U.S. transport plane to a peace conference in Ethiopia just a few weeks later.[25] The problem with this approach hardly needs to be spelled out: the certainty that American forces would soon be gone removed any incentive on the part of the Somali warlords to mend their ways. Something very similar happened in September 1994, when the Clinton administration—once again acting under a UNSC resolution (940)—sent twenty thousand troops to Haiti to restore the elected president Jean-Bertrand Aristide, who had been ousted by the military three years before. Six months later the United States handed over responsibility to a UN mission, leaving only a few hundred men on the island and allowing Aristide to resume the normal routine of Haitian politics: theft, murder, intimidation, corruption.

In ethnically homogeneous Haiti, where 95 percent of the population are the descendants of African slaves, there can never be such a thing as genocide; there can be only mass homicide. Yet genocide, meaning the murder of a tribe or people, loomed ever larger than plain murder in the course of the 1990s. The term is itself a neologism dating back to 1944, when it was coined by Raphael Lemkin in his book *Axis Rule in Occupied Europe*. Lemkin was a Polish-Jewish refugee from nazism, whose family was all but obliterated in the Holocaust (forty-nine of his relatives died, including his parents; only his brother and his brother's wife and children survived). It was his single-handed campaign that turned a made-up word into one of the foundations of postwar international law. By the end of 1948 it seemed that Lemkin had triumphed. Not only had the UN General Assembly unanimously passed a resolution condemning genocide in 1946, but by 1948 it had passed—again *nem con*—a Convention on the Prevention and Punishment of the Crime of Genocide.[26]

Yet there proved to be a nearly fatal flaw in Lemkin's project. The country that had granted him asylum, the United States—in other words, the country best placed to do something to stop genocide, whether by economic pressure or military intervention—refused to ratify the convention. Indeed, it was not until 1985 that opposition in the Senate was finally overcome (in an attempt by the Reagan administration to repair the damage done by the president's ill-judged visit to the Bitburg War Cemetery in West Germany, where forty-nine Waffen SS officers turned out to be buried). Hardbitten realists still argued that the UN convention ought not to be ratified since it would tend to enhance the standing of the International Court of Justice. Indeed, Senator Jesse Helms sought to water down the terms of ratification with a number of so-called reservations, understandings and declarations. Nevertheless, as the study and memorializing of the Holocaust came to occupy an ever more important place in American cultural life, such realism grew less respectable. Democratic and Republican presidents alike took their turns to insist that genocide must never be allowed to happen again. Thus Jimmy Carter in 1979: "We must forge an unshakable oath with all civilized people that never again will the world fail to act in time to prevent this terrible crime of genocide." Thus Ronald Reagan in 1984: "Like you, I say in a forthright voice, 'Never again!'" And thus Bill Clinton in 1993, opening the Holocaust Museum in Washington: "We must not permit that to happen again." Unfortunately, "never again" turned out in the 1990s to mean "no more than once or twice a decade."

There is no need here to detail the events that led to the disintegration of the multiethnic Yugoslav federation into twelve territorial fragments. The crucial point is that where this disintegration was violent—notably though not exclusively in Bosnia and Herzegovina, Krajina and Kosovo—

it posed a profound challenge to all those who had pledged never to permit another genocide (least of all in Europe). The deal struck between the Serbian leader Slobodan Milošević and the Croatian leader Franjo Tudjman in March 1991 to partition Bosnia was always intended to lead to "cleansing of the ground" (*ciscenje terena*) of Muslims (hence "ethnic cleansing"); as Tudjman later remarked, there was intended to be "no Muslim part," despite the fact that Muslims accounted for two-fifths of the population. From the moment the Bosnian Serbs proclaimed their own independent republic centered on Pale and began their attacks on Sarejevo (April 1992) the world was faced with an unmistakable case of genocide as defined in the UN convention.[27] What is more, although atrocities against civilians were perpetrated by all the three sides in the conflict, there was from an early stage evidence that most of the genocidal acts were the responsibility of the Serbian authorities in Pale and their masters in Belgrade. According to the State Department, only 8 percent of recorded atrocities during the war were the responsibility of Bosnian Muslims. And of all the crimes perpetrated during the war, none came close in its premeditated savagery to the massacre of more than seven thousand Bosnian Muslim men in Srebrenica by Serbian forces.

Here was genocide. Where was the United Nations? The answer is that it was right there; indeed, with grotesque irony, its forces effectively presided over the worst of the genocidal atrocities.

The initial efforts to avoid a conflict in Yugoslavia had in fact been left to an *ad hoc* international conference under the former British foreign secretary Lord Carrington. But in 1991 the United Nations turned to an American, the former secretary of state Cyrus Vance, to negotiate the deployment of peacekeeping forces (UNPROFOR), which were duly sent to Croatia and later Bosnia. Specified towns were designated as "safe areas," which UNPROFOR was charged with protecting. At the same time, the UN imposed sanctions on the whole of Yugoslavia, including Bosnia, a circumstance that greatly handicapped the Bosnian Muslims, who had no significant internal source of arms and other supplies; the Bosnian Serbs, by contrast, received substantial assistance from Belgrade.

It is important to recollect that much of the responsibility for this woefully ill-conceived response lay with the European powers that had proclaimed their ability to cope with the Yugoslav crisis without American assistance. Supposedly, this was to be "the hour of Europe." But Europe, as usual, spoke with multiple voices. It had been the German foreign minister Hans-Dietrich Genscher, euphoric after the ease with which his country's reunification had been achieved in 1990, who had accelerated the disintegration of the Yugoslav federation by his precipitate recognition of Slovenian and Croatian independence in the autumn of the following year. By contrast, the British government adopted a posture of studious, not to say shameless, neutrality, insisting as the conflict escalated that it was a civil war between morally equivalent foes, obsessed with their own "ancient hatreds." Successive British foreign secretaries willfully ignored the evidence of the sustained campaign by Milošević to whip up murderous nationalism among the Serbs and instead concentrated on blocking any effective intervention—by anyone.

In fact, the Bush administration had contemplated "a sort of mini-Iraq thing" as early as the winter of 1991, drawing up contingency plans for a military strike against the Serbs. It was decided instead to take the Europeans at their word. "They will screw it up," argued Secretary of State Lawrence Eagleburger, "and this will teach them a lesson."[28] Eagleburger's successor, Warren Christopher, was also inclined to keep out of what he called "a problem from hell." And during the 1992 presidential campaign, Clinton himself had argued that American troops should not be sent "into a quagmire that is essentially a civil war."[29] This was a line echoed on numerous occasions by key figures, not least Colin Powell, still chairman of the Joint Chiefs of Staff ("No American President could defend to the American people the heavy sacrifice of lives it would cost to resolve this baffling conflict") and Defense Secretary William Cohen, who unwittingly gave a "green light" to Serbian attacks on Gorazde when he declared that the United States would not enter the war to avert its fall.[30] Nevertheless, the arguments for intervention never went away in Washington.[31] And with every harrowing news report from Bosnia, they grew stronger.

American indignation took time to overcome European appeasement, however. In May 1993 the British government smothered American proposals to lift sanctions and launch air strikes against the Serbs ("lift and strike"). In November the following year the Foreign Office protested indignantly when the United States unilaterally ceased to enforce the arms embargo.[32] American planes flew supplies of medicine to Sarajevo and enforced a UN-authorized no-fly zone (as if ethnic cleansing were being carried out from fighter planes). But air strikes against Serb positions were opposed by the British on the ground that they would leave UNPROFOR forces vulnerable to Serb reprisals. It took an atrocity on the scale of the massacre at Srebrenica—a town supposedly under the protection of Dutch blue helmets—to tip the balance belatedly in favor of American intervention. Now the United States insisted that NATO bomb the Serbs in earnest. Sure enough, Operation Deliberate Force, coinciding as it did with a major Croatian offensive and a rift between Milošević and the Bosnian Serb leader Radovan Karadjić, forced the Serbs to retreat.

The institutional framework within which American policy over Bosnia evolved was bewildering in its complexity. Not only the UN but also NATO, to say nothing of the Conference on (later Organization for) Security and Cooperation in Europe, the Council of Europe and the West European Union; all, it seemed, had to have their say.[33] Yet the overwhelming impression remains that if one institution got it completely wrong in Bosnia, it was the United Nations. And its failures were in large measure a result of the conduct of two permanent members of the Security Council: Britain and, to a lesser extent, France. (Significantly, it had been at Jacques Chirac's insistence that the UN troops in charge of the so-called safe areas were commanded by a French general.)[34] In the end, the Dayton Accords drawn up and forced upon the recalcitrant Serbs—after the Croats and Muslims had struck a deal of their own—were the work of none of these august bodies but of an informal Contact Group, composed of the United States, Britain, France, Germany and Russia, the nineteenth-century great powers doing business as of old, but now under firm American leadership in the person of Richard Holbrooke.[35] With sublime insouciance, the French foreign minister still insisted: "One cannot call it an American peace," even requesting that the Dayton agreement be referred to as the "Treaty of the Élysée."[36] The reality was very different. It was the threat of American air strikes that forced the Serbs to accept a smaller share of the partitioned Bosnia. It was the presence of twenty thousand American troops—a third of the Implementation Force (IFOR)—that ensured they did not renege on the agreement.

The disintegration of Yugoslavia had begun in Kosovo; it also ended there. It had been at a rally in Kosovo in 1989—to mark the 600th an-niversary of the battle of Kosovo Polje—that Milošević had first revealed his mutation from Communist to radical nationalist. In one respect the case of Kosovo was clear-cut: unlike in Bosnia, there was a large ethnic major-ity, since Albanians accounted for more than three-quarters of the popu-lation, a proportion that had risen during the 1980s owing to the higher Albanian birthrate. But although Tito had granted its inhabitants a mea-sure of autonomy in 1974, Kosovo had remained a province of Serbia. Whereas both the European Union and the United States had not hesi-tated to recognize Bosnian independence, which amounted to the seces-sion of one of the republics from the Yugoslav federation, they felt unable to do the same for Kosovo. The trouble was that even as the Serbs were forced to compromise in Bosnia, so they stepped up their long-running campaign of violence and intimidation against the Albanian majority in Kosovo. Ethnic cleansing resumed: at Drenica in March 1998 eighty-five Kosovar Albanians were killed; at Racak ten months later, another forty-five. Support for the militant Kosovo Liberation Army (KLA) grew. Peace-able Albanians began to seek refuge across the border.

The compromise that emerged at Rambouillet from the mediating ef-forts of the Organization for Security and Cooperation in Europe was de-signed to stop the violence simply by postponing a decision on Kosovo's constitutional status: for three years the province would come under NATO control, after which a referendum would determine its future.[37] The Serbs rejected this. The United States knew how to change their minds. Yet three things were different about the decision to unleash the full might of the U.S. Air Force against not just the Serbian forces in Kosovo but Serbia as a whole. First, the Clinton administration did not seek the approval of the United Nations Security Council; it was NATO, not the UN, that went to war. Secondly, this was an intervention that very clearly violated the sovereignty of Serbia, precisely why approval from the UNSC was not sought. At the time a number of commentators (this author among them) worried that the war violated not only Article 2 of the UN Charter but also the Helsinki Accords Final Act and indeed NATO's own defensive rationale.[38] There was a plausible ground for intervention—to avert genocide—but it required a UN resolution to be legitimate. Thirdly, the air strikes had the unanticipated effect of worsening the situation of those on whose behalf they were launched. Altogether between December 1998 and May 1999 an estimated thirty thousand Albanians were killed and nearly a million people were forced from their homes. Most of this happened after the bombing began on March 24, 1999. With war declared, Milošević felt able to pursue ethnic cleansing with almost Hitlerian ruthlessness. He underestimated American resolve, however, and after seventy-eight days of bombing was forced to capitulate. Once again airpower sufficed to eliminate Serb resistance; American troops could be deployed—as seven thousand of a fifty-five-thousand-strong Kosovo Force (KFOR)—without a shot's needing to be fired, though it may be that Milošević gave in only to avert an assault by U.S. land forces in support of the KLA.[39]

In 2003 this simple fact seemed to be generally forgotten: There was no United Nations approval for the NATO war against Serbia. Only after the war—on June 10, the day after Milošević's surrender—did the UNSC provide a resolution (1244) on which the military occupation of Kosovo could be based, leading to the creation of the UN Mission in Kosovo (UNMIK), which currently governs the province. Also generally forgotten, at the time of writing, is the fact that the Kosovo question has in no sense been answered. Violence in the province has not ceased, despite KFOR-sponsored "fun runs" and other wholesome initiatives: in August 2003 two youths were murdered in the tiny Serbian enclave of Gorazdebac.[40] Nor has the Serb government shown any sign of abandoning its claim to sovereignty. Kosovo remains a civil war on hold.

Nevertheless, something highly significant had happened. In the words of Michael Ignatieff, the war's most astute observer, "Humanitarian intervention in Kosovo . . . was never exactly what it appeared. It was never just an attempt to prevent Milošević from getting away with human rights abuses in Europe's backyard. It was also a use of imperial power to support a self-determination claim by a national minority—a claim that used violence in order to secure international notice and attention."[41] True, as Max Boot noted, the United States was "trying to play the role of imperialist on the cheap," inhibited by the Clinton administration's "'no casualties' mindset," while at the same time remaining indifferent to the "collateral damage" that inevitably resulted from high-altitude bombing.[42] But the discovery that the United States could shoot first and seek UNSC resolutions afterward was a revelation. Almost equally important was the realization on the part of the American commander General Wesley Clark that decision making within the structure of NATO was only slightly less cumbersome than decision making within the UN.[43] The American appetite for untrammeled command over its military ventures had already been whetted, more than two years before September 2001.

Superficially, the crises in Yugoslavia and Iraq had much in common. Both were multiethnic polities created after World War I. Both had been held together in the 1980s by ruthless dictators guilty of human rights abuses. In both cases economic sanctions had unintended consequences. Both had revealed the limits of the United Nations as an entity. And both had showcased the daunting capability of the American military. To some observers in the aftermath of the war against Serbia, there was an obvious conclusion. Serbia and Iraq would continue to be sources of violence and instability as long as they were ruled by Slobodan Milošević and Saddam Hussein. Their overthrow was something that the United States was capable of effecting. But it might well have to act without the authority of the UN.[44]

Much had been done in the name of humanitarianism in the 1990s; some skeptics were even moved to grumble about the "imperialism of human rights." Yet the most disastrous violation of human rights, an indubitable case of genocide, was greeted by both the United States and the United Nations with a lamentable apathy. This was the systematic massacre of Rwanda's Tutsi minority instigated by the leaders of the country's Hutu majority.

Those who are sentimentally attached to the United Nations as an institution should be forced to study its abject failure to respond to the ghastly events that unfolded in Rwanda in the mid-1990s, which claimed at least half a million lives. It is well known that the Clinton administration's attitude was determined, as usual, by the fear of American casualties. The decision to send a laughably small force of two hundred U.S. troops to Kigali airport in 1994 was based on the repulsive calculation that "one American casualty is worth about 85,000 Rwandan dead."[45] The American insistence that any UN force be kept as small as possible; the American delaying tactics over proposals to send reinforcements; the American insistence that any U.S. troops be paid for by the UN in advance; the American refusal to jam Hutu radio broadcasts—these were acts of shameful negligence in the face of a genocide vastly greater than anything that happened in the Balkans.[46] But those who today see the French president Jacques Chirac as the keeper of the conscience of the international community should also ponder France's role in this nightmarish episode. For it was France that since the early 1990s had lent military support to the Hutu-dominated government of Juvénal Habyarimana. It was France that conceived of the Ugandan intervention in support of the Tutsi Rwandan Patriotic Front as an "Anglo-Saxon" plot against *la francophonie* in Africa. It was the French who sent troops to create "safe areas" for Hutus—among them the perpetrators of the massacres—in the southwest of the country. And it was the French who objected furiously when the crisis in Rwanda engulfed their client state Zaire, leading to the fall of one of the most egregious tyrants of the postcolonial era, Marshal Mobotu Sese Seku.[47] When Chirac visited New York in the summer of 1995, he disconcerted UN officials by telling them, "If you want to find idiotic behavior you can always count on the Americans."[48] This took some nerve.

CLAUSEWITZ REDIVIVUS

Even before 9/11 the Bush administration made no secret of its impatience with United Nations–sponsored military operations. The new president's stated intention was to eschew "open-ended deployments and unclear military missions," to achieve "an orderly and timely withdrawal from places like Kosovo and Bosnia." His policy was "humbly" to "propose our principles," not arrogantly to "impose our culture."[49] Yet when, as a candidate for the presidency, George W. Bush had criticized Clinton's overseas adventures in these ways, it was not the idea of overseas military intervention *per se* he was repudiating, merely the idea that such interventions should be constrained by the UN. As he said during the 2000 campaign, "I don't think our troops ought to be used for nation-building. I think our troops ought to be used to fight and win war. I think our troops ought to be used to help overthrow a dictator when it's in our best interests. But in this case [he was referring to Somalia] it was a nation-building exercise."[50] "Nation-building" was a dirty word because it was associated with the UN. An American-led "regime change" was another matter.

The great significance of this became clear in the aftermath of the terrorist attacks of September 2001. From very early on, President Bush insisted that in its retaliation the United States would "make no distinction between those who planned those acts and those who harbor them" and that if the Taliban regime in Kabul did not hand over bin Laden and other members of al Qa'eda in Afghanistan, then it would be overthrown. It was he of all the senior members of the administration who was most "kinetic" in pressing for swift and decisive regime change in Afghanistan.[51] It was he who was most insistent that the war against terror should involve more than "firing a $2 million missile at a $10 empty tent and hit[ting] a camel in the butt."[52] It was he who pressed the CIA and the Defense Department to get "boots on the ground" in Afghanistan. It was Bush who wanted to respond to terrorism with outright, full-scale war.

In the most famous line of his masterwork, *On War,* published in 1832, Carl von Clausewitz called war "not merely an act of policy, but a true political instrument, a continuation of political intercourse, carried on with other means." "The political object is the goal," he argued; "war is the means of reaching it."[53] There is no question that in its readiness to use war to achieve its objectives, the Bush administration after 9/11 was more Clausewitzian than its predecessor. Admittedly, Clausewitz would have found it hard to imagine enemies equipped with hijacked jets, dirty bombs, anthrax and sarin, and capable of striking anywhere from Manhattan to Mombasa. In the words of the "National Security Strategy" published in 2002, the enemy in this new war consisted of "shadowy networks of individuals [who] can bring great chaos and suffering to our shores for less than it costs to purchase a single tank." The campaign against such a foe could only be unspectacular: an arrest at Frankfurt Airport or in a seedy Pakistani flophouse, an assassination in a Baghdad villa or a Palestinian back street. In some ways, the war against terrorism retained the espionage of the cold war without any of the front-of-the-house hardware: no serried ranks of missiles and tanks, just an ever-wider range of cameras, some hidden in matchboxes, others orbiting in outer space. But it was also like the old Great Game—once again a game played in the Middle East, Central Asia and Afghanistan, but now a game played with gizmos. The war against terrorism needed to counter the terrorist's new technological advantages (the power and compactness of modern explosives) with the modern spy's (the unprecedented power of modern surveillance technology).

What Clausewitz would have had no difficulty in recognizing was the parallel war that the Bush administration embarked on: against states "harboring" or otherwise supporting terrorist organizations. One consequence of 9/11 was to shatter forever the illusion that Americans could retreat to enjoy the fruits of their productivity behind a missile defense shield, leaving the benighted countries of the world to take their own paths to perdition. For terrorism bred in precisely the "rogue" regimes and strife-torn "failed" states that some Republicans had once believed America could ignore. This kind of war—intervention to overthrow bad governments—is not novel, nor is it unrealistic. Indeed, it was precisely what the Victorians excelled at. A typical example was the war against the Sudanese Mahdists, Wahhabist zealots whose killing of General Charles Gordon at Khartoum was (in its public impact) a Victorian 9/11, and who were ultimately brought to book in 1898 by a small but lethally well-armed expeditionary force in the spectacularly asymmetrical battle of Omdurman.[54] This was the kind of reckoning Bush had in mind. Though there was no existing plan for a regime change in Afghanistan, the CIA and Central Command scrambled to put one together.[55] Airpower was once again used to devastating effect. But what made Operation Enduring Freedom distinctive was the role of more than a hundred CIA operatives and over three hundred Special Forces personnel in galvanizing the anti-Taliban Northern Alliance and persuading other Afghan warlords to defect to their side.[56] The first American air strikes took place on October 7, less than a month after the destruction of the World Trade Center. Within two months the Taliban leadership had been driven from Kabul. Hamid Karzai was sworn in as head of an interim government before the year was out.

An Afghan Omdurman was not something the United Nations could object to, least of all in the febrile atmosphere of late 2001. The Taliban regime had given Osama bin Laden shelter since May 1996. Though the operational details of the September 11 attacks were worked out in Europe and the United States, the mastermind behind them was plainly bin Laden; yet the Taliban declined to extradite him. From the point of view of the UN, it was therefore a legitimate act of self-defense on the part of the United States to act as it had done. Already in July 2001 the Security Council had described the Taliban regime as "a threat to international peace and security in the region" (resolution 1363). The day after the 9/11 attacks, it stressed in a new resolution "that those responsible for aiding, supporting or harboring the perpetrators, organizers and sponsors of these acts will be held accountable" (resolution 1368). After the war started the Security Council studiously avoided any reference to the United States, confining itself to anodyne expressions of support for "the efforts of the Afghan people to replace the Taliban regime" (resolution 1378). But since the Bush administration wasted no time in setting up a new Afghan government, there was no reason for the other members of the Security Council to complain. The other NATO members also readily accepted the invitation to assist with the postwar occupation. For all these reasons, the regime change was broadly welcomed by the "international community," despite the very obvious precedent that had been set.

In a speech at West Point in June 2002 President Bush revived the old notion of "preemptive" war, the case for which was set forth more fully three months later by the White House in the thirty-three-page "National Security Strategy of the United States." Because (in Vice President Cheney's words) "weapons of mass destruction in the hands of a terror network or murderous dictator . . . constitute as grave a threat as can be imagined," the president asserted his right as commander in chief to forestall any "mortal threat" to American security. "As a matter of common sense and self-defense," America would "act against such emerging threats before they are fully formed."[57] Many critics seized upon this "Bush doctrine" as a dangerous, even revolutionary departure from post-1945 American practice.[58] Yet the idea that preemptive action might be necessary in the face of an imminent threat was not a major departure in American policy.[59] The radical aspect of the Bush doctrine was not so much the theory as the practice. The point was simply that when President Bush said he was prepared to fight for freedom and against terror in "every corner of the world," he really meant to. And if the only way to defeat terrorism was to overthrow regimes that sponsored it, he would not hesitate.

Who would be next? Throughout the 1990s there had been elements within the Republican Party who yearned for a settling of accounts with Saddam Hussein. Almost immediately after 9/11, Defense Secretary Donald Rumsfeld began pressing for the planned war against terror to be directed against Iraq as well as Afghanistan, a view echoed by Vice President Dick Cheney. It was Bush who argued against this, insisting that the initial focus must be on the Taliban, who were harboring the perpetrators of the attacks on New York and Washington. But this did not mean that Bush was opposed to regime change in Baghdad at some future date. In his State of the Union address on January 29, 2002, he explicitly identified Iraq as one of three prime targets in an "axis of evil," along with Iran and North Korea. Now the only question was whether he could rely on the established alliances and multilateral institutions—whose importance, incidentally, his "National Security Strategy" had in no way denied.

There were many legitimate reasons for a UN-authorized war against Saddam Hussein—almost too many. Throughout the 1980s the Iraqi government had not only developed biological and chemical weapons (it had used the latter—including mustard gas and sarin—against the Kurds of Halabja) but had also attempted to acquire nuclear weapons. The United Nations Special Commission set up after the Gulf War by Security Council resolution 687 was charged with ensuring that Iraq's weapons of mass destruction (WMD) were removed or rendered harmless; until UNSCOM certified that this had been done, an embargo remained in force, preventing the country from exporting its oil.[60] From the outset Saddam frustrated the efforts of the special commission. Time and again Iraqi declarations on what proscribed weapons had been produced turned out to be false. In 1994 the Iraqis ceased to cooperate with UNSCOM and allowed the inspectors to resume work only when faced with the threat of military action. This happened again in 1997, when inspectors were banned from specific sites, prompting a further threat of military action, a step that was averted only when Kofi Annan flew to Baghdad in February 1998 and secured yet another pledge from Saddam that the inspections could resume. Cooperation lasted just a few months. So damning was the final UNSCOM report that the United States and Britain launched air strikes (Operation Desert Fox) against suspected Iraqi WMD facilities. A new inspections team (UNMOVIC) was set up in 1999, but it was not allowed into Iraq until November 2002.[61]

Abuses of human rights, if not quite genocide; sponsorship of terrorist organizations, notably Abu Nidal; contravention of the conventions on chemical and biological weapons; attempted acquisition of nuclear weapons—the charge sheet against Saddam's regime was long indeed by the beginning of the new century. All that was clearly missing from it was any conclusive evidence of involvement in the 9/11 attacks. Considering the list of Saddam's violations of international law and his manifest contempt for the numerous UN Security Council resolutions he had inspired—seventeen in just four years[62]—the only mystery is why Iraq was not invaded before 2003.

The explanation must be sought in the attitude of the other permanent members of the Security Council. It might have been thought that they would have shared the American desire to see Saddam disarmed. Britain did. Yet France, Russia and China all subtly encouraged Iraqi noncompliance with the weapons inspection regime. It was the United States and the United Kingdom alone that threatened and carried out military action to enforce the inspection regime. By the end of 1999 the chairman of UNSCOM, Richard Butler, was so incensed by the conduct of the other permanent members that he accused them of trying to "kill" the special commission.[63] They certainly showed no great enthusiasm for reviving the apparently defunct inspection program. It was not the last time that the French in particular were to use their power on the Security Council to obstruct not just American foreign policy but the clearly expressed wishes of the Security Council itself.

Much has been written in the past year about the "failure" of American diplomacy in 2003. When the United States went to war against Iraq, leading Democrats lined up to blame the president for his ineptitude. "I am saddened, saddened that this president failed so miserably at diplomacy," declared Tom Daschle, the Senate minority leader. "Probably the least successful handling of allies that we've had in a long period of time," was the verdict of Congressman Steny Hoyer. "When did we become a nation that ignores and berates our friends and calls them irrelevant?" demanded Robert Byrd, the venerable Democratic senator. Such views were echoed by more cerebral commentators, notably Stanley Hoffman, as well as members of the previous administration's foreign policy team.[64] Yet it might equally well be argued that President Bush and his advisers were *too* diplomatic in their approach. For it was above all their desire *not* to act uni-laterally that led to the fiasco of the entirely superfluous "second resolution" (which would, had it been passed, have been closer to a twenty-second res-olution on the subject of Iraq). The core aim of American policy, never-theless, was consistent and was achieved—namely, to overthrow Saddam Hussein once and for all. The United States also succeeded in doing this with the support of some, though not all, of its traditional allies, building an ad hoc "coalition of the willing" in precisely the way the president's National Security Strategy had envisaged. It was not American diplomacy that failed. It was the diplomacy of those who believed they could stop the war or at least isolate the United States.

The Bush administration's patience with Saddam ran out in the second half of 2002. Vice President Dick Cheney had publicly expressed his dis-gust with Saddam's "game of cheat and retreat" as early as August 26. Ken-neth M. Pollack's book *The Threatening Storm* had concluded: "The only prudent and realistic course of action left to the United States is to mount a full-scale invasion of Iraq to smash the Iraqi armed forces, depose Sad-dam's regime and rid the country of weapons of mass destruction." This, he argued plausibly, would be preferable to an indefinite continuation of the policy of containment, which was what the combination of sanctions, weapons inspections, no-fly zones and the American military presence in neighboring states amounted to.[65] Still, the decision was taken, partly in deference to the wishes of the British prime minister Tony Blair, once again to refer the matter to the Security Council.[66] The result was UNSC resolution 1441, which rehearsed—at considerable length—Saddam's many sins of omission and commission, defiance and noncompliance but offered Iraq "a final opportunity to comply with its disarmament obliga-tions under relevant resolutions of the Council," demanding within thirty days "a currently accurate, full, and complete declaration of all aspects of its programs to develop chemical, biological, and nuclear weapons" and envisioning a resumption of weapons inspections. The resolution con-cluded with a somewhat unconvincing reminder of the UNSC's previous

warnings that Iraq "will face serious consequences as a result of its continued violations of its obligations."[67] For the Americans, the final straw—
perhaps the final bale of straw—was the twelve-thousand-page declaration
delivered by the Iraqis in response to this demand, which they dismissed as
"not even a credible document."[68]

Bush and his advisers now had two good grounds for acting. These
were:

1. that Iraq had consistently failed to comply with UNSC resolutions
   and *might*—no one could of course be sure, precisely because of
   Iraqi noncooperation—have retained or recovered the capability to
   use or to export chemical or biological weapons and
2. that Saddam was a bloody tyrant who had committed crimes against
   humanity, if not outright genocide.

Quite apart from these legitimate justifications for a war of disarmament
and/or liberation, three further practical arguments for action seem to
have been advanced:

3. that the overthrow of Saddam might help to break the gridlock of
   the Middle Eastern peace process by sending an unequivocal signal
   of hostility to any regime that defied the United States—*pour en-
   courager les autres,* as much as to get rid of Saddam himself,
4. that creating a democratic Iraq might also begin a wholesale
   "transformation of the Middle East" (in the words of Condoleezza
   Rice), with Iraq once again setting an example for the other Arab
   states and
5. that controlling Iraq might create alternative bases for U.S. troops
   in the Middle East, allowing them to leave Saudi Arabia (and
   thereby meeting at least one of the radical Islamists' demands).[69]

Not all elements within the Bush administration accepted these supplementary arguments for intervention—there were differences of opinion even
inside the Defense Department—but the president himself apparently saw
all three as legitimate. It was now time for the Clausewitzian application of
war to the pursuit of these political goals.

There then ensued an unsuccessful but very damaging attempt by the French government, supported by the German and Russian governments, to stop the war. On January 20 the French foreign minister, the poet and historian Dominique de Villepin, declared at a press conference following a meeting of the Security Council that the French would not "associate ourselves with military intervention that is not supported by the international community."[70] Two days later President Chirac echoed this sentiment in a speech celebrating the thirtieth anniversary of the Franco-German Élysée Treaty, in which he appeared to endorse the recently reelected German chancellor Gerhard Schröder's vote-grabbing opposition to any American "military adventure" in Iraq. On February 10, at a meeting of the North Atlantic Council in Brussels, France and Germany were joined by Belgium in blocking an American-inspired Turkish request for assistance in the event of a war with Iraq. That same day the Russian president Vladimir Putin visited his French counterpart in Paris to proclaim Russia's opposition to the war.

Much opprobrium was subsequently heaped on Defense Secretary Donald Rumsfeld for his dismissive comment that the opposition came only from "old Europe." In fact, it would be more accurate to say that it came from roughly a quarter of old Europe plus America's erstwhile Eurasian rival. On the other side, expressing support for the American position, were Britain, Spain, Denmark, Portugal and Italy—all long-standing EU members—and Poland, Hungary and the Czech Republic, three of the EU's ten incoming members. Their pro-American letter to the *Wall Street Journal* on January 30, which accused the Security Council of allowing Saddam "systematically to violate" its resolutions and strongly implied that Saddam had blown his "last chance to disarm," was echoed by ten smaller East European countries, including the three Baltic states and Bulgaria. It was therefore a clear *majority* of European states (eighteen in all) that took the American side, hardly surprising given the condemnation of Iraqi behavior by the chief UN weapons inspector himself just a few days before. The French had been comprehensively outgunned, as evinced by Chirac's petulant attack on the East European states in the wake of the publication of the two letters.[71] Moreover, even the European countries that did not support the war generally offered some limited assistance, such as the use of their airspace, antichemical weapons specialists or humanitarian aid. Arguably, the sole American mistake was at this point, when President Bush was persuaded by his British counterpart to seek yet another UNSC resolution explicitly authorizing war. This made the pro-American majority in Europe irrelevant since, besides Britain, only two of its members (Spain and Bulgaria) were on the Security Council. In the glare of publicity they now attracted, none of the other nonpermanent members— Syria, Pakistan, Cameroon, Angola, Guinea, Chile and Mexico—had any desire to be seen as backing an "American" war. Ironically, in view of the subsequent fuss about a transatlantic "rift," Europe proved to be the most pro-American of all the continents represented on the Security Council. Still, the key point is that it was President Chirac's veto, delivered preemptively on French television, and not a formal vote on the Security Council, that doomed Blair's "second" resolution, which was duly withdrawn.

Shortly after the first missiles struck Baghdad, Chirac accused the United States of "breaching the legitimacy of the United Nations and putting a premium on the use of force." Quite what France had thus far done for the legitimacy of the UN is hard to say. Chirac had declared that France would veto a second resolution "whatever the circumstances might be." Yet Jean-David Levitte, the French ambassador to the United States, added a highly significant rider: "If Saddam Hussein were to use chemical or biological weapons, this would change the situation completely and immediately for the French government." Chirac himself added another rider: he would in fact consider "all the options, including war," if Saddam was still in material breach of resolution 1441 after a further thirty days.[72] This gave the lie to the French position. In essence, they were willing to countenance a war against Iraq only if Saddam used chemical or biological weapons first. If he merely possessed them in some hidden cache, there was no need for war. Another empty ultimatum would do. As far as the French were concerned, the inspectors could play missile tag around Mesopotamia indefinitely, and the United States could keep its troops in the gulf as spectators for the duration. The sole French concern was to avoid a war—much as Britain's had been throughout the Bosnian crisis. For all the posturing of Chirac and Villepin, their policy was nothing more or less than a policy of appeasement. And it left the United States to bear nearly all the costs of the containment that policy implied.

MR. BLAIR'S SPECIAL PLEADING

Might Saddam be able to use chemical or biological weapons, assuming he did have some hidden? This became a question of vital importance for Tony Blair, whose own Labour Party was riven with doubts about the wisdom of supporting what was now perceived to be an "American" war. Two members of his own cabinet resigned on the issue. Had he been defeated in the House of Commons on the night of March 18, he too would very probably have felt obliged to resign. In Blair's mind, there was only one remedy. Good evidence that Saddam not only possessed WMD but was already in a position to use them would persuade hesitant backbenchers that Britain was acting in self-defense.

That the prime minister made the most of intelligence reports that pointed in that direction seems beyond doubt, though he was perhaps acting more like a barrister who chooses only the best circumstantial evidence to make his case than as the perjurer a BBC reporter accused him of being. In the preface to a British intelligence dossier published on September 24, Mr. Blair clearly stated: "I am in no doubt that the threat is serious and current." Saddam Hussein's "military planning allows for some of the WMD to be ready within 45 minutes of an order to use them."[73] That same day he told the House of Commons: "Iraq has chemical and biological weapons. . . . Saddam has continued to produce them. . . . He had existing and active military plans for the use of chemical and biological weapons, which could be activated in 45 minutes."[74] Quite apart from the ambiguity of that last sentence—was it the plans or the weapons that could be activated?— there appears to have been a significant discrepancy between the impression the prime minister conveyed and the original intelligence on which his remark was based. Asked by Lord Hutton in August last year to comment on which kinds of weapons British intelligence believed might be ready for use within three quarters of an hour, the chairman of the Joint Intelligence Committee John Scarlett gave the revealing answer that "it related to munitions, which we had interpreted to mean battlefield mortar shells or small calibre weaponry, quite different from missiles."[75]

When he addressed the Commons on March 18, the prime minister gave what was surely the most brilliant speech of his career. He linked together, far more deftly than his American counterpart was ever able to do, the threat posed by Saddam Hussein's tyranny and the threat posed by Islamist terrorism. He argued for a war not merely to disarm Iraq but to liberate the Iraqi people, to reactivate the Middle East peace process and—perhaps most cleverly—to salvage the credibility of the UN Security Council. The case for the war was never more persuasively made. Yet at the heart of his speech was a fantastic piece of elision, in which the chemical and biological weapons the UN inspectors had not been able to trace in Iraq were connected to the possibility of a terrorist attack comparable with 9/11. The two passages in question, which were separated by some minutes and several interruptions from the floor, deserve to be quoted at length:

> On 7 March, the inspectors published a remarkable document . . . detailing all the unanswered questions about Iraq's WMD. It lists 29 different areas where they have been unable to obtain information. For example, on VX it says: "Documentation available to UNMOVIC suggests that Iraq at least had far reaching plans to weaponize VX." On biological weapons, the inspectors' report states: "Based on unaccounted-for growth media, Iraq's potential production of anthrax could have been in the range of about 15,000 to 25,000 liters. . . . Based on all the available evidence, the strong presumption is that about 10,000 litres of anthrax was not destroyed and may still exist. . . ."
>   Let me explain the dangers. Three kilograms of VX from a rocket launcher would contaminate a quarter of a square kilometer of a city. Millions of lethal doses are contained in one liter of Anthrax. 10,000 litres are unaccounted for. 11 September has changed the psychology of America.[76]

Mr. Blair's ingenuity and eloquence carried the day. But it is hard to escape the conclusion that he set out to create in the minds of his listeners the impression that Saddam was himself capable of a chemical or biological version of 9/11—perhaps in London itself. And if, despite Lord Hutton's absolution, Mr. Blair's credibility should never recover in the eyes of British voters, he has only himself to blame. The case for war against Saddam Hussein was quite good enough without invoking the wholly unrelated threat of al Qa'eda.

.   .   .

The Americans took it for granted that they could count on "the Brits." "Two years from now," Bush had declared just a week after 9/11, "only the Brits may be with us."[77] The fact that this was so—that no other country so consistently supported U.S. policy after September 2001—was both important and surprising. It was important not only because it assured the United States of the support of one other permanent member on the Security Council, but also—a point Americans themselves may not have grasped—it significantly added to the imperial flavor of the U.S. invasions of both Afghanistan and Iraq. It was surprising because the United Kingdom had not been nearly as enthusiastic about American military action during the Bosnian crisis. And when Blair had backed the U.S. decision to go to war over Kosovo, he had been supporting a much more congenial president in a much more congenial cause. Clinton's war for human rights was a very different thing from Bush's wars against terror (and for regime change).

The question nevertheless remains: What was in it for Britain? It is easy to see why President Bush went so far to meet Blair's requests for a United Nations mandate for war. Having Britain on board lent credibility to the American claim to be leading a coalition against Saddam and ensured that U.S. troops would be reinforced by a substantial British contingent, which, though rather less numerous and much less well equipped than their American counterparts, proved to be rather better at the constabulary duties that swiftly fell to the victorious invaders. But why exactly did the British prime minister risk his political life for a plan of action against Iraq that was designed in Washington with American needs primarily in mind? From a narrowly British vantage point, the costs of backing the United States were immediately obvious: Britain incurred a share of the costs of the war and the subsequent occupation, while at the same time becoming the Islamist zealots' third-favorite target after Israel and the United States. But if the spoils went, as they traditionally do, to the victor, what share would the victor's spear-carrier get? It seemed highly unlikely, to give just one example, that British oil companies would secure a significant role in the postwar reconstruction of the Iraqi oil fields. And the next time President Bush should feel the need to raise an import tariff for domestic political reasons, British exporters certainly would not be exempted, since all of Britain's trade negotiations must be conducted through the European

Union. In war and peace there may be "old" and "new" Europe. In trade there is only Brussels. The benefits to Britain of the special relationship seemed strangely intangible in 2003.[78]

Of course, nearly all British prime ministers since the war have been seduced by the idea of a special relationship with the United States, a relationship personified in its strange mixture of affection and mutual disappointment by Winston Churchill. At the time of the coup in Iraq that ended British rule there, the eighty-three-year old statesman, now retired, was tempted to make a speech on the subject of the Anglo-American role in the Middle East. His notes survive and seem quite prescient forty-six years later:

> *America & Britain* must work together,
>   reach *Unity* of purpose.
> The complications which the problem presents
>   can be cured if & only *if,*
>   they are dealt with by united forces
> & common principles
>   not merely increase of strength.
> When we divide we lose.[79]

Churchill's point, which he decided in the end not to make, was that in precipitating the first American expedition to Lebanon, the 1958 coup in Baghdad might be an intimation of some future American Suez crisis. "It wd. be too easy to mock USA," Churchill toyed with saying. "This is not time for our trying to balance a long account. The accounts are balancing themselves."[80] But *do* the accounts of the special relationship balance?

Not all prime ministers have automatically assumed that they do. Harold Wilson wisely resisted all pressure from the Americans to send even a token force to Vietnam. "Be British," pleaded one American official when the foreign secretary George Brown went to Washington in January 1968. "How can you betray us?"[81] Dean Rusk would have settled for "just one battalion of the Black Watch." "When the Russians invade Sussex," he grumbled when this too was denied, "don't expect us to come and help you."[82] Yet even Wilson was not wholly immune to American blandishments. "The ceremonies of welcome went far beyond anything I have had before," he told Barbara Castle, one of his cabinet ministers, after a visit to Washington in 1975.[83] That may give us a clue to why so many premiers have clung to the special relationship, even when its fruits have been so hard to pick. In the end it is simply more pleasant to visit the White House (or even Crawford, Texas) than the Élysée Palace, much less the German Federal Chancellery. Given the choice between Brussels and the Beltway, most British prime ministers opt for the latter. The only authentic exception to this rule was Edward Heath, who relished telling Richard Nixon that from now on he would have to deal with all nine members of the European Economic Community as one.[84] Even Tony Blair, who once appeared instinctively to prefer Tuscany to Texas, proved unable to resist the allure of the special relationship.

So who won? One answer is that Clausewitz did. The United States once again pursued its political goals through war, one that its colossal economic and military superiority ensured was swift and cost few American lives: just ninety-one combat-related fatalities between the start of the war on March 20 and President Bush's declaration of victory on the deck of the *USS Abraham Lincoln* six weeks later. This was a different war from those fought in the 1990s. After much talk of "shock and awe," the preliminary air bombardment was short and selective, and much more of the fighting was left to highly mobile ground forces, which swept toward the main cities, encountering only desultory resistance. Saddam was toppled. After a nine-month manhunt he was found skulking in a "spider hole." As it turned out, he had been bluffing: initial searches found little, if any, trace of weapons of mass destruction or even facilities to make them. But more fool Saddam. Had he simply told the truth to the inspectors instead of duping the CIA, he might have survived to a ripe old age amid the gaudy comforts of his numerous repulsive palaces. Even his conventional weapons proved virtually useless, for most of the men armed with them simply fled rather than fight.

The war against Iraq therefore ended up being much more a war of humanitarian intent than anyone had anticipated. In the absence of conspicuous piles of WMD, attention turned to the second stated aim of the coalition, the liberation of the Iraqi people from tyranny. Here it became apparent within a very short time that not only Clausewitz but the United States had won. They might have reservations about President Bush, but

when asked in June 2003 about the consequences of the war in Iraq, fully
three-quarters of French, Italian and German respondents to the Pew
Global Attitudes survey agreed that the Iraqi people were better off without
Saddam Hussein.[85] Even more striking, ordinary Iraqis seemed to share the
same view. The first rigorously conducted poll of Baghdad, published in
September last year, revealed that 62 percent of Baghdad residents believed
"the ousting of Saddam Hussein was worth any hardships they might have
personally suffered since the . . . invasion." Moreover, two-thirds (67 percent) believed that Iraq would be somewhat (35 percent) or much (32 percent) better off five years from now than it was before the American action.
Support for the regime change was especially strong in poor areas of the
city.[86] The only consolation for the opponents of the war was that the most
popular Western politician in Iraq was none other than Jacques Chirac.[87]

There is no gratitude in international affairs; as the saying goes, no
good deed goes unpunished. In 2003 the United States went to war against
a regime that had repeatedly broken international law, repeatedly defied
the United Nations Security Council and—according to the organization
Human Rights Watch—repeatedly murdered its own citizens, perhaps as
many as three hundred thousand of whom Saddam caused to be executed
and interred in mass graves. Most European governments supported the
American decision to overthrow Saddam. Most rational people in Europe
and in Iraq itself welcomed the fact that he was gone. Yet a great many of
the same people complained that the United States had acted "unilaterally"; that it, rather than Iraq, was the "rogue nation." This was nonsense.
Already before 9/11 it was obvious that the United Nations was too weak
an institution to deal effectively with renegade states engaged in military
aggression and/or genocide. Bosnia and Kosovo had shown that American
military leadership was the only effective solution to such challenges.
Afghanistan had shown that the United States could achieve *military* success more or less single-handedly. But there was never any intention to act
in complete isolation, there or in Iraq. There was a role for the UN—and
indeed for NATO and all the other components of the international community—after the tyranny had been overthrown. That role was to assist in
the very different task that turned out to be the inevitable concomitant of
regime change: precisely that nation building of which President Bush and
his closest advisers were so suspicious.

Asked at a press conference during the Afghan War what the United States would do after the Taliban were overthrown, Secretary Rumsfeld gave a revealing answer. "I don't think [it] leaves us with a responsibility to try to figure out what kind of government that country ought to have," he declared. "I don't know people who are smart enough from other countries to tell other countries the kind of arrangements they ought to have to govern themselves."[88] This was also the president's view. "I oppose using the military for nation-building," he told a meeting of his National Security Council three days after Rumsfeld's statement, "Once the job is done, our forces are not peacekeepers. We ought to put in place a U.N. protection and leave. . . ." He was notably sympathetic to his secretary of state Colin Powell's notion of a "UN mandate plus third country forces ruling Kabul."[89] Like the dichotomy between unilateralism and multilateralism, however, this distinction between U.S. regime change and UN nation building was a chimera. In practice, the United States simply could not walk away from Afghanistan or from Iraq the moment the obnoxious regime it was fighting was no more.

Even before the invasion of Iraq, what Michael Ignatieff has called "a distinctive new form of imperial tutelage called nation building"—"Empire Lite" in his witty coinage—was already under way in at least three countries.[90] In each case it was American military intervention, though at no stage positively requested by the United Nations, that made nation building (to be precise, state building) by the UN possible. In each case it was the United Nations that gave the American presence international legitimacy and thereby reinforcements. The goals of both parties had certainly changed over time. In the Balkans the objective had been humanitarian: to halt genocide and an exodus of refugees. Ousting the Taliban from Afghanistan had obvious humanitarian benefits, but these were, as economists say, "externalities." The main object had been to "root out" terrorists and their sponsors. The fundamental tendency, however, was imperialism in the name of internationalism. Whether they liked it or not, and whether the enemy was genocide or terrorism, the United States and the United Nations were now operating together as a kind "semi-empire."[91] This was also bound to be true in Iraq, despite the UN's skepticism about the American rationale for regime change. Regime change and nation building were not after all distinct activities, as President Bush had hoped.

The one shaded inevitably into the other, and while the United States might be capable of unilateral (or at least UN-less) regime change, it was not capable of nation building on its own. Nor, unfortunately for Bush and Rumsfeld, was the United Nations. By the end of 2003 it was an ineluctable reality that to reconstruct Iraq the United States and United Nations must put aside differences and unite.

PART II

FALL?

CHAPTER 5

THE CASE FOR
LIBERAL EMPIRE

Imperialists don't realize what they can do, what they can create! They've robbed this continent [Africa] of billions, and all because they are too short-sighted to understand that their billions were pennies, compared to the possibilities! Possibilities that *must* include a better life for the people who inhabit this land.

FRANKLIN D. ROOSEVELT, 1943[1]

It would be ignorant, dangerous nonsense to talk about grants of full self-government to many of the dependent territories for some time to come. In those instances it would be like giving a child of ten a latch-key, a bank account, and a shot-gun.

HERBERT MORRISON, 1943[2]

NO TO EMPIRE?

Nation-states are a novelty compared with empires, for there have been empires since the beginning of written records. Colonization—the establishment of new settlements by large and organized groups of migrants—is of course a process that predates recorded history. Civilization—the emergence of complex social structures with urban centers—can be traced back to the fourth millennium before Christ. Empire, however, denotes something more sophisticated still: the extension of one's civilization, usually by military force, to rule over other peoples. It is one of history's truisms that empires rise and fall. One less commonly understood implication is that there are periods in history in which there is no dominant empire,

indeed sometimes no empire at all. In the 1990s the world faced this possibility. To put it starkly, the choice after the collapse of the Soviet Empire
was between a world of independent nation-states, some but not all of them
democracies, and an American *imperium*. Those opponents of the Bush administration whose slogan in 2003 was "No to Empire" took it for granted
that the former was and remains a viable world order. Ironically, this was also
the view of President Bush himself and indeed of most of his most senior
advisers. As we have seen, though willing to use American military power to
effect changes of government in rogue regimes and failed states, they had little appetite for "nation building," a euphemism for a new kind of "multilateral empire" in which the United States and United Nations together took
over and ran countries in the aftermath of regime changes. In theory, this
imperialism of internationalism could last indefinitely in countries palpably
incapable of stable self-rule. But as far as Bush was concerned, the American
presence in Bosnia, Kosovo, Afghanistan and Iraq was no more than a temporary expedient; this was not nation building in the Clintonian sense but
merely an interim, provisional form of administration, paving the way
back to self-government for the countries in question.

In short, both opponents and proponents of war to overthrow Saddam
Hussein agreed that a swift return to full political sovereignty for Iraq was
desirable; the same applied to the other countries under international administration. The question this chapter addresses is whether or not it is
correct to regard national independence—what Woodrow Wilson called
self-determination—as a universally viable model. Might it not be that for
some countries some form of imperial governance, meaning a partial or
complete suspension of their national sovereignty, might be better than
full independence, not just for a few months or years but for decades?[3]
Paradoxically, might the only hope for such countries ever to become successful sovereign states (especially if we regard democracy as a key criterion
of success) be a period of political dependence and limited power for their
representative institutions?[4] To answer that question, we need to compare
the costs and benefits of both empire and independence in the modern
period.

FROM EMPIRES TO NATION-STATES

The age of empires reached its zenith in the century stretching from the 1880s until the 1980s. For most of that period a relatively small number of empires governed nearly all of the world. On the eve of the First World War, Britain, France, Belgium, Holland and Germany, which among them accounted for less than 1 percent of the world's land surface and less than 8 percent of its population, ruled in the region of a third of the rest of the world's area and more than a quarter of its people.[5] All of Australasia, 90 percent of Africa and 56 percent of Asia were under some form of European rule, as were nearly all the islands of the Caribbean, the Indian Ocean and the Pacific. And although only around a quarter of the American continent—mainly Canada— found itself in the same condition of dependence, nearly all the rest had been ruled from Europe at one time or another in the seventeenth and eighteenth centuries. In both the north and the south, the polities of the American republics were fundamentally shaped by the colonial past.

Nor do these calculations about the extent of the West European maritime empires tell the whole story of nineteenth-century empire. Most of Central and Eastern Europe was under Russian, German or Austrian imperial rule. Indeed, the Russian empire stretched from the Baltic to the Black Sea and from Warsaw to Vladivostok. And still intact, though in a position of increasing inferiority to the European empires, were the Ottoman Empire in the Middle East and the Chinese empire in the Far East. Independent nation-states, in short, were the exception to a worldwide imperial rule. Even Japan, the best-known example of an Asian state that had resisted colonization (though its economy had been forcibly opened to trade by the United States), had itself already embarked on empire building, having conquered Korea. And as we have seen, the United States, though forged in the crucible of anti-imperial war, had taken its first steps on the road to empire, having annexed Texas in 1845, California in 1848, Alaska in 1867 and the Philippines, Puerto Rico, Hawaii and Guam in 1898. Indeed, its nineteenth-century history can be told as a transition from continental to hemispherical imperialism.

Yet the twentieth century rejected empire, in principle, if not in practice. The rejection may be said to have begun with the publication of one of the most influential of all anti-imperialist tracts, J. A. Hobson's *Imperialism: An Essay,* the central thrust of which—that the British Empire was a racket, run for the sole benefit of a tiny elite of financiers and their clients—later inspired Lenin's tract *Imperialism: The Highest Stage of Capitalism.* To Lenin, the First World War was a direct result of imperialist rivalries. Its consequences were, however, to overthrow no fewer than four Central and East European emperors (though Lenin himself ensured that the Romanov empire was reborn in a more malevolent form under Bolshevik rule). The five surviving West European empires limped through the 1920s and 1930s but were shattered in the 1940s by the German, Italian and Japanese bids to build new empires in Europe, Africa and Asia. The two superpowers that emerged victorious from the world wars, though empires in all but name, were both decidedly anti-imperial in their rhetoric. Elaborating on his predecessor Woodrow Wilson's first draft for a new world order, Franklin Roosevelt conceived of the Second World War as a war to end empire. The Soviet Union, for its part, consistently equated fascism and imperialism and did not take long after 1945 to accuse the United States of sponsoring one and practicing the other. Both these anti-imperial empires believed they would derive strategic advantages from decolonization.

Roosevelt envisaged a system of temporary[6] trusteeships for all former colonies, as a prelude to their independence on the basis of the Wilsonian principle of self-determination (which the peacemakers after the previous world war had emphatically ruled out for non-European peoples). Despite the best efforts of Churchill, he got his way.[7] Decolonization happened after the Second World War in a succession of great waves, postponed only where (as in the Middle East or Indochina) the Americans were willing to subsidize European colonial governments against Communist "insurgency."[8] The First World War had already dismantled three empires—the Habsburg, Hohenzollern and Ottoman—but many of their possessions had ended up in the hands of other empires, having enjoyed only the most fleeting tastes of independence. After 1945 it was different. Not only the British but also the French, Dutch, Belgian and Portuguese empires were wound up, rapidly in some regions of the world, slowly and painfully elsewhere, until by the 1970s little more than vestiges remained. Only three empires endured: the Russian and Chinese (which Roosevelt conceived of as somehow different from the West European empires because their colonies were not overseas and, perhaps, because their ideologies were overtly egalitarian) and, of course, the unspoken American empire.[9] The result was a leap in the number of independent states in the world, which more than doubled. In 1920 there were 69 sovereign states in the world. By 1950 the number had risen to 89, and in 1995, by which time the Russian empire had finally fallen apart, there were 192, with the two biggest increases coming in the 1960s (mainly Africa, where no fewer than 25 new states were formed between 1960 and 1964) and the 1990s (mainly Eastern Europe).[10]

Thus, impelled forward by a combination of European exhaustion, non-European nationalism and American idealism, the world embarked on an epochal experiment, an experiment to test the hypothesis that it was imperialism that caused both poverty and wars and that self-determination would ultimately pave the way to prosperity and peace.

WHY DECOLONIZATION FAILED

That hypothesis has been largely proved false. The coming of political independence has brought prosperity only to a small minority of former colonies. And although the former imperial powers no longer fight one another, decolonization has in many cases been followed by recurrent conflict between newly independent states and, even more often, within them. This has been the great double disappointment of the sixty years since the end of World War II. Nor has the disappointment ended there. Self-determination was supposed to go hand in hand with democracy. But decolonization has often led not to democracy but, after the briefest of interludes, to indigenous dictatorship. Many of these dictatorships have been worse for the people living under them than the old colonial structures of government: more corrupt, more lawless, more violent. Indeed, it is precisely these characteristics that explain why standards of living have actually worsened in many sub-Saharan African countries since they gained their independence.[11]

Most of the former colonies of the Middle East are wealthier only because nature endowed some of them with underground deposits of oil, full exploitation of which came only after they had gained their independence. But with few exceptions their polities are little better than despotisms. Colonialism was not all good, of course, and independence has not been all bad. But it is not convincing (though it is certainly convenient for the likes of the Zimbabwean despot Robert Mugabe) to blame all the problems of the developing world today on the malign after-effects of colonial rule. In the words of the African Development Bank's 2003 report, "More than four decades of independence . . . should have been enough time to sort out the colonial legacies and move forward."[12] The experience of much of Africa and the Middle East since 1945, as well as large parts of Asia, makes it clear that Roosevelt's faith in decolonization was misplaced.

Take poverty. Although historical statistics for *per capita* incomes are very far from complete or exact, it is possible to measure approximately how former empires and former colonies have fared in the period from high imperialism to post-imperialism. Long-run *per capita* gross domestic product figures are available for forty-eight countries, eight of which can be considered empires before the world wars and fourteen of which were colonies. Two things are immediately apparent from table 6, which compares both sets of countries in 1913 and in 1998. The first is that only one former colony has significantly improved its relative economic position: Singapore, which in 1913 had a *per capita* GDP of a quarter of that of the United States, but which by 1998 had overtaken all the former European imperial powers. The other ex-colony to improve its position, Malaysia, has done so only modestly, raising its *per capita* GDP from 17 percent to 26 percent of the American level. All the others have fallen farther behind the United States than they were in 1913, in some cases very far behind. The second point, which follows from the first, is that the gap between the world's former empires and most of their former colonies has widened sharply. In 1913 the Philippines, Egypt, India, Vietnam, Ghana and Burma all had *per capita* GDP of between 13 and 20 percent of the American level. In 1998 the average income in all six was less than a tenth of the average U.S. income. By comparison, all the former empires have remained within sight of the world's economic leader, with the exception of the United Kingdom, which is distinctly worse off in relative terms than it was in 1913.

Yet these figures understate the extent of the global divergence between rich and poor, because they omit many of the poorest countries in

TABLE 6. PER CAPITA GROSS DOMESTIC PRODUCT OF
EMPIRES AND COLONIES DURING AND AFTER THE AGE
OF EMPIRE (IN 1990 INTERNATIONAL DOLLARS)

	1913 USA=100	Rank	1998 USA=100	Rank	Change in Ranking
USA	5,301	100	2	27,331	100	1	1
Singapore	1,279	24	28	22,643	83	3	25
Canada	4,447	84	5	20,559	75	7	-2
Australia	5,715	108	1	20,390	75	8	-7
Netherlands	4,049	76	8	20,224	74	9	-1
France	3,485	66	12	19,558	72	10	2
Belgium	4,220	80	7	19,442	71	11	-4
United Kingdom	4,921	93	4	18,714	68	14	-10
Germany	3,648	69	11	17,799	65	16	-5
Italy	2,564	48	17	17,759	65	17	0
New Zealand	5,152	97	3	14,779	54	19	-16
Portugal	1,244	23	29	12,929	47	21	8
Malaysia	899	17	36	7,100	26	29	7
South Africa	1,602	30	24	3,858	14	37	-13
Sri Lanka	850	16	38	3,349	12	39	-1
Indonesia	904	17	35	3,070	11	41	-6
Philippines	1,066	20	32	2,268	8	43	-11
Egypt	732	14	45	2,128	8	44	1
India	673	13	47	1,746	6	45	2
Vietnam	754	14	42	1,677	6	46	-4
Ghana	739	14	44	1,244	5	47	-3
Burma	685	13	46	1,024	4	48	-2

Source: Angus Maddison, *The World Economy*. Rankings are based on the forty-eight countries for which Maddison provides data. The calculations are for real GDP *per capita*, measured in constant U.S. dollars of 1990, adjusted for purchasing power parity.

the world for which historical data simply do not exist. When one concentrates on the period between 1960 and 1989, a critical era for the postcolonial states of Africa, Asia and the Middle East, it is possible to discern more striking evidence of the economic failure of independence. Among forty-one former British colonies, only fourteen succeeded in narrowing the gap between their own *per capita* GDP and that of their erstwhile British rulers during those thirty years.[13] Indeed, in all but two former African colonies (Botswana and Lesotho), the ratio of British to former colonial income significantly increased.[14]

In one respect, this great postcolonial divergence may be slackening as

India, the most populous of all the former European colonies, enters a long-overdue era of economic growth. However, most ex-colonies continue to lag ever farther behind the elite of wealthy countries. According to the World Bank, there are only fourteen countries in the world with *per capita* GDP of three-quarters or more of the American level. Of these, all but two are European; the others (Japan and Hong Kong) represent the extremes of Asian experience, the former having never been a colony, the latter having remained under British rule for more than a century and a half. At the other end of the scale, however, there are twenty countries where *per capita* GDP is 3 percent or less of the American level. In more than thirty of the world's countries the average income is less than $1 a day.[15] All but six[16] of these are African countries that have gained independence since the Second World War. In the poorest of the former British colonies, Sierra Leone, *per capita* income is now $140 per year; the average Briton is more than two hundred times better off. In 1965 the difference in income was a factor of just eight. Gambia, the condition of which so appalled Roosevelt in 1943, has fared only slightly better. Incomes there are 0.8 percent of the British level, a far wider differential than at the time of independence in 1965. According to the World Bank, its GDP *per capita* has grown in real terms by just 14 percent since 1970, despite the fact that it has received aid totaling $1.6 billion since independence—equivalent, on average, to nearly 20 percent of its national income.

In short, the experiment with political independence, especially in Africa, has been a disaster for most poor countries. Life expectancy in Africa has been declining and now stands at just forty-seven years. This is despite aid, loans and programs of debt forgiveness. Only two sub-Saharan countries out of forty-six, Botswana and Mauritius, have bucked the trend of economic failure.[17]

Why have so many newly independent countries failed so badly to achieve economic growth? Why have only a tiny handful improved their relative position since the days of imperial rule? There are those who claim that the big divergence in *per capita* incomes between rich and poor countries since the 1960s has been a direct consequence of globalization. But this is a flawed argument. In theory, globalization, meaning simply the international integration of international markets for commodities, services and capital and labor, should tend to maximize economic efficiency, yielding gains for all concerned. The real problem of the early twenty-first century is not globalization but its absence or inhibition. Indeed, the sad truth about globalization is that it is not truly global at all.

Part of the problem is that world trade is still far from being truly free. At least some of the blame for this can be laid at the door of the world's richest countries, which continue to pay subsidies to their farmers equivalent to the entire gross domestic product of Africa.[18] American producer support still amounts to around 20 percent of gross farm receipts; the figure for the European Union is more than 30 percent.[19] To give a single example, the subsidies paid to American cotton producers reduce the value of cotton exports from Benin, Mali, Chad and Burkina Faso by a quarter of a billion dollars a year, equivalent to nearly 3 percent of their combined national income.[20] But it is not just rich countries that are at fault. Many poor countries have hedged their economies around with a bewildering variety of restrictions that tend to hamper commerce. It has been convincingly shown that one of the principal reasons for widening international inequality in the 1970s and 1980s was in fact protectionism in less developed economies. A comparison of *per capita* GDP among developing countries found that the more "open" economies grew at an annual rate of 4.5 percent, while the "closed" countries managed barely 0.7 percent.[21] These findings have been widely interpreted as making the case for present-day globalization—that is to say, demonstrating that countries that reduce impediments to trade are much more likely to achieve rapid growth than those that incline toward autarky.

A similar point can be made with respect to flows of labor. It is now well established that international migration (or the restriction of it) plays a crucial role in determining the extent of international inequality. The more free movement there is of labor, the more international income levels tend to converge. One reason that modern globalization is associated with high levels of inequality is that there are so many restrictions on the free movement of labor from less developed to developed societies.[22] One recent estimate suggests that a liberalization of the global labor market would yield aggregate benefits twenty-five times larger than the expected benefits of further liberalization of flows of goods and capital.[23]

Above all, consider the evidence on international capital flows, another key component of globalization. Development economists have spent many decades trying to work out how to raise the level of investment in backward agrarian societies. The most obvious solution has been for them to import capital from where it is plentiful—namely, the developed world. According to the basic classical model of the world economy, this ought to happen of its own accord; capital should automatically flow from developed to less developed economies, where returns are likely to be higher. But as the Nobel laureate Robert Lucas pointed out in a seminal article published in 1990, this does not seem to happen in practice.[24] Although some measures of international financial integration indicate that the 1990s saw exceptionally large cross-border capital flows, in reality most of today's overseas investment goes on *within* the developed world. In 1994 only 36 percent of foreign direct investment and 10 percent of portfolio investment went to poor countries (defined as countries with incomes a third or less of the OECD average);[25] by 2000 the poor countries' share had fallen to around 12 percent and 2 percent, respectively.[26] The very poorest countries nowadays receive almost no investment from abroad.[27] Most cross-border capital flows are in fact *among* the United States, the European Union and Japan. Quite simply, investors in rich countries prefer to invest in other rich countries. The large gross capital flows of recent decades thus have little to do with widening international inequalities; the culprit is the absence of net capital flows from rich countries to poor.

According to one school of thought, geography, climate and the incidence of disease provide a sufficient explanation for the widening of global inequalities. Countries that are far from major sea routes, located in tropical zones where people are prey to diseases like malaria are more likely, if not simply doomed, to be poor.[28] However, there is good reason to believe that the key to economic success lies in the adoption of legal, financial and political institutions conducive to investment and innovation—regardless of location, mean temperature and the prevalence of disease-bearing insects.[29] Thus investors prefer to put their money in countries where rights of private property are effectively protected, though that should be regarded as a minimum requirement. In *The Wealth and Poverty of Nations,* David Landes summed up this view by postulating that "the ideal growth-and-development" government would:

1. secure rights of private property, the better to encourage saving and investment;
2. secure rights of personal liberty . . . against both the abuses of tyranny and . . . crime and corruption;
3. enforce rights of contract . . .
4. provide stable government . . . governed by publicly known rules . . .
5. provide responsive government . . .
6. provide honest government . . . [with] no rents to favor and position
7. provide moderate, efficient, ungreedy government . . . to hold taxes down [and] reduce the government's claim on the social surplus. . . .[30]

In a cross-country study of postwar economic growth, the economist Robert Barro concluded that there were six significant variables that correlated closely to a country's economic performance. Among them were the enforcement of the rule of law and the avoidance of excessive government expenditures and inflation.[31] It is widely accepted now that property rights are more likely to be respected in a country where the sovereign is constrained by a representative assembly.[32] And constitutional regimes based on the rule of law are in turn more likely to experience the financial revolutions that encourage both foreign investment and domestic capital formation. A representative legislature, a transparent fiscal system, an independent monetary authority and a regular market for securities create the institutional environment within which all kinds of corporations, particularly limited liability companies, can flourish.[33] Democracy in the sense of a universal suffrage-based legislature is not indispensable for growth; witness the recent economic success of China, Malaysia, Singapore, South Korea, Taiwan and Thailand. Democratization may even slow a country's economic development if an overhasty widening of the franchise unleashes popular demands for economically detrimental fiscal and monetary policies. On the other hand, democratic societies are more likely to invest in public education and public health, which also tend to enhance a society's economic performance.[34] Though authoritarian regimes in Asia have fared well economically, most in the rest of the world have not. Exceptions such as post-1973 Chile may have had the rule of law in the economic sphere, but they certainly lacked it in the sphere of human rights; under Augosto Pinochet's dictatorship, property had more rights than people.

It is in this realm of economic, legal and political institutions that so many poor countries fall down. There have been numerous attempts in the past fifty years to address the problems of economic backwardness by means of loans and aid. Indeed, Western countries gave away around $1 trillion (in 1985 dollars) in unrequited transfers to poorer countries between 1950 and 1995. But these efforts have yielded pitiful results, in large measure because the recipient countries lacked the political, legal and financial institutions necessary for aid to be productive.[35] Arbitrary and corrupt rulers bear a large share of the responsibility for this economic failure.[36] Much of the money that has poured into poor countries has simply leaked back out— often to bank accounts in Switzerland—as corrupt rulers have stashed their ill-gotten gains abroad.[37] One study of thirty sub-Saharan African countries calculated that total capital flight for the period 1970 to 1996 was in the region of $187 billion, which, when accrued interest is added, implies that Africa's ruling elites had private overseas assets equivalent to 145 percent of the public debts their countries owed. The authors conclude that "roughly 80 cents on every dollar borrowed by African countries flowed back as capital flight in the same year."[38] There seems to be a close correlation between sub-Saharan economic failure and the generalized absence of the rule of law and political accountability; only five out of nearly fifty countries can be classified today as liberal democracies.[39]

Perhaps the best evidence for the institutional argument is that even a poorly situated country can prosper with the right institutions. Botswana has enjoyed the fastest rate of growth of *per capita* income in the world over the past thirty-five years, despite being little better endowed in terms of geography, climate and natural resources than other sub-Saharan African countries. According to a recent analysis, the main reason for Botswana's success is simply that it managed to adopt good institutions:

> The basic system of law and contract worked reasonably well. State and private predation have been quite limited. Despite the large revenues from diamonds, this has not induced domestic political instability or conflict for control of this resource. The government sustained the minimal public

service structure that it inherited from the British and developed it into a meritocratic, relatively noncorrupt and efficient bureaucracy. . . . Moreover, the government invested heavily in infrastructure, education and health. Fiscal policy has been prudent in the extreme and the exchange rate has remained closely tied to fundamentals.[40]

In particular, Botswana has managed to develop functioning institutions of private property, "which protect the property rights of actual and potential investors, provide political stability, and ensure that the political elites are constrained by the political system and the participation of a broad cross-section of the society."[41]

Helpfully, controlled experiments were carried out in both Europe and Asia after 1945 to see how practically identical populations—in terms of environment, situation and culture—would fare economically under quite different institutional regimes. The widely divergent experiences of the two Germanies and the two Koreas confirm that institutions do indeed play the decisive role in development. So too did the experiment of keeping one Chinese city, Hong Kong, under Britain's liberal imperial system and one Chinese island, Taiwan, under a not dissimilar American-sponsored system, while the rest of the country endured the miseries of Mao's Marxist tyranny.

Most poor countries stay poor because they lack the right institutions—not least the right institutions to encourage investment. Because they are not accountable to their subjects, autocratic regimes are more prone to corruption than those where the rule of law is well established. Corruption in turn inhibits economic development in a multitude of ways, diverting resources away from capital formation and the improvement of human capital through better health care and education. According to the African Union, the costs of corruption are equivalent to around one-quarter of African GDP.[42] Moreover, poor countries are more likely to succumb to civil war than rich ones, making them poorer still. In the absence of nonviolent means of bringing dictators to account, political violence is of course more likely to occur. Having begun, however, civil war can quickly become a way of life. A truly vicious circle now exists in many poor countries, as rival warlords fight for the control of mineral deposits, narcotics plantations and even flows of foreign aid, recruiting cohort after cohort of poor, illiterate youths with little prospect of employment other than warfare and even less expectation of long life.[43] The problem is not confined to Africa; Colombia is in the grip of just such a downward spiral.

No doubt each of the "failed states" of the world has failed in its own distinctive way. But they also have much in common. Among the very poorest countries in the world are the Central African Republic, Uganda, Rwanda, Chad, Tajikistan, Niger, Eritrea, Guinea-Bissau, Liberia, Sierra

TABLE 7. POVERTY, UNFREEDOM AND CIVIL WAR

Country	GNI per Capita, Atlas Method (Current U.S. $)	UN HDI Value (U.S.=0.937)	Freedom House Political Rights (Best 1, Worst 7)	Freedom House Civil Liberties (Best 1, Worst 7)	Periods of War
Central African Republic	260	0.363	5	5	2001
Uganda	250	0.489	6	4	1971–72, 1977–79, 1981–91, 1994–95, 1996–2001
Rwanda	230	0.422	7	5	1990–94, 1998–2001
Chad	220	0.376	6	5	1965–88, 1989, 1990, 1991–94, 1997–2001
Tajikistan	180	0.677	6	5	1992–93, 1994–96, 1998
Niger	170	0.292	4	4	1990–92, 1994, 1996, 1997
Eritrea	160	0.446	7	6	1998–2000
Guinea-Bissau	150	0.373	4	5	1963–64, 1965–73, 1998, 1999
Liberia	150	NA	6	6	1980, 1989–96, 2000–01
Sierra Leone	140	0.275	4	4	1991–2000
Burundi	100	0.337	6	5	1965, 1990–92, 1995–96, 1997–2001
Ethiopia	100	0.359	5	5	1960, 1962–67, 1968–73, 1974–91, 1996–97, 1998–2001
Democratic Republic of Congo	90	0.363	6	6	1960–62, 1964–65, 1967, 1977, 1978, 1996, 1997, 1998–2000, 2001
Afghanistan	NA	NA	6	6	1978–2001
Somalia	NA	NA	6	7	1978, 1981–96

Source: World Bank, *World Development Indicators* database; United Nations Human Development Report, 2003; Freedom House; International Peace Research Institute, Oslo (PRIO), Department of Peace and Conflict Research, Uppsala University.

Leone, Burundi, Ethiopia, the Democratic Republic of Congo, Afghanistan and Somalia. Besides extreme poverty and (in nearly every case) average life expectancy of little more than forty years, all these countries fall far short of being liberal democracies, and all have experienced in the recent past, or continue to experience, some form of war.[44] In most cases, their only hope for the future would seem to be intervention by a foreign power capable of constructing the basic institutional foundations that are indispensable for economic development.

GLOBALIZATION

Think, then, of liberal empire as the political counterpart to economic globalization. If economic openness—free trade, free labor movement and

TABLE 8: GLOBALIZATION: AN OVERVIEW

Given (More or Less)	Flows	Mechanism	Agency	Policy	International Regime
Laws of physics: gravity, second law of thermo- dynamics etc.	Disease	Natural	None	Free migration	Anarchic
Climate	Goods	Transport technology	Corporations	Free trade	**Liberal**
Topography	Capital	Communica- tions tech- nology	Other nongovernmental organizations	Free capital flows	**Hegemonic**
Resource endowment	Labor		Governments	Free information flows	Imperial
Prevalence of organisms hostile to man	**Technology**		The rule of law		
Human biology	**Services**		**Fiscal transparency**	Monetary standards	
	Institutions				
	Knowledge Crises				

free capital flows—helps growth, and if capital is more likely to be formed where the rule of law exists and government is not corrupt, then it is important to establish not only how economic activity becomes globalized but also how—by what mechanism—economically benign institutions can be spread around the world.

The fact that globalization applies to politics as well as economics is one of the messages of table 8. The first column lists what can be regarded as givens about the globe we inhabit; the second, those things that can flow around it; the third, the mechanisms that facilitate such flows; the fourth, the agencies operating these mechanisms; the fifth, the policies that allow those mechanisms to operate and the sixth, the possible international regimes.

Economists and economic historians alike tend to focus their attention on flows of commodities, capital and labor when talking about the history of globalization. However, there are other flows that can also occur on a global scale, not only flows of technology and services but also flows of institutions, knowledge and culture. A particular event like a revolution or a bank failure can also be transmitted by a kind of mimesis around the world.[45] And disease was globalized before any of these. The history of the fourteenth century would be incomprehensible without some knowledge of the bubonic plague, just as the conquest of the Americas by Europeans from the late fifteenth century until the mid-nineteenth would not have happened so easily without the export of infectious diseases, which more than decimated native populations. As well as infections, the conquistadors and colonists brought technology, institutions and ideas: gunpowder and the horse, Christianity and its various churches, West European notions of property, law and governance. Slow and erratic though it has been, the process of global democratization since the 1770s illustrates the way both institutions and ideas can be spread internationally as readily as goods can be traded across borders or money invested abroad. And the phenomenon of contagion, familiar to students of international financial markets, has its political counterpart in the international revolutionary epidemics after 1789, 1848, 1917 and 1989.

If one leaves aside the mechanisms of the natural world, which can only really transmit infectious diseases (and not very far without man-made assistance), all these different things have been able to traverse the world only because of advances in the technology of transport and communications. It was above all improvements in the design of oceangoing ships, and increases in their number, that globalized the world economy in the nineteenth century, though the foundations of this revolution were laid earlier by advances in navigation, medicine and propulsion. Yet continued advances in the technology of transport and communications—the advent of aircraft, wireless transmission and satellites in space—were by themselves no guarantee of continued economic globalization. Much depended, and still depends, on the private and public agencies that control the means of communication. In the mid-twentieth century the encroachments of governments into economic life did much to reverse the economic integration of the pre-1914 period as more and more regimes adopted policies inimical to free international exchange.

Economic historians tend to pay more attention to the ways governments can facilitate globalization by various kinds of deregulation (the first four items in the fifth column of the table) than to the ways they can promote globalization more actively. Yet the history of the integration of international commodity markets in the seventeenth and eighteenth centuries is inseparable from the process of imperial competition among Portugal, Spain, Holland, France and Britain. The creation of global markets for spices, textiles, coffee, tea and sugar were the work of monopoly companies like the Dutch and English East Indian companies, simultaneously engaged in a commercial and a naval contest for market shares. In the same way, the spread of free trade and the internationalization of capital markets in the nineteenth century were intimately linked to the expansion of British imperial power. On the other hand, the eclipse of globalization in the middle of the twentieth century was in large measure a consequence of the immensely costly and destructive challenges to British hegemony mounted by Germany and its allies in 1914 and 1939. Nothing did more than the world wars to promote alternative models of economic organization to that of the international free market. War was actively waged against seaborne trade, while it was the various wartime experiments with the control of trade and foreign exchange, the centralized allocation of raw materials and the rationing of consumption that provided the inspiration for theories of peacetime economic planning in the Soviet Union and elsewhere. The globalization of warfare in the twentieth century must bear a large share of the responsibility for the midcentury breakdown of international trade, capital flows and migration.

It is certainly far from self-evident that an international order based on a multiplicity of notionally equal independent nation-states is the one best designed to maximize economic integration and to spread the institutions conducive to the success of free markets.[46] In an ideal world, of course, free trade would be naturally occurring. But history and political economy tell us that it is not. The period after the Second World War saw great strides to reduce the tariff barriers that had arisen in the beggar-my-neighbor mood of the Depression, but under the Bretton Woods system, international capital movements were tightly regulated and indeed stayed that way even after the system of fixed exchange rates had broken down, until the 1980s. Nor has the resistance to liberal economic policies wholly disappeared even in our own era of globalization; there still remain formidable barriers to the movement of workers and agricultural products. No matter how persuasive the arguments for economic openness, it seems, nation-states cling to their tariffs, quotas and subsidies. By contrast, in the first era of globalization, from the mid-nineteenth century until the First World War, economic openness was imposed by colonial powers not only on Asian and African colonies but also on South America and even Japan.[47] To be more precise, free trade spread because of Britain's power and Britain's example. It is to that first age of "Anglobalization" that we now turn, in order to assess both its costs and its benefits.

ANGLOBALIZATION

From the 1840s until the 1930s the British political elite and electorate remained wedded to the principle of laissez-faire, laissez-passer—and the practice of "cheap bread." That meant that certainly from the 1870s, Britain's tariffs were significantly lower than those of its European neighbors;[48] it also meant that tariffs in much of the British Empire were kept low. Abandoning formal control over Britain's colonies would almost certainly have led to higher tariffs being erected against British exports in their markets and perhaps other forms of trade discrimination; witness the protectionist policies adopted by the United States and India after they secured independence, as well as the tariff regimes adopted by Britain's imperial rivals from the late 1870s onward. Whether one looks at the duties on primary products or those on manufactures, Britain was the least protectionist of the imperial powers. In 1913 average tariff rates on imported manufactures were 13 percent in Germany, over 20 percent in France, 44 percent in the United States and 84 percent in Russia. In Britain they were zero.[49]

According to one estimate, the economic benefit *to Britain* of enforcing free trade could have been anywhere between 1.8 and 6.5 percent of GNP.[50] But what about the benefit to the rest of the world? In the words of the Whig free trader Sir John Graham, Britain was "the great Emporium of the commerce of the World."[51] Its domestic market and much of its empire were more or less open to all comers to sell their wares as best they could. The evidence that, in an increasingly protectionist world, Britain's contin-ued policy of free trade was beneficial to its colonies seems unequivocal. Between the 1870s and the 1920s the colonies' share of Britain's imports rose from a quarter to a third.[52] More generally, British colonial authori-ties resisted protectionist backlashes to the dramatic falls in factor prices caused by late-nineteenth-century globalization.[53] That said, a distinction needs to be made between the majority of colonies, which had free trade thrust upon them, and the elite few that secured, through the granting of "responsible government," the right to set their own tariffs. Canada did so in 1879, an example soon followed by Australia and New Zealand.[54] Moreover, there appears to have been a positive correlation between the imposition of these tariffs and the economic growth of what became the Dominions—an apparently awkward finding for the proponents of uncon-ditional economic "openness."[55] This has important implications for any economic history of the British Empire. If Canada and the other Domin-ions benefited from protection, then the question becomes: would India have done better with tariffs? Happily for economic liberals, there is a dif-ficulty with this line of argument. First, the tariffs imposed by Canada and others were designed to raise revenue, not to exclude imports. Canadian growth came from exports of agricultural products, not import substitu-tion by domestic manufacturers.[56] Secondly, the argument ignores the far more damaging effects of unfree trade on primary producers during the 1930s. The Depression was hard on everyone, but significantly harder on primary producers outside the system of imperial preference than those inside it.

The evidence looks incontrovertible, then, that the British Empire fostered the integration of global markets for commodities and manufactures. Nor would there have been so much international mobility of labor without the British Empire. True, the independent United States was the most attractive destination for nineteenth-century emigrants. But as American restrictions on immigration increased, the significance of the white Dominions as a destination for British emigrants grew markedly, attracting around 59 percent of all British emigrants between 1900 and 1914, 75 percent between 1915 and 1949 and 82 percent between 1949 and 1963.[57] This had important distributional consequences. It is often argued that the lion's share of the returns on empire flowed to a tiny group of politically influential investors. But the effect of mass migration to land-rich, labor-poor colonies like Canada, Australia and New Zealand was to reduce global inequality.[58] Nor should we lose sight of the vast numbers of Asians who left India and China to work as indentured laborers, many of them on British plantations and mines in the course of the nineteenth century. Perhaps as many as 1.6 million Indians emigrated under this system, which lay somewhere between free and unfree labor.[59] There is no question that the majority of them suffered great hardship; some indeed might have been better off staying at home.[60] But once again we cannot pretend that this mobilization of cheap and probably underemployed Asians to harvest gum or dig gold had no economic significance.

Above all—and this is where Roosevelt and other critics of empire got it most wrong—the British Empire was an engine for the integration of international capital markets. Between 1865 and 1914 more than £4 billion flowed from Britain to the rest of the world, giving the country a historically unprecedented and since unequaled position as a global net creditor, "the world's banker" indeed, or, to be exact, the world's bond market. By 1914 total British assets overseas amounted to somewhere between £3.1 and £4.5 billion, as against British GDP of £2.5 billion.[61] This portfolio was authentically global: around 45 percent of British investment went to the United States and the colonies of white settlement, 20 percent to Latin America, 16 percent to Asia and 13 percent to Africa, compared with just 6 percent to the rest of Europe.[62] Out of all British capital raised through public issues of securities, as much went to Africa, Asia and Latin America between 1865 and 1914 as to the United Kingdom itself.[63] This pattern was scarcely changed by the effects of the First World War and the Great Depression.[64] As is well known, British investment in developing economies principally took the form of portfolio investment in infrastructure, especially railways and port facilities. But the British also sank considerable (and not easily calculable) sums directly into plantations to produce new cash crops like tea, cotton, indigo and rubber.

It has been argued that there was therefore something of a Lucas effect in the first era of globalization—in other words, that British capital tended to gravitate toward countries with higher *per capita* GDP, rather than relatively poor countries.[65] Yet the bias in favor of rich countries was much less pronounced than it is today. In 1997 only around 5 percent of the world's stock of capital was invested in countries with *per capita* incomes of a fifth or less of U.S. *per capita* GDP. In 1913 the proportion was 25 percent.[66] The share of developing countries in total international liabilities was 11 percent in 1995, compared with 33 percent in 1900 and 47 percent in 1938.[67] Very nearly half the total stock of international capital in 1914 was invested in countries with *per capita* incomes a third or less of Britain's,[68] and Britain accounted for nearly two-fifths of the total sum invested in those poor economies. The contrast between the past and the present is striking: whereas today's rich economies prefer to "swap" capital with one another, largely bypassing poor countries, a century ago the rich economies had very large, positive net balances with the less well-off countries of the world.

Investing money in faraway places is always risky; what economists call informational asymmetries are generally greater, the farther the lender is from the borrower.[69] Less developed economies also tend to be rather more susceptible to economic, social and political crises. Why, then, were pre-1914 investors willing to risk such high proportions of their savings by purchasing securities or other assets overseas? One possible answer is that the adoption of the gold standard by developing economies offered investors a kind of "good housekeeping seal of approval."[70] In 1868 only Britain and a number of its economic dependencies—Portugal, Egypt, Canada, Chile and Australia—had currencies that were convertible into gold on demand. France and the other members of the Latin Monetary Union, as well as Russia, Persia and some Latin American states were on the bimetallic (gold and silver) system, while most of the rest of the world was on the silver standard. By 1908, however, only China, Persia and a handful of Central American countries were still on silver. The gold standard had become, in effect, the global monetary system, though in practice a number of Asian economies, notably India, had a gold exchange standard (with local currencies convertible into sterling rather than actual gold), while some "Latin" economies in Europe and America did not technically maintain convertibility of notes into gold.[71] This system of international fixed exchange rates may have encouraged international trade. Adherence to gold was also a signal of monetary and fiscal rectitude that allegedly facilitated access by peripheral countries to West European capital markets. It was a commitment mechanism, a way of affirming that a government would eschew irresponsible fiscal and monetary policies such as printing money or defaulting on debt.[72] A commitment to gold convertibility, according to one estimate, reduced the yield on a country's bonds by around forty basis points.[73] To put it simply, that meant that countries on the gold standard could borrow more cheaply when they went cap in hand to the London bond market.

As a *contingent* commitment, however, membership of the gold standard was nothing more than a promise of self-restraint under certain circumstances. Countries on gold retained the right to suspend convertibility in the event of an emergency, such as a war, a revolution or a sudden deterioration in the terms of trade. Such emergencies were in fact quite common before 1914. Argentina, Brazil and Chile all experienced serious financial and monetary crises between 1880 and 1914. By 1895 the currencies of all three had depreciated by around 60 percent against sterling. This had serious implications for their ability to service their external debt, which was denominated in hard currency (usually sterling) rather than domestic currency. Argentina defaulted in 1888–93, and Brazil in both 1898 and 1914. In other words, investors who pinned their faith in a country's adoption of the gold standard had no guarantee that the country would not default. (Indeed, some countries made the chances of a default more likely by going on to gold during the years of relative gold shortage between the mid-1870s and the mid-1890s, since falling commodity prices made it harder for them to earn from exports the hard currency they needed to service their external gold-denominated debts.)

Altogether different was the kind of commitment that came with the imposition of direct British rule. This amounted to an unconditional "no default" guarantee; the only uncertainty investors had to face concerned the expected duration of British rule. Before 1914, despite the growth of nationalist movements in colonies from Ireland to India, political independence still seemed a distinctly remote prospect; even the major colonies of white settlement had been granted only a limited political autonomy. Moreover, the British imposed a distinctive set of institutions on their colonies that was very likely to enhance their appeal to investors: not only a gold-based currency but also economic openness (free trade as well as free capital movements) and balanced budgets—to say nothing of the rule of law (specifically, British-style property rights) and relatively noncorrupt administration.[74] In other words, while investors who put their money in independent gold standard countries got little more than a promise not to print money, investors who put their cash in colonies could count not just on sound money but on the full range of Victorian "public goods." It would therefore be rather puzzling if investors had regarded Australia as no more creditworthy than Argentina or Canada as no more creditworthy than Chile.

We can measure the "empire effect" on international capital flows in two ways: the volume of capital that went to British colonies and the interest rates those colonies paid. According to the best available estimates, more than two-fifths (42 percent) of the cumulative flows of portfolio investment from Britain to the rest of the world went to British possessions. The imperial proportion of stocks of overseas investment on the eve of the First World War was even higher: 46 percent.[75] It also seems clear that imperial possessions were able to borrow at lower rates of interest than independent countries (or the colonies of other powers). Britain and its principal possessions had among the lowest average bond yields for the period 1870 to 1914. By comparison, the yields on bonds issued by the Latin American economies, which also attracted substantial inflows of British capital without actually coming under British rule, were significantly higher. Argentine yields, to give just one example, were more than two hundred basis points higher than those on Indian bonds.[76] Among twenty-three countries for which bond yield figures are readily available for the period 1870 to 1914, it is very striking that the five states that were members of the British Empire had the lowest rates, all averaging less than 4 percent. Only Norway and Sweden were able to borrow in London at rates lower than New

Zealand and Australia. Egypt, which began the period outside the empire but became a *de facto* colony in 1882, saw a dramatic decline in its average yield from to 10.1 percent (1870–81) to 4.3 percent (1882–1914).[77] The differential was even more pronounced in the interwar period, which saw major defaults by numerous independent debtor countries, including Argentina, Brazil, Chile, Mexico, Japan, Russia and Turkey.[78] By the 1920s, at the latest, membership of the empire was therefore confirmed as a better "good housekeeping seal of approval" than gold.[79] Experience showed that money invested in a *de jure* British colony such as India, or in a colony in all but name like Egypt, was more secure than money invested in an independent country such as Argentina. In turn, the low-risk premium paid by British colonies when they raised capital in London made it less likely that they would fall into the kinds of debt traps that claimed other emerging markets, whose interest payments out to foreign creditors exceeded the amounts of money flowing in from new loans and being generated by the foreign-financed investments.

That imperial membership offered better security to investors than mere adoption of the gold standard should not surprise us. At the turn of the century legislation was introduced, in the form of the Colonial Loans Act (1899) and the Colonial Stock Act (1900), which gave colonial bonds the same trustee status as the benchmark British government perpetual bond, the "consol."[80] At a time when a rising proportion of the national debt was being held by Trustee Savings Banks, this was an important boost to the market for colonial securities.[81] Moreover, after the First World War, it was agreed between the Treasury and the Bank of England that new bond issues by British possessions should be given preference over new issues by independent foreign states.[82] Even colonial constitutions had been drafted with at least one eye on creditor preferences.[83] It was inconceivable, declared one colonial governor in 1933, that the interest due on Gold Coast bonds should be compulsorily reduced; why should British investors "accept yet another burden for the relief of persons in another country who have enjoyed all the benefits but will not accept their obligation"?[84] When the self-governing dominion of Newfoundland came to the brink of default in the early 1930s, a royal commission under Lord Amulree recommended that its Parliament be dissolved and its government entrusted to a six-man commission and royal governor appointed from London. Amulree's report made it clear that he and his committee regarded the end of representative government as a lesser evil than default.[85]

Small wonder an increasing share of British overseas investment ended up going to the empire after the First World War. In the period from 1900 to 1914, around two-fifths (39 percent) of British overseas capital went to the empire. But after the First World War the balance shifted. In the 1920s the empire accounted for around two-thirds of all new issues on the London market.[86] Writing in 1924, John Maynard Keynes observed caustically that it was "remarkable that Southern Rhodesia—a place in the middle of Africa with a few thousand white inhabitants and less than a million black ones—can place an unguaranteed loan on terms not very different from our own [British] War Loan." It seemed equally "strange" to him that "there should be investors who prefer[red] . . . Nigeria stock (which has no British Government guarantee) [to] . . . London and North-Eastern Railway debentures."[87] Keynes's point was that this state of affairs was not in the economic interests of Britain itself. With unemployment stubbornly stuck above prewar levels and mounting evidence of industrial stagnation, capital export seemed like a misallocation of resources. But Keynes did not consider the benefits reaped by colonial economies from this kind of cheap access to British savings. From an imperial rather than a narrowly national point of view, it was highly desirable that savings from the wealthy metropolis be encouraged to flow to the developing periphery. Besides ensuring that British investors got their interest paid regularly and their principal paid back, the imperial system was conducive to *global* economic growth—more so, certainly, than an alternative policy of the sort Keynes had in mind, which would have prioritized the industrial production and employment of the United Kingdom.

IMPERIAL SINS OF OMISSION

The results of imperial globalization were in many ways astounding. The combination of free trade, mass migration and low-cost British capital propelled large parts of the empire to the forefront of world economic development. In terms of the production of manufactured goods per head of population, Canada, Australia and New Zealand ranked higher than Germany in 1913. Indeed, *per capita* GDP grew more rapidly in Canada than in the United States in the ninety years before World War I.[88]

But there is a problem. The performance of the Dominions was not matched in the rest of the empire, and least of all in Asia, where the jewel in the imperial crown was supposedly situated. This raises a crucial question. Why was Indian economic performance so much worse than that of the dominions? India attracted £286 million of all the capital raised in London between 1865 and 1914—18 percent of the total placed in the empire, second only to Canada. Yet Indian *per capita* GDP grew at a miserably slow rate. Between 1857 and 1947—between the mutiny and independence, in other words—it rose by just 19 percent, compared with an increase in Britain of 134 percent.[89] Between 1820 and 1950 it grew at a mere 0.12 percent per annum—barely at all by the standards of the "white" empire and slow even by comparison with British Africa.

Here is one of the central conundrums of modern economic history. India, more than any other major economy, had free trade and Western commercial norms imposed upon it. Yet the result was deindustrialization and economic stagnation. The United States, by contrast, had thrown off British rule and adopted the kind of protectionist tariff rates—averaging 44 percent on imported manufactures—that we would now condemn in a developing economy. The result? By the end of the nineteenth century the United States had overtaken the United Kingdom by most measures of economic performance. If India's relative economic decline can be blamed on the British, the case against liberal empire begins to look dauntingly strong.

The nationalist explanation for Indian "underdevelopment" under British rule has four essential components. First, the British deindustrialized India by opening it to factory-produced textiles from Lancashire, whose manufacturers were initially protected from Indian competition until they had established a technological lead.[90] Secondly, they imposed excessive and regressive taxation. Thirdly, they "drained" capital from India, even manipulating the rupee-sterling exchange rate to their own advantage. Finally, they did next to nothing to alleviate the famines that these policies caused. One recent historian has gone so far as to speak of "Late Victorian Holocausts" in the 1870s and 1890s.[91] This negative view of the British role in India, which can be traced back as far as Naoroji Dadabhai's *Poverty and Un-British Rule in India* (1901), continues to enjoy wide currency.[92] It is perhaps the single most powerful piece of evidence in the case against liberal empire.

No doubt it benefited the Indian economy little to maintain one of the world's largest standing armies as, in effect, a mercenary force at Britain's disposal.[93] Yet recent research casts doubt on other aspects of the nationalist critique. The Indian historian Tirthankar Roy has shown that the destruction of jobs in the Indian textile industry was probably inevitable, regardless of who ruled India, and that an equal, if not greater, number of new jobs were created in new economic sectors built up by the British.[94] Even in the case of textiles, by the 1920s the government of India was clearly giving preference to Indian manufacturers over Lancashire's mills. It is also far from clear that taxation under the British was excessive, since the land tax burden fell from around 10 percent of net output in the 1850s to 5 percent by the 1930s.[95] The supposed "drain" of capital from India to Britain turns out to have been comparatively modest: only around 1 percent of Indian national income between the 1860s and the 1930s, according to one estimate of the export surplus (which was what nationalists usually had in mind).[96] In any case, a large proportion of the notorious Home Charges remitted to Britain were paying for services that India needed but could not have provided for itself.[97] Finally, the famines that beset the Indian economy were far more environmental than political in origin, and after 1900 the problem was in fact alleviated by the greater integration of the Indian market for foodstuffs. The Bengal famine of 1943 arose precisely because improvements introduced under British rule collapsed under the strain of the war.[98]

British rule had some distinctly positive effects in India. It greatly increased the importance of trade, from between 1 and 2 percent of national income to over 20 percent by 1913.[99] The British created an integrated Indian market: they unified weights, measures and the currency, abolished transit duties and introduced a "legal framework [that] promoted private property rights and contract law more explicitly." They invested substantially in repairing and enlarging the country's ancient irrigation system; between 1891 and 1938 the acreage under irrigation more than doubled.[100] They transformed the Indian system of communications, introducing a postal and telegraph system, deploying steamships on internal waterways and building more than forty thousand miles of railway track (roughly five times the amount constructed in China in the same period). This railway network alone employed more than a million people by the last decade of British rule. Finally, there was a significant increase in financial intermediation.[101] As Roy concludes: "The railways, the ports, major irrigation systems, the telegraph, sanitation and medical care, the universities, the postal system, the courts of law, were assets India could not believably have acquired in such extent and quality had it not developed close political links with Britain. . . . British rule appears to have done far more than what its predecessor regimes and contemporary Indian regimes were able to do."[102] It is also possible (and the British no doubt believed) that their rule in India tended to reduce social inequality.[103] Certainly, by comparison with their counterparts in the other big Asian economy, which remained under Asian political control throughout the period, Indians fared quite well. Chinese *per capita* GDP actually shrank by around 17 percent between 1870 and 1950, roughly the amount by which Indian incomes rose. Though China's troubles were in large measure due to the disruptive effects of informal European imperialism and then Japanese colonization, it is at least arguable that the country would have fared better economically if formal British rule had been extended beyond the outposts of the so-called treaty ports like Hong Kong.

If one leaves aside their fundamentally different resource endowments, the explanation for India's underperformance compared with, say, Canada lies not in British exploitation but rather in the insufficient scale of British interference in the Indian economy. The British expanded Indian education—but not enough to make a real impact on the quality of human capital. The number of Indians in education may have risen sevenfold between 1881 and 1941, but the proportion of the population in primary and secondary education was far below European rates (2 percent in India in 1913, compared with 16 percent in Britain). The British invested in India—but not enough to pull most Indian farmers up off the base line of subsistence and certainly not enough to compensate for the pitifully low level of indigenous capital formation, worsened by the custom of hoarding gold.[104] The British built hospitals and banks—but not enough of them to make significant improvements in public health and credit networks.[105] These were sins of omission more than commission. Unfortunately for Indians, the nationalists who came to power in 1947 drew almost completely the wrong conclusions about what had gone wrong under British rule, embarking instead on a program of sub-Soviet state-led autarky, the achievement of which was to widen still further the gap between Indian and British incomes. This reached its widest historic extent in 1979.[106]

LESSONS OF LIBERAL EMPIRE

Economic historians will doubtless continue to debate the causes of the "great divergence" of economic fortunes that has characterized the last half millennium. If environmental factors provide a sufficient explanation for the widening of global inequalities, then the policies and institutions exported by British imperialism were of marginal importance; the agricultural, commercial and industrial technologies developed in Europe from 1700 onward were bound to work better in temperate regions with good access to sea routes. However, if—as seems more likely—the key to economic success lies in the adoption of the right legal, financial and political institutions, then it matters a great deal that by the end of the nineteenth century a quarter of the world was under British rule. Even in the tropics, the British endeavored to introduce the institutions that they regarded as essential to prosperity: free trade, free migration, infrastructural investment, balanced budgets, sound money, the rule of law and incorrupt administration. If the results were much less impressive in Africa and India than they were in the colonies of British settlement, that was because even the best institutions work less well in excessively hot, disease-ridden, or landlocked places. There the investments that were needed to overcome geography, climate and its attendant deleterious effects on human capital were beyond the imaginings of colonial rulers schooled in the Victorian fiscal tradition of balanced budgets with low taxes. Certainly, the very different policies adopted by postindependence governments have been more successful in only a tiny minority of cases.

In November 2002 the British foreign secretary, Jack Straw, told the *New Statesman* magazine: "I'm not a liberal imperialist. There's a lot wrong with liberalism, with a capital L, although I am a liberal with a small L. And there's a lot wrong with imperialism. A lot of the problems we are having to deal with now are a consequence of our colonial past." Central to my argument is that there was such a thing as liberal imperialism and that on balance it was a good thing. From the 1850s until the 1930s the British approach to governing their sprawling global *imperium* was fundamentally liberal both in theory and in practice. Free trade, free capital movements and free migration were fostered. Colonial governments balanced their budgets, kept tariffs low and maintained stable currencies. The rule of law was institutionalized. Administration was relatively free of corruption, especially at the top. Power was granted to representative assemblies only gradually, once economic and social development had reached a level judged to be propitious. This policy "mix" encouraged British investors to put a substantial portion of their capital in poor countries and to demand relatively low-risk premiums in return. New technologies like railways and steam power were introduced to poor countries sooner and at a lower cost than if these countries had been politically independent. The results of liberal imperialism were mixed, no doubt. Not everywhere grew as rapidly as the colonies of white settlement. But even those countries (like India) that achieved only very slow increases in *per capita* income almost certainly fared better than they would have under alternative regimes.

Two conclusions follow from all this. The first is simply that in many cases of economic "backwardness," a liberal empire can do better than a nation-state. The second, however, is that even a very capable liberal empire may not succeed in conferring prosperity evenly on all the territories it administers. With that *caveat,* we may therefore make what might be called an altruistic argument for the United States to engage in something resembling liberal imperialism in our time. A country like—to take just one example—Liberia would benefit immeasurably from something like an American colonial administration.[107] Liberia is one of those countries listed in table 7 where nearly everything has gone wrong. Misgovernment and civil war have reduced it to the very bottom of the international rankings for human development. In 2003, as the country plunged still deeper into anarchy following the flight of its dictator Charles Taylor, the United States came under pressure to send troops to Monrovia to impose order there. From one point of view, of course, this was precisely the kind of humanitarian intervention Republicans had previously criticized the Clinton administration for undertaking; what was manifestly needed here was nation building rather than mere regime change. Yet if there is one country in Africa for which the United States has a historic responsibility, it is Liberia, the only African country to have been colonized by Americans in the nineteenth century (so that former slaves could return "home" after their emancipation). If liberal empire is a serious possibility in the twenty-first century, where better for it to begin its work than in wretched Liberia, a place where political independence has been a curse, not a blessing, and self-determination has turned out in practice to mean self-destruction?

The fact that as I write, the American intervention in Liberia is already being wound up brings us to the next—and in many ways the paramount—question: Is the United States capable of the kind of long-term engagement without which the liberal imperial project, by whatever euphemistic name it goes, is bound to fail?

CHAPTER 6

GOING HOME OR
ORGANIZING HYPOCRISY

Our armies do not come into your cities and lands as conquerors or enemies, but as liberators. . . . It is [not] the wish of [our] government to impose upon you alien institutions. . . . [It is our wish] that you should prosper
even as in the past, when your lands were fertile, when your ancestors gave
to the world literature, science and art and when Baghdad city was one of
the wonders of the world. . . . It is [our] hope that the aspirations of your
philosophers and writers shall be realized and that once again the people of
Baghdad shall flourish, enjoying their wealth and substance under institutions which are in consonance with their sacred laws and their racial ideals.

GENERAL F. S. MAUDE to the people of Mesopotamia, March 19, 1917

The government of Iraq, and the future of your country, will soon belong
to you. . . . We will end a brutal regime . . . so that Iraqis can live in security. We will respect your great religious traditions, whose principles of
equality and compassion are essential to Iraq's future. We will help you build
a peaceful and representative government that protects the rights of all citizens. And then our military forces will leave. Iraq will go forward as a unified, independent and sovereign nation that has regained a respected place
in the world. You are a good and gifted people—the heirs of a great civilization that contributes to all humanity.

PRESIDENT GEORGE W. BUSH to the people of Iraq, April 4, 2003

Wheresoever the Roman conquers, he inhabits.

SENECA

MESOPOTAMIA REVISITED

Anyone who doubts that there are at least some resemblances between the liberal empire of the United States today and that of the United Kingdom roughly a century ago should consider the epigraphs to this chapter. The very rhetoric used by the British commander who occupied Baghdad in 1917 was unmistakably, though doubtless unconsciously, echoed by President Bush in his television address to the Iraqi people shortly after the American occupation of Baghdad began. In both cases, Anglophone troops had been able to sweep from the south of the country to the capital in a matter of weeks. In both cases, their governments disclaimed any desire to rule Iraq directly and proceeded, after some prevarication, to install Iraqi governments with at least the appearance of popular legitimacy. In both cases, imposing law and order proved much harder than achieving the initial military victory: British troops were being picked off by gunmen throughout 1919, and massive airpower had to be used to quell a major insurrection in the summer of 1920, which left 450 British personnel dead.[1] In both cases, there were times when it was tempting to pull out altogether rather than incur further costs.[2] Finally, in both cases, the presence of substantial oil reserves—confirmed by the Anglo-Persian Oil Company in 1927—was not a wholly irrelevant factor, though it was not the main reason for the occupation.[3]

Yet there are differences. One of these is the tension that has arisen between the United States and the United Nations over the future of Iraq. Britain did not have such difficulties after the First World War, when the League of Nations, the UN's forerunner, more or less unquestioningly legitimized British rule in Mesopotamia by designating Iraq as one of its "mandates."[4] It is impossible to imagine Winston Churchill, as colonial secretary, appealing to the League of Nations for reinforcements in 1921 in the way that President George W. Bush was forced to appeal to the United Nations for assistance in September 2003. Nor is that the only difference between the British and American experience in Iraq. In two fundamental respects, British rule was based on a long-term commitment. Whatever the formal arrangements—and the British conceded in 1923 that their mandate would run for just four years rather than the twenty originally envisaged—their intention was to stay in control of Iraq for the foreseeable future. Secondly, there were enough Britons willing to spend substantial portions of their lives in Baghdad to make British influence an enduring reality there for forty years. The British and American occupiers both promised they would soon hand over power to Iraqis and leave. The difference is that the Americans *mean* it. They sincerely want to go home.

"Don't even go there!" is one of those catchphrases heard on a daily basis in New York. It sums up the problem exactly. Despite their country's vast wealth and lethal weaponry, Americans have little interest in the one basic activity without which a true empire cannot enduringly be established. They are reluctant to "go there"—and if they must go, then they count the days until they can come home. They eschew the periphery. They cling to the metropolis.

DISPOSABLE EMPIRE

The world did not have to wait long for a perfect symbol of the transience of American rule in Iraq. On April 9, 2003, the day Baghdad fell, Marine Corporal Edward Chin draped an American flag over the head of the statue of Saddam Hussein in al-Firdos (Paradise) Square. Seconds later, however, Chin removed the Stars and Stripes and replaced it with a pre–Gulf War Iraqi flag.[5] The quick change was presumably intended to reassure watching Iraqis that they were indeed experiencing liberation rather than conquest. As President Bush put it in his television address to Iraq aired shortly after the fall of their capital city, "The government of Iraq, and the future of your country, will soon belong to you. . . . We will help you build a peaceful and representative government that protects the rights of all citizens. *And then our military forces will leave.*"[6]

But when exactly? In the last letter that Corporal Kemaphoom Chanawongse sent home before he and his unit entered Iraq, the young soldier joked that his camp in Kuwait reminded him of the television series *M*A*S*H*—except that the acronym in this case would need to be M*A*H*T*S*F: "Marines Are Here to Stay Forever." Corporal Chanawongse was killed a week later, when his amphibious assault vehicle was blown up in Nasiriya. The implication of his poignant final joke was that he and his comrades could not wait to get their mission over and come

home. It was a desire to which President Bush directly alluded in his somewhat premature victory speech on board the *Abraham Lincoln* aircraft carrier on May 1: "Other nations in history have fought in foreign lands and
remained to occupy and exploit. Americans, following a battle, want nothing more than to return home."[7]

The duration of an American occupation of Iraq remains, at the time
of writing, clear in only one respect: it will be short. In a prewar speech to
the American Enterprise Institute, President Bush kept his options open:
"We will remain in Iraq as long as necessary and not a day more."[8] It was
striking, however, that the unit he used was a "day." Speaking a few days
before the fall of Baghdad, Deputy Defense Secretary Paul Wolfowitz suggested that General Jay Garner, the first American put in charge of the
country, would run his Office of Reconstruction and Humanitarian Assistance for at least six months; Garner himself talked of ninety days.[9]
Since then the time frame has varied from week to week. The outgoing
commander of the U.S. Central Command, General Tommy Franks,
seemed to suggest an occupation of between two and four years. In July,
however, the new "occupation administrator," L. Paul Bremer, told reporters: "The timing of how long the coalition stays here is effectively
now in the hands of the Iraqi people," adding, "We have no desire to stay
a day longer than necessary."[10] Later that same month he predicted that
elections would take place by the middle of 2004, followed by a handover
of power from Bremer's Coalition Provisional Authority to an elected
government, after which, as he put it, "my job here will be over."[11] On
September 26 Secretary of State Colin Powell told the *New York Times* that
the American-appointed Iraqi Governing Council would be given six
months to draw up a new constitution for the country; after that, elections
would be held and power handed over to the winners.[12] Bremer reiterated
on November 1 that it was his aim "to turn sovereignty to the Iraqi people as quickly as practicable."[13] Later the same month he was summoned
back to Washington to discuss how the transfer of power might be expe-
dited. On November 15 it was announced that an Iraqi provisional government—to be nominated rather than elected—would take over this July,
leaving elections and the constitution for next year.

In short, when the Americans say they come as liberators, not conquerors, they seem to mean it. If, as so many commentators claim, Amer-

ica is embarking on a new age of empire, it is shaping up to be the most ephemeral empire in all history. Other empire builders have fantasized about ruling subject peoples for a thousand years. This would seem to be history's first thousand-day empire. It is not so much "lite" as disposable.

Besides the obvious constraint imposed on American administrations by the electoral system, which requires that overseas interventions show positive results within two or at most four years, an important explanation for this chronic short-windedness is the difficulty the American empire finds in recruiting the right sort of people to *run* it. America's higher educational institutions excel at producing very capable young men and women. Indeed, there is little question that the best American universities are now the best in the world. But few, if any, of the graduates of Harvard, Stanford, Yale or Princeton aspire to spend their lives trying to turn a sun-scorched sandpit like Iraq into the prosperous capitalist democracy of Paul Wolfowitz's imaginings. America's brightest and best aspire not to govern Mesopotamia but to manage MTV; not to rule the Hejaz but to run a hedge fund. Unlike their British counterparts of a century ago, who left the elite British universities with an overtly imperial ethos, the letters ambitious young Americans would like to see after their names are CEO, not CBE.*

Like the United States today, the British after the First World War felt compelled by both domestic and Iraqi opinion to hand over power to an Iraqi government. But they did it slowly and incompletely. In the first three years of their occupation, the country was run by a civil commissioner, Sir Arnold Wilson.[14] He and his assistant, Gertrude Bell, were skeptical about the viability of Mesopotamian self-rule. They drew up a scheme for a unitary Iraqi state with almost no local consultation, simply ignoring those who advised against yoking together Assyria and Babylonia, Sunni and Shia. "There was no real desire in Mesopotamia for an Arab government," Wilson confidently assured the British cabinet in 1920. "The Arabs would appreciate British rule."[15] Only after the insurrection of 1920 and a fierce public denunciation of official policy by T. E. Lawrence, the hero of the Arabian campaign, did policy change. At a conference held

*Commander of the Order of the British Empire.

in Cairo in March 1921, it was decided to offer Lawrence's friend and wartime ally the Hashemite Prince Faisal the throne of the country, which would be transformed into a British-style constitutional monarchy.[16] A tame Council of Ministers presided over by the Naqib of Baghdad invited Faisal to Baghdad as a "guest" of the nation and on July 11 unanimously adopted a resolution declaring him king. Sayyid Talib of Basra, the most dangerous of the rival contenders, was arrested and deported to Ceylon for daring to use the slogan "Iraq for the Iraqis."[17] A plebiscite was duly held that endorsed Faisal's elevation and on August 23 he was crowned. Thus did the British create the country henceforth known as Iraq, which means, ironically, "well-rooted country."[18]

Faisal was no mere puppet. It was he who insisted that the British mandate be reduced from twenty to just four years. But even after the Anglo-Iraqi Treaty of 1922, there was no doubt who was really running the place. Controlling Iraq was strategically vital. It gave Britain a position of unrivaled dominance in the Middle East. It was also economically attractive. When two geologists from the American Standard Oil Company entered Iraq on a prospecting expedition, the British civil commissioner handed them over to the chief of police of Baghdad.[19] In 1927 the British takeover paid a handsome dividend when oil was struck at Baba Gurgur. Although they formally relinquished all power to the ruling dynasty, the British remained more than merely influential in Iraq throughout the 1930s. In April 1941 they had little difficulty in sending an expeditionary force from Amman to reverse a pro-Axis coup in Baghdad. Indeed, they only really lost their grip on the country with the assassination of their clients Faisal II and his prime minister Nuri es-Said in the revolution of 1958. In short, there were British government representatives, military and civilian, in Baghdad uninterruptedly for almost exactly forty years. When the British went into Iraq, they stayed.

Will there be Americans playing such a role in Baghdad in 2043? It seems, to put it mildly, improbable.

Gertrude Bell was the first woman to graduate from Oxford with a first-class degree. She learned to speak Arabic during an archaeological visit to Jerusalem in 1899 and, like T. E. Lawrence, became involved in British military intelligence. In 1917 she was appointed oriental secretary to the British civil commissioner in Baghdad. It was a posting she relished. "I don't care to be in London much," she wrote. "I like Baghdad, and I like Iraq. It's the real East, and it is stirring; things are happening here, and the romance of it all touches me and absorbs me."[20] Dotted all over the British Empire were thousands of "Orientalists" like Gertrude Bell, simultaneously enamored of the exotic "Other" and yet dominant over it. Her account of Faisal I's coronation in 1921 perfectly illustrates their mode of operation: "Faisal looked very dignified but much strung up—it was an agitating moment. He looked along the front row and caught my eye and I gave him a tiny salute. Then Saiyid Husain stood up and read [the British commissioner's] proclamation in which he announced that Faisal had been elected king by 96% of the people in Mesopotamia, long live the King! with that we stood up and saluted him, the national flag was broken on the flagstaff by his side and the band played God Save the King—they have no national anthem yet."[21] To a woman like Gertrude Bell, being there, in order discreetly to supervise this carefully choreographed regime change, was evidently very good fun. She had absolutely no desire for an "exit strategy" that would have sent her back to England.

Admittedly, most Britons who moved abroad preferred to migrate to the temperate regions of a select few colonies—Canada, Australia, New Zealand and South Africa—that soon became semiautonomous Dominions. Between 1900 and 1914 around 2.6 million Britons left the United Kingdom for imperial destinations (by 1957 the total had reached nearly 6 million); three-quarters of them went to Canada or the Antipodes.[22] Nevertheless, a significant number went to the much less hospitable climes of Asia and Africa. There were around 168,000 Britons in India in 1931.[23] The official Colonial Service in Africa was staffed by more than 7,500 expatriates.[24]

The British went abroad in multiple roles: not only as soldiers and administrators but also as businessmen, engineers, missionaries and doctors. Like America's informal empire today, Britain's empire had its nongovernmental character; there were Victorian multinational corporations and Victorian "nongovernmental organizations." But the key point is that whichever role the British played, they generally stayed—until retirement or, as countless colonial cemeteries testify, death. The substantial expatriate communities they established were crucial to the operation of the British Empire. These were the indispensable "men on the spot" who learned the local languages, perhaps adopted some local customs—though not to the fatal extent of "going native"—and acted as the intermediaries between a remote imperial authority and the indigenous elites upon whose willing collaboration the empire depended.

Of crucial importance in this regard was the role of the Indian Civil Service, which became a magnet for the very best products of the university system. The proportion of Oxford and Cambridge graduates in the Indian Civil Service was remarkably high, rising steadily after the 1880s to over 70 percent. Two-thirds of ICS men who served in the 1930s had been educated in England's exclusive public schools; three-quarters had attended either Oxford or Cambridge. All but one of the eight provincial governors in India in 1938 were Oxonians.[25] John Maynard Keynes, who by the 1920s had become quite disparaging about the empire, experienced one of the few reverses of his dazzling Cambridge career when he came in second rather than first in the ICS examination.[26] Oxbridge products also staffed the less exalted Colonial Service, which administered the British colonies in Africa and other parts of Asia. Of the 927 recruits to the Colonial Service between 1927 and 1929, nearly half had been to Oxford or Cambridge.[27] There were also significant numbers of Oxbridge graduates in the other governmental and private-sector agencies that operated in the colonies.[28]

The key question is why so many products of Britain's top universities were willing to spend their entire working lives so far from the land of their birth, running infernally hot, disease-ridden countries. Consider the typical example of Evan Machonochie, an Oxford graduate who passed the ICS exam, set off for Bengal in 1887 and spent the next forty years in India.[29] One clue lies in his Celtic surname. The Scots were heavily overrepresented not just in the colonies of white settlement but also in the commercial and professional elites of cities like Calcutta and Hong Kong and Cape Town. The Irish too played a disproportionate role in enforcing British rule, supplying a huge proportion of the officers and men of the British army. Not for nothing is Kipling's representative Indian Army NCO named Mulvaney. This was because Scotland (especially the north) and Ireland (especially the south) were significantly poorer than England. For young men growing up on the rainy, barren fringes of the United

Kingdom, the empire offered opportunities. The potential benefits of emigration seemed to outweigh the undoubted risks of the tropics. Like the "porridge traps" that Hong Kong banks were supposed to set in order to recruit their predominantly Scottish clerks, Balliol College functioned as a channel through which ambitious young Scots could pass from "North Britain" via Oxford to the empire.

Yet economics alone cannot explain what motivated a man like Machonochie or, indeed, a female Oxonian like Gertrude Bell. The imperial impulse arose from a complex of emotions: racial superiority, yes, but also evangelical zeal; profit, perhaps, but also a sincere belief that spreading "commerce, Christianity and civilization" was as much in the interests of Britain's colonial subjects as in the interests of the imperial metropole itself.

The contrast with Americans today could scarcely be more stark. To put it bluntly, one of the most serious difficulties the United States currently faces is its chronic manpower deficit. There are simply not enough Americans out there to make nation building work.

At the time of writing, the shortage of military personnel in Iraq was acknowledged by nearly every informed observer outside the Office of the Secretary of Defense. Of the army's thirty-three front-line brigades, sixteen were in Iraq in September 2003; by the end of the year, active duty force levels had been increased by 33,000, and 165,000 members of the National Guard and Reserve had been called up, a substantial number of whom went to Iraq. Even with the support of other countries, however, a total U.S. presence of around 120,000 was not sufficient to impose order on the country.[30] The crisis was such that the administration was forced to swallow its pride and seek foreign reinforcements—even from the very countries that had opposed the war at the outset.[31] This can be seen as a direct consequence of the sustained contraction in the size of the American armed forces since the early 1970s (when the total number of active service personnel peaked at 3 million, compared with under 1.4 million today). True, the United States in 2002 had around the same number of service personnel overseas as the United Kingdom did back in 1881, just over a quarter of a million in each case.[32] But there the resemblance ends. In those days, less than a third of Britain's total armed forces were stationed in the United

Kingdom itself. By contrast, more than four-fifths—82 percent—of Americans on active military duty are based in the United States.[33] Even the B-2 stealth bombers that pounded Serbia into quitting Kosovo in 1999 were flying out of Knob Noster, Missouri. It is also striking that when American service personnel are posted abroad they generally do not stay for very long. The introduction of yearlong tours of duty in Iraq marks a break with the system of minimal overseas stints introduced thirty years ago after Vietnam.

Twelve months, to be sure, are longer than the average duration of a foreign trip by a Wall Street investment banker, which can be measured in days, but it is scarcely long enough to acquire much local knowledge. In any case, it is worth remembering that more than half of America's seventy-three major overseas bases are in Western Europe, and no fewer than twenty-five of them in Germany, near towns like Heidelberg and Kaiserslautern, where living standards are higher than in some American states.[34] Unlike the British, who built barracks in hostile territories precisely in order to subjugate them, the Americans today locate a quarter of their overseas troops in what is one of the most prosperous and arguably one of the most pacifist countries in the world. (Significantly, when the Pentagon detects serious local hostility to one of its overseas outposts, as in the case of Subic Bay in the Philippines, the base is hastily shut down.)

The problem of manpower is not purely military, however. Unlike the United Kingdom a century ago, the United States is an *im*porter of people, with a net immigration rate of 3 per 1,000 and a total foreign-born population of 32 million (nearly 1 in 9 U.S. residents).[35] Moreover, when Americans do opt to reside abroad, they tend to stick to the developed world. There are an estimated 3.8 million Americans currently resident abroad. That sounds like a great many, but it is just one eighth of the number of foreign-born residents of the United States. And of the expatriate Americans, more than three-quarters live in the two next-door countries (1 million in Mexico, 687,000 in Canada) or in Europe (just over 1 million). Of the 290,000 who live in the Middle East, nearly two-thirds are to be found in Israel. A mere 37,500 live in Africa.[36] This, in other words, is an empire without settlers, or rather the settlers come *to* the metropolis rather than leave it for distant lands. How far it is possible to exert power outside a country's borders by drawing foreigners inside those borders is debatable, to say the least. It can be argued that luring foreign elites to study at America's universities is a kind of indirect rule, in the sense that it involves a form of collaboration and cooptation, not to say acculturation, of indigenous elites. Much, however, depends on how long these foreign students stay in the United States. Since quite a large proportion of them never return to their native lands, it is not clear how much influence is in fact thereby exerted.[37]

A further important contrast with the British experience is that the products of America's elite educational institutions seem especially reluctant to go overseas, other than on flying visits and holidays. The Americans who serve the longest tours of duty are the volunteer soldiers, a substantial proportion of whom are African-Americans (12.7 percent of the U.S. population, 28.9 percent of Army enlisted personnel).[38] Hence Timothy Garton Ash's pun on Kipling when he visited Kosovo after the 1999 war: here (as in Vietnam) "the white man's burden" was visibly being borne by a disproportionate number of black men.[39] It is of course just possible that the African-Americans will turn out to be the Celts of the American empire, driven to overseas adventure by comparatively poor opportunities at home, just as the Irish and the Scots were in the nineteenth century. Indeed, if the occupation of Iraq is to be continued for any length of time, it can hardly fail to create career opportunities for the growing number of African-American officers in the army. The Central Command's most effective press spokesman during the war, General Vincent K. Brooks, exemplifies the type.

The British, however, were always wary about giving the military too much power in their imperial administration. Parliamentarians at Westminster had read enough Roman history to want to keep generals subordinate to civilian governors. The "brass hats" were there to inflict the Victorian equivalent of "shock and awe" whenever the natives grew restive; otherwise, colonial government was a matter for Oxbridge-educated mandarins. It would be interesting to know, by way of comparison, how many members of Harvard's or Yale's class of 2004 are seriously considering careers in the postwar administration of Iraq. The number is likely to be small. In 1998–99 there were 43,683 undergraduate course registrations at Yale, of which just 335 (less than 1 percent) were for courses in Near Eastern languages and civilization. There was just one, lone undergraduate majoring in the subject (compared with 17 doing film studies).[40] After graduation too the members of America's academic elite generally subscribe to the Wizard of Oz principle: "There's no place like home." According to a 1998 survey, there are currently 134,798 registered Yale alumni. Of these, little more than 5 percent live outside the United States. Scarcely any, just over 50, live in Arab countries.[41] At Oxford and Cambridge a hundred years ago ambitious students dreamed of passing the ICS exam and embarking on careers as imperial proconsuls. Today the elite products of the Ivy League set their sights on law school or business school; their dream is by definition an American dream. This, then, is not only an empire without settlers, but also an empire without administrators. Though he himself was an experienced diplomat whose past postings ranged from Afghanistan to Malawi, L. Paul Bremer and his staff were manifestly short of Middle Eastern expertise. It is a sobering statistic that just 3 of his initial team of officials were fluent in Arabic.[42]

It may be that the bolder products of Harvard's Kennedy School are eager to advise the Iraqi Governing Council on its constitutional options. And a few of the country's star economists may yearn to do for Iraq what they did for post–Soviet Russia back in the early 1990s. But we may be fairly certain that their engagement will take the form of a series of week-long trips rather than long-term residence: consultancy, not colonization. As far as the Ivy League nation builders are concerned, you can set up an independent central bank, reform the tax code, liberalize prices and privatize the major utilities—and be home in time for your first class reunion.

It can of course be argued that the American tendency to pay flying visits to their putative *imperium*—rather than settle there—is just a function of technology. Back in the 1870s, by which time the British had largely completed their global network of railways and steamships, it still took a minimum of eighty days to circumnavigate the world, as Jules Verne celebrated in the story of Phileas Fogg. Today it can be done in less than three. The problem is that along with the undoubted advantages of modern technology comes the disadvantage of disconnection. During the diplomatic crisis over Iraq in early 2003, Secretary of State Colin Powell was criticized for conducting his foreign policy by telephone. Powell retorted that he had traveled abroad twice that year already, but the destinations and durations of these trips were revealing: one was to Davos, Switzerland, for the World

Economic Forum (January 25–26) and the other was to the Far East (February 21–25).[43] We can only guess at what these trips achieved—and what Secretary Powell might have achieved if instead he had paid visits to Paris and Ankara.

It is not just the most senior American officials who prefer the comforts of sweet home. Shortly before the terrorist attacks of September 2001, a former CIA man admitted that the agency "probably doesn't have a single truly qualified Arabic-speaking officer of Middle Eastern background who can play a believable Muslim fundamentalist who would volunteer to spend years of his life with shitty food and no women in the mountains of Afghanistan." "For Christ's sake," he went on, "most case officers live in the suburbs of Virginia. We don't do that kind of thing." In the immortal words of one such case officer, "Operations that include diarrhea as a way of life don't happen."[44] This was precisely the attitude that another CIA officer sought to counter in the wake of the terrorist attacks when he hung a sign outside his office that read as follows: "Officers wanted for hazardous journey. Small wages. Bitter cold. Long months of complete darkness. Constant danger. Safe return doubtful. Honour and recognition in case of success." Significantly, this was the recruiting poster used by the British explorer Ernest Shackleton before his 1914 expedition to the Antarctic.[45] At the time of the invasion of Iraq, the short-lived Office for Reconstruction and Humanitarian Assistance also sought British imperial inspiration: it relied on retired British army Gurkhas from Nepal to provide the security around its Kuwait base.[46]

What, then, about the much-vaunted role of the voluntary sector, the governmental and nongovernmental aid agencies? Might they provide the Americans on the ground who are so conspicuously hard to find in government service? The institution that, since the 1960s, has done most to channel the idealism of young Americans into what we now call nation building is of course the Peace Corps. Since 1961 more than 168,000 Americans have joined it, serving in a variety of civilian capacities in no fewer than 136 countries. Today there are some 6,678 Peace Corps volunteers, an improvement on the low point of 5,380 in 1982, and they can be found in 69 countries.[47] The Peace Corps certainly attracts the right type of person: among the universities that have sent the most volunteers are Berkeley and Harvard;

disproportionate numbers also come from the exclusive liberal arts colleges like Dartmouth, Tufts and Middlebury.[48] Yet the total number of volunteers remains just two-thirds of the target of 10,000 set by Congress in 1985, a target that was supposed to be attained by 1992.

We should not, in any case, pin too much hope on agencies like the Peace Corps. Civilian aid agencies can, like the missionaries of old, be as much an irritant as a help to those trying to run a country like Iraq. It is one of the unspoken truths of the new "imperialism of human rights" that around every international crisis there soon swarms a cloud of aid workers, whose efforts are not always entirely complementary. If the United States successfully imposes law and order in Iraq, economic life will swiftly revive and much aid will simply be superfluous. If it fails to impose order, on the other hand, aid workers will simply get themselves killed.

After Kipling, John Buchan was perhaps the most readable writer produced by British imperialism. In his thriller *Greenmantle* (1916) he memorably personifies imperial Britain in the person of Sandy Arbuthnot, an Orientalist so wily that he can pass for a Moroccan in Mecca or a Pathan in Peshawar. Arbuthnot's antithesis is the dyspeptic American millionaire John Scantlebury Blenkiron, "a big fellow with a fat, sallow, clean-shaven face [with] a pair of fully sleepy eyes, like a ruminating ox." "These eyes have seen nothing gorier than a Presidential election," he tells Buchan's hero, Richard Hannay. The symbolism is a little crude, but it has something to it.

Since September 2001 the Blenkirons have certainly been seeing something gorier than an election. But will it whet their appetites for an empire in the British mode? Only, it would seem, if Americans radically rethink their attitude to the world beyond their borders. Until there are more U.S. citizens not just willing but eager to shoulder the "nation builder's burden," ventures like the occupation of Iraq will lack a vital ingredient. For the lesson of Britain's imperial experience is clear: you simply cannot have an empire without imperialists—out there, on the spot—to run it.

Could Blenkiron somehow mutate into Arbuthnot? Could the United States work out how to produce men like John Buchan himself, whose career led him from the obscurity of a Scottish manse, by way of Oxford, to the post of Governor-General of Canada? Perhaps. After all, it has happened before. In the years after the Second World War the generation that had just missed out on fighting left Harvard and Yale with something like Buchan's zeal for global rule. Many of them joined the Central Intelligence Agency and devoted their lives to fighting communism in far-flung lands from Cuba to Cambodia. Yet as Graham Greene foresaw in *The Quiet American,* their efforts at what the British would have called indirect rule were vitiated by the low quality of the local potentates they backed and constrained by the need to shore them up more or less covertly. Today the same fiction that underpinned American strategy in Vietnam—that America was not attempting to resurrect French colonial rule in Indochina—is being peddled in Washington to rationalize what is going on in Iraq. It may look like the resurrection of British colonial rule. But all Americans want to do is give the Iraqi people democracy and then go home.

THE INCENTIVE TO COLLABORATE

It is perhaps inherent in the nature of a democratic empire that it should operate with a short time horizon. The constraints imposed on the executive by the election cycle are tight, and there is strong evidence from previous conflicts—not only Korea but Vietnam—of a negative correlation between the level of American casualties and the popularity of an executive at war. There are those who insist that the Vietnam syndrome was finally "kicked" in the 1990s. In reality, however, the sensitivity of the American electorate to casualties seems to have grown more acute since the cold war. Between April and October 2003, there was a 29 percent drop in the popularity of the war in Iraq, yet only a little over 350 U.S. service personnel lost their lives in that period, only two-thirds of whom were killed as a result of hostile action (see figure 11). Compare that with Vietnam, where it took around three years and more than thirty thousand "killed in action" to reduce popular support for the war by a comparable amount. Small wonder American politicians have a tendency to start looking for an exit some time before the drama has been concluded.

Unfortunately, there is a fatal flaw to the project of short-term nation building, and that is the extreme difficulty of securing local support when an American pledge to depart imminently has been announced and—more important—is believed by the inhabitants of the occupied country in question. Perhaps more than anything else, the British Empire was an empire based on local collaboration; how else could fewer than a thousand ICS men have governed a population of four hundred million Indians? But why should any Iraqi have risked collaborating with a fly-by-night occupier like L. Paul Bremer? No sooner had he created a Governing Council for Iraq than he began talking of packing his bags. What is especially striking is that this desire for an American withdrawal was not at first shared by a majority of the Iraqi population. In a poll conducted in Baghdad in July 2003, people were asked: "Right now, would you prefer to see the U.S. (and Britain) stay in Iraq or pull out?" Only 13 percent favored immediate withdrawal. Nearly a third—31 percent—answered that the coalition "should stay for a few years"; a further 25 percent said "for about a year."[49]

FIGURE 11

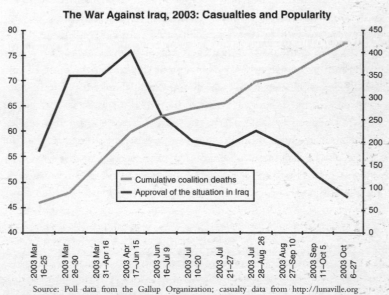

The War Against Iraq, 2003: Casualties and Popularity

Source: Poll data from the Gallup Organization; casualty data from http://lunaville.org /warcasualties/ Summary.aspx.

This brings us to a critical point. It is simply that the time frame is the key to successful nation building.[50] It is no coincidence that the countries where American military intervention has been most successful have been those in which the United States has maintained a prolonged military presence. As we have seen, President Bush is fond of citing Japan and West Germany after 1945 as examples of what successful American intervention can achieve. "America has made and kept this kind of commitment before," he argued in February 2003, drawing an implicit parallel with 1945. "After defeating enemies we did not leave behind occupying armies, we left constitutions and parliaments."[51] This overlooks the awkward fact that the formal occupation regimes lasted seven years in the Japanese case and ten in the West German, and that—even to this day—the deployments of American troops in those two countries remain among the largest anywhere in the world. It is also worth remembering a third success story, South Korea, which took until the late 1980s to become a genuine democracy, after nearly forty years of an American military presence.[52] By contrast, relatively little good, and probably a good deal of ill, came of the numerous short-term American interventions in Central America and the Caribbean, which began in 1898. Unfortunately, the time frames contemplated for Iraq (not to mention Afghanistan) are closer to these dismal episodes than to the post-1945 success stories. Baghdad simply cannot be turned into the capital of a Western-style democracy in the space of two years. The goal in itself is not wholly unrealistic, despite the very obvious social and cultural differences between Iraq in 2003 and West Germany in 1945.* In September 2003 nearly two-fifths (39 percent) of those polled by Gallup in Baghdad picked multiparty parliamentary democracy as the form of government they would most like to see established in Iraq. Slightly more—42 percent—thought this was the system their country was most likely to have in five years' time. However, more than half—51 percent—

---

*The conventional wisdom has it that democratization was bound to succeed in postwar Germany because German society was highly advanced and homogeneous and there was a clear memory of how democracy worked from the 1920s. Such comparisons overlook the extent to which the Third Reich had revolutionized German political culture with one of the most extreme *ideologies* in all history. Hitler's Germany was a rogue regime far more dangerous than Saddam Hussein's Iraq. Only with the benefit of hindsight does its transformation into a stable Western democracy look easy.

believed the outcome would be the result of direct American influence.[53] That seems to suggest that many Iraqis expected the Americans to stay longer than the Americans themselves were planning to and that they anticipated political benefits from an ongoing American presence. Unfortunately, if the United States does walk away from Iraq in the course of 2005, those Iraqi hopes will almost certainly be dashed. Premature elections, held before order has been restored and economic life resumed, would almost certainly fail to produce a stable government. They would be much more likely to accentuate the ethnic and religious divisions within Iraqi society.[54]

Is there any way to reconcile the American impulse to get home fast and the manifest need for long-term commitment in Iraq if nation building is to work? Again, there is something to be learned in this regard from the British experience, though the place to look for a lesson is not Iraq but Egypt. Iraq was, after all, a relatively late addition to the British Empire, more or less run on a shoestring. The British never quite had their hearts in the matter, and financial constraints would have checked them even if they had. Egypt was another story. It was acquired in the 1880s at the very height of Britain's economic and strategic power. It was run until the Second World War as the very model of what a liberal empire could do. Yet from the outset the British publicly insisted that Egypt was being run not by them but by the Egyptians.

The resemblances between Britain's occupation of Egypt 121 years ago and America's current occupation of Iraq are indeed uncannily close. There is also an obvious lesson the Bush administration might learn from the earlier case. There is in fact a great deal to be said for promising to leave—provided you do not actually mean it or do it.

In 1882 a nationalist army officer named Said Ahmed Arabi seized power in Egypt, overthrowing the pro-British khedive Tewfik. First the differences. Arabi was no Saddam, and the pretext for foreign intervention was not the same: violence against European residents in Alexandria, as opposed to noncompliance with international calls for disarmament. However, the deeper causes and consequences of intervention strikingly prefigure today's imbroglio in Iraq. For a start, the newly elected British government had pledged during the 1879 election campaign *not* to behave in an imperialistic way. The Liberal leader, William Ewart Gladstone, had expressly condemned his archrival, Benjamin Disraeli, for meddling in Egyptian affairs. "Our first site in Egypt," Gladstone had warned, "be it by larceny or be it by emption, will be the almost certain egg of a North African Empire, that will grow and grow until . . . we finally join hands across the Equator with Natal and Cape Town. . . ."[55] In the third of his famous speeches to the voters of Midlothian, Gladstone had set out his six principles of Liberal foreign policy. They included the preservation of peace, good relations with the other European powers, the avoidance of needless overseas entanglements, equal rights for all nations and "the love of freedom." It was hardly a manifesto for unilateral imperialist intervention. Indeed, as late as January 1882, Gladstone was still arguing that "Egypt for the Egyptians" would be "the best, the only solution of the 'Egyptian question.'"[56] He never ceased to hope for "real movement towards institutions & local self-government" in Egypt.[57]

Secondly, however, Britain had substantial economic interests in the country. What the oil in Iraq is today, so the Suez Canal was then. More than 80 percent of the traffic going through the canal was British—indeed, 13 percent of Britain's entire trade went through the canal—and in 1876 Britain had acquired a substantial shareholding in the canal company itself. Moreover, the Egyptian economy had emerged during the American Civil War as an alternative source for the raw cotton insatiably consumed by Britain's textile industry. As if that were not enough, a substantial chunk of the Egyptian external debt was held by British bondholders, including the new prime minister himself. Today's liberal commentators fret about the links between the Bush administration and oil companies like Halliburton. But Halliburton's share price declined by a third in the three years after former chief executive Dick Cheney became vice president, whereas Gladstone's substantial investments in Egyptian loans soared in value—by over 40 percent—as a direct result of his decision to invade the country. Had this fact become known at the time, it is hard to say what the effect would have been on Gladstone's reputation for sea-green incorruptibility. Even without it, there was widespread suspicion that the government's motives were at least partly mercenary; one critic detected the hand of financial interests "whose only wish is to convert Egypt into a coupon-paying machine directed by European controllers and administered solely for European Employées."[58]

A third factor was the expectation that any resolution of the crisis would need to involve the French, who were also substantial holders of Egyptian bonds and canal shares, and who had indeed been responsible for the construction of the canal itself. Since the Egyptian debt default of 1876, the country's finances had been under a joint Anglo-French control commission. Gladstone's immediate response to the crisis was to continue with this cross-Channel partnership. There was a widespread belief that decisions governing what was then known as the Near East should be settled among all the five great powers—Britain, France, Germany, Austria and Russia—with Turkey (which still exercised formal suzerainty over Egypt) bullied as much as consulted. To repeat, the regular great power conferences were the Victorian equivalent of the United Nations Security Council today, and in the 1880s they were about as productive. Gladstone, good internationalist that he was, tried to secure foreign backing for military action against Egypt, just as George W. Bush sought explicit authorization from the UN for his action against Iraq. In both cases, the failure to achieve this, followed by the decision to act anyway, strained great power relations, and especially relations with France. Gladstone kept insisting that he had been a "labourer in the cause of peace" and that Egypt had been "neutralized by European act."[59] The French just sneered, while the Germans gloated. A fourth resemblance is that as in Iraq today, there was at least some popular opposition to a foreign occupation. As that arch-cynic Lord Salisbury shrewdly put it, "The Musselman feeling is still so strong that I believe we shall be safer and more powerful as wire-pullers than as ostensible rulers."[60] Egyptian resentment never went away.

Just as happened in 2003 over Iraq, the public at home was at first delighted by the swiftness of the military victory that ensued after the order was given to invade Egypt. At Tel el Kebir Sir Garnet Wolseley smashed Arabi's army in a matter of hours and with minimal British casualties (fifty-four British dead, as against at least two thousand on the other side).[61] This was the kind of victory the nascent popular press adored; indeed, even the high-minded Mr. Gladstone was infected by the euphoric mood. "We and the whole country are in a state of rejoicing," he wrote

shortly after Wolseley's victory, "We certainly ought to be in a good hu-
mour, for we are pleased with our army, our navy, our admirals, our generals & our organization."[62] One noteworthy difference is that this mood
lasted much longer than the comparable mood in the United States in
2003. Indeed, British newspaper readers soon became enthused by the
prospect of extending British rule to neighboring Sudan too, especially
when a radical Islamic revolt erupted there under the leadership of the
charismatic Mahdi.

Finally, there was the Egyptian economy. It swiftly became clear to the
British administrators charged with the task that Egypt's finances could be
stabilized only with sweeping reforms, but that these would be possible
only if there were an ongoing British military presence. In the supremely
condescending words of Evelyn Baring, the all-powerful British agent and
consul-general in Egypt from 1883 to 1907, "We need not always enquire
too closely what these people . . . themselves think is in their own interests. . . . It is essential that each special issue should be decided mainly with
reference to what, by the light of Western knowledge and experience . . .
we conscientiously think is best for the subject race."[63] As Gladstone put it
in his diary, the challenge was "how to plant solidly western & beneficent
institutions in the soil of a Mohamedan community?"[64] It clearly could
not be done overnight.

To recapitulate, then: a government reluctant to be labeled "imperialist," compelling economic reasons for intervention, a failure to arrive at a
multilateral solution, indigenous resistance to occupation, popular support
for it at home and technocratic reasons to maintain a military presence for
an unspecified period. The net result offers an intriguing template for the
United States in Iraq.

Having occupied Egypt, the British almost immediately began promising to leave. "Should the Khedive desire it," declared Gladstone, "a small
British force may remain in Egypt, at the charge of that country, until his
authority is solidly established & placed beyond risk."[65] But shortly after
that there appeared, in the words of Gladstone's biographer, "the first of
what were to be at least sixty-six protestations of the temporary nature of
the British presence in Egypt."[66] As early as August 1883 Gladstone himself had already made no fewer than five public pledges to leave Egypt.[67]
However, all attempts to agree a departure date with the other powers

foundered. With the outbreak of the First World War, the British felt em-
boldened to convert their "veiled Protectorate" into a real one. But in
1922 they formally declared Egypt independent, and in 1936 they pronounced their military occupation at an end. The only *caveat* was that the
British troops did not actually leave. As late as October 1954, eighteen years
after the occupation had supposedly ended, there were still eighty thousand British troops in the canal zone, a huge military base covering an area
the size of Massachusetts. It was not until June 1956 that they were finally
compelled—seventy-four years after the original invasion and largely as a
result of economic weakness at home—to honor their multiple pledges to
go. Even then, as we have seen, they made a desperate last-ditch attempt
to return after Nasser nationalized the canal. In short, from 1882 until the
Suez crisis—as Lord Salisbury had said almost from the occupation's outset—the independence of Egypt had been a "screaming farce."[68]

Is this, then, how American policy should be conducted in Iraq: sixty-
six promises to leave and seventy-two years of occupation? One way of
answering that question is to ask how well the British project for Egyptian
economic reform went. That, after all, was the primary rationale for the
original occupation. In many ways, there was a very modern quality to
what happened. The British administration of Egyptian finances had
much in common with an International Monetary Fund mission—or
rather the way an IMF mission would operate if it could call on the Royal
Navy to enforce its prescriptions. Evelyn Baring, later Lord Cromer, ran
Egypt's finances much like a modern structural adjustment program. The
results were a fiscal triumph. When the British took over Egyptian finances, debt service was consuming two-thirds of all tax revenue.[69] Indeed, crippling taxation and cuts in the army's budget had been among the
principal causes of Arabi's nationalist coup. By 1885, however, a debt
rescheduling agreement had been reached with the foreign bondholders
that gave the Egyptian economy a two-year breathing space and a new, internationally guaranteed loan of £9 million. By 1892 the debt crisis was
over, and in the subsequent two decades the ratio of debt to revenue was
halved, from 10:1 to 5:1.[70]

Fiscal reform paved the way for new foreign lending from British and
other European investors (who reaped the benefits of the British occupation while publicly decrying it). Total capital flows from the London mar-

ket to Egypt amounted to £40 million.[71] And precisely because it was under British rule, and therefore guaranteed not to default, Egypt could borrow abroad at roughly half the rate of interest it had previously needed to pay. New loans helped to finance substantial investments in the country's infrastructure, notably the first Aswan Dam, built between 1902 and 1906, which stored summer floodwater and then released it, doubling or tripling the crops peasant farmers could produce.[72] Between 1886 and 1953 the area under cultivation expanded by nearly half. The railway network grew in size by a factor of four. Egypt's trade expanded rapidly until the onset of the Great Depression and again during and after the Second World War. Egypt's peasants benefited directly not only from better infrastructure but also from lower taxation and access to affordable credit. The proportion of the population attending schools also quadrupled. All this was achieved by a combination of "English heads and Egyptian hands," as the British liked to say. The number of the former was remarkably small; there were just 662 British officials in Egypt in 1906.[73]

Yet there was a catch. So far as it can be estimated, Egyptian *per capita* gross domestic product stagnated between 1913 and 1950.[74] Why? As was true in British India during the same period, economic advances were largely negated by the extraordinary growth in population, which nearly doubled between 1882 and 1917 and grew by half again in the succeeding thirty years. Matters were not helped by the vulnerability of the economy's principal export, cotton, to the vagaries of global demand. In short, though Egypt got richer as a country, the average Egyptian did not. Indeed, there was no improvement whatever in the shockingly poor state of public health. Between 1917 and 1934 infant mortality actually rose.

What should Americans conclude from all this? The first thing is that it is possible to occupy a country for decades, while consistently denying that you have any intention of doing so. This is known as hypocrisy, and it is something to which liberal empires must sometimes resort. But the second thing is that running Iraq—trying to make it conform to Western institutional ideals—could prove to be a frustrating business, yielding only meager returns. In many ways, Cromer and his successors got both the policies and the institutions right. Indeed, some development economists today would give them close to full marks: they rescheduled the debt, balanced the budget, reformed the tax system, stabilized the currency, attracted new foreign investment in infrastructure, reduced corruption, enforced the rule of law and improved education. Yet the economic results were less than spectacular. And the Egyptian elites never ceased to resent British rule. Indeed, a modern nationalist movement, the Wafd, was well established before the First World War.

Is that an argument against trying the same tactics today in Iraq? No. Egypt may not have experienced a *Wirtschaftswunder* under British rule. But nor did it experience an economic disaster, which the fiscal irresponsibility of successive Egyptian rulers might well have caused. The question we need to ask is what Egyptian incomes would have been in the absence of British-guaranteed foreign investment. More important, perhaps, Egypt proved an invaluable strategic asset during the two world wars. It was from Egypt that the British were able to wage war on the pro-German Ottoman Empire during World War I. It was from Libya into Egypt that first the Italians and then the Germans marched in their bid to secure the southern Mediterranean in World War II. With good cause, historians regard the British victory at the second battle of El Alamein, just fifty miles west of Alexandria, as one of the turning points of the war against the Axis. For similar strategic reasons, the United States simply cannot afford to walk away from post-Saddam Iraq; the last thing it needs is another Iran, an oil-rich country governed by Islamic fundamentalists, or a Middle Eastern version of Yugoslavia, descending into internecine war. No matter how much foreign critics and American voters may pine for an early American exit, in truth the only credible option is to hang on and try to make a success of economic and institutional reform.

Let us therefore be specific about what can be learned from Britain's experience in Egypt. First, there must be limits on how much power can be entrusted to the interim Iraqi government, to say nothing of any elected National Assembly. Control of the country's military, fiscal and monetary policies needs to remain, at least for the foreseeable future, partly in American hands. This will not be easy. Repeatedly, during their time in Egypt, the British had to resist the efforts of the country's nominal rulers to go it alone. In 1884, 1888, 1891 and again in 1919 the British effectively sacked recalcitrant Egyptian ministers. In both world wars they had to use force to get their way, deposing the khedive in 1914 and surrounding the palace of his successor with tanks in 1942. Anti-British forces fought back.

In 1924 the British-appointed commander of the Egyptian army, Sir Lee Stack, was assassinated.

Secondly, the United States needs to commit significant sums to the postwar reconstruction of the Iraqi economy, just as the City of London helped stabilize Egyptian finances in the 1880s. In the medium term, Iraq can hope to attract foreign investment and to finance some of its own recovery from exploiting its oil reserves. But confidence needs to be kindled; Iraq needs something equivalent to the big loans floated by the Rothschild bank in the 1880s and 1890s that were used to stabilize Egyptian finances. The trouble is that Iraq's existing foreign debts are daunting: $120 billion to foreign governments, multilateral lenders and commercial banks, to say nothing of up to $125 billion in reparations claims arising from Saddam's wars of aggression. This is why the International Monetary Fund, the modern equivalent of the Rothschilds, needs to be involved, and soon, in overhauling Iraq's finances.[75] Without substantial debt forgiveness, the country's economy will be crippled.

But the third and most important lesson is a diplomatic one. Like Gladstone, Bush was not so giddy with military success as to disregard international opinion about Iraq's future. Just as Gladstone sought to reach agreement with France and Germany about the timing of Britain's withdrawal from Egypt, so Bush returned to the United Nations to secure a lifting of the sanctions on Iraq and to offer the UN a limited role in postwar reconstruction—not least to take on some of the unglamorous work of peacekeeping that the American military so dislikes. Like Gladstone, Bush needed to give his foreign protectorate at least a semblance of international legitimacy, especially if he wanted the assistance of foreign troops. In the real world of international relations, as the Victorians knew better than some modern analysts of American foreign policy, there is no straight choice between unilaterism and multilateralism. Even after they had invaded Egypt, the British could not disentangle themselves from the interests of the other European powers. The French continued to be represented on the Caisse de la Dette Publique, set up to administer Egyptian finances after the 1876 default. Up until 1914 Egypt still owed formal allegiance to Ottoman Turkey, which came increasingly under German influence. In the same way, the future of Iraq simply cannot be decided without the involvement of the European powers today, and that would be true even if the United States were willing to shoulder all the costs of peacekeeping. For these reasons, President Bush and other U.S. officials have no real option but to keep on promising the imminent withdrawal of U.S. troops from Iraq. Still, as the British showed in Egypt, it is possible to make a great many promises to leave a country, over quite a long period of time, without actually having to go.

Benjamin Disraeli once called a conservative government "an organized hypocrisy." Perhaps the best thing we can hope for is that the same will one day be said of "liberated" Iraq. A formal return to Iraqi self-government clearly had to be announced in 2004. But there also needed to be continuing limitations on the country's sovereignty in order to ensure economic recovery, internal political stability and the future security of those countries Iraq once menaced.[76] Ambassador Negroponte must be prepared to be Iraq's Lord Cromer, viceroy in all but name for decades. And if no American wants the job after 2005, we may be reasonably sure that under the right terms and conditions a European will volunteer.

In an important but underreported speech he gave in June 2003, the former leader of the British Liberal Democrat Party, Paddy Ashdown, reflected on the "principles of peacemaking" he had learned in his capacity as high representative in Bosnia and Herzegovina (a post created by the Dayton peace accords). His seven principles were as follows:

1. [To have] a good plan and stick to it. This plan needs to be drawn up, not as an after-thought, but well in advance, as an integral part of the planning for the military campaign.
2. [To] establish the rule of law—and do so as quickly as possible. . . . It is much more important to establish the rule of law quickly than to establish democracy quickly. Because without the former, the latter is soon undermined.
3. [To] establish your credibility straight away. The more robustly a peacekeeping force deals with any initial challenges to its authority, the fewer challenges there will be in the future.
4. To start as quickly as possible on the major structural reforms—from putting in place a customs service or reliable tax base, to reforming the police and the civil service, to restructuring and screening the judiciary, to transforming the armed forces.

5. [To ensure] that the international community organizes itself in [the] theatre in a manner that can work and take decisions.

6. [To establish] an exceptionally close relationship between the military and civilian aspects of peace implementation.

7. [To] avoid setting deadlines, and settle in for the long haul. . . . Installing the software of a free and open society is a slow business. It cannot be done . . . in a year or so. . . . Peace-keeping needs to be measured not in months but decades. What we need here . . . is "sticktoitiveness" . . . the political will, the unity of purpose, and the sheer stamina as an international community to see the job through to lasting success. That means staying on, and sticking at it, long after the CNN effect has passed.[77]

There is wisdom in all seven of Ashdown's principles, above all the last one. It is nevertheless significant that such sentiments could be expressed more easily by a Briton running an international protectorate in a European country than by an American running a provisional authority in a Middle Eastern one. No less noteworthy was Ashdown's eighth and final principle:

8. [To give] peace-building . . . a political destination. For Iraq, that may be a democratic and prosperous state in a peaceful and secure Middle East. For Bosnia, it is Europe.

It is time now to consider just how plausible a "political destination" Europe actually is, not just for Bosnia but also for all the actual and potential members of the European Union. For if any counterweight currently exists in the world to the power of the United States, it is the European Union.

CHAPTER 7

"IMPIRE": EUROPE BETWEEN BRUSSELS AND BYZANTIUM

A EUROPEAN DREAM NOW BECOMES REALITY.
International Herald Tribune headline, 2001

COUNTERWEIGHT?

There is a plausible role for the European Union as the partner of an American empire: the peacekeeper that follows in the wake of the peacemaker. The war in Iraq, however, raised the possibility of a diametrically different role for Europe: as a potential imperial rival to the United States. This is a role that Europe's political leaders would much prefer to play. The French president Jacques Chirac is said by a former adviser to want "a multipolar world in which Europe is the counterweight to American political and military power." The former German chancellor Helmut Schmidt has declared that his country and France "share a common interest in not delivering ourselves into the hegemony of our mighty ally, the United States."[1] In a speech in October 2002, the EU commissioner for external affairs Chris Patten explicitly called for Europe to become "a serious player . . . a serious counterweight and counterpart to the United States."[2] And the Italian prime minister Silvio Berlusconi declared on the eve of taking over the EU presidency in July 2003 that "Europe will only be able to look at the United States as something other than a subordinate if it becomes a great Europe."[3] Even that most subtle of British commentators Timothy Garton Ash has lately found himself yearning for a more globally assertive Europe. "America," he argued in the *New York Times* in April 2002, "has too much power for anyone's good, including its own."[4]

In economic terms, China may conceivably catch up with the United States at some point in the next forty years. But for the present only the European Union comes close to matching U.S. output. The solution— presumably for everyone's good, but certainly for Europe's—must therefore be for the EU to become more politically powerful, to punch its economic weight. Such sentiments have been expressed with increasing frequency since the Anglo-American invasion of Iraq.

In the eyes of many commentators, that was precisely the aim of the new Treaty Establishing the Constitution of the European Union, drafted by the former French president Valéry Giscard d'Estaing's European Convention and submitted in June 2003 to the European Council in Thessaloniki. Consider what the treaty has to say on the subject of Europe's military power. Article I-11, clause 4, explicitly declares: "The Union shall have competence to define and implement a common foreign and security policy, including the progressive framing of a common defense policy." Article I-40, clause 3, states "that Member States shall make civilian and military capabilities available to the Union for the implementation of the common security and defense policy" and that they shall also "undertake progressively to improve their military capabilities."[5] While British Euroskeptics have focused, predictably, on the cryptofederalist aspects of the draft treaty, some American commentators have seen it as the latest manifestation of Europe's "anti-American" tendency. "There is only one rationale for such a proposal at this time," according to the journalist Andrew Sullivan, and that is "to check U.S. power." When Giscard d'Estaing himself says that he wants the EU to be "respected and listened to as a political power that will speak as an equal with the largest powers on the planet," that does seem a plausible inference.[6]

Of course, this kind of talk elicits nothing more than derision in some quarters. In his popular polemic on the subject, Robert Kagan has heaped scorn on the "relative weakness" of Europeans, in contrast to the martial vigor of Americans. "Europe's military weakness," Kagan argues, "has produced a perfectly understandable aversion to the exercise of military power. Indeed, it has produced a powerful European interest in inhabiting a world where strength doesn't matter. . . . [But] Europe's rejection of power politics, [and] its devaluing of military force as a tool of international relations, have depended on the presence of American military forces on European soil."[7] One could in fact go further than Kagan. It is not just the searing experiences of two world wars that have turned Europeans from Mars to Venus. It is also the fact that in relative terms their continent is much less important than it was in the nineteenth century. Its share of world population is half what it was in 1820. Its share of world output is down to a fifth, compared with over a third in 1870. And this relative decline seems almost certain to continue in the foreseeable future. To many Americans, Europe's principal significance these days is not as a strategic rival but as a tourist destination.[8]

Yet Kagan's insistence on Europe's weakness remains something of a minority view in the American academy. A substantial number of commentators have followed the lead of Samuel Huntington in seeing European integration as "the single most important move" away from the "unipolar" world of the post–cold war hiatus toward a "truly multipolar" twenty-first century.[9] Charles Kupchan predicts that "Europe will soon catch up with America . . . because it is coming together, amassing the impressive resources and intellectual capital already possessed by its constituent states. Europe's political union is in the midst of altering the global landscape." According to Kupchan, "a collective Europe" is "next in line" to challenge American power.[10] Drawing an intriguing analogy with the ancient world, he portrays the EU as "an emerging pole, dividing the West into American and European halves."[11]

The EU as the new Byzantium? Kupchan's views are less idiosyncratic than they seem at first sight. Classical analogies have also inspired the British diplomat Robert Cooper to call for "a new kind of imperialism, one acceptable to a world of human rights and cosmopolitan values . . . an imperialism which, like all imperialism, aims to bring order and organization but which rests today on the voluntary principle." Significantly, Cooper sees not the United States but the European Union as the institution best able to become such a postmodern *imperium*:

The postmodern E.U. offers a vision of cooperative empire, a common liberty and a common security without the ethnic domination and centralized absolutism to which past empires have been subject, but also without the ethnic exclusiveness that is the hallmark of the nation state. . . . A cooperative empire might be . . . a framework in which each has a share in the government, in which no single country dominates and in which the governing principles are not ethnic but legal. The lightest of touches will be required from the centre; the "imperial bureaucracy" must be under control, accountable, and the servant, not the master, of the commonwealth. Such an institution must be as dedicated to liberty and democracy as its constituent parts. Like Rome, this commonwealth would provide its citizens with some of its laws, some coins and the occasional road.[12]

There is, however, no need to invoke the memory of either Rome or Byzantium to make the case that Europe is capable of spoiling America's unipolar party. Joseph Nye too sees Europe as already America's equal in the economic sphere, where "the United States is not a hegemon, and must often bargain as an equal with Europe."[13] Though more perturbed by the rise of China, John Mearsheimer is also concerned by the two possible challenges to American power that he expects to emanate from Europe: "Either the U.S. will leave Europe . . . because it does not have to contain an emerging peer competitor, in which case the region becomes less stable, or the U.S. will stay engaged to contain a formidable rival in what is likely to be a dangerous situation."[14] The historian Paul Kennedy has added his voice to the chorus, emphasizing the demographic significance of European consolidation and enlargement. "Even now," he wrote on the first anniversary of the terrorist attacks of September 2001, "[Europe] has a substantially larger population than has the United States . . . and a roughly similar or perhaps slightly higher share of total world product. With plans to add more members, and with the use of the euro deepening, here is a trend that clearly knows of no September 11 watershed."[15] The successful conclusion of accession agreements with ten new member countries—not to mention the sustained appreciation of the euro against the dollar since Kennedy's article appeared—has seemingly vindicated this analysis. So too, in the eyes of some commentators, has the vociferous and not wholly ineffectual opposition of at least some EU member states to American policy in Iraq. If the United States has an imperial rival today, then the European Union appears to be it.

PRO

In what ways does the European Union genuinely represent a counter-weight—let us avoid the overblown word *threat*—to the United States?

DEMOGRAPHY

As Kennedy rightly says, the population of the European Union is already more than a quarter larger than that of the United States. One effect of the enlargement of the union in 2004 has been to widen the demographic gap still further, increasing the EU's population to just under 450 million, more than one and a half times that of the United States.

OUTPUT

In terms of total economic output, the European Union is indeed not far behind the United States, depending on which measure is used. According to the World Bank, the combined gross domestic product of the fifteen preenlargement EU member states in 2002 was $8.6 trillion, compared with a figure of $10.4 trillion for the United States. In other words, the European economy was about 82 percent the size of the American. Adjusting on the basis of purchasing power parity reduces the gap somewhat—on that basis EU output is still nearly 6 percent less—but it does not eliminate it. Only when output is measured in constant prices (expressed in 1995 dollars) can European GDP be said to be higher.[16] The ten countries who joined the EU in 2004 did not significantly add to its combined output.[17] The GDP of the EU-25 is also bigger than that of the "U.S.-50" on the basis of purchasing power parity, though it is still around 15 percent smaller in current dollar terms.

PRODUCTIVITY

The West European economies have spent most of the past half century rapidly catching up with the United States when performance is measured in terms of productivity. In 1950 gross domestic product per hour worked in the United States was three times what it was in Germany; today German productivity is just 23 percent lower, while French productivity is a trifling 2 percent less than American. Between 1973 and 1998 U.S. productivity grew at an average annual rate of just 1.5 percent, compared with a French rate of growth of 2.4 percent.[18]

TRADE

The United States has large deficits on its external accounts, whether one considers just "visible" trade or the current account in its entirety. The same cannot be said of the European Union. Not only does the EU account for a slightly larger share of total world exports (20 percent compared with 18 percent), it also runs a small trade surplus.[19] There is no question that in trade negotiations, the United States must treat the European Union as an equal. Nor is the EU as dependent on inflows of foreign capital as the United States (a point to be examined more closely in the next chapter). It is in fact a net exporter of capital.

THE SINGLE CURRENCY

To an extent that is not widely appreciated, the European Economic and Monetary Union has transformed the international capital market. The volume of government bonds denominated in European currencies was very large even before the single currency was introduced; in 1998 the outstanding volume of Eurozone government bonds was roughly half the outstanding volume of U.S. government bonds.[20] However, as the rapid convergence of Eurozone bond yields shows, monetary union has greatly reduced what investors call country risk, so that all Eurozone members' bonds are now regarded as being (almost) as good as the old German bunds. The EMU has significantly boosted the market for European securities. According to the Bank for International Settlements, around 47 percent of net international bond issuance has been denominated in euros since the first quarter of 1999, compared with 45 percent in dollars. For the equivalent period of time before the introduction of the euro the respective shares were just 29 percent for the currencies that merged to form the euro and 51 percent for the dollar.[21] Moreover, for all its crudeness, the Stability and Growth Pact imposed tight constraints on the fiscal policies of the Eurozone countries, though whether or not the rule restricting deficits to 3 percent of GDP will be reimposed remains to be seen. In theory, at least, the pact has merely been "suspended" since November 2003.

The possibility that investors may come to regard the euro as being as good as the dollar when it comes to denominating low-risk securities cannot therefore be excluded. Indeed, they may already be doing so. In the year after February 2002 the dollar declined against the euro by 45 percent. U.S. long-term bond yields have been between ten and seventy basis points higher than Eurozone yields since 1997, having been lower for all but two of the previous twenty years.[22] According to one projection, foreign direct investment over the next five years will be substantially higher in the EU than in the United States.[23] When he urged his country's state oil company to price its gas and oil in euros rather than dollars, the Malaysian prime minister, Datuk Seri Mahathir Mohamad, was doubtless aiming to score a political point at the expense of the United States. But his proposal (made in June 2003) was far from absurd. It is not without significance that Arab cartoonists have seized on the appreciation of the euro as evidence of American weakness. A cartoon published in 2003 by *Al Jazeera* depicted a euro note being run up a flagpole in place of a depreciated dollar, to the chagrin of a weeping Uncle Sam.[24]

A FEDERAL CONSTITUTION

Ostensibly, the European Convention's treaty establishing an EU constitution does *not* create a European federation. We know this because the phrase *United States of Europe* barely made it off the drawing board and because the word *federal* was deleted from an early version of Article I-1, clause 1. The original version read as follows: "Reflecting the will of the peoples and States of Europe to build a common future, this Constitution establishes a Union . . . within which the policies of the Member States shall be coordinated, and which shall administer certain common competences on a federal basis." The final version was rather different: "Reflecting the will of the citizens and States of Europe to build a common future, this Constitution establishes the European Union, on which the Member States confer competences to attain objectives they have in common. The Union shall coordinate the policies by which the Member States aim to achieve those objectives, and shall exercise in the Community way [*sic*] the competences they confer on it."[25] The question is of course how far the constitution nevertheless remains in practice a federalist document. Some people certainly intended it to be. When the 105-member convention was itself called into being at Laeken in December 2001, it was declared that its aim would be "the construction of a political union" to complement the Economic and Monetary Union created at Maastricht nine years before. In a joint statement before the Laeken meeting, the French president and the German chancellor expressed the wish that the convention should transform the EU into a "federation of nation-states." The Greek premier went further, urging in January 2002 that "the enlarged European Union must evolve into a fully-fledged Political Union with strong governmental institutions and policies of a federal nature."[26]

In some respects, it should be emphasized, the EU already has a quasi-federal character. This is most obvious in the legal sphere. EU legislation now accounts for around half of all new legislation in Europe.[27] Article I-10 of the constitution simply reiterates—though it perhaps also reinforces—what has long been an established principle—namely, that EU law is superior to national law. Europe already has a Convention of Human Rights, which is upheld by the autonomous Court of Human Rights in Strasbourg. However, the constitution includes a new Charter of Fundamental Rights, which it would fall to the European Court of Justice to interpret, thus enhancing the standing of that court (which is based in Luxembourg) as Europe's Supreme Court. The constitution also proposes the creation of a new category of cross-border crimes, which would become the purview of a European prosecutor, thus extending the EU's competence into the field of criminal law.

If only on paper, the European Union also has many of the political institutions that one would expect a federation to have: not only a Supreme Court but also what the Germans would call a *Bundesrat* (the Council of Ministers, representing the governments of the member states), a Parliament, a central bank and a permanent bureaucracy. The principal institutional changes envisaged by the constitution treaty are partly designed to give this protofederation not just legal but actual personality. Thus the presidency of the quarterly European Council (of heads of state) will no longer be held successively by all the member states for six-month periods; it will be held by one individual, elected by the members of the council, for up to five years. The president of the European Commission, by contrast, will be nominated by the European Council but will require a majority in the European

Parliament to be confirmed in office. Which post will emerge as the dominant one? Almost certainly the latter, given the much more frequent meetings of the commission. There will also be a single commissioner to play the part of foreign minister, a role currently and confusingly performed by two separate people.

However, the most implicitly federal clauses of the constitution are those that spell out the respective competences of the EU, its member states and their regions and localities. Only a limited number of spheres of policy—thirty-four, to be exact—have up until now been subject to the weighted system known as qualified majority voting on the EU Council of Ministers. Decisions in other fields have required unanimity; in other words, they have been subject to veto by as few as one of the member states. The constitution does not eliminate the national veto, but it confines its use to decisions concerning foreign policy, defense and taxation. Qualified majority voting would now apply in seventy areas, including immigration and social policy. In perhaps its most sweeping articles, the constitution asserts EU competence not only over foreign and defense policy but over the "coordination of the economic and employment policies of the member states" (Articles I-11 and I-14) as well as over "common commercial policy" (Article I-12). It also authorizes the EU to raise whatever funds it regards as "necessary to attain its objectives and carry through its policies" (Article I-53). The sops to national sovereignty—"the principle of conferral" and "the principle of subsidiarity"—seem rather nebulous by comparison with this bald assertion of fiscal power. Crucially, the right to propose EU legislation would remain the monopoly of the commission. According to one assessment, the extension and modification of qualified majority voting on the Council of Ministers would significantly increase the chances of draft bills' becoming directives.[28]

For all these reasons, there is at least a *prima facie* case that the European Union would become, in practice, something close to a federal United States of Europe, were the new constitution to be accepted by its members.

CULTURE

There is little doubt (indeed it is almost a cliché) that Europe's political culture is becoming more self-consciously different from—and hostile to—the United States. A 2003 survey by the Pew Research Center shows that substantial majorities in France, Spain, Italy and Germany now favor a more independent (less American-influenced) European foreign policy (see table 9).[29] This is undoubtedly a consequence of widespread public disapproval of the American-led war against Iraq. In 1999–2000 no fewer than 83 percent of Britons surveyed had a "favorable" view of the United States; by March 2003 the figure had fallen to 48 percent. In France over the same period the pro-American proportion halved, from 62 to 31 percent. In Italy it went from three-quarters to a third; in Germany from more than three-quarters to barely a quarter; in Spain from half to just 14 percent.[30] The brief duration of the war and the postwar revelations about the viciousness of Saddam Hussein's regime have brought a partial but not a complete reversal of these trends.[31]

Nor is this the only evidence of a divergence of political cultures. Assumptions still commonly made by Americans about the fundamental unity of "Western civilization" look increasingly questionable in view of Europe's precipitously declining religiosity (see table 10). In the Netherlands, Britain, Germany, Sweden and Denmark fewer than one in ten of the population now attend church at least once a month, a dramatic decline since the 1960s. Only in Catholic Italy and Ireland does more than a third of the population worship on a monthly basis or more often.[32] In the Gallup Millennium Survey of religious attitudes (conducted in 1999), 49 percent

TABLE 9. PUBLIC VIEWS OF THE U.S.–EUROPEAN
ALLIANCE, 2003

	U.S.-Europe Alliance Should Remain as Close	Our Country Should Be More Independent
France	23	76
Spain	28	62
Italy	37	61
Germany	42	57
Britain	51	45
U.S.	53	39

Source: Pew Global Attitudes Project, "Views of a Changing World," June 2003.

TABLE 10. A TALE OF TWO CIVILIZATIONS? RELIGIOUS
ATTITUDES IN NORTH AMERICA AND EUROPE

	North America	Western Europe	Eastern Europe
Percentage attending religious services once a week or more	47	20	14
Percentage regarding God as important or very important	83	49	49
Percentage who don't think there is any sort of God, spirit or life force	2	15	9
Percentage agreeing that there is no essential truth in religion	6	17	11

Source: Gallup International.

of Danes, 52 percent of Norwegians and 55 percent of Swedes said that God did not matter to them at all. In North America, by comparison, 82 percent of respondents said that God was "very important" to them. Nor is this a peculiarity of Western (or "old") Europe. According to Gallup, 48 percent of people living in Western Europe almost never go to church; the figure for Eastern Europe is just a little lower at 44 percent. Six out of ten North Americans believe in God as a person, but the ratio in Eastern Europe is just four out of ten. Nearly two-thirds of Czechs regard God as not mattering at all in their lives—a higher proportion even than in Sweden.

The corollary of this widening transatlantic cultural rift is a growing European self-consciousness. Only one in ten Europeans now regards EU membership as an unequivocally "bad thing." Even in Euroskeptical Britain, the proportion of people in this camp has fallen from 34 percent in 1973 to just 21 percent today. Nearly half of Europeans want the EU to play a bigger role in their lives in five years' time. And almost a third of Europeans surveyed in 2002 saw the EU as standing for "a stronger say in world affairs."[33]

EXTERNAL RELATIONS

Finally, we should not underestimate the European Union's potential power on the international stage. Although there is no question that the European countries lag far behind the United States in terms of arms technology, their military capability is far from negligible. The U.S. defense budget is nearly double the combined defense budgets of the fifteen EU members.[34] In financial terms, the American contribution to NATO exceeds that of the EU members of NATO by around 30 percent.[35] But that still makes the

EU countries' combined military expenditures substantially more than those of Russia, Japan or China. Indeed, in terms of crude manpower, the EU countries are now ahead of the United States (around 1.8 million to 1.5 million service personnel) and second only to China, which has around 2.5 million. Of course, Europe's armies are less well trained and much less well equipped than America's; only a tiny fraction of enlisted men can be regarded as "combat-effective." But there is an obvious and important role for European troops that does not require them to possess the full range of American weapons technology: as peacekeepers in the growing number of "postconflict situations." In the years 2000 and 2001 around seven times as many troops from EU countries took part in United Nations peacekeeping operations as troops from the United States.[36]

The European Union countries also outstrip the United States significantly in terms of aid to developing countries. If official aid budgets are adjusted to take account of a variety of relevant factors, it emerges that the combined aid budgets of the EU members are nearly three times larger.[37] When these indicators are combined with a variety of others—openness to international trade, investment in developing countries, openness to legal immigration and adoption of "responsible" environmental practices— the United States ranked an ignominious twentieth out of twenty-one developed economies in its "commitment to development."[38] It is not without importance that fifteen of the nineteen countries ranked ahead of the United States are members of the European Union.

Of course, the Europeans' commitment to development needs to be attributed to the altruism of national governments rather than to the EU itself. Nevertheless, the fact that the EU's member states do so much more than the United States in these fields must have some geopolitical implications. Moreover, the EU is playing an increasing role in its own right through the commission's Humanitarian Office, the European Agency for Reconstruction and the European Bank for Reconstruction and Development. It is not without significance that in UN-occupied Kosovo the Banking and Payments Authority and the Central Fiscal Authority are under EU control; indeed, the province now has the euro as its official currency.[39]

Recent global surveys have tended to focus on the increasingly negative attitudes of people in developing countries toward the United States. It seems likely that their attitudes toward the European Union are more posi-tive. Whatever "soft power" means, the EU seems intent on accumulating it.

For all these reasons, it does not seem irrational for the United States to consider the European Union a potential, if not yet an actual, rival.

CONTRA

Yet there is another side to this balance sheet, which tends to be ignored by those who would posit a nascent transatlantic competition, if not an-tagonism. When the debit side of the European Union's account is exam-ined, it becomes clear that Americans have little, if anything, to worry about. Far from being a rival empire in the making, the introverted char-acter of the EU suggests that it is better understood as an "impire," an en-tity that directs most of its efforts toward the preservation of its own inner equilibrium rather than toward the exercise of power beyond its borders.

AGING POPULATIONS

Europe is getting old. The median age in Germany will rise from forty to-day to forty-seven by 2050; the median age in France from twenty-eight to forty-five; the median age in Hungary from thirty-eight to fifty. (Amer-ica too is aging, of course, but not so fast. In the next fifty years the median age in the United States will rise from thirty-five today to forty.) The im-plications are sobering. According to the European Commission, the rising dependency ratio could reduce annual growth by up to three-quarters of a percentage point by 2040—no insignificant reduction in view of the EU's recent low rate of growth (see below).[40] That calculation may even under-state the problem. According to estimates of the generational imbalances in the fiscal systems of the world's economies, the majority of EU members urgently need to increase taxation or to cut government transfers if they are to avoid imposing unprecedented peacetime tax burdens on the next generation. In the case of Austria, Finland and the Netherlands, cuts in government transfers would need to be of the order of 20 percent to achieve generational balance.[41] It is no coincidence that wrangles about pensions currently take up so much of the time of German and French politicians. The reforms needed to avert a collapse of the European states' welfare systems require immediate sacrifices by powerful vested interests.

ECONOMIC PERFORMANCE

Ever since the 1940s European integration has consistently been marketed to voters in terms of its economic benefits. The coincidence of the first wave of European integration and the *Wirtschaftswunder* of the 1950s and 1960s seemed to bear this out, though the causal relationship between the two was actually quite weak.[42] Recently, however, the claim that integration enhances growth has become much more obviously implausible. No one could dispute that the Single European Act (1986) and the Maastricht Treaty (1992) increased the integration of the West European economy. Nontariff barriers to trade in goods and services have been significantly reduced. The creation of a single currency has, if nothing else, made it much easier to compare prices across the borders of twelve out of the fifteen EU states. Yet Europe's economic performance since these measures came into force has been disappointing, to say the least. Between 1950 and 1973 the average annual growth rate of *per capita* GDP in Western Europe (broadly defined) was 4.1 percent. Between 1973 and 1998 it slumped to 1.8 percent. In the latter period there was no significant difference between the growth experienced by the "first wave" members of European Economic Community, the new members that joined after 1973 and the nonmembers.[43] What is especially striking is the poor performance of the countries that have participated in monetary union since 1999. According to the International Monetary Fund, the "output gap" widened in all the Eurozone economies between 2000 and 2003 and currently lies somewhere between −2 and −3.5 percent of GDP.[44]

By comparison, the American economy has fared better. In every year but one in the last decade (that year was 2001) the annual growth rate of the EU economy has been below that of the U.S. economy.[45] The real growth rate of U.S. GDP averaged approximately 3.6 percent per annum between 1995 and 2001, according to the Organization for Economic Cooperation and Development. The figure for the EU was a meager 2.1 percent. Between 1970 and 1983 unemployment in Europe was consistently lower than in the United States. Now it is substantially higher. In the second half of the 1990s EU unemployment rose above 10 percent, while

U.S. unemployment fell below 5 percent. Even in the past three years of American job losses, European unemployment has remained between two and three percentage points above the American rate. In seven out of fifteen EU countries, unemployment was in excess of 7 percent in 2002.[46] Nowhere is this underperformance more striking than in Germany, formerly the pride and the powerhouse of the European economy. Since 1996 the German economy has been, in the words of the *Economist,* the "sick man of Europe," with an average growth rate of just 1.1 percent, half the Eurozone average.[47] Nor is relief in sight. German unemployment stood at 4.5 million in mid-2003 (10.6 percent of the workforce); the economy contracted by 0.2 percent in both the first and the second quarters of 2003.

Finally, European productivity growth may have been more rapid than American for most of the postwar period, but in the last seven years the tables have been turned. According to the Conference Board, American GDP per hour worked grew at an average annual rate of just under 2 percent in the period 1995–2002, whereas for the EU the figure was closer to 1.2 percent. Only one EU country—Ireland—achieved higher productivity growth than the United States.[48]

EUROPE'S "LEISURE PREFERENCE"

Europe's poor economic performance *despite* measures designed to enhance economic integration begs the obvious question why? One widely held explanation is that Europe's labor market is insufficiently flexible, not just because of the obvious linguistic barriers but also because of regulations introduced over the years in response to the demands of trade unions.

A recent study by the International Monetary Fund considered the evidence from the period 1960 and 1998 and asked a simple question: What would the effect on European unemployment be if the EU labor market were Americanized? To be precise, the study envisaged:

Increasing the participation rate (the proportion of the population in the labor force),
reducing the replacement rate (the ratio of benefits to past earnings),
reducing employment protection,

reducing the tax rate on labor (introducing fiscal reforms to elimi-
    nate poverty traps),
weakening trade unions, and
decentralizing wage bargaining (where nationwide collective
    agreements demonstrably cause big differentials in regional un-
    employment rates).

Table 11 summarizes the projected short-, medium- and long-term
impacts of three of these policies. Its message is clear: Only by doing all
three would European unemployment come down to American levels—
and that only in the "long term." This suggests that labor market reform is
bound to be difficult. Very radical changes are necessary, but the payoffs
would be slow to manifest themselves.

A further difference between the European Union and the United States
not captured in such calculations—or, indeed, by standard measures of
productivity—is the widening gap between the amount of time Americans work and the amount of time West Europeans work. According to a
recent OECD study, the average American in employment works just under 2,000 hours a year (1,976). The average German works just 1,535—
fully 22 percent less. The Dutch and Norwegians put in even fewer hours.
Even the British do roughly 10 percent less work than their transatlantic
cousins. The extraordinary thing is how much of this divergence has oc-
curred in the past twenty years. Between 1979 and 1999 the average American working year lengthened by fifty hours, or nearly 3 percent. But the
average German working year shrank by 12 percent, and the average

TABLE 11. EFFECTS ON EUROZONE UNEMPLOYMENT OF
"AMERICANIZING" THE LABOR MARKET

	Impact on Eurozone Unemployment Rate (%)		
	Short-Term	After 3 Years	Long-Term
Reduction in replacement rate from Eurozone to U.S. level	-0.26	-0.62	-1.24
Reduction in employment protection to U.S. level	-0.35	-0.83	-1.65
Reduction in taxes on labor to U.S. level	-0.08	-0.20	-0.40
Combined effect of three policies	-0.69	-1.65	-3.29

Source: International Monetary Fund, *World Economic Outlook* (April, 2003).

Dutch year by 14 percent.[49] It is a relatively new state of affairs that Americans get ten days of holiday a year, and Europeans thirty.

In fact, these figures understate the extent of the European "leisure preference," since they take no account of the fact that a much larger proportion of Americans actually work. Between 1973 and 1998 the percentage of the American population in employment rose from 41 to 49. But in Germany and France the equivalent percentages fell to, respectively, 44 and 39. The overall employment rate for the working-age population in the United States is 73 percent; in the EU it is just 64 percent.[50] Unemployment rates in most European countries are also markedly higher than in the United States—over 10 percent in Belgium and Spain, more than twice the American rate. And then of course there are the strikes. Between 1992 and 2001 the Spanish economy lost, on average, 271 days per thousand employees as a result of industrial action. For Denmark, Italy, Finland, Ireland and France the figures lie between 80 and 120, compared with less than 50 for the United States.[51]

This, then, is the main reason why the U.S. economy has surged ahead of its European competitors in the past two decades. It is not that Americans are markedly more productive. It is not about efficiency. It is simply the fact that Americans work *more*. It is the fact that Europeans take longer holidays and retire earlier. It is the fact that so many more European workers are either unemployed or on strike. Europe's political leaders are belatedly waking up to this problem. In June 2003 a German politician took his career in his hands by daring to suggest that if Germans made do with fewer holidays, their economy might grow faster. Such views are no longer taboo in France either. But a century of European social democracy has created habits of mind that are extremely hard to break. From almost its very inception in the late nineteenth century, the German Social Democratic Party campaigned for shorter working hours and, more recently, shorter working lives. For their French counterparts, securing a maximum working week of thirty-five hours was one of the great achievements of the recent past. This tradition dies hard. A striking feature of the proposed EU constitution is that it seeks to enshrine as "fundamental rights" a number of the things that make the European population so much less active than their American counterparts. It alarms British business leaders that Article II-27 enshrines the right of workers to be consulted by the management about the running of the companies that employ them. But just as significant is Article II–31: "Every worker has the right to limitation of maximum working hours, to daily and weekly rest periods and to an annual period of paid holiday."[52]

THE COMMON AGRICULTURAL POLICY

Europe may be running a trade surplus, but part of the reason is the relatively slow growth of domestic demand. Another relevant factor is the European Union's continued protectionism, which is most evident in the agricultural sector. At the time of writing (June 2003), an agreement had belatedly been reached to reform the Common Agricultural Policy, which at present accounts for nearly half the EU budget. The system whereby the subsidies paid to farmers are linked to the volume of production is to be partly dismantled.[53] The prices at which the EU commits itself to buy farm produce are to be reduced, though not entirely scrapped. CAP payments to farmers in the ten new member states will be paid at just a quarter of the level paid to existing members.[54] But these reforms do nothing to reduce the tariffs currently imposed on agricultural imports to Europe. American proposals to the World Trade Organization prior to the abortive Cancún conference included the phasing out of agricultural export subsidies over five years as well as the reduction of subsidies to 5 percent of the value of farm production and of tariffs to a maximum of 25 percent. Before Cancún the EU indicated its willingness to reduce subsidies, which prior to last year's reforms were around 33 percent of the value of production, compared with around 21 percent in the United States. Without a global trade agreement, however, these subsidies will continue.[55] This state of affairs is simply indefensible—and politically almost incomprehensible given that barely 4 percent of the EU workforce is now employed in agriculture.

The United States is not significantly more virtuous in these respects.[56] But Europe's addiction to agricultural subsidies and tariffs nevertheless needs to be borne in mind when judgments are being made about the EU's positive contributions toward developing countries. Europe may be more generous in its aid policy than the United States. But so long as the Common Agricultural Policy remains in existence—even in its reformed incarnation—the EU will be giving with one hand while taking away with the other. Worse, it will be offering dependence on aid as a substitute for economic development based on agricultural exports. Were the EU to break the stranglehold of what are now numerically weak protectionist lobbies, the benefits—not least for developing countries around its Mediterranean and Slavic periphery—would be immense. There would be real benefits for West European consumers too. Only a relatively small number of inefficient farmers, notably in France, would lose out. And those who protest that the French countryside benefits aesthetically from subsidized agriculture should think again. If what is at issue is the look of the Gallic landscape, then farmers can quite easily be paid to act as glorified gardeners, charged with the task of keeping France pretty, but not paid to produce food that could come more cheaply from outside the EU.

THE EUROPEAN CENTRAL BANK AND GERMAN DISINFLATION

The Common Agricultural Policy also makes food expensive for European families, reducing their disposable income twice: by taxing their incomes and by inflating their food bills. But it is not the principal cause of Europe's recent economic underperformance. Of far more importance is the mismanagement of Eurozone monetary policy since the creation of the single currency in January 1999.

The success of the euro as a substitute for the dollar in some international transactions masks a deeper failure. This failure has consisted in systematically underestimating the disinflationary and perhaps even deflationary pressures on the German economy of a monetary policy devised to achieve price stability in twelve quite different economies.[57] Between 1999 and 2001 the Economic and Monetary Union meant higher interest rates for Germany, compensated for by exchange rate depreciation.[58] In 2002 and 2003 it meant belated and insufficient interest rate cuts and a real monetary tightening through exchange rate appreciation. Some symptoms of deflation have already manifested themselves in Germany. Although the official consumer price inflation rate remains (just) positive, there is reason to think that this may conceal actual deflation. The main producer price index fell in 2002, and agricultural prices have been falling since mid-

2001.[59] Uniquely among the major Western economies, Germany's real estate prices have fallen—by as much as 13 percent in real terms—over the past decade. [60]

The problem has been compounded because German fiscal policy is also circumscribed by European rules. The misnamed Stability and Growth Pact—ironically, demanded as a sine qua non of monetary union by the Germans themselves—implied that Germany could be fined by the EU if, as seemed likely, Berlin ran deficits in excess of 3 percent of GDP for three years running (2002–04). In large measure, these deficits merely reflect the operation of automatic stabilizers in a recession or near recession. The idea that they could be made larger by the imposition of fines (a mechanism that was designed to elicit good fiscal behavior from Italy and other historically profligate member states) is among the most grotesque of the unintended consequences of monetary union. Small wonder the Stability and Growth Pact was hastily suspended in November 2003.

One way of seeing where the European Central Bank has gone wrong is to ask where German interest rates would be today if the German central bank, the Bundesbank, had not been emasculated. Given the Bundesbank's record—which includes at least five episodes when rates were cut quite steeply in response to a recession (in 1967, 1975, 1982–83, 1987 and 1994–96)—it seems reasonable to assume that rates would be lower. Were it not for the ECB's need to target inflation not just in Germany but also in Greece and Ireland, German base rates in 2003-4 would very probably have been closer to American rates—i.e., nearer to 1 percent than to 2 percent.[61]

Under the circumstances, it is scarcely surprising that after much circumlocution, the British government has avoided committing itself to joining the Eurozone in the near term. Although one study in the voluminous June 2003 Treasury report on the subject suggested that euro membership might boost British economic growth, it was only by a modest amount—at best, 0.25 percent of GDP per annum; at worst, 0.02 percent.[62] Even these calculations (which assumed that switching to the euro would boost cross-Channel trade and that this in turn would raise productivity) must be viewed with skepticism in view of the dismal performance of the Eurozone since its creation.[63] The ten countries that have just joined the EU should also think twice about converting to the euro. They could lose more than they gain if, in order to qualify, they are required to spend two years of purgatory in a second-generation exchange rate mechanism, given the volatile flows of speculative capital such a system would tend to attract.[64] The government deficits of Poland, Hungary and the Czech Republic all were in excess of 4 percent in 2002; indeed, the Hungarian deficit was close to 10 percent. It is fortunate for these countries, too, that the Stability and Growth Pact is in abeyance.[65]

If enlargement turns out to mean that the low-productivity economies of Eastern Europe acquire both a West European welfare system and a West European currency, its macroeconomic effects could conceivably be like a slow-motion replay of German reunification, which threw millions of East Germans out of work. Productivity levels in the Czech Republic, Poland, Slovakia and Hungary are around a third of the French level. Put crudely, what this means is that unless wages in those countries are set at around a third of French levels, their workers will not be able to compete with their West European counterparts. Unfortunately, European Union labor legislation is designed to prevent what the West Europeans disingenuously label "social dumping," a pejorative term for competition from low-wage economies. East Europeans are currently able to compensate for their low productivity by working longer hours even than Americans. The average Czech worker does more than two thousand hours of work a year, a figure that has been steadily rising since the collapse of communism, even as working hours in Western Europe have been declining. EU accession is likely to reverse that tendency, obliging Czechs to work less or not at all by giving them legal entitlements to shorter working weeks, longer holidays, stronger unions, higher minimum wages and, of course, generously funded unemployment when their employers go bust because of all this. Joining the EMU would remove the last vestige of economic flexibility, the possibility of currency depreciation.

THE RESCUE OF THE NATION-STATE, CONTINUED

What, then, of Europe's steps toward a federal constitution? Here, as always, there is a need to distinguish between rhetoric and reality. Some French and German politicians have been using the language of European federalism for years. Yet the reality has always lagged far behind, for the simple reason that the very same politicians—when it comes to actions rather than words—have consistently defended their countries' respective national inter-

ests. Alan Milward's dictum that the first phase of European integration had
more to do with the rescue of the nation-state than the construction of a federation still applies today.[66] There is little reason to think this will cease to
be true even if Giscard's constitution is eventually adopted. Indeed, a close
reading of the constitution—and of comments made by the convention's
president during its deliberations—suggests that the real point of the exercise was to prevent an irrevocable swamping of the four biggest West European countries by the smaller states in the wake of eastward enlargement.

A cynic might say, for example, that the new offices of president of the
European Council and EU foreign minister are the perfect jobs for a certain kind of French elder statesman—not unlike the post of president of
the constitutional convention. Giscard envisaged freezing the number of
European commissioners at fifteen, in other words scrapping the rule that
gives each member state at least one commissioner. If that did not happen,
so his argument ran, the seven smallest countries in an enlarged EU—
accounting for less than 2 percent of the union's GDP—would provide
more commissioners than the six largest countries, despite the fact that the

TABLE 12. THE EUROPEAN UNION IN PERCENTAGES

	GDP	Population	Seats in European Parliament	Votes on Council of Ministers*	Commissioners	Judges on European Court	Population per Council of Ministers Vote
Germany	23.4	21.8	15.8	11.5	10	6.7	8,219,300
United Kingdom	18.0	15.9	13.9	11.5	10	6.7	5,983,200
France	16.6	15.8	13.9	11.5	10	6.7	5,952,100
Italy	13.8	15.3	13.9	11.5	10	6.7	5,784,400
Spain	7.4	10.5	10.2	9.2	10	6.7	4,936,250
Netherlands	4.8	4.2	5.0	5.7	5	6.7	3,196,600
Belgium	2.9	2.7	4.0	5.7	5	6.7	2,052,400
Sweden	2.7	2.4	3.5	4.6	5	6.7	2,220,750
Austria	2.4	2.2	3.4	4.6	5	6.7	2,030,250
Denmark	2.0	1.4	2.6	3.4	5	6.7	1,783,000
Greece	1.5	2.8	4.0	5.7	5	6.7	2,102,200
Finland	1.5	1.4	2.6	3.4	5	6.7	1,727,000
Portugal	1.4	2.7	4.0	5.7	5	6.7	2,004,600
Ireland	1.3	1.0	2.4	3.4	5	6.7	1,273,333
Luxembourg	0.2	0.1	1.0	2.3	5	6.7	220,500

*System before the Nice Treaty of 2001.
Source: John McCormick, *Understanding the European Union;* OECD.

latter group's share of total EU output exceeds 80 percent. Giscard also raised the idea of making representation in the European Parliament more proportionate to national population sizes. "You have to take the populations into account because we operate in a democracy here," he declared in April 2003.[67] Perhaps most important, changes to the system of qualified majority voting on the Council of Ministers would mean that EU legislation could be passed if it had the support of just half the member states, provided they represented at least 60 percent of the European Union population—a much better deal for the big four than the system agreed to at Nice in December 2000.

Giscard had a point. EU institutions as presently constituted do substantially overrepresent the smaller countries, as table 12 shows. For many years, this overrepresentation of the small and underrepresentation of the large has had a fiscal dimension too. Almost from its genesis in the European Coal and Steel Community (1951), the European Union has been predi-

FIGURE 12

Germany's Share of European Union Resources and Institutions (Percentages)

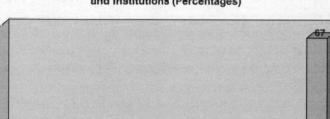

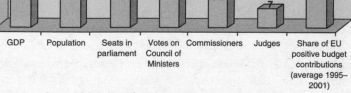

Source: John McCormick, *Understanding the European Union;* OECD.

cated on transfers of resources from the larger, wealthier countries to the smaller, poorer countries. In the 1950s the inefficient Belgian coal industry received tens of millions of dollars from the other members of the ECSC, principally Germany. After the Treaty of Rome, France's former colonies (which the French ingeniously managed to slip into the Common Market) received $380 million in development assistance from the other five signatories, again principally Germany. The Common Agricultural Policy, which by 1969 accounted for 70 percent of the European Economic Community's budget, also effectively obliged German consumers to pay for dearer French and Dutch produce.[68] According to German budgetary data, the total amount of unrequited transfers from Germany to the other member states some years ago exceeded in nominal terms the celebrated 132 billion marks demanded of Germany by the victorious powers after the First World War.[69]

Yet it is inconceivable that this system can survive for very long. Apart from anything else, EU enlargement brings into the fold a number of countries markedly poorer in relative terms than any previous new members. In past enlargements the *per capita* GDP of the richest existing member—invariably Luxembourg—has been roughly two or two and a half times that of the poorest new member (Ireland in 1974, Greece in 1981, Portugal in 1986 and Finland in 1995). But the accession of the former Communist economies of Eastern Europe is an altogether bigger challenge. The average Luxembourgeois is roughly five times better off than the average Lithuanian. At Copenhagen it was agreed that the "maximum enlargement-related commitments" for the ten new states would not exceed 40.8 billion euros in the three years 2004–06. But who exactly is going to finance these transfers? It is very hard to see how German politicians can continue to justify paying the largest net contributions to the EU budget at a time when the German economy is growing so sluggishly. Clearly, German altruism has played an important role in the history of European integration since 1945. Still, there must be limits to how much more "tacit reparations" German taxpayers are willing to pay to the rest of Europe.

One little-noticed finding of recent Eurobarometer surveys is that there are significant discrepancies between the numbers of people who think the European Union is a "good thing" in general and the numbers who think it is good for their own country. There may well be a connection between these discrepancies and the workings of the EU budget. In countries that are net recipients of substantial sums—Greece, Ireland and Portugal, all of which received sums greater than 2 percent of GDP between 1995 and 2001—the proportion of voters who regard the EU as good for their specific country is significantly larger than the proportion who regard it as a good thing generally. Conversely, a larger number of voters in a number of the big donor countries—Germany, Belgium and Luxembourg—regard the EU as a good thing generally than regard it as good for their own country.[70] If nothing else, that suggests a recognition on the part of voters in some, if not all, member states that there is a distinction between the European interest and the national interest.

THE LIMITS OF "EUROPEANNESS"

While it is tempting to represent "European" attitudes as increasingly "anti-American" and more self-consciously European, this is at best a caricature. First, as the Pew Center data clearly show, most Europeans draw a sharp distinction between Americans in general and the Bush administration. No less than 74 percent of French people with a negative view of the United States regard "the problem" as being "mostly Bush," compared with just 21 percent who think it is "America in general" and 4 percent who blame both. The proportions are very similar in Germany and Italy. Secondly, and somewhat ironically, there are at least some aspects of President Bush's foreign policy that Europeans support. Three-quarters of French, Italian and German respondents to the Pew survey agreed that the Iraqi people are better off without Saddam Hussein. Clear majorities in all the major European countries continue to favor the U.S.-led war against terrorism. More generally, there are no real transatlantic differences in attitudes toward economic and cultural globalization. It should also be noted that anti-American sentiment is not deterring young Europeans from learning the English language. Excluding Britain and Ireland, 92 percent of secondary school students in the EU are studying English—nearly three times the number studying French and seven times the number studying German.[71]

At the same time, Europeans remain far less "European" than French, British, German, Italian and so on. Nine out of ten Europeans feel "fairly attached" or "very attached" to their countries. But fewer than five out of ten—45 percent—feel as "attached" to the EU. In some countries—

Sweden, Holland, Britain and Finland—between two-thirds and three-quarters of citizens describe themselves as "not very attached" or "not at all attached" to the EU. Only a tiny proportion of Europeans identify themselves exclusively as "European"; nearly half see themselves primarily as members of a traditional nationality and only secondarily as European. Moreover, the popularity of EU membership within the fifteen current members is in decline. In 1990 more than 70 percent of Europeans thought membership a good thing; the most recent surveys show a drop to just 55 percent. Just under half of Europeans regard EU membership as having "as many advantages as disadvantages." In the light of these figures, European identity seems less than securely established.

Moreover, the impact of immigration to Europe, which will almost certainly need to continue and indeed increase to counter the rising dependency ratios discussed above, is tending to reduce rather than increase European cultural cohesion. Millions of people have moved into the European Union in the past decade, whether as economic migrants, asylum seekers or ethnic Germans. These migrants are following previous influxes, notably of former subject peoples from the defunct colonial empires in the 1960s and 1970s. According to recent estimates, between 3 and 4 percent of the populations of Holland, Germany and Britain are now Muslims; in France the proportion is nearly double that, 7.5 percent.[72] Recent trends in applications by asylum seekers and their success rates suggest that some countries are likely to end up with larger immigrant populations than others. In the years 1990 to 2000, Denmark, Germany, the Netherlands, Austria and Sweden admitted the largest numbers relative to their respective populations. For the foreseeable future there is certain to be a profound tension between the economic need to attract more legal immigrants to Western Europe and the political antagonism toward newcomers that tends to be felt most acutely in (or close to) the relatively poor neighborhoods where they settle.

It would be an exaggeration to depict recent successes by politicians with explicitly anti-immigrant platforms as manifestations of a revival of extreme nationalist or racist politics in Europe. The politicians concerned, ranging from Jean-Marie Le Pen to Jörg Haider to the late Pim Fortuyn, have too little in common and have achieved such ephemeral successes that it would be more accurate to speak of a rash of protest votes with xenophobic overtones. Still, hostility to immigrants is widespread. A survey conducted in 2000 found that more than half of Europeans think that ethnic minorities abuse national welfare systems and that immigrants increase unemployment. Nearly two-fifths think that even legal immigrants should be sent back to their countries of origin.[73] It is hardly surprising that unscrupulous populists are tempted to pander to such sentiments. The implications for those who dream of a federal Europe are dispiriting. Asked by Eurobarometer pollsters what the EU meant to them, more than a fifth of European voters checked the box marked "Not enough border controls." Whatever restrictions are initially left in place, enlargement seems certain to heighten the perception that the EU encourages migration by creating new opportunities for young men in Eastern Europe and the Mediterranean to move westward. A few demagogues are already linking hostility to immigration and hostility to European integration. More in this vein seems almost inevitable.

And then there is the Turkish question. The Turks first applied to join the European Union as early as 1987. Hitherto their advances have been rebuffed, mainly on the ground of Turkey's somewhat checkered political, civil and human rights record; implicitly (and sometimes explicitly) because Turkey is overwhelmingly a Muslim country. The economic case for membership has, however, been growing stronger. According to some estimates, *per capita* income in Turkey is in fact higher than in Hungary, Latvia or Lithuania, all of which are now members of the EU, and more than double that of most of the Balkan states. The religious argument, by contrast, has become a politically incorrect embarrassment, as Giscard himself discovered when he injudiciously advanced it last year. The notion that Europe is by definition Christian will no longer hold water; as we have seen, there are just too few observant Christians and too many non-Christian immigrants. Nor can it any longer be claimed that Turkey is not a functioning democracy. A moderately Islamist party came to power there in free and fair elections; the army has not intervened, as it might have done in the past. Meanwhile the strategic arguments for binding Turkey to the West by new institutional ties are compelling. The Turkish Parliament's refusal to facilitate a U.S. invasion of northern Iraq demonstrated that its members, if no one else, have read and understood the North Atlantic Treaty, which does not have a clause justifying preemptive war. By overthrowing Saddam

Hussein, the United States has clearly demonstrated the perils of being a "rogue regime" in the Middle East. But what better way could there be to signal the rewards of being a democratic and religiously moderate regime than to admit Turkey to the EU?

Here is the only way in which Charles Kupchan's notion of Europe as a new Byzantium might be seen as (unintentionally) prescient. Should Turkey join the EU, and should the Muslim communities in Western Europe continue growing, there may one day be good reason to draw parallels between Brussels and Byzantium—or rather, Ottoman Constantinople.

"THE HOUR OF EUROPE"

Though immigration to France has not been especially high compared with other EU countries, the presence of large Muslim communities in France—now into their third generation—may help explain the success of the National Front leader Jean-Marie Le Pen in the first round of the French presidential elections of 2002. To be certain of victory in the second round, Jacques Chirac had to distance himself from Le Pen's stance on immigration, and that in turn may help explain why he was so reluctant to be associated with military action against Iraq in 2003.

Such domestic political considerations—or, to be precise, the diversity of domestic political constellations—are the principal reason why it has proved so difficult to coordinate the diplomacy of the EU member states. In theory, a Common European Foreign and Security Policy is an appealing idea; in practice, it has proved exceedingly difficult. Over Bosnia, as we have seen, the "hour of Europe" manifestly failed to strike; the disagreements between the EU states led to a kind of political paralysis. Over Iraq even deeper fissures opened up within the EU. Would the creation of a European foreign minister change that? It seems highly unlikely.

Europe's, in short, is a curious kind of union, a confederation that fantasizes about being a federation without ever quite becoming one. It has an executive, a legislature, an upper house, a supreme court, a central bank, a common currency, a flag and an anthem. But it has only a tiny common budget and the barest bones of a common army. Many more decisions than its architects intended are still taken by the national governments at meetings of the Council of Europe or at intergovernmental conferences. The EU lacks a common language, a common postal system, a common soccer team, even a standardized electric socket. To some critics—perhaps most famously the late Conservative cabinet minister Nicholas Ridley—it threatens to become a "Fourth Reich," not only dominated by Germany, but German in its institutional structure. To others—notably the Oxford professor of politics Larry Siedentop—it is the French who really run the union in the style of their own less than accountable bureaucracy, preventing its evolution into an American-style United States.[74] Siedentop's EU is more like a third Bonapartist empire than a Fourth German Reich.

A better analogy than either of these might be with Switzerland, a country where economics tends to count for more than politics and where the cantons are more powerful than the central government. Yet even the idea of a super-Switzerland understates the importance of the two glaring democratic deficits that characterize the EU. The first is well known— namely the weakness of the European Parliament relative to the European Commission, an institution that glories in its lack of transparency and seems barely accountable to anyone. The EU may not be Byzantium, but its inner workings are certainly Byzantine. The second democratic deficit is the less obvious but perhaps more important deficit that condemns the individual German voter to a far smaller say in European affairs than his fellow European in Luxembourg or Ireland. It may well be that both these deficits are necessary to the existence of the EU, since an authentically democratic system might unleash the xenophobia felt by many ordinary Europeans or revive the long-dormant German question in the minds of both the Germans and their neighbors. But under these circumstances the EU seems unlikely to achieve that increase in its legitimacy without which a common foreign and security policy is inconceivable.

Already significant moves have been made in the direction of what is known, euphemistically, as variable geometry. Only twelve EU members have thus far adopted the euro; shortly before this book was completed, a second Swedish referendum went decisively against EMU membership, further reducing the odds of an imminent British vote on the subject. Britain and Ireland have not signed the Schengen Agreement to relax border controls within the EU. Between 1989 and 1997 the British also opted out of the Social Charter, one of the three "pillars" of the EU proclaimed at Maastricht. In a similar fashion, the new members of the EU will not immediately implement all the terms and conditions of membership. The concept of constructive abstention introduced in the Amsterdam Treaty and the concept of enhanced cooperation in Giscard's constitutional treaty (Article I-43) point the way to more such *à la carte* arrangements. No one can seriously expect this to strengthen the EU. The more opt-outs there are, the less coherent the union is bound to become. A multispeed Europe can hardly achieve the Treaty of Rome's goal of "ever closer union." On the contrary, union will tend to become more remote. Instead there will be a multiplicity of petty unions, from the Treaty of Rome, in short, to a political spaghetti junction of partially overlapping "coalitions of the willing"— with the mission in each case defining the coalition. It was symptomatic of this tendency that, following the postponement of a decision on the constitutional treaty at the Brussels summit in December 2003, the leaders of France and Germany spoke openly of their countries as the "vanguard" of what is by implication a two-tier Europe.*

MYTHS, STORIES AND PARADES

The conclusion of this chapter is straightforward. The United States has nothing much to fear from either the widening or the deepening of the European Union—not least because the two processes stand in contradiction to each other. Talk of a federal Europe's emerging as a counterweight to the United States is based on a complete misreading of developments. The EU is populous but senescent. Its economy is large but sluggish. Its productivity is not bad but vitiated by excessive leisure. It is a successful but still insufficiently liberal customs union. It contains a monetary union that has depressed rather than enhanced its members' economic growth. It is certainly a legal union, but too much of its law emanates from an unelected and unaccountable commission for it to enjoy legitimacy. And as a political entity it seems likely to remain confederal for the foreseeable future. What de Gaulle said in 1962 remains fundamentally true today: "At the

---

*The ostensible reason for the failure of the Brussels summit was the refusal of Spain and Poland to accept the relative dilution of their influence on the Council of Ministers implied by the proposed new rules on qualified majority voting. The Nice system suits them better.

present time there cannot be any other Europe than a Europe of States, apart, of course, from myths, stories and parades." And even these myths do not command much respect. Although there are traces of a common European culture that is distinct from the amorphous, American notion of "the West," national identities still predominate, and immigration is doing little to diminish them. For all these reasons, a common foreign and security policy seems a remote and perhaps unattainable ambition.

Who needs a counterweight anyway? In the final analysis, both the United States and the European Union have far more to gain from cooperation than from competition. The bottom line is that they need, even depend on, each other. This is most obvious in the economic sphere. Very nearly a quarter of EU exports go to the United States, while a fifth of EU imports come from there. The United States accounted for 65 percent of foreign direct investment into the EU in 1999; the same proportion of European FDI went to the United States. No less than 45 percent of the stock of U.S. FDI is in the EU.[75] A substantial share of the U.S. government debt as well as the debts of American corporations are held in the portfolios of European investors and institutions. There is, then, something to be said for Richard Rosecrance's characterization of the relationship as a partnership between "Caesar and Crocsus."[76] But Euro-American common interests are cultural too; those who grumble at the ubiquity of McDonald's throughout Europe overlook the immense number of French and Italian restaurants in the United States. As Disney chief executive Michael Eisner has been heard to remark, "*Sleeping Beauty* is culture, and that's French; *Peter Pan* is English, *Pinocchio* Italian, *Snow White* German."[77] Above all, there can be no question that Americans and Europeans have a common interest in combating terrorism. The efforts of a small number of zealots to cause murder and mayhem, whether in Manhattan or Mombasa, will be defeated only if the intelligence agencies and police forces of the United States and Europe work together.[78] Nation-building projects in Bosnia, Kosovo, Afghanistan and Iraq are also more likely to succeed if there is meaningful transatlantic cooperation.

Those in the United States of America who fret about the "rise" of a United States of Europe should therefore relax. And those in Europe who fantasize about precisely the same thing should get real. Brussels is still—both literally and metaphorically—a very long way from Byzantium.

CHAPTER 8

THE CLOSING DOOR

... the interesting subject of the finances of the declining empire.

EDWARD GIBBON[1]

THE GREAT RECONVERGENCE?

For most of the period between the decline of the Roman Empire and the rise of the European Union, the characteristic condition of Europe has been political fragmentation. Periods of imperial unity—from Charlemagne to Hitler, by way of Charles V and Napoleon—have been the exceptions, not the rule. On the other side of the world, in East Asia, the opposite has been true. Since the third century B.C., when Shih Huang-ti, the first Ch'in emperor, united China and built the Great Wall, imperial unity has been the norm. Indeed, despite occasional eras of civil war and dynastic weakness, China has been the longest-lived empire in world history—as well as one of the largest. In the 1820s the Manchu dynasty directly ruled a vast territory, roughly coterminous with today's People's Republic; in addition, Korea, Indochina, Siam, Burma and Nepal all were Chinese vassals. For most of modern history, China has been home to between a quarter and a third of the world's population—perhaps as many as 37 percent in 1820. Prior to the Industrial Revolution, China was also the titan of the world economy. Between 1500 and 1820 its share of world output was never less than a fifth, and it may have risen as high as a third in 1820.[2]

Yet the nineteenth and twentieth centuries saw a disastrous collapse of living standards in China. Between 1820 and 1950 gross domestic product *per capita* fell by roughly a quarter. By 1973 Chinese income per head was around a fifth of the world average, worse than in many parts of Africa. China's share of world output, which had been close to 33 percent in 1820, fell below 5 percent. Why this happened remains a hotly debated question. The Chinese themselves tend to attribute their decline to the negative effects of Western imperialism after the Anglo-Chinese wars of the mid-nineteenth century (the so-called Opium Wars of 1839–42 and 1856–60) A more recent Western hypothesis is that China's long-term political unity had a stifling effect on the country's technological and strategic development at a time when Europe was divided into rival nation-states. It was their competition at home and abroad that gave the Occident its decisive economic and military edge over the more populous Orient.[3] The acquisition of colonies in the New World, according to Kenneth Pomeranz, was what propelled Europe ahead of China. By the end of the early modern period, both Western Europe and the Yangtze Valley had faced ecological crises associated with deforestation, but the Europeans could draw on American silver and Caribbean sugar—not to mention their own conveniently located coal—to commercialize and industrialize their way out of the Malthusian trap.[4]

China's fate in the twentieth century was a miserable one. The Europeans brought economic transformation to the Chinese periphery, but only in a few cities—notably Hong Kong—did they introduce the full array of legal and administrative institutions they had brought to the post-Mughal empire in India. At British instigation, the rival Occidental powers (including, by the late nineteenth century, the United States) agreed on the policy of the "Open Door": China would be a huge free trade zone, but one that would retain its own political institutions, the decrepit remnants of the Ch'ing, or Manchu, empire.[5] The transition from empire to republic in 1911 was abortive, above all because of the disastrous consequences of Japanese imperialism in the 1930s and the ensuing civil war. Victory in this went to the Marxist Mao Zedong, who successfully mobilized the impoverished peasantry, only to plunge Chinese society into the worst man-made famine in history (the "Great Leap Forward") and one of the worst government-inspired social disruptions (the Cultural Revolution). Communist China continued to function as a successful empire, pursuing its foreign policy goals with a realism that deeply impressed Henry Kissinger. But its economic weakness placed serious limitations on Chinese power.

Since the reforms initiated in the late 1970s by Deng Xiaoping, however, China has experienced a startling economic recovery. Unlike the Soviet Union, which sought simultaneously to liberalize its planned economy and to democratize its political system (with the result that both collapsed), the Chinese have concentrated on modifying rather than jettisoning their existing economic institutions, while making only limited political changes.[6] The result has been a dramatic increase in the rate of economic growth.[7] In the past twenty years the average annual growth rate of real Chinese GDP has been between 8 and 12 percent. Adjusted on the basis of purchasing power parity, China's share of world output has risen from 4 to 12 percent since 1983.[8] Its share of global exports has also soared. According to a study by Goldman Sachs, the Chinese economy could overtake the American economy in size in 2041.[9] Small wonder that so many students of international relations have jumped to the conclusion that China is the strategic challenge of the future.[10] In narrowly economic terms, at least, it seems a more plausible candidate for the role of counterweight to the United States than the European Union. The great divergence, it seems, is giving way to a "great reconvergence," which will see China regain its rightful place in the "world system."[11] Renewed historical interest in China's past achievements, symbolized by the eunuch admiral Cheng Ho's fifteenth-century voyages of discovery across the Indian Ocean, echo such expectations of the future.

Nevertheless, like the febrile forecasts that the world would "turn Japanese" in the 1980s, such predictions must be treated with caution. For one thing, such runaway growth rates may very well bring instability as well as prosperity to China. The example of tsarist Russia a century ago is instructive. Under Alexander II and his two successors, the Russian empire embarked on a comparable program of industrialization, opening its economy to foreign trade and capital and achieving exceptionally rapid growth by the standards of the time. But the social consequences of this economic boom placed enormous strains on the institutions of the Romanov autocracy, which, when it sought to harness the country's new wealth for war, fell victim to revolution. A new Chinese revolution is not in the cards; no matter how wide the inequalities, a society does not embark on a new revolution with the memory of not one but two great political upheavals so painfully fresh. Yet there are conceivable scenarios in which some kind of internal crisis could beset Beijing, if only a crisis of the country's fragile banking and financial system.[12] One possibility that cannot be ruled out is that China's new reliance on free trade and foreign direct investment is nothing more than a return to the Open Door era of a century ago, the political consequences of which were less than happy. Linked to this is a second and more immediate limitation on Chinese power, and that is the growing *interdependence* between it and the United States. Far from being strategic rivals, these two empires have the air of economic partners. The only question is which of the two is the more dependent; which, to be precise, stands to lose more in the event of a crisis in their amicable relationship, now over thirty years old. Today, just as was true a century ago, there is an open door between America and China. But could that door close?

OVERSTRETCH REVISITED

Toppling three tyrannies within four years is no mean achievement by the standards of any past global empire. Since 1999 Slobodan Milošević, the Taliban, and now Saddam Hussein all have been overthrown as a result—admittedly an indirect result in the first case—of American military intervention against their armed forces. What makes this so remarkable is that it comes little more than a decade after a wave of anxiety about American decline. In 1987 Paul Kennedy warned that the United States was running "the risk . . . of what might roughly be called 'imperial overstretch.'" America, he maintained, was spending too high a proportion of national income on its military commitments. This was already having an impact on the performance of the American economy compared with more or less demilitarized Germany and Japan, which were able to spend much more on civilian research and development. Could the United States hope to preserve its cold war position as a superpower? "The only answer to the question," wrote Kennedy, "is 'no.'"[13] Indeed, Kennedy went further, hinting at the dire domestic political consequences that might ensue from imperial overstretch. Citing the defense-driven growth in the federal debt under President Reagan, he drew a parallel with prerevolutionary France, "the only other example which comes to mind of a Great Power so increasing its indebtedness in *peacetime*."[14]

As Keynes once said, when the facts change, one ought to change one's opinion.[15] Writing in September 2002 about America's subsequent ascent from superpower to "hyperpower," Kennedy invoked the *deus ex machina* of the "revolution in military affairs" to explain why his predictions of overstretch had not been fulfilled. All that investment in military research and development, of which he had been so disapproving back in the 1980s, had paid an unforeseen dividend.[16] Not only did the Soviet Union collapse as it strained to match the Reagan-Weinberger arms extravaganza, but the United States also went on to collect a triple peace dividend in the 1990s: falling defense spending as a share of GDP, accelerating economic growth and a quantum leap in military capability that left other powers far behind.

The irony is that Kennedy's original thesis of *fiscal* overstretch might yet be vindicated—despite his decision to abandon it. America's fiscal overstretch is far worse today than anything he envisaged sixteen years ago. The key point—and here the resemblance to Kennedy's earlier argument ends—is that this overstretch has almost nothing to do with the United States' overseas military commitments. It is the result of America's chronically unbalanced *domestic* finances. And the magnitude of the problem is such that most Americans, including those who consider themselves well informed about the nation's finances, find it quite simply incredible. Indeed, the main reason why America's fiscal crisis remains latent is precisely that people refuse to believe in its existence.[17] And they are able to do this because the United States has imperceptibly come to rely on East Asian capital to stabilize its unbalanced budgets. Many commentators have noted the very muted, even quiescent reaction of China to recent American military interventions.[18] Fewer have appreciated the extent to which China now helps underwrite American power.

Like Britain's liberal empire a century ago, America's nascent liberal empire is surprisingly inexpensive to run. That is largely because the American economy is so very large. Since 1980 U.S. GDP, measured in current dollar terms, has risen from a low point of just 10 percent of world output to 31 percent in 2002. That makes it two and half times larger than the Japanese economy, eight and a half times larger than the Chinese and thirty

times larger than the Russian. U.S. military expenditure exceeds the combined defense budgets of the EU, China and Russia. Yet the cost of the
U.S. military has declined steeply in relative terms, from an average of 10
percent of GDP in the 1950s to just 4 percent in the 1990s and a forecast
3.5 percent in the first half of the present decade.

Many Americans worry about the cost of the American occupation of
Iraq. That is in large measure because they were encouraged to imagine that
it would cost nothing. In April 2003 some Bush administration spokesmen
talked as if the country's reconstruction would somehow be self-financing.
The first Gulf War had been effectively free to Americans because a broadly
based coalition, including Germany and Japan, had paid between 80 and 90
percent of its total military costs.[19] But in the second Gulf War the United
States did more than defeat Iraq; it occupied it. And it did so with the support of fewer wealthy allies. For much of 2003 America's leaders seemed
reluctant to confront this reality. "Iraq is a wealthy nation," the president's
spokesman Ari Fleischer blithely declared. "Iraq will have a huge financial
base from within, upon which to draw . . . because of [its] oil wealth." The
motto of America's biggest corporation, Wal-Mart, is simple and to the
point: "Always Low Prices. Always." The same principle was initially
adopted by the Bush administration after 9/11. Regime change was the
policy, but the means allocated to it were small change.

It is worth remembering that as late as September 2003 the Bush administration had still spent relatively little on the reconstruction of Afghanistan,
where nation building had supposedly been under way for a year and a
half. According to CARE International, the amount per person per year
pledged to Afghanistan by that date—by all foreign donors—was no more
than a quarter of the amount actually spent on postconflict recovery in
Kosovo, despite the fact that Afghanistan's needs were obviously far more
acute. In any case, the Center on International Cooperation calculated in
June 2003 that no more than $1.6 billion had actually been "disbursed" for
Afghan reconstruction, of which just $947 million had been "activated"
(which often meant it had been spent on vehicles and computers for Western "needs assessment" teams). Barely $192 million had been spent on
projects that had been completed.[20] The future stability in Afghanistan
plainly depends on the success of the Interim Administration established
in Kabul under President Hamid Karzai. Yet at the time of writing, less

than a fifth of postwar funding had gone to the Afghan government's designated trust funds; far more had been distributed via international donors. By May 2003 the United States had disbursed a paltry *$5 million* to the main Afghan Interim Administration Fund.[21]

Such tightfistedness cannot be blamed on the Bush administration alone, however. The decline in America's foreign aid budget—from its peak in the years after the Second World War, when it averaged close to 1.8 percent of U.S. gross national product, to its present level of barely 0.2 percent[22]—is the result of many years of cheeseparing by American legislators. In the early stages of the war in Iraq there was a surreal meeting of House and Senate negotiators to determine how—and where—the $79 billion initially requested by the Bush administration to cover the cost of the war should be spent. By the time they finished, $2.9 billion had been earmarked to bail out American airlines, whose profits have been squeezed by the increased international insecurity since 9/11. Another $275 million had been diverted to workers recently laid off by the airlines. There was even a farcical moment when Senator Patrick J. Leahy of Vermont proposed that $3.3 million of the war budget should be spent on reconstructing a dam near his house in Waterbury. Given the choice between local pork and national security, there are always some members of Congress who can be relied on to opt for the former.

Yet attitudes changed discernibly in the course of 2003; witness the congressional approval of the administration's request in October of that year for $87 billion to fund the occupation and reconstruction of Iraq and Afghanistan. There is, after all, a difference between aid that is simply disbursed to unreformed foreign states and aid that goes to make a success of an American regime change. And American lawmakers are not blind to the benefits as well as the costs of overthrowing Saddam Hussein.

At substantially less than the requested $79 billion—probably closer to $48 billion—the war itself was relatively cheap.[23] Moreover, as economists at the University of Chicago pointed out, the United States might even have made a saving by getting rid of Saddam since it was costing around $13 billion a year just to contain the military threat he posed.[24] No doubt $87 billion sounds like a great deal of money to most Americans. But it is equivalent to just 0.8 percent of U.S. GDP, and given the impossibility of forecasting how much failure in Iraq would cost, it seems a reasonably low price to pay to establish a stable and friendly system of government in that country—if one assumes this can be achieved. Admittedly, most of the $87 billion will be absorbed by the purely military costs of the U.S. presence. Just over $20 billion has been earmarked for reconstruction, a quarter of which will go on modernizing the Iraqi security forces.[25] Repairs to the dilapidated oil wells, pipelines and refineries alone could cost over $5 billion; overhauling the electricity system, more than twice that. Still, $20 billion is still a large sum in relation to Iraq's miserably low GDP; it is proportionately a far bigger stimulus than Marshall Plan aid was to West Germany in the late 1940s, since the German economy never collapsed as completely under Hitler as Iraq's has under Saddam.[26] Moreover, international donors have already offered around $13 billion toward the cost of postwar reconstruction.

Why should the expenditure of up to $100 billion on security and reconstruction not suffice to bring about an Iraqi recovery? After all, the country has the second-largest oil reserves in the world. Before they were plunged into poverty by Saddam's despotism, the average Iraqi's income was between a quarter and a half of his American counterpart, depending on the method of calculation used. By 1999, however, two decades of war, state control, state theft and sanctions had reduced the average Iraqi's income to three-quarters of 1 percent of the average American's.[27] Twenty years are not long enough to eradicate the collective memory of how a market economy works; the experiences of Poland and Russia in the 1990s make it clear that even forty-five years do not suffice, though after seventy-five years the slate has largely been wiped clean. Under the right circumstances, then, Iraq could bounce back quite rapidly to pre-1979 standards of living. For economic recovery to begin, of course, three things are urgently needed: the effective imposition of law and order, the repair and restoration of basic infrastructure (in particular, water and electricity) and substantial expenditure on reconstruction to modernize the dilapidated oil fields and stimulate economic activity in other sectors. But these things can be achieved, provided the occupation is not prematurely terminated and stable economic and legal institutions are given time to take root.

The Bush administration did not invade Iraq because of the country's oil reserves, contrary to the widely believed conspiracy theory.[28] However, reviving oil production is a necessary precondition for the success of the

American transformation of Iraq. That Iraq has a lot of oil under the ground nobody doubts, though the exact quantity of the country's reserves is hotly debated by industry experts. But whether Iraq has just 78 billion barrels or 300 billion barrels is a matter of purely academic interest in the short run. The real question is how much oil will be pumped out of the ground this year, next year and the year after, and what price will each barrel of it fetch? Table 13 offers three possible scenarios for an occupation optimistically assumed to last four years. In the best scenario, Iraq is able to increase production to 3.5 million barrels a day by 2006, and the price of oil remains at the high level of $30 a barrel, producing a total of around $100 billion over four years. In reality, supply is likely to grow more slowly and average prices to be lower, so that revenues for the whole period might end up being somewhat less than $40 billion. Note also that these are gross revenue projections; all kinds of costs would have to be deducted from these figures. Nor should we forget Iraq's existing foreign debts, $120 billion to foreign lenders plus up to $125 billion in reparations claims. Only a cancellation of these "odious debts"—odious because they were incurred by the tyrant Saddam—would free future oil revenues to finance reconstruction. Nevertheless, the outlook is not hopeless. At least some of the costs of Iraq's stabilization should ultimately be covered by oil sales.

TABLE 13. IRAQ'S OIL REVENUES: SOME PROJECTED
REVENUES, 2003–06

	2003	2004	2005	2006	Total
Middle					
Price per barrel ($)	25	25	25	25	
Barrels per day (million)	1.7	2.5	2.5	2.5	
Barrels per year (million)	620.5	912.5	912.5	912.5	
Revenue per year (billion $)	3.9	22.8	22.8	22.8	72.3
Lower					
Price per barrel ($)	15	15	15	15	
Barrels per day (million)	1.7	2	2	2	
Barrels per year (million)	620.5	730	730	730	
Revenue per year (billion $)	2.3	11.0	11.0	11.0	35.2
Upper					
Price per barrel ($)	30	30	30	30	
Barrels per day (million)	1.7	2.5	3	3.5	
Barrels per year (million)	620.5	912.5	1095	1277.5	
Revenue per year (billion $)	4.7	27.4	32.9	38.3	103.2

Source: Author's own calculations.

Finally, if stabilization is successful, not only will the country's economy grow, but American exports to Iraq will also grow, just as happened when Germany and Japan revived in the later 1940s. Critics of the Bush administration grumble that American companies are being awarded contracts for the reconstruction of Iraq's infrastructure. They should instead celebrate the fact that postwar policy is already creating jobs for some American workers, for without such material payoffs magnanimous policies to former foes quickly forfeit public support. The arithmetic of occupation is not the zero-sum game it sometimes appears to President Bush's more radical critics, who insist that every dollar spent in Iraq is a dollar less for American schools or hospitals.[29] On the contrary, success in Iraq could pay significant dividends—and not just to those companies that take the risk of accepting contracts for the country's reconstruction.

GUNS AND BUTTER

It is not, then, the cost of regime change and nation building that threatens the American empire with overstretch. It is expenditure much closer to home. For the American economy has come to rely to a greater extent than at any time in its history on consumption and credit—both public and private. Since America's external power is predicated on the strength of the economy, there is therefore a paradox. Traditionally, empires faced a choice between guns or butter—between military expenditures and consumption—and were constrained by excessive indebtedness. But the American empire needs consumption to fuel its economic growth, out of which its military expenditures can so easily be afforded. And it seems to be able to borrow unprecedented sums in order to maintain the growth of consumption. It is a guns *and* butter empire.

The paradox is perfectly embodied in the high-mobility multipurpose wheeled vehicle, otherwise known as the Hummer. In its original incarnation, the Hummer was designed by AM General in 1979 as a light personnel carrier for the U.S. military, and it has become the transportation of choice for American patrols in nearly all the conflict zones where U.S. troops are deployed. Yet the Hummer is also a consumer durable. Since the rights to produce them for civilian use were sold to General Motors in

1999, Hummers have begun to appear in a variety of unmilitary hues on highways all over America, beginning in California.[30] Is the Hummer for conquest or consumption? The answer is both. Indeed, with its low mileage to the gallon (on average 11 mpg) and its huge weight and width, it exemplifies the profligacy of American fossil fuel use.

Some would of course close the circle by saying that Hummers are needed in Iraq in order to keep Hummers in California supplied with cheap gasoline. But this once again exaggerates the importance of oil in the decision for war against Saddam Hussein. For the paradox of the empire of guns and butter can also be illustrated by comparing the contrasting economic fortunes of two American companies since the election of President Bush. Anyone who invested in the oil field engineering company Halliburton in late 2000 in the expectation that the company would benefit from a Republican election victory has been disappointed. In the three years to November 2003 the company's shares declined by more than a third and did not benefit significantly from the more aggressive Middle Eastern policy supported by its friends in high places. An investor who put his money in Wal-Mart shares in late 2000 would, by contrast, have made a capital *gain* of a fifth. From a strictly economic point of view, investment in the quintessential consumer sector company has proved much more profitable than investment in the firm supposedly at the heart of the military-petroleum complex.

The growing importance of personal consumption in American economic growth has been one of the most striking developments of the past four decades. As a percentage of GDP it has risen from around 62 percent in the 1960s to nearly 70 percent in 2002. The corollary of this has been a decline in savings: the personal savings rate has dropped from an average of 9 percent from 1959 until 1992 to just over 4 percent in the subsequent eleven years. Indeed, Americans have financed a substantial part of their increased consumption by borrowing. Household sector credit market debt rose from 44 percent of GDP in the 1960s and 1970s to 78 percent in 2002.

Nor is it only ordinary Americans who are relying on credit to cover their rising expenditures on consumption. The federal government admitted in July 2003 that the budget surplus of $334 billion that it forecast two years before had—thanks to a combination of recession, war and tax cuts—become a deficit of at least $475 billion.[31] This figure came as a shock to many Americans. During the Clinton administration, after all, the Congressional Budget Office projected budget surpluses stretching as far as the eye could see. However, these projections were based on the assumption that regardless of inflation or economic growth, the federal government would spend precisely the same number of dollars, year in and year out, on everything apart from Social Security, Medicare and other entitlements. At the same time, the CBO confidently assumed that federal tax revenues would grow at roughly 6 percent per year. In 2001 the CBO decided that failing to adjust projected discretionary spending for inflation (but not economic growth) was no longer "useful or viable." Making this adjustment reduced the projected 2002–11 surplus from $6.8 trillion to $5.6 trillion. But that was nothing compared with the impact of subsequent unforeseen events. Two years later, after a recession, a huge tax cut and 9/11, the CBO's projected ten-year surplus had fallen to $20 billion. Nevertheless, the CBO was still able to predict a medium-term decline in the federal debt in public hands from 35.5 percent of GDP to 16.8 percent over ten years.[32] To generate this result, the CBO assumed, conveniently, that discretionary spending would remain fixed over the next decade even as the economy grew. In fact, these purchases, which include the additional military and security costs since September 2001, have risen more than twice as fast as economic output over the last three years. At the time of writing, the CBO has revised its projections again. It now predicts a deficit for 2004 of close to half a trillion dollars, and for the ten-year period from 2002 to 2011 the erstwhile surplus has become a $2.7 trillion deficit. That is $9.5 trillion more new debt than the CBO was anticipating before the last presidential election, less than four years ago.

Yet even the CBO's latest projections still grossly understate the true size of the federal government's liabilities because its "bottom line" is only that part of the liabilities that takes the form of bonds.

Americans like security. But they like Social Security more than national security. It is their preoccupation with the hazards of old age and ill health that will prove to be the real cause of their country's fiscal overstretch, not their preoccupation with the hazards of terrorism and the "axis of evil." Today's latent fiscal crisis is the result not of excessive overseas military burdens but of a chronic mismatch between earlier Social Security legislation, some of it dating back to the New Deal, and the changing demographics of American society.

In just three years, the first of around seventy-seven million baby boomers will start collecting Social Security benefits. In six years they will start collecting Medicare benefits. By the time they all are retired, an official estimates, the United States will have doubled the size of its elderly population but increased by barely 15 percent the number of taxpaying workers able to pay for their benefits. Economists refer to the government's commitment to pay pension and medical benefits to current and future elderly as part of the government's "implicit" liabilities. But these liabilities are no less real than the obligation to pay back the principal plus the interest on government bonds. Indeed, politically, it may be easier to default on explicit debt than to stop paying Social Security and Medicare benefits. While no one can say for sure which liability the government would renege on first, one thing is clear: the implicit liabilities dwarf the explicit ones.

The scale of these implicit liabilities was laid bare in 2003 in a paper by Jagadeesh Gokhale, a senior economist at the Federal Reserve Bank of Cleveland, and Kent Smetters, the former deputy assistant secretary of economic policy at the U.S. Treasury. They asked the following question: Suppose that today the government could get its hands on all the revenue it can expect to collect in the future, but had to use it, also today, to pay off all its future expenditure commitments, including debt service. Would the discounted present value of all its future revenues suffice to cover the discounted present value of all its future expenditures? The answer is a decided no. According to their calculations, the shortfall amounts to $45 trillion.[33] To put that figure into perspective, it is twelve times larger than the current official debt held by the public and roughly four times the country's annual output. Gokhale and Smetters also asked by how much taxes would have to be raised or expenditures cut—on an immediate and permanent basis—to generate, in present value, $45 trillion. They offer four alternative answers (see table 14). The government could, starting today, raise income taxes (individual and corporate) by 69 percent, or it could raise payroll taxes by 95 percent, or it could cut Social Security and Medicare benefits by 56 percent, or it could cut federal discretionary spending altogether—to zero.

TABLE 14: PERCENTAGE INCREASES IN TAXATION OR CUTS IN
EXPENDITURE REQUIRED TODAY TO ACHIEVE GENERATIONAL
BALANCE IN U.S. FISCAL POLICY

Policy	Percentage Change
Increase federal income taxes	+ 69
Increase payroll taxes	+ 95
Cut federal purchases	– 100
Cut Social Security and Medicare	– 56

Source: Jagadeesh Gokhale and Kent Smetters, "Fiscal and Generational Imbalances."

Another way of expressing the problem is to compare our own lifetime
tax burden with the lifetime tax burden the next generation will have to
shoulder if the government does not do one of the above—hence the term
often used to describe calculations like these: *generational accounting*. What
such accounts imply is that anyone who has the bad luck to be born in
America today, as opposed to back in the 1940s or 1950s, is going to be sad-
dled throughout his working life with very high tax rates, potentially twice
as high as those his parents or grandparents faced. Notwithstanding the Bush
administration's tax cuts, Americans today are scarcely undertaxed. So the
idea of taxing the next generation at twice the current rate seems, to say
the least, fanciful.

There is, however, one serious problem with these figures, not with
the calculations that underlie them but with their *acceptance*. To put it
bluntly, this news is so bad that scarcely anyone believes it. It is not that
people are completely oblivious of the problem. It is common knowledge
that Americans are living longer and that paying for the rising proportion
of elderly people in the population is going to be expensive. What people
do not yet realize is just how expensive. One common response is to say
that the economists in question have a political ax to grind and have therefore made assumptions calculated to paint the blackest picture possible. But
the reality is that the Gokhale-Smetters study was commissioned by Paul
O'Neill when he was treasury secretary and was prepared while Smetters
was at the Treasury and Gokhale at the Federal Reserve. Moreover, far
from being a worst-case scenario, the Gokhale and Smetters figures are
based on what are arguably optimistic official assumptions about growth in

future Medicare costs and longevity. Historically, the annual growth rate in real Medicare benefits per beneficiary has exceeded that of labor productivity by 2.5 percentage points. But official projections assume only a 1 percentage point differential in the future. (They also assume, optimistically, that it will take fifty years for Americans to achieve current Japanese life expectancy.) Under somewhat different assumptions the total fiscal imbalance could be even larger than $45 trillion.

Nobody can be surprised that in the American political system such unpleasant fiscal arithmetic gets marginalized. No sane presidential candidate would campaign with the slogan "Hike taxes by two-thirds." Nor is any rational incumbent likely to cut Social Security and Medicare benefits by more than half. It is therefore safe to assume that in the short run almost nothing will be done to address the problem of generational imbalance. Unfortunately, this means the problem will get still worse. According to Gokhale and Smetters, if policy were left unchanged until 2008, income taxes would have to go up even higher—by 74 percent—to close the intergenerational gap. In other words, the arithmetic of generational accounting implies a distributive reckoning at some point in the future. The government sooner or later has to reduce its spending commitments or increase its tax revenues. Regrettably, the Bush administration's approach to the latent federal fiscal crisis seems so far to have been a variation on Lenin's old slogan: "The worse the better." Faced with mounting deficits, the president and his men elected to push three major tax cuts through Congress. Administration officials have sometimes defended these measures as a stimulus to economic activity, a version of the "voodoo economics" once upon a time derided by the president's father. There are good reasons to be skeptical about this, however, not least because the principal beneficiaries of these tax cuts are wealthy individuals.

One possible fiscal solution to the problem of generational imbalance has in fact already been implemented in Britain; that is simply to scrap the mechanism that allows welfare entitlements to rise ahead of general inflation. In 1979 the newly elected government of Margaret Thatcher discreetly reformed the long-established basic state pension, which was increased each year in line with the higher of two indices, the retail price index or the average earnings index. The first Thatcher budget amended the rule so that the pension would rise in line only with the retail price index, breaking the link with average earnings.[34] The short-run fiscal saving involved was substantial, since the growth of earnings was much higher than inflation after 1980. The long-run saving was greater still. The United Kingdom's unfunded public pension liability today is a great deal smaller than those of most continental governments, as little as 5 percent of GDP for the period to 2050, compared with 70 percent for Italy, 105 percent for France and 110 percent for Germany.[35] This and other Thatcher reforms are the reason the United Kingdom is one of the elite of developed economies that do not have major holes in their generational accounts.[36]

In the present American situation, the vital thing must be to bring Medicare spending under control, for it is in fact responsible for the lion's share—82 percent—of the $45 trillion budget black hole. Just cutting the growth rate of payments per beneficiary by half a percentage point per year would shave $15 trillion off the $45 trillion long-term budget gap. There must be a way of capping the program's growth without jeopardizing its ability to deliver medical services to the less well-off elderly. Unfortunately, by subsidizing the cost of prescriptions, the Medicare reform put forward by President Bush and enacted by Congress in 2003 will have the very opposite effect.[37] A second policy option (now under serious consideration) would be to privatize Social Security.[38]

Will either of these policies be implemented? The answer is that it seems unlikely in view of the growing political organization and self-consciousness of the American elderly. Social Security is sometimes referred to as the third rail by American politicians, because politicians who touch it by suggesting any cut in benefits tend to receive a violent political shock from the American Association of Retired Persons (AARP). Mindful of the British experience in the 1980s, the AARP has already commissioned a study showing what the effect would be if an American government replaced the link between the state pension and wages with a link to inflation. It concludes that price indexation would cause the average replacement rate (benefit as a percentage of preretirement income) to drop by half over a period of seventy-five years, "fundamentally changing the relationship between workers' contributions and the benefits they receive."[39] Quite why today's elderly should worry about the level of pensions three-quarters of a century hence is not altogether clear. Nevertheless, such arguments resonate not only among the retired but also among the soon-to-retire. The baby boomers are now so old that they have a bigger stake in preserving their future benefits than in lowering their current payroll taxes. Indeed, many have already joined the AARP, which sends Americans application forms on their fiftieth birthdays. So long as attitudes toward old age remain unchanged and so long as the retired and soon-to-be-retired remain so well organized, radical reform of the U.S. welfare state—and hence a balancing of federal finances—seems a distant prospect.

GOING CRITICAL

Conventional wisdom predicts that if investors and traders in government bonds anticipate a growing imbalance in a government's fiscal policy, they will sell that government's bonds. There are good reasons for this. A widening gap between current revenues and expenditures is usually filled in two ways. The first is by selling more bonds to the public. The second is by printing money.[40] Other things being equal, either response leads to a decline in bond prices and a rise in interest rates, the incentive people need to purchase bonds. That incentive has to be larger when the real return of principal plus interest on the bond is threatened by default or inflation. The higher the anticipated rate of inflation is, the higher interest rates will rise because nobody wants to lend money and be paid back in banknotes whose real value has been watered down by rising prices. The process whereby current fiscal policy influences expectations about future inflation is a dynamic one with powerful feedback effects. If financial markets decide a country is broke and is going to inflate, they act in ways that make that outcome more likely. By pushing up interest rates, they raise the cost of financing the government's debt and hence worsen its fiscal position. Higher interest rates may also depress business activity. Firms stop borrowing and start laying off workers. The attendant recession lowers tax receipts and drives the government into a deeper fiscal hole. In desperation, the government starts printing money and lending it, via the banking system, to the private sector. The additional money leads to inflation, and the higher inflation rates assumed by the market turn into a self-fulfilling prophecy. Thus the private sector and the government find themselves in a game of chicken. If the government can convince the private sector it can pay its bills without printing money, interest rates stay down. If it cannot, interest rates go up, and the government may be forced to print money sooner rather than later.

Figures like those produced by Gokhale and Smetters might therefore have been expected to precipitate a sharp drop in bond prices. But at the time their study appeared, financial markets barely reacted. Yields on ten-year treasuries have in fact been heading downward for twenty years. At their peak in 1981 they rose above 15 percent. As recently as 1994 they were above 8 percent. By mid-June 2003—two weeks after the $45 trillion fiscal imbalance figure had appeared on the front page of the *Financial Times*—they stood at 3.1 percent, the lowest they had been since 1958.[41] Six months later they were just 1 percent higher.

One possible explanation for this apparent *non sequitur* is that bond traders found themselves in a similar predicament to that experienced by their colleagues trading equities just five years ago. At the time it was privately acknowledged by nearly everyone on Wall Street and publicly acknowledged by most economists that American stocks, especially those in the technology sector, were wildly overvalued. In 1996 Alan Greenspan famously declared that the stock market was suffering from "irrational exuberance." Over the next three years a succession of economists sought to explain why the future profits of American companies could not possibly be high enough to justify their giddy stock market valuations. Still the markets rose. It was not until January 2000 that the bubble burst.[42] Perhaps something similar subsequently happened in the bond market. Just as investors and traders knew that most Internet companies could never earn enough to justify their 1999 valuations, investors and traders in 2003 knew that future government revenues could not remotely cover both the interest on the federal debt and the transfers due on the government's implicit liabilities. But just as participants in the stock market were the mental prisoners of a five-year bull market, so participants in the bond market last year were the mental prisoners of a twenty-year bond bull market that had seen the price of long-term treasuries rise by a factor of two and a half. Everyone knew there was going to be a "correction." Yet nobody wanted to be the first player out of the market—for fear of having to sit and watch the bull run continue for another year. Between January 2000 and October 2002 the Dow Jones Industrials index declined by almost exactly 38 percent as irrational exuberance gave way to rational gloom. In the middle of 2003 it was not difficult to imagine a similar correction to the bond market.[43]

When trying to make financial matters more vivid, writers often invoke imagery from the natural world. Bubbles burst. Bears chase bulls. So vast is America's looming fiscal crisis that it is tempting to talk about the fiscal equivalent of the perfect storm—or the perfect earthquake, if you prefer; perhaps the perfect forest fire. In this case, however, nature offers more than mere literary color. For the dynamics of fiscal overstretch really do have much in common with the dynamics of natural disasters. We can know only that, like a really big earthquake, a big fiscal crisis will happen. What we cannot know is when it will strike, or the size of the shock. Adopting the language used by scientists who study the unpredictable pattern of natural disasters, we are condemned to wait and see when our fiscal system will enter "self-sustaining criticality"—in other words, when it will go critical, passing with dramatic speed and violence from one equilibrium to another.[44]

The simplest example of this phenomenon is what happens when you try to add to a pile of dry sand. If you drop more sand on top of the pile, one grain at a time, it keeps growing higher for a while. Then suddenly—and there is no way of knowing which grain will make it happen—the pile collapses. That collapse is when the pile of sand goes critical. Something not wholly dissimilar happens when one of the earth's tectonic plates pushes once too often against another along a fault line, causing an earthquake. Now translate this into the world of mammals, which, unlike particles of sand, have consciousness. Imagine a herd of cattle quietly grazing while a man and his badly disciplined dog take a walk through a field. At first, one or two cows on the periphery spot him; then a couple more. They start to feel a little nervous. But it is only when the dog barks that the whole herd stampedes. A stampede is the self-sustaining criticality of mammals panicking.

What might panic the mammals who buy and sell long-term U.S. bonds for a living? Here the sand pile is composed of the *expectations* of millions of individuals. Like grains of sand, little bits of bad news are dropped on us, day after day, week after week. Like the sand pile, we can hold steady for some time before the cumulative weight of these grains of bad news causes us to alter our fundamental expectations. But one day something happens—maybe just one extra grain of bad news—that triggers the shift from equilibrium into self-sustaining criticality. Everything therefore depends on what traders and investors expect the government to do about the $45 trillion black hole and what might happen to change the expectations they currently hold. Here, then, is one possible scenario. Bondholders will start to sell off as soon as a critical mass of them recognize that the government's implicit and explicit liabilities are too much for it to handle with conventional fiscal policy and conclude that the only way the government will be able to pay its bills is by printing money, leading to higher inflation. What commonly triggers such shifts in expectations is an item of bad financial news.[45]

One reason this scenario has superficial plausibility is that it echoes past events. Although few bond traders have history degrees, they recollect that the high bond yields of the early 1980s were in large measure a consequence of the inflationary fiscal and monetary policies of the previous decade. Nor do the 1970s furnish the only historical precedent for inflationary outcomes of fiscal crises. Governments in fiscal difficulties have often resorted to printing money because doing so helps in three ways. First, they get to exchange intrinsically worthless pieces of paper for real goods and services. Secondly, inflation waters down the real value of official debt. Thirdly, if the salaries of government workers are paid with a lag or are only partially adjusted for inflation, inflation will lower their real incomes. The same holds true for other government transfer payments.

Yet there are reasons to be skeptical about the idea of a new inflation. For one thing, there are strong deflationary pressures at work in the United States today. Overcapacity generated during the 1990s boom, investor hesitancy in the wake of the bust, consumer anxiety about job losses—all these things meant that virtually the only sector of the U.S. economy still buoyant in mid-2003 was housing, for the simple reason that mortgage rates were at their lowest in two generations. In April 2003 one of the lead stories on Bloomberg described *de*flation as the "great bugaboo menacing the markets and the economy in the early 2000s."[46] A month later the chairman of the Federal Reserve, Alan Greenspan, acknowledged that there was a "possibility" of deflation in his testimony before the Joint Economic Committee of Congress.[47] A second argument against the higher inflation scenario is more pragmatic: only a modest proportion of the federal government's $45 trillion fiscal imbalance would in fact be reduced through a jump in inflation in the ways described above. First, much of the government's tradable debt is of short maturity; indeed, fully a third of it has a maturity of one year or less.[48] That makes it much harder to inflate away because any increase in inflationary expectations forces the government to pay higher interest rates when it seeks to renew these short-dated bonds. Secondly, Social Security benefits are protected against inflation through an annual inflation adjustment. Medicare benefits are also effectively inflation-proof because the government unquestioningly pays whatever bills it receives. Thirdly, government workers are not likely to sit idly and watch prices outpace their wages. For all these reasons, a rerun of the 1970s would not in fact solve the federal government's fiscal problems.

There is one other, more drastic possibility, however. Bond markets worry about default on the government's explicit, tradable liabilities, not its implicit liabilities such as Social Security. A default on the government's nontradable liabilities may seem hard to imagine, but it has a historical precedent. In *ancien régime* France the biggest burden on royal finances did not take the form of bonds but the salaries due to tens of thousands of officeholders, men who had simply bought government sinecures and expected in return to be paid salaries for life. All attempts to reduce these implicit liabilities within the existing political system simply failed. It was only after the outbreak of the Revolution—arguably a direct consequence of the fiscal crisis of the monarchy—that the offices were abolished. The officeholders were compensated by cash payments in a new currency, the *assignats,* which within a few years were reduced to worthlessness by the revolutionary printing presses.[49] Vested interests that resist necessary fiscal reforms can end up losing much more heavily from a revolutionary solution.

Perhaps, then, Paul Kennedy was not so wrong to draw parallels between modern America and prerevolutionary France. Bourbon France, like America today, had pretensions to imperial grandeur but was ultimately wrecked by a curious kind of overstretch. It was not their overseas adventures that did it for the Bourbons. Indeed, Louis XVI's last foreign war, in support of the rebellious American colonists, was a huge strategic success. The French overstretch was internal, and at its very heart was a black hole of implicit liabilities. In the same way, the decline and fall of America's undeclared empire may be due not to terrorists at the gates or to the rogue regimes that sponsor them, but to a fiscal crisis of the welfare state at home.

This fiscal crisis is not of course a problem unique to America. It afflicts the world's second- and third-largest economies even more seriously. But neither Japan nor Germany any longer has pretensions to be a global hegemon, so their decline into economic old age has minimal strategic implications. That is not true in the American case. As Gibbon said, the finances of a declining empire do indeed make an interesting subject.

THE DEBTOR EMPIRE

Yet the extent of the fiscal problems of the United States and the timing of their manifestation cannot be discussed with reference to American expectations alone. This is a world of globalized capital flows, and no American foreign policy initiative can be divorced from one crucial fact: that this is a debtor empire.

It is an unusual, though not unprecedented, state of affairs. In the heyday of the European empires, the dominant power was supposed to be a creditor, investing a large proportion of its own savings in the economic development of its colonies. Hegemony, in short, also meant hege*money*. When the last great Anglophone empire bestrode the globe a hundred years ago, capital export was one of the foundations of its power. Between 1870 and 1914 net flows out of London averaged between 4 and 5 percent of gross domestic product; at their peak on the eve of the First World War they reached an astonishing 9 percent. This was not merely an extraordinary diversion of British savings away from home. It was also a remarkable attempt to transform the global economy by investing in the construction of commercial infrastructure—docks, railways and telegraph lines—in what we would now call less developed countries. Whatever its undoubted

shortcomings in other respects, one undeniable benefit of British hegemony was that it encouraged investors to risk their money in such countries, something they are significantly less willing to do in our own time.

This was not just a British idiosyncrasy. When the United States was fit-
fully asserting itself in Central America, the Caribbean, Europe and Asia in
the first half of the twentieth century, it was able to engage in "dollar diplomacy" because it was a substantial net capital exporter. By 1938 the gross
value of U.S. assets abroad amounted to $11.5 billion.[50] Having bankrolled
the victors during both world wars, the United States bankrolled the reconstruction of the losers in peacetime too. The most famous example of
U.S. capital export was, as we have seen, the Marshall Plan, the high water-
mark of official unrequited transfers to foreign governments. However, private American foreign lending continued to fuel the world's economic
recovery for a further two decades. Between 1960 and 1976 the United
States ran current account surpluses totaling nearly $60 billion.

Those days are gone. Today, even as it boldly overthrows one rogue
regime after another, the United States is the world's biggest borrower.
Since 1982 the country has run a current account deficit totaling nearly $3
trillion. In 2002 the deficit was 4.8 percent of GDP; in 2003 it was even
higher.[51] According to one estimate, gross foreign claims on the United
States in 2003 amounted to around $8 trillion of U.S. financial assets, in-
cluding 13 percent of all stocks and 24 percent of corporate bonds. The
country's international investment position has changed dramatically, from
net assets equivalent to 13 percent of GDP in 1980 to net liabilities worth
23 percent in 2002. In March 2003 the *Wall Street Journal* posed the question: "Is the U.S. hooked on foreign capital?"[52] The answer is yes, and it applies to the government even more than to the private sector. According to
the Federal Reserve's September 2003 estimate, foreign investors currently
hold around 46 percent of the federal debt in private hands—more than
double the proportion they held ten years ago.[53] These are extraordinary
levels of external indebtedness, more commonly associated with emerging
markets than empires. Indeed, Brazil's net international indebtedness is now
lower than that of the United States. At a press conference in April 2003,
the International Monetary Fund chief economist Ken Rogoff remarked
that he would be "pretty concerned" about "a developing country that had

gaping current account deficits year after year, as far as the eye can see, of five percent or more, with budget ink spinning from black into red, with the likely deficit to GDP ratio for general government exceeding five percent this year [and] open-ended security costs." Of course, he hastily added, the United States is "not an emerging market." But "at least a little bit of that calculus still applies."[54] Perhaps more than a little.

Given that domestic political gridlock will surely lead to a stream of deficits in the coming decades, a great deal depends on whether or not foreign investors will be willing to absorb increasing quantities of U.S. treasuries. According to one line of argument, there is nothing to worry about on this score. The reason that so much overseas capital flows into the United States, so it is said, is that the American economy is the engine of global growth and foreign investors simply want a "piece of the action." Yet foreign investors seem willing to settle for markedly lower returns when they invest in the United States than the returns Americans get when they invest overseas.[55] Far from acquiring equity in America's dynamic corporations, many foreign investors turn out to be mainly interested in buying government bonds. Why is this? The explanation lies in the fact that a substantial and rising share of the foreign holdings of American bonds are in fact in the hands of East Asian central banks, which have been buying up dollar assets in order to keep their own currencies from appreciating against the dollar. Between April 2002 and August 2003 the central banks of China and Hong Kong bought ninety-six billion dollars of U.S. government securities.[56] The Bank of Japan was equally active.

From a strictly economic point of view, this may give no grounds for anxiety since the Asian central banks have as strong an interest in the arrangement as the big borrower itself. China's exports to the United States are one of its principal engines of growth and job creation. Looked at another way, there is a neat symmetry between the American propensity to consume and the Chinese propensity to save. As figure 13 shows, China is essentially playing the role that Japan played in the 1980s, channeling its surplus savings into the American current account and fiscal deficits. But what are the strategic implications of the fact that for its economic stability—to be precise, for its ability to finance federal borrowing at around 4 percent per annum—the United States is reliant on the central bank of the People's Republic of China?

FIGURE 13

**Net National Savings as a Percentage of Gross National Income,
China, Japan and the United States, 1982–2001**

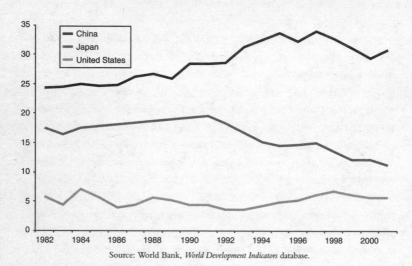

Source: World Bank, *World Development Indicators* database.

There are two ways of thinking about this symbiotic relationship between Asian savers and American spenders. One is that it gives the Asians leverage over the United States, in the conventional way that a creditor has leverage over a debtor. In the event of a disagreement over a foreign policy issue—the obvious examples that spring to mind are Taiwan and North Korea—the Chinese might consider reducing their exposure to U.S. bonds by selling a few billion off. That would apply pressure on the dollar and on U.S. interest rates. Yet this commonsense reasoning overlooks what such a strategy would cost the Chinese themselves. For the appreciation of their currency would immediately have an impact on their exports. It would also have a strong deflationary effect on their economy as a whole. And—more important, perhaps—it would inflict severe losses on Chinese institutions left holding dollar assets. Given the way Asian banks generally hold dollars in their reserves but lend long in their local currencies, dollar devaluation could punish the Chinese by tipping their banking system (which is far from healthy as things stand) into crisis.[57]

The crux of the matter is that the Asian-American economic relationship is not symmetrical. Twentieth-century history handed the United States a privileged position in the world economy; its currency became and has remained the world's favorite. Since 1945 it has been used more than any other for denominating international transactions, and that has made it the preferred currency for central bank reserves.[58] A century ago sterling enjoyed something of the same status. But sterling was strictly pegged to gold, just as the dollar was by somewhat different means during the years of the Bretton Woods system. De Gaulle complained in the 1960s that the United States was abusing its position as printer of the world's reserve currency, but as long as the dollar retained the link to gold, there were limits to how far such abuse could be taken. Only from the 1970s onward, when the dollar became a pure fiat currency with its supply dictated by the Federal Reserve regardless of gold convertibility, was the United States really able to exploit the dollar's unique appeal to foreigners. Ever since, the United States has periodically collected from foreigners the special tax known as seigniorage, the transfer from the holders of a currency to its issuer that automatically happens when the value of that currency is diminished. Dollar devaluations have been the device Americans have periodically used to reduce the real value of their external liabilities, most spectacularly in the mid-1980s. No other economy in the world reaps such benefits from devaluation as the United States. The cost in terms of more expensive imports is offset not just by the textbook stimulus to exports but, more important, by the real reduction in the value of America's external liabilities.

It was not so long ago that the dollar fell precipitously on the world's foreign exchange markets; it happened between 1985 and 1987. The second half of 2003 may have seen the start of a similar depreciation. Although the dollar's real trade-weighted exchange rate has risen slightly, its nominal rate has already declined by more than two-fifths against the euro since February 2002. This raises an important question, touched on in the previous chapter: could the dollar's reserve currency status be challenged by the euro? Recall that since the creation of the new European currency, international investors have acquired a whole new range of securities in which to invest, which are widely seen as being substitutes for dollar-denominated assets. Admittedly, the Eurozone economies seem to be stagnating compared with the United States by most measures of economic

performance. On the other hand, Europe has acquired the endearing characteristic of not wanting to fight wars, even when they are right on its
doorstep. French and German leaders are also markedly less keen to confront Islamist extremists than their American counterparts. These things
have their subtle benefits. For investors, the most important thing about a
safe haven is, after all, that it should be safe.

In any case, the Bush administration at times seems intent on biting the
hand that lends to it. The relationship between the United States and
China described above is in no way based on Chinese altruism. The Chinese buy dollar-denominated bonds not to help George W. Bush out, but
to maintain the exchange rate of their own currency against the dollar and
hence the competitiveness of their own products in the eyes of American
consumers.[59] Last year China had a $105 billion trade surplus with the
United States. The real reason for this—indeed the key to the whole Sino-
American interdependence—is, as we have seen, that Chinese households
save significantly more of their incomes than do their American counterparts. But to those Americans whose companies come under pressure from
cheaper Chinese competition, it is tempting to take another view: that
China is unfairly undercutting American firms. This explains the mounting pressure in Washington during 2003 for either a revaluation of the
Chinese currency relative to the dollar (code for a dollar devaluation) or
tariffs on Chinese imports.[60]

There are two reasons why such calls are ill advised, to say the least.
The first, to repeat, is that a dollar devaluation would have grave implications for Chinese financial institutions, many of which hold their reserves
in dollars but have renminbi-denominated assets. The consequence could
be deflation spreading throughout the Chinese economy.[61] The second
reason is that anti-Chinese measures would hurt American firms, a growing number of which are investing directly in China to exploit its combination of cheap but relatively good-quality labor in an apparently stable
institutional setting. Foreign direct investment in China now totals around
40 percent of Chinese GDP, a level of Western participation in the Chinese economy not seen since the era of the imperial Open Door.

Low long-term interest rates are the key to the postponement of
America's fiscal reckoning. So long as the debt can be financed abroad at
rates of little more than 4 percent, there will be no incentive to grasp the

political nettles that surround Medicare and Social Security. The price of these low rates, however, is that the United States cannot expect to devalue the dollar; it must live with a static or even rising real exchange rate because its trading partners in Asia are buying dollar-denominated securities precisely to maintain nominal exchange rates as they are. Put like that, the world sounds as if it has arrived at a more or less happy state of equilibrium. In history, however, no equilibrium goes unpunctuated. In the decade before 1914, it seemed to many observers as if economic interdependence between Britain and Germany were making a war between the two great empires unlikely, if not impossible. Still war came. In the months after the Wall Street stock market bubble burst in October 1929, it seemed as if the United States would experience nothing more than a conventional recession. The Smoot–Hawley tariff bill, enacted in June 1930, triggered a global depression.

None of us can know what will trigger a shift from last year's equilibrium to something quite different.[62] It could be domestic anxieties about a default on welfare entitlements; it could be a strategic change of heart in East Asia. Nor can any of us know when the shift will happen or how big it will be. As with an earthquake, its timing and magnitude are simply impossible to forecast. We cannot even be sure where the effects will be most severe. The possibility cannot be discounted that, as in the 1980s, a dollar devaluation might be more costly to East Asia's banks than to the United States economy. If that is the case—if China suffers the fate of Japan and is tipped into deflation by the vagaries of American economic policy—the future of the dollar as the world's favorite currency will surely cease to be assured. Today's open door between America and Asia could close with a surprisingly loud bang.

CONCLUSION:
LOOKING HOMEWARD

La comperai
per novecentonovantanove anni,
con facoltà, ogni mese,
di rescindere i patti.
Sono in questo paese
elastici de, par, case e contratti.

[I've bought it
for nine hundred ninety-nine years,
but I can cancel the arrangement at a month's notice.
It seems that in this country
both houses and contracts are elastic.]

GIACOMO PUCCINI, *Madama Butterfly,* Act I

Each of us is all the sums he has not counted: subtract us into nakedness and night again, and you shall see begin in Crete four thousand years ago the love that ended yesterday in Texas. The seed of our destruction will blossom in the desert. . . .

THOMAS WOLFE, *Look Homeward, Angel*[1]

PINKERTON AND SCHWARZENEGGER

The United States today is an empire—but a peculiar kind of empire. It is vastly wealthy. It is militarily peerless. It has astonishing cultural reach. Yet by comparison with other empires it often struggles to impose its will beyond its shores. Its successes in exporting American institutions to foreign lands have been outnumbered by its failures.

In many respects, this American empire shares the same aspirations and ambitions as the last great Anglophone hegemon. Despite originating in a revolt against British imperialism, the United States inherited many of its begetter's defining characteristics. Styling itself, in good Whig terminology, an "empire of liberty," the fledgling Republic embarked on an astonishingly rapid colonization of the central belt of the North American continent. If anything, the independent Americans were even more ruthless in the way they expropriated indigenous peoples than they had been as British subjects.[2] However, the differences between the British and American empires became more apparent as the United States sought to extend its influence overseas.[3] Its experiment with overt imperialism after 1898 had distinctly mixed results, ending unhappily in both the Pacific and the Caribbean, with the notable exceptions of Hawaii and Puerto Rico. Like the fickle Lieutenant Pinkerton in Puccini's *Madama Butterfly*, American overseas interventions went through three phases: ardent in Act I, absent in Act II, anguished in Act III.

Only when the United States could cast itself in an anti-imperialist role—first against the British Empire during the Second World War and then (more wisely) against the Soviet Union during the cold war—were Americans able to perform their own cryptoimperial role with self-confidence. Even then, there were clear limits to American stamina. The doctrine of limited war led to a draw in Korea and a defeat in Vietnam. Contradictory commitments undermined U.S. predominance in the Middle East too. It took a succession of humanitarian disasters abroad in the 1990s and terrorist attacks at home in 2001 to rekindle public enthusiasm for a more assertive American foreign policy, though even this had to be cloaked in euphemism, its imperial character repeatedly denied.

The United States has invaded and occupied many countries over the past two centuries. Yet in terms of their economic and political institutions relatively few of these have evolved into anything remotely resembling miniature Americas. Will things go any better in Kosovo, Afghanistan and Iraq? And can President Bush live up to his implied threats to deal sooner or later with the other members of the "axis of evil," Iran and North Korea—to say nothing of Cuba, Libya and Syria, added to the list of rogue states in May 2002, as well as Burma and Zimbabwe, also singled out for presidential opprobrium in November last year?[4]

At the time of writing, simply imposing order in Iraq was proving difficult enough, even with British and Polish assistance. After all the bravado of the Three-Week War, the Bush administration felt constrained to request assistance from the United Nations for its Coalition Provisional Authority. To have any hope of securing this, the United States had to promise to expedite the transfer of power from the Anglo-American coalition to an elected Iraqi government. American power also looked circumscribed in the Middle East. When George W. Bush visited the region in June 2003, some expressed the hope that the overthrow of Saddam would help break the deadlock in the Middle Eastern peace process, sending a signal to Syria and Iran that their support for terrorist organizations bent on the destruction of Israel would no longer be tolerated, bolstering the moderates among the Palestinian leadership and encouraging a skeptical Israeli government to take the route marked on the American "road map." By the fall, however, Yasser Arafat had reasserted his control over the Palestinian administration, Ariel Sharon was building a replica of the Berlin Wall around the Palestinians and for the first time Americans were being targeted by terrorists in the occupied territories. At the same time, al Qa'eda began to attack the one Arab autocracy that the United States had pledged itself to preserve, the house of Saud.

The Bush administration had meanwhile made equally little headway in dealing with what was surely the most dangerous of all the world's rogue regimes, North Korea. Pyongyang's development of long-range missiles and its research into nuclear, chemical and biological weapons—to say nothing of its huge conventional armed forces—plainly posed a huge threat to the stability of East Asia. In December 2002 the North Koreans had repudiated a 1994 agreement shutting down its nuclear reactors and had expelled UN monitors; in October 2003 a North Korean Foreign Ministry spokesman threatened, somewhat opaquely, to "open [North Korea's] nuclear deterrent to the public as a physical force." Could the United States do anything about this? Apparently not—despite the fact that the country continued to depend on American aid to feed its half-starved population. Insisting that it be given not just handouts but a fully fledged nonaggression treaty with the United States, this repulsive little dictatorship defied the American hyperpower with impunity.

The United States even hesitated before sending a tiny force to the one basket case country in Africa for which it can be said to have any historical responsibility, Liberia. In August 2003 three ships, carrying around 4,500 sailors and marines, were sent to Liberia after repeated requests for American intervention. In all 225 U.S. personnel went ashore, of whom 50 succumbed to malaria. Two months later the Americans were gone.

This halfhearted African adventure seemed to exemplify the limits of American power. But how are we to explain these limits? As we have seen, by most conventional measures of power—economic, military and cultural—there has never been an empire mightier than the United States today. Its recent difficulties in achieving its foreign policy goals cannot simply be blamed on the Bush administration's alleged diplomatic ineptitude. Rather, we need fundamentally to rethink what we mean by power, for all too often we confuse that concept with other, quite different things—wealth, weaponry and a winning way with "soft power." It is in fact perfectly possible to have a great deal of all these things, yet to have only limited power. Indeed, that is precisely the American predicament.

The election of the actor Arnold Schwarzenegger as governor of California in October 2003 offered an important clue to the nature of American power. In his most recent film, *Terminator 3,* Schwarzenegger plays a musclebound and almost indestructible robot, programmed to protect a young man who is destined to save the world. The film abounds in irony, not all of it intentional. In the climactic scene, the Terminator's operating system becomes corrupted; instead of rescuing the future savior, he comes close to killing him. As his original program battles this contradictory command, the word *ABORT* flashes in bright red letters in his head, all but paralyzing him.

In three distinct ways the Terminator is a perfect, if unwitting, metaphor of American power. Though he has the body of a man half his age, Schwarzenegger himself is in fact just a few years short of his sixtieth birthday. His determination to remain forever Mr. Universe typifies the determination of an entire generation never to grow old, though grow old they must—with significant economic consequences. The Terminator is also a very American hero for the simple reason that there is only one of him. In this he personifies the chronic manpower shortage that currently constrains American nation building. Above all, the Terminator exemplifies the limits of American power because the word *ABORT* starts flashing in his head before he has completed his mission. Outwardly, Arnold Schwarzenegger is without question a colossus; it is hard to imagine the male body looking any bigger and stronger. He is to the human frame what the United States is to the capitalist economy. Yet his character embodies the three key deficits that explain why America only *looks* immensely strong without actually *being* immensely strong.

THREE DEFICITS

In this book I have tried to show that there are three fundamental deficits that together explain why the United States has been a less effective empire than its British predecessor. They are its economic deficit, its manpower deficit and—the most serious of the three—its attention deficit.

In the space of four years Americans intervened militarily against three rogue states in the Balkans, Central Asia and the Middle East. As I write, American troops patrol the streets of Kosovo, Kabul and Kirkuk. Whatever the rationale, each U.S. incursion has led to a change of political regime, of military occupation and an attempt at institutional transformation euphemistically described as nation building. But where will the money come from to make these undertakings successful? How many Americans will be willing to go to these places to oversee how that money is spent? And how long will the American public at home be prepared to support a policy that costs not only money but also lives—even if the quantities in both cases are comparatively modest?

There may be ways of bridging two of these three deficits, at least for a time. Since 1985, as we have seen, the United States has gone from being a net international creditor to being the world's biggest debtor; its net international liabilities are now equivalent to around a quarter of gross domestic product. However, that is far from being the maximum ever run up by a developed economy. In the 1990s Australia's net foreign debt touched 60 percent of GDP, while New Zealand's came close to 90 percent.[5] It may therefore be possible to carry on borrowing from abroad since there seems to be an insatiable appetite on the part of foreign investors for dollar-denominated securities, no matter how low the return on them.[6] Unlike

Australia and New Zealand, after all, the United States gets to issue debt denominated in the global reserve currency.

Admittedly, America's reliance on foreign capital is a balancing act on a very high wire. One conceivable and troubling scenario is that foreign expectations could shift, leading to simultaneous pressure on the exchange rate and bond prices, with higher interest rates threatening American growth more than a weak dollar boosts it.[7] No one should rule out the possibility that American fiscal profligacy, even with the most accommodating monetary policy in the history of the Federal Reserve system, could still coincide with a Japanese-style deflation rather than a return to inflation, especially if American consumers began to save more and attempt to reduce their indebtedness. Two generations with no experience of sustained declines in prices would struggle to adjust their behavior in appropriate ways. In particular, people with large accumulations of mortgage and consumer debt would find apparently low nominal interest rates becoming painfully high in real terms if prices fell by more than 1 or 2 percent a year.

Yet the costs of such a crisis would be heavier outside the United States than inside. Even a modest reduction in the growth of American consumer demand in the years ahead would have serious consequences for the rest of the global economy, given that nearly 60 percent of the total growth in world output since 1995 has come from the United States.[8] And if the United States were to press for a devaluation of the dollar and some measure of protection against Chinese imports, there could be a deflationary chain reaction throughout the world economy.[9] A deflationary world would not necessarily be a disastrously depressed world; it might be more like the 1880s than the 1930s. The original Great Depression that began in the aftermath of the 1873 crash and lasted until 1895 saw prices depressed much more than output (which more than doubled in the United States), and although the period was associated with increases in tariffs, these were not so large as to choke off global trade. If such a Great Deflation were to happen again, America's latent fiscal crisis would not go away, of course; indeed, it might get even worse if real interest rates rose above the real growth rate or if the costs of Medicare continued to rise at a time when other prices were declining. As in the depression of the 1880s, the deflation losers might well turn to radical forms of politics to express their disgruntlement. Populism and socialism thrived as falling prices squeezed

farmers and workers, while white-collar workers and small-business owners often turned to new strains of xenophobic nationalism. These were the
first harbingers of the "end of globalization" in the mid-twentieth century.[10] On the other hand, the British Empire's strategic position was
positively enhanced by the late Victorian slowdown, not least because it
discouraged the strategic ambitions of potential rivals. It was only after the
deflation was over that the Germans began to build their navy and to pursue their "world policy." A Great Deflation would be likely to hurt Europe
and China more than it hurt America.

Nor is America's manpower deficit insuperable. There is undoubtedly
something perplexing about the apparent lack of American combat-
effective troops at a time when the U.S. population is growing at 1.25
percent per annum, unemployment is proving stubbornly resistant to
economic recovery (by one estimate there are 4 million victims of the current "job gap")[11] and the American prison population exceeds 2 million—
1 in every 142 American residents.[12] If one adds together the illegal
immigrants, the jobless and the convicts, there is surely ample raw material
for a larger American army. One of the keys to the expansion of the Roman Empire was, after all, the opportunity offered to non-Romans to earn
citizenship through military service. One of the mainsprings of British colonization was the policy of transportation that emptied the prison hulks of
eighteenth-century England into ships bound for Australia. Reviving the
draft would not necessarily be unpopular, so long as it was appropriately
targeted.

The only alternative is to rely on foreign armies to provide auxiliary
forces. There are precedents for this too. Without the Indian Army, Britain's
empire would have suffered from a chronic manpower deficit. India was, as
Lord Salisbury memorably remarked, "an English barrack in the Oriental
Seas from which we may draw any number of troops without paying for
them."[13] The British relied heavily on their empire to provide manpower
in wartime: roughly a third and just under a half of total British forces during World War I and World War II, respectively. Having rashly dissolved
the Iraqi Army, L. Paul Bremer belatedly came to see that resurrecting it
might be his best hope of establishing order and reducing unemployment.
The alternative, as we have seen, is to go begging to the UN or NATO for

reinforcements. If Americans themselves are reluctant peacekeepers, they must be the peacekeepers' paymasters, and strike such bargains as the mercenaries of the "international community" may demand.

Of the three deficits, however, it is the third that may prove the most difficult to overcome—namely, the attention deficit that seems to be inherent in the American political system and that already threatens to call a premature halt to reconstruction in both Iraq and Afghanistan.[14] This is not intended as a term of abuse. The problem is systemic; it is the way the political process militates against farsighted leadership. In the words of retired General Anthony Zinni:

> There is a fundamental question that goes beyond the military. It's, "What is our obligation to the world?" We preach about values, democracy, human rights, but we haven't convinced the American people to pony up. . . . There's no leadership that steps up and says, "This is the right thing to do." . . . That's the basic problem. . . . There's got to be the political will and support for these things. We should believe that a stable world is a better place for us. If you had a policy and a forward-leaning engagement strategy, the U.S. would make a much greater difference to the world. It would intervene earlier and pick fights better.[15]

But a "forward-leaning engagement strategy" is much easier for a soldier to imagine than for an elected politician. It is not just that first-term American presidents have only two and a half years in office before the issue of securing reelection begins to loom. It is the fact that even sooner, midterm congressional elections can have the effect of emasculating their legislative program. It is the fact that American politics operates on three tiers simultaneously: the national, the state and the local. How could Californians be expected to pay full attention to the problems of nation building in Baghdad in the summer of 2003, when a self-selected mob of amateur politicians was noisily bidding to recall their incumbent governor? It is the fact that the federal executive itself is anything but a homogeneous entity. Interdepartmental rivalry is of course the norm in most human institutions of any size. But there were times in 2003 when the complete absence of coordination among the Defense Department, the State Department and the Treasury—to say nothing of the Commerce Department, the trade representative, the U.S. Agency for International Development and the host of institutions now notionally concerned with "homeland security"—recalled the worst "polycracy" of Wihelmine Germany.[16] The presidency is of course an elected rather than a hereditary office, but its recent incumbents have sometimes appeared to conduct business in the style of the last German kaiser, allowing policy to be determined by interagency competition rather than forging a sense of collective responsibility. Small wonder so many American interventions abroad have the spasmodic, undiplomatic quality of Wilhelm II's *Weltpolitik*. Imperial Germany too practiced what Michael Ignatieff has called imperialism in a hurry. It too was "impatient for quick results."[17]

Unlike the kaiser's Germany, however, the United States disclaims any interest in acquiring new "places in the sun." Its conquests are not merely temporary; they are not even regarded as conquests. The Victorian historian J. R. Seeley famously joked that the British had built their empire "in a fit of absence of mind." Americans, however, have gone one better; here absent-mindedness has become full-blown myopia. Few people outside the United States today doubt the existence of an American empire; that America is imperialistic is a truism in the eyes of most educated Europeans.[18] But as the theologian Reinhold Niebuhr noted as long ago as 1960, Americans persist in "frantically avoiding recognition of the imperialism [they] in fact exercise."[19]

Does imperial denial matter? The answer is that it does. Successful empire is seldom solely based on coercion; there must be some economic dividends for the ruled as well as the rulers, if only to buy the loyalty of indigenous elites, and these dividends need to be sustained for a significant length of time. The trouble with an empire in denial is that it tends to make two mistakes when it chooses to intervene in the affairs of lesser states. The first may be to allocate insufficient resources to the nonmilitary aspects of the project.[20] The second, and the more serious, is to attempt economic and political transformation in an unrealistically short time frame. As I write, the United States would seem to be making the second of these mistakes in both Iraq and Afghanistan. By insisting—and apparently intending—that they will remain in Iraq only until a democratic government can be established "and not a day longer," American spokespeople have unintentionally created a further disincentive for local people to co-operate with them. Who in these countries can feel confident that if he lends support to American initiatives, he will not lay himself open to the charge of collaboration as soon as the Americans go? "If the people of the Balkans realized America would be there," General John Shalikashvili remarked in the late 1990s, "it would be great. . . . Why is it such a crime to suggest a similar longevity [to the occupations of West Germany and Japan] in Bosnia and Kosovo?"[21] The answer is a political one. Today's GIs must be brought home, and soon.

These two points help explain why this vastly powerful economy, with its extraordinary military capability, has had such a very disappointing record when it has sought to bring about changes of political regime abroad. The worst failures—in Haiti, Cuba and Vietnam—were due, above all, to this fatal combination of inadequate resources for nonmilitary purposes and a truncated time horizon. It would be a tragedy if the same process were to repeat itself in the Balkans, Afghanistan and Iraq. But not a surprise.

TOWARD APOLARITY?

Consuming on credit, reluctant to go to the front line, inclined to lose interest in protracted undertakings: if all this conjures up an image of America as a sedentary colossus—to put it bluntly, a kind of strategic couch potato—then the image may be worth pondering. According to the standard measure of obesity, the body mass index,[22] the percentage of Americans classified as obese has nearly doubled in the past decade, from 12 percent in 1991 to 21 percent in 2001. Nearly two-thirds of all American men are officially considered overweight, and nearly three-quarters of those aged between forty-five and sixty-four.[23] In other words, for every superfit Schwarzenegger there are now three fat Frank Cannons. International comparisons, insofar as these are possible, suggest that only western Samoans and Kuwaitis are fatter.[24] Today, it seems, "the white man's burden" is around his waist.[25]

Yet this should not be taken to vindicate those pessimists who predict imminent decline for the United States, whether relative to Europe or to

China. The trouble with "realist" fears of a coming shift from "unipolarity" to "multipolarity" is that they overlook the possibility of generalized impotence—or, if you like, apolarity. Those fixated on a Bismarckian model of the balance of power tend to assume that international relations resemble the interplay of magnets, with the larger powers attracting satellites as if they were iron filings, sometimes joining together, but more often repelling each another. But what if the great powers of today ceased to be magnetic, losing their powers both to attract and to repel? What if even the United States, ever more preoccupied with its own internal problems, became the strategic equivalent of an inert lump of old iron? In many ways, this is already the fate that has overtaken Japan and the European Union; once economic titans, they are now senescent societies and strategic dwarfs. Nor will China be exempt from demographic "graying." One legacy of the one-child policy will be a rising dependency ratio in the coming decades.

The *absence* of great power conflict is a concept that is unfamiliar in modern international history. In his classic 1833 essay "The Great Powers," Ranke portrayed European history since the sixteenth century as a succession of bids for hegemony by one empire or another, each of which had been successfully resisted by the others: first the Habsburgs, then France in the seventeenth century and again France between 1793 and 1815. Had he lived for another ninety years, Ranke would have been able to add Germany between 1914 and 1945. For Ranke, Europe's natural order was truly multipolar; power was shared by a pentarchy composed of France, Austria, England, Russia and Prussia, each in its different way an imperial power.[26] From 1945 until 1989, of course, we lived in a bipolar world, which would have astonished Ranke (though not his contemporary Alexis de Tocqueville), a world divided between two continental empires, each accusing the other of being the imperialist. Then in the early 1990s it seemed as if the United States had established a unipolar order. Yet today's transnational threats such as terrorism, nuclear proliferation and organized crime—to say nothing of disease pandemics, climate change and water shortages—put a premium on cooperation, not competition, between states. The attractions of unilateralism are undeniable, since demanding allies can be more irksome than invisible foes, but a solo strategy offers little prospect of victory against any of these challenges; the successful prosecution of the "wars" against all of them depends as much on multilateral institutions as does the continuation of international free trade. There is, in any case, nothing more dangerous to a great empire than what the Victorian Conservatives called, with heavy irony, splendid isolation. Then as now, the great Anglophone empire needs perforce to work in concert with the lesser—but not negligible—powers in order to achieve its objectives. As G. John Ikenberry has argued, American success after both the Second World War and the cold war was closely linked to the creation and extension of international institutions that at once limited and yet legitimized American power.[27]

Consider again the question of peacekeeping. It has become abundantly clear that the United States is not capable of effective peacekeeping—that is to say, constabulary duties—in countries as far apart as Kosovo, Afghanistan and Iraq without some foreign assistance. Peacekeeping is not what American soldiers are trained to do, nor do they appear to have much appetite for it. It also seems reasonable to assume that the American electorate will not tolerate a prolonged exposure of U.S. troops to the unglamorous hazards of "low-intensity conflict": suicide bombers at checkpoints, snipers down back streets, rocket-propelled grenades fired at patrols and convoys. The obvious solution, short of a substantial expansion of the U.S. Army, is to continue the now well-established practice of sharing the burdens of peacekeeping with other United Nations members—in particular, America's European allies, with their relatively generous aid budgets and their large conscript armies. If they are not used for peacekeeping, it is hard to see what these soldiers are for, in a Europe that has declared perpetual peace within its own borders and is no longer menaced by Russia.

Those, like Robert Kagan, who dismiss the Europeans as Kant-reading Venusians—as opposed to America's Hobbes- (and Clausewitz-) reading Martians—overlook the crucial significance of Pluto in the process of nation building. War and love are all very well, but all empires depend in some measure on money. Without hefty investment in enforcing the rule of law, countries like Afghanistan and Iraq will stagnate and perhaps disintegrate. Unless the United States is prepared radically to alter its attitudes toward low-intensity conflict, it will have little option but to cooperate with the more generous Europeans. Unilateralism, like isolation, is not so splendid after all. Indeed, it is seldom a realistic option for an empire.

The danger is that great power cooperation could simply break down, not because of rivalry between the United States and the European Union but because neither lacks the will to act beyond its own borders. The internal problems of these huge and complex entities may simply distract them from the problems of failed states and rogue regimes. Some would say that such a Spengleresque decline of the West might create a vacuum that only the rising powers of Asia could fill. Yet those who look at China as a future hegemon may discover that it too has enough to contend with in managing the social and political consequences of its second "Great Leap Forward," this time to the capitalist free market. Likewise, those who see Islam as the West's principal antagonist in a war of civilizations will find it difficult to imagine a political accompaniment to the indisputable demographic expansion of Muslim societies. The future, in short, might prove for a time to be *a*polar, a world without even *one* dominant imperial power.

THE TERMINATOR

The paradox of globalization is that as the world becomes more integrated, so power becomes more diffuse. Thanks to the dynamism of international capitalism, all but the poorest people in the world have significantly more purchasing power than their grandfathers dared dream of. The means of production were never more productive or—as China and India achieve their belated economic takeoffs—more widely shared. Thanks to the spread of democracy, a majority of people in the world now have markedly more political power than their grandfathers. The democratic means of election were never more widely accepted as the optimal form of government. The means of education too are accessible in most countries to much larger shares of the population than was the case two or three generations ago; more people than ever can harness their own brainpower. All these changes mean that the old monopolies on which power was traditionally based—monopolies on wealth, political office and knowledge—have in large measure been broken up. Unfortunately, thanks to the proliferation of modern means of destruction, the power to inflict violence has also become more evenly distributed. Firepower has also been shared out as never before.

Power, let us not forget, is not just about being able to buy whatever you want; that is mere wealth. Power is about being able to get whatever you want at below the market price. It is about being able to get people to perform services or part with goods that they would not ordinarily offer to sell at any price. For empires, those ambitious states that seek to exert power beyond their own borders, power depends on both the resolve of the masters and the consent of the subjects. Yet power diminishes as it is shared. One country with one nuclear bomb is more powerful, if the rest of the world has none, than a country with a thousand nuclear bombs, if everyone else has one.

And this brings us to the final respect in which the United States resembles Arnold Schwarzenegger's Terminator. In military confrontations, the United States has the capability to inflict amazing and appalling destruction, while sustaining only minimal damage to itself. There is no regime it could not terminate if it wanted to—including North Korea's. Such a war might leave South Korea in ruins, of course, but the American Terminator would emerge from the rubble more or less unscathed. What the Terminator is *not* programmed to do, however, is to rebuild. In his wake he leaves only destruction.

During the fall of 2003 President Bush sought to stiffen American morale by declaring that he was "not leaving" Iraq; that America "doesn't run"; that the Middle East "must be a focus of American policy for decades to come." If, nevertheless, the United States finally submits to political pressure at home and abroad by withdrawing from Iraq and Afghanistan before their economic reconstruction has been achieved, the scene will not be wholly unfamiliar. The limits of American power will be laid bare when the global Terminator finally admits: "I won't be back."

In my book *The Cash Nexus,* written in 2000 and published in the spring of 2001, I tried to make the argument that the United States not only *could* afford to play a more assertive global role but could not afford *not* to. Any historian who ventures to make prognostications has a duty to review them with the benefit of hindsight. The key points I made were as follows:

1. "The means of destruction have never been cheaper. . . . The main
   beneficiaries [of cheap weaponry] have been and remain the guerrilla armies of the Middle East and sub-Saharan Africa, the terrorist
   groups of Western Europe and the drug gangs of the Americas."[28]
2. "Plainly, it is highly unlikely that any state would contemplate a direct attack on the United States in the foreseeable future; though a
   terrorist campaign against American cities is quite easy to imagine."[29]
3. "Nearly all of the increase in the number of wars in the world since
   1945 is due to the spread of civil war. . . . [But] the United Nations
   [has a] very patchy record as a global policeman. . . . Between 1992
   and 1999 the Security Council authorized a series of humanitarian
   interventions. . . . The majority were at best ineffective, and at worst
   disastrous."[30]
4. "The question has frequently been asked, and deserves repetition:
   would it not be desirable for the United States to depose these tyrants
   and impose democratic government on their countries? The idea of
   invading a country, deposing its dictators and imposing free elections at gunpoint is generally dismissed as incompatible with American 'values.' A common argument is that the United States could
   never engage in the kind of overt imperial rule practiced by Britain
   in the nineteenth century—though this was precisely what was
   done in Germany and in Japan at the end of the Second World War,
   and with great and lasting success."[31]
5. "Far from retreating like some giant snail behind an electronic shell,
   the United States should be devoting a larger percentage of its vast
   resources to making the world safe for capitalism and democracy.
   Contrary to the naïve triumphalism of the 'end of history,' these are
   not naturally occurring, but require strong institutional foundations
   of law and order. The proper role of an imperial America is to establish these institutions where they are lacking, if necessary . . . by
   military force. There is no economic argument against such a policy,
   since it would not be prohibitively costly. Imposing democracy on all
   the world's 'rogue states' would not push the U.S. defense budget
   much above 5 per cent of GDP. There is also an economic argument
   for doing so, as establishing the rule of law in such countries would
   pay a long-run dividend as their trade revived and expanded."[32]

Writing in the dying days of the Clinton administration, I concluded—somewhat heatedly—that "the greatest disappointment facing the world in the twenty-first century [is] that the leaders of the one state with the economic resources to make the world a better place lack the guts to do it." Little did I imagine that within a matter of nine months, a new president, confronted by the calamity of September 11, would embark on a policy so similar to the one I had advocated. Since the declaration of the war against terrorism, the question has ceased to be about guts. It is now about grit, the tenacity to finish what has been started.

Unlike most European critics of the United States, then, I believe the world needs an effective liberal empire and that the United States is the best candidate for the job. Economic globalization is working. The rapid growth of *per capita* incomes in the world's two most populous countries, China and India, means that international inequality is finally narrowing.[33] But there are parts of the world where legal and political institutions are in a condition of such collapse or corruption that their inhabitants are effectively cut off from any hope of prosperity. And there are states that, through either weakness or malice, encourage terrorist organizations committed to wrecking a liberal world order. For that reason, economic globalization needs to be underwritten politically, as it was a century ago.

The United States has good reasons to play the role of liberal empire, both from the point of view of its own security and out of straightforward altruism. In many ways too it is uniquely well equipped to play it. Yet for all its colossal economic, military and cultural power, the United States still looks unlikely to be an *effective* liberal empire without some profound changes in its economic structure, its social makeup and its political culture.

American neoimperialists like to quote Kipling's "White Man's Burden," written in 1899 to encourage President McKinley's empire-building efforts in the Philippines. But its language—indeed the entire nineteenth-century lexicon of imperialism—is irrevocably the language of a bygone age. Though I have warned against the dangers of imperial denial, I do not mean to say that the existence of an American empire should instead be proclaimed from the rooftop of the Capitol. All I mean is that whatever they choose to call their position in the world—hegemony, primacy, predominance or leadership—Americans should recognize the *functional* resemblance between Anglophone power present and past and should try to do a better rather than a worse job of policing an unruly world than their British predecessors. In learning from the history of other empires, Americans will learn not arrogance but precisely that humility which, as a candidate for the presidency, George W. Bush once recommended to his countrymen.

There is another poem by Kipling, written two years before "The White Man's Burden," which perhaps strikes a more apposite chord. Entitled simply "Recessional," it is a somber intimation of imperial mortality, perfectly crafted to temper late Victorian delusions of grandeur:

> *Far-called, our navies melt away;*
> *On dune and headland sinks the fire:*
> *Lo, all our pomp of yesterday*
> *Is one with Nineveh and Tyre!*
> *Judge of the Nations, spare us yet,*
> *Lest we forget—lest we forget!*

These are words the Colossus of our time needs to heed, even as it seems to bestride the globe, unrivaled. As Tony Blair put it succinctly in his address to Congress in July 2003, "All predominant power seems for a time invincible, but in fact, it is transient."[34] The question Americans must ask themselves is just how transient they wish their predominance to be. Though the barbarians have already knocked at the gates—once, spectacularly—imperial decline in this case seems more likely to come, as it came to Gibbon's Rome, from within.

Statistical Appendix

TABLE 1: MAJOR AMERICAN OCCUPATIONS OF FOREIGN TERRITORY, 1893–2003

Territory	Occupied	Departed	Duration (years)	Status	Per Capita Income Today*	Democracy Today (FH Score)†
Hawaii	1893	No	110	State of the U.S.	30,001	1
Puerto Rico	1898	No	105	Commonwealth united with U.S.	11,091	N/a
Guam	1898	No	105	U.S. possession	20,664	N/a
The Philippines	1898	1946	48	Independent	1,020	2
American Samoa	1899	No	104	U.S. possession	7,279	N/a
Panama (Canal Zone)	1903	1979	76	Independent	4,020	1
Virgin Islands	1916	No	87	U.S. possession	13,139	N/a
Dominican Republic	1916	1924	8	Independent	2,320	2
Haiti	1915	1934	19	Independent	440	6
West Germany	1945	1955	10	Independent	22,670	1
Japan	1945	1952	7	Independent	33,550	1
Northern Mariana Islands	1947	No	56	Commonwealth united with U.S.	12,500	N/a
Palau	1947	1994	47	Free association with U.S.	7,140	1
Micronesia	1947	1986	39	Free association with U.S.	1,980	1
Marshall Islands	1947	1986	39	Free association with U.S.	2,350	1
South Korea	1950	No	53	Independent	9,930	2
South Vietnam	1965	1972	7	Annexed by North Vietnam	430	7
Afghanistan	2002	?	1.5	Interim Government	N/a	6
Iraq	2003	?	0.5	Coalition Authority	N/a	7

*Gross national income per capita, Atlas method (current US$).

†Freedom House index of political freedom: 1 = wholly free, 7 = wholly unfree.

TABLE 2. AMERICAN CASUALTIES IN MAJOR WARS

Conflict	Enrolled in Military	Deaths Combat	Deaths Other	Total Wounded	Total Casualties	KIA	Percentages Dead	Casualty	Duration Months	Rate KIA/Month
Revolutionary War	200,000	4,435	N/a	6,188	10,623	2.2	2.2	5.3	80	55
War of 1812	286,000	2,260	N/a	4,505	6,765	0.8	0.8	2.4	30	75
Mexican War	78,700	1,733	11,550	4,152	17,435	2.2	16.9	22.2	20	87
Civil War: Union	2,803,300	110,070	249,458	275,175	634,703	3.9	12.8	22.6	48	2,293
Civil War: Confederate*	1,064,200	74,524	124,000	137,000	335,524	7.0	18.7	31.5	48	1,553
Civil War: Combined	3,867,500	184,594	373,458	412,175	970,227	4.8	14.4	25.1	48	3,846
Spanish–American War†	306,800	385	2,061	1,662	4,108	0.1	0.8	1.3	4	96
World War I	4,743,800	53,513	63,195	204,002	320,710	1.1	2.5	6.8	19	2,816
World War II	16,353,700	292,131	115,185	670,846	1,078,162	1.8	2.5	6.6	44	6,639
Korean War	5,764,100	33,651	N/a	103,284	136,935	0.6	0.6	2.4	37	909
Vietnam War	8,744,000	47,369	10,799	153,303	211,471	0.5	0.7	2.4	90	526
Gulf War‡	2,750,000	148	145	467	760	0.0	0.0	0.0	1	148

NOTE: "Combat deaths" refers to troops killed in action. KIA = killed in action. "Other" includes deaths from disease, privation and accidents and includes losses among prisoners of war.

*Confederate nonbattle deaths and wounded estimated.

†Only one month of combat.

‡Only six weeks of sustained combat.

Source: Department of Defense.

ACKNOWLEDGMENTS

This book would not have been written had I not gone to live in the United States in January 2003. It is the first fruit of what has proved to be a revitalizing transatlantic migration. I arrived in New York with a hypothesis about "American empire" in my luggage. Working in the world metropolis has forced me to do more than unpack it. The result is a synthesis—not just of the published and unpublished works cited in the bibliography, but also of innumerable conversations on the subject of American power, past, present and future. The past is, of course, the proper concern of the historian. However, what I have to say about recent events and possible futures gains, I hope, from being located in what is primarily a work of history. My principal aim is simply to encourage Americans to relate their country's current predicament to the experiences of empires past. I write not as a carping critic but as an avid admirer of the United States who wants it to succeed in its imperial undertakings and who fears the consequences if it should fail.

More than any previous book I have written, this book is the result of intercourse with people and institutions as well as with published and unpublished texts. My first and largest debt is to New York University, and in particular to the Leonard N. Stern School of Business. When the-then dean of the Stern School, George Daly, suggested that I might like to come and teach at NYU it seemed at first a fantastic idea. It turned out to be a fantastically good idea. I am grateful not only to him but also to his successor, Tom Cooley, as well as to all the faculty and administrative staff at Stern. I owe a special debt to Dick Sylla, whose friendship and intellectual companionship were among the strongest arguments for my move to West Fourth Street, and to Luis Cabral, his successor as chair of the economics department. It is usually invidious to name some names when an entire institution has been so welcoming, but a number of my colleagues at Stern and at NYU deserve special thanks, usually because they commented on seminar papers and other writings that eventually mutated into chapters of this book. My thanks, then, to David Backus, Tom Bender, Adam Brandenburger, Bill Easterly, Nicholas Economides, Shepard Forman, Tony Judt, Fabrizio Perri, Tom Sargent, Bill Silber, George Smith, Larry White and Bernard Yeung. Thanks for administrative and secretarial support are also due to Kathleen Collins, Melissa Felci and Janine Lanzisera (in New York), Katia Pisvin (in Oxford) and Maria Sanchez (in Stanford).

After nearly fifteen years of giving undergraduate tutorials and supervisions at Oxford and Cambridge, I approached the challenge of teaching large classes of American graduates with apprehension. It was a relief to find that the experience was not merely painless but pleasurable. Sergio Fonseca and Gopal Tampi did sterling work as my first teaching assistants at Stern. But with such excellent students my duties were very far from burdensome. I should like to thank all those who took my classes; I learned as much from them as they from me. This is an appropriate place, too, for an expression of gratitude to President John Sexton, a truly charismatic pedagogue.

One thing I have come to understand about American academic institutions is that they owe much of their vitality to the continuing involvement of alumni in their affairs. Two in particular gave me both generous support and friendship during my time in New York: William Berkley and John Herzog. To them and their wives, Marjorie and Diana, I shall always be grateful. It was John and Diana who endowed the chair in financial history of which I am the first occupant. To them, by way of thanks, I dedicate this book.

Thanks are also due to the many people who simply made me feel welcome as a new boy in New York—in particular, Martha Bayona, Mike Campisi, Jimmy Casella, Cesar Coronado, Joseph Giordano, Phil Greene, Jorge Lujo, Saleh Muhammed, Hector Rivera, Neville Rodriguez and Giovanni di Salvo.

Last year I was also fortunate to become associated with one of the great American centers of historical research: the Hoover Institution at Stanford University. I would like to thank the director and fellows of the Hoover Institution for electing me to a senior fellowship. They and all the staff at Hoover gave me a wonderfully warm welcome to California last fall—the first, I trust, of many.

A further institutional debt of gratitude is to my alma mater, Oxford

University, which made me a visiting professor, so that I did not wholly vanish from my old haunts last year. I should also like to thank the principal and fellows of Jesus College, Oxford, for electing me to a senior research fellowship, and the master and fellows of Oriel College, for providing me with a study during my visits to Oxford. I owe a particular debt to Jeremy Catto. I have also been extremely fortunate to have had an Oxonian research assistant, the superb Ameet Gill.

Some of the material in this book had its genesis in journalism. Among the editors who showed me the ropes of American newspaper writing, I should like to thank Anne Burrowclough, Erich Eichman, Tony Emerson, Nikolas Gvosdev, Damjan de Krnjevic-Miskovic, Dean Robinson, Gideon Rose, Allison Silver, Robert Silvers, Zofia Smardz, Tunku Varadarajan, Michael Young and Fareed Zakaria. Thanks also to George Ames, Ric Burns, Peter Kavanagh, Brian Lehrer, Kevin Lucey, Tom Moroney, Peter Robinson and Geoffrey Wawro for some memorable discussions "on air."

Sections of Chapter 3 first appeared as "Clashing Civilizations or Mad Mullahs: The United States Between Informal and Formal Empire" in *The Age of Terror,* edited by Strobe Talbott (Basic Books, 2001). Sections of Chapter 5 were published as "The British Empire and Globalization" in *Historically Speaking.* Sections of Chapter 6 were first published as "The Empire Slinks Back" in *The New York Times Magazine* and "True Lies" in *The New Republic.* Finally, sections of Chapter 8 were coauthored by Laurence Kotlikoff and appeared as "Going Critical: The Consequences of American Fiscal Overstretch" in the fall 2003 issue of *The National Interest.* I am grateful to all those journals for allowing me to reprint the passages in question.

Other parts of the book have been improved by being read in draft by others. Richard Cooper spotted numerous flaws in a draft of the introduction. Eric Rauchway kindly cast his eye over the earlier chapters and helped to improve my freshman-level American history. Chapter 4 owed much to the friendship and counsel of Diego Arria. Judith Brown offered invaluable suggestions for Chapter 6. Chapter 7 was read in draft and much improved by my friends Timothy Garton Ash of St. Antony's College, Oxford, and Martin Thomas at the Bank of England. Chapter 8 was significantly reshaped in light of comments by David Hale and Deirdre McCloskey on an earlier version delivered as a lecture at the Chicago Humanities Festival, as well as conversations with Ronald McKinnon at Stanford.

Many others deserve thanks for having read and commented on drafts, for having listened and responded to seminar papers or for having proffered hospitality during the writing of the book. My gratitude to Graham Allison, Anne Applebaum, Chris Bassford, Max Boot, Amy Chua, Gordon Cravitz, Larry Diamond, Gerald Dorfman, Maureen Dowd, Michael Edelstein, Frank and Ronita Egger, Gerry and Norma Feldman, Marc Flandreau, Ben and Barbara Friedman, Andrew and Barbara Gundlach, John Hall, Patrick Hatcher, Paul Heinbecker, Michael Ignatieff, Harold James, Robert Kagan, Harry Kreisler, Melvyn Leffler, Peter Lindert, Eileen Mackevich, Charles Maier, Norman Naimark, Joseph Nye, Patrick O'Brien, Kevin O'Rourke, Lynn and Evelyn de Rothschild, Simon Schama, Moritz Schularick, Peter Schwartz, Zach Shore, Radek Sikorski, Lawrence Summers, Giuseppe Tattara, Alan M. Taylor, Mike Tomz, Marc Weidenmier, Barry Weingast, James Wolfensohn, Ngaire Woods and Minky Worden.

The incomparable Andrew Wylie and his excellent team at the Wylie Agency have expertly managed my Atlantic crossing as an author. At The Penguin Press in New York, I would like to thank Ann Godoff and my editor, Scott Moyers, whose critical reading of early drafts much improved the finished article. Equally astute were the suggestions for deletion and addition made by his counterpart at Penguin in London, Simon Winder. An author could not wish for better editors. Thanks are also due to Anthony Forbes-Watson, Helen Fraser and Stefan McGrath, not forgetting my copy editor, Pearl Hanig, Chloe Campbell, Sarah Christie, Sophie Fels, Rosie Glaisher, Rachel Rokicki and the many other indispensable Penguin employees whom the author of a book never gets to meet but nevertheless depends upon.

From its inception *Colossus* was intended to accompany a British television documentary and I should like to thank Janice Hadlow and Hamish Mykura at Channel 4 for their encouragement; as well as Denys Blakeway and the wonderful production team assembled by Blakeway Productions: Russell Barnes, Tim Cragg, Melanie Fall, Kate Macky and Ali Schilling. Thanks also to Kassem Derghan, Reyath Elibrahim, Mathias Haentjes, and Nguyen Hu Cuong.

But my biggest debt is to my wife, Susan, and our children, Felix, Freya and Lachlan, whom I have neglected unforgivably in order to write this book but who are, nevertheless, its main source of inspiration.

NOTES

PREFACE TO THE PAPERBACK EDITION

1. Ron Suskind, "Without a Doubt," *New York Times Magazine*, October 17, 2004.
2. Woodward, *Plan of Attack*, p. 443.
3. It is symptomatic that John Lewis Gaddis interprets the present predicament of the United States with reference to John Quincy Adams: Gaddis, *Surprise, Security, and the American Experience* (Cambridge, Mass., 2004).
4. Ash, *Free World*, p. 102.
5. Text of President Bush's speech, *New York Times*, April 13, 2004.
6. My emphasis; first presidential debate, September 30, 2004, text from FDCH E-Media. See also David M. Halbfinger and David E. Sanger, "Bush and Kerry Clash Over Iraq and a Timetable," *New York Times*, September 7, 2004.
7. On the significance of the frontier in imperial history, see Maier, *Among Empires*.
8. Remarks by the President at the Twentieth Anniversary of the National Endowment for Democracy, November 6, 2003; http://www.whitehouse.gov/news/releases/2003/11/20031106-2.html.
9. President Bush's speech to the Republican Party Convention, *New York Times*, September 2, 2004.
10. "We're pursuing a strategy of freedom around the world . . ."; first presidential debate, September 30, 2004.
11. See Fukuyama, *State Building*.
12. Roger Cohen, "'Imperial America' Retreats from Iraq," *New York Times*, July 4, 2004.
13. Daniel Drezner, "Bestriding the World, Sort Of," *Wall Street Journal*, June 17, 2004.
14. Michiko Kakutani, "Attention Deficit Disorder in a Most Peculiar Empire," *New York Times*, May 21, 2004.
15. See my *Empire*.
16. By the end of August 2004, there had been around 300 allegations of mistreatment of detainees; 155 had so far been investigated, of which 66 had been substantiated; *Wall Street Journal*, August 26, 2004.
17. Ibid.
18. Woodward, *Plan of Attack*, p. 249.
19. "The Best-laid Plans?," *Financial Times*, August 3, 2003.
20. Woodward, *Plan of Attack*, pp. 150, 270.
21. See the remarks of UN Secretary General Kofi Annan in an interview with the BBC in September 2004.
22. Daniel Barnard, "The Great Iraqi Revolt: The 1919–20 Insurrections against the British in Mesopotamia," paper presented at the Harvard Graduate Student Conference in International History, April 23, 2004, http://www.fas.harvard.edu/~conih/abstracts/Barnard_article.doc.
23. "White House Says Iraq Sovereignty Could Be Limited," *New York Times*, April 22, 2004.
24. My own calculations based on Budget

of the United States Government, 2005 historical tables, http://frwebgate.access.gpo.gov/cgi-bin/multidb.cgi.

25. Budget of the United States Government, 2005, table 1.3, http://www.gpoaccess.gov/usbudget/fy05/sheets/hist01z2.xls

26. "Kennedy, Reagan, and Bush Tax Cuts in Historical Perspective," http://www.taxfoundation.org/bushtaxplan-size.htm.

27. Economic Report of the President, table B-81, http://wais.access.gpo.gov.

28. Suskind, *The Price of Loyalty*, p. 291.

29. Ibid.

30. Source: Congressional Budget Office.

31. See Michael P. Dooley, David Folkerts-Landau, and Peter Garber, "An Essay on the Revived Bretton Woods System," *NBER Working Paper*, 9971 (September 2003) and "The Revived Bretton Woods System: The Effects of Periphery Intervention and Reserve Management on Interest Rates and Exchange Rates in Center Countries," *NBER Working Paper*, 10332 (March 2004).

32. Source: Treasury Bulletin, June 2004, http://www.fms.treas.gov/bulletin/. Cf. Pÿivi Munter, "Most Treasuries in Foreign Hands," *Financial Times*, June 14, 2004.

33. See most recently Peterson, *Running on Empty*. According to the April 2004 report of the Medicare trustees, the system obligations to future retirees are unfunded by $62 trillion: see Joe Lieber-mann, "America Needs Honest Fiscal Accounting," *Financial Times*, May 25, 2004.

34. Niall Ferguson, "A Dollar Crash? Euro Trashing," *The New Republic*, June 21, 2004.

35. See Paul Krugman, "Questions of Interest," *New York Times*, April 20, 2004. For a different view, see David Malpass,

"Don't Blame the Deficits for America's Rate Hikes," *Financial Times*, May 3, 2004.

36. Niall Ferguson, "Who's Buried by Higher Rates," *Fortune*, June 14, 2004. On the macroeconomic implications of the decline of the American savings rate, see Lawrence H. Summers, "The United States and the Global Adjustment Process," Third Annual Stavros S. Niarchos Lecture, Institute for International Economics, Washington, D.C., March 23, 2004.

37. "Kerry's Acceptance: There Is a Right Way and a Wrong Way to Be Strong," *New York Times*, July 30, 2004.

38. Robert Manchin and Gergely Hideg, "E.U. Survey: Are Transatlantic Ties Loosening?" http://www.gallup.com/content/default.aspx?ci=12247&pg=1.

39. The phrase was originated by Charles Maier.

40. Population Division of the Department of Economic and Social Affairs of the United Nations Secretariat, *World Population Prospects: The 2002 Revision*, http://esa.un.org/unpp.

41. Edward C. Prescott, "Why Do Americans Work So Much More than Europeans?," *NBER Working Paper*, 10316 (February 2004). For a different interpretation, see Olivier Blanchard, "The Economic Future of Europe," *NBER Working Paper*, 10310 (February 2004).

42. Dominic Wilson and Roopa Purusho-thaman, "Dreaming with the BRICs: The Path to 2050," *Goldman Sachs Global Economics Paper*, 99 (October 1, 2003).

43. Nikola Spatafora, Yongzheng Yang, and Tarhan Feyzioglu, "China's Emergence and Its Impact on the Global Economy," *International Monetary Fund World Economic Outlook* (March 2004), pp. 82–99.

44. Niall Ferguson, "Eurabia?," *New York Times Magazine*, April 4, 2004. The neologism was coined by the Egyptian-born writer Bat Ye'or.

45. For an optimistic view, see Held, *Global Covenant*. Rather more pessimistic—and more aware of medieval visions of a global "civil society"—is Linden, *A New Map of the World*.

INTRODUCTION

1. Secretary of State Donald Rumsfeld, interview with Al Jazeera TV, February 27, 2003, press release, Department of Defense.

2. Bowden, *Black Hawk Down*, p. 228.

3. For an archetypal rant from the French Left, see Julien, *America's Empire*.

4. See, e.g., Nearing, *American Empire*; Freeman and Nearing, *Dollar Diplomacy*.

5. For an early example, see Williams, *Tragedy of American Diplomacy*. See also Lerner, *America as a Civilization* and Williams's later *Empire as a Way of Life*.

6. Kolko and Kolko, *Limits of Power*. Also Kolko, *Politics of War*; Kolko, *Roots of American Foreign Policy*; Kolko, *Vietnam*. For a good example of the way Vietnam encouraged talk of American empire, see Buchanan, "Geography of Empire." See also Magdoff, *Age of Imperialism*; McMahon, *Limits of Empire*; Swomley, *American Empire*. The odd contrarian defended American imperialism in the 1960s: see Liska, *Imperial America*; Steel, *Pax Americana*. One was even a Frenchman: Aron, *Imperial Republic*.

7. Tucker and Hendrickson, *Imperial Temptation*, pp. 53, 211.

8. Johnson, *Blowback*; Blum, *Rogue State*; Hudson, *Super Imperialism*. See also Smith, *American Empire*.

9. See, for example, Eric Hobsbawm, "America's Imperial Delusion," *Guardian*, June 14, 2003. Predictable commentaries have also come from Edward Said and Noam Chomsky.

10. Vidal, *Decline and Fall of the American Empire*.

11. Patrick Buchanan, *Republic*, p. 6. See also idem, "What Price the American Empire?," *American Cause*, May 29, 2002.

12. Prestowitz, *Rogue Nation*.

13. See, e.g., Bacevich, *American Empire*, p. 243: "Although the U.S. has not created an empire in any formal sense . . . it has most definitely acquired an imperial problem. . . . Like it or not, America today *is* Rome, committed irreversibly to the maintenance and, where feasible, expansion of an empire that differs from every other empire in history. This is hardly a matter for celebration; but neither is there any purpose served by denying the facts." See also Rosen, "Empire," p. 61: "If the logic of an American empire is unappealing, it is not at all clear that the alternatives are that much more attractive." For a superbly nuanced and subtle contribution to the debate, see Maier, "American Empire?"

14. Quoted in Bacevich, *American Empire*, p. 219.

15. Ibid., p. 203.

16. Thomas E. Ricks, "Empire or Not? A Quiet Debate over U.S. Role," *Washington Post*, August 21, 2001.

17. Max Boot, "The Case for an American Empire," *Weekly Standard*, October 15, 2001.

18. Boot, *Savage Wars*, p. xx: "Unlike nineteenth-century Britain, twenty-first century America does not preside over a formal empire. Its 'empire' consists not of far-flung territorial possessions but of a family of democratic, capitalist nations that eagerly seek shel-

ter under Uncle Sam's umbrella." However, Boot later adds that "the U.S. has more power than Britain did at the height of its empire, more power than any other state in modern times;" p. 349. On the distinctly mixed reception of Kipling's poem, see Gilmour, *Long Recessional,* pp. 124–29.

19. Kaplan, *Warrior Politics.*

20. Emily Eakin, "It Takes an Empire," *New York Times,* April 2, 2002.

21. Ibid.

22. Dinesh D'Souza, "In Praise of an American Empire," *Christian Science Monitor,* April 26, 2002.

23. Mallaby, "Reluctant Imperialist," p. 6. Cf. Pfaff, "New Colonialism." For similar arguments in favor of European neo-imperialism, see Cooper, "Postmodern State."

24. Ignatieff, *Empire Lite,* pp. 3, 22, 90, 115, 126. See, however, "Why Are We in Iraq? (And Liberia? And Afghanistan?)," *New York Times Magazine,* September 6, 2003.

25. Kurth, "Migration," p. 5.

26. James Atlas, "A Classicist's Legacy: New Empire Builders," *New York Times,* May 4, 2003, Section 4, p. 4.

27. "Interdicting North Korea," *Wall Street Journal,* April 28, 2003, p. A12.

28. Max Boot, "Washington Needs a Colonial Office," *Financial Times,* July 3, 2003.

29. Quoted in Bacevich, *American Empire,* p. 44.

30. "Strategies for Maintaining U.S. Predominance," Office of Net Assessment, Office of the Secretary of Defense, Summer Study, August 1, 2001, esp. p. 22.

31. Priest, *Mission,* p. 70.

32. Ferguson, *Empire,* p. 370. For a suggestive discussion, see Williams, *Empire as a Way of Life,* p. ix.

33. Quoted in Bacevich, *American Empire,* p. 242.

34. Quoted in Mead, *Special Providence,* p. 6.

35. Speech at the Council on Foreign Relations, 1999, quoted in *Washington Post,* August 21, 2001.

36. Quoted in Bacevich, *American Empire,* p. 201.

37. "Transcript of President Bush's Speech," *New York Times,* February 26, 2003.

38. Transcript from the Office of International Information Programs, U.S. Department of State, http:usinfo.state.gov.

39. "Transcript of President Bush's Remarks on the End of Major Combat in Iraq," *New York Times,* p. A16.

40. Colin L. Powell, "Remarks at The Elliott School of International Affairs, George Washington University," http:www.state.gov/secretary/rm/2003/23836.htm.

41. Minxin Pei, "The Paradoxes of American Nationalism," *Foreign Policy,* May–June 2003, p. 32.

42. However, see Davies, *First English Empire.*

43. Zelikow, "Transformation," p. 18.

44. Schwab, "Global Role." "American empire," in the words of Michael Mandelbaum, "was given up in the twentieth century:" Mandelbaum, *Ideas,* p. 87.

45. Kupchan, *End,* p. 228.

46. Mandelbaum, *Ideas,* p. 88.

47. Bobbitt, *Shield of Achilles.* Bobbitt sees imperialism as a thing of the past, having been one of the "historic, strategic and constitutional innovations" of the "state-nation" in the two centuries between 1713 and 1914.

48. I am extremely grateful to Graham Allison for inviting me to open this series. This book owes much to the rigorous and constructive criticism of the seminar's participants.

49. See, e.g., Kagan, *Paradise and Power*, p. 88; Kupchan, *End*, p. 266.

50. Johannson, "National Size," p. 352n.

51. A hegemonic power was "a state . . . able to impose its set of rules on the interstate system, and thereby create temporarily a new political order," and which offered "certain extra advantages for enterprises located within it or protected by it, advantages not accorded by the 'market' but obtained through political pressure": Wallerstein, "Three Hegemonies," p. 357.

52. This notion can be traced back to Charles Kindleberger's seminal work on the interwar world economy, which described a kind of "interregnum" after British hegemony, but before American. See Kindleberger, *World in Depression*.

53. See, e.g., Kennedy, *Rise and Fall*.

54. Calleo, "Reflections." See also Rosecrance, "Croesus and Caesar."

55. O'Brien, "Pax Britannica."

56. Gallagher and Robinson, "Imperialism of Free Trade."

57. See Robert Freeman Smith, "Latin America," pp. 85–88. Cf. Cain and Hopkins, *British Imperialism*.

58. Lieven, *Empire*, p. xiv.

59. See for an attempt at a formal economic theory of empire, Grossman and Mendoza, "Annexation or Conquest?"

60. Davis and Huttenback, *Mammon and the Pursuit of Empire*.

61. Lundestad, *American "Empire."*

62. Zakaria, *Future of Freedom*, esp. p. 162.

63. Krugman, *Great Unravelling*, passim.

64. See Kupchan, *End*, p. 153.

65. For some recent examples, see Joseph Nye, "The New Rome Meets the New Barbarians: How America Should Wield Its Power," *Economist*, March 23, 2002; Jonathan Freedland, "Rome, AD . . . Rome DC," *Guardian*, September 18, 2002; Robert Harris, "Return of the Romans," *Sunday Times*, August 31, 2003.

66. American Samoa, Baker Island, Guam, Howland Island, Jarvis Island, Johnston Atoll, Kingman Reef, Midway Island, Navassa Island, Northern Mariana Islands, Palmyra Atoll, Puerto Rico, Virgin Islands and Wake Island.

67. Joseph Curl, "U.S. Eyes Cuts at Germany, S. Korea Bases," *Washington Times*, February 12, 2003.

68. *Statistical Abstract of the United States, 2002*, table 495.

69. Transcript in *New York Times*, February 26, 2002.

70. Ian Traynor, "How American Power Girds the Globe with a Ring of Steel," *Guardian*, April 21, 2003.

71. Paul Kennedy, "Power and Terror," *Financial Times*, September 3, 2002.

72. Gregg Easterbrook, "American Power Moves Beyond the Mere Super," *New York Times*, April 27, 2003.

73. Kennedy, *Rise and Fall of the Great Powers*, p. 519.

74. Porter (ed.), *Atlas of British Overseas Expansion*, p. 120.

75. See, e.g., O'Hanlon, "Come Partly Home, America."

76. I am grateful to Dr. Christopher Bassford of the National War College for drawing this map to my attention.

77. Priest, *Mission*, p. 73.

78. The term *great power* is yet another euphemism. At the time it was current, all the five states designated as such—Great Britain, France, Russia, Austria and the German Reich—were or possessed empires.

79. Kennedy, *Great Powers*.

80. Although Hanson's *Decline of the American Empire* appeared as early as 1993.

81. According to Charles Kupchan, for ex-

ample, "Europe [would] soon catch up with America . . . because it is coming together, amassing the impressive resources and intellectual capital already possessed by its constituent states": Kupchan, *End,* pp. 119, 132.

82. John Mearsheimer concluded his economically deterministic *Tragedy of Great Power Politics* with this grim verdict: "The United States has a profound interest in seeing Chinese economic growth slow considerably in the years ahead." Should China keep growing, in other words, the United States would cease to be the dominant power in Asia: Mearsheimer, *Tragedy,* p. 402. Cf. ibid., p. 383f. Oddly, Russia is double-counted in Mearsheimer's tables, and the comparable American data are omitted.

83. See Huntington, "Lonely Superpower," p. 88.

84. Todd, *Après l'Empire.*

85. Calculations based on data in Maddison, *World Economy,* appendix A. A study by Goldman Sachs estimates that Chinese output could exceed American by 2041.

86. Maddison, *World Economy,* p. 261, table B-18.

87. World Bank, *World Development Indicators* database. An international dollar is an imaginary unit that has the same purchasing power over the gross domestic product of any country as the U.S. dollar has in the United States. This adjustment eliminates the effects of exchange rate movements and differentials in prices for equivalent goods between countries (a Big Mac costs more in the United States than in China). Measuring income and output in current dollars gives very different results. In 1980, using current dollars, the U.S. share of world output was just

10.6 percent, nearly a third what it is today. Seven years later it was up to a quarter, its highest share since 1960, and between 1995 and 2002 it rose from a quarter to a third. Note that income here is gross national income, which (in the World Bank's definition) is "the sum of value added by all resident producers plus any product taxes (less subsidies) not included in the valuation of output plus net receipts of primary income (compensation of employees and property income) from abroad." The measure of output is gross domestic product, which (again in the World Bank's definition) "is the sum of gross value added by all resident producers in the economy, plus any product taxes and minus any subsidies not included in the value of the products. It is calculated without making deductions for depreciation of fabricated assets or for depletion and degradation of natural resources."

88. Though this is not strictly speaking the right comparison. If we add together Maddison's estimates for the gross domestic product of Britain and all its colonies in 1913, the total (adjusting for purchasing parity) comes to over 20 percent of his estimate for world GDP. It might be more accurate to say, then, that the U.S. economy today and the combined economies of the British Empire a century ago account for roughly similar shares of world output.

89. http:grassrootsbrunnet.net/keswick-ridge/mcdonalds/history_of_expansion.htm. Technically, McDonald's does not own these restaurants, but it sells franchises to restaurant proprietors. There is widening latitude for these to adapt McDonald's products to suit local tastes. However, its inspectors

ensure that franchisees conform to the standards of service and food quality set by McDonald's in the United States.

90. Neil Buckley, "Eyes on the Fries," *Financial Times*, August 29, 2003.

91. *Coca-Cola Company 2002 Annual Report 2002*, p. 44.

92. Office of the Undersecretary of Defense (Comptroller), "National Defense Budget Estimates for FY 2004" (Green Paper), March 2003.

93. Kennedy, *Rise and Fall*, p. 609, n. 18.

94. Nye, *Paradox*, p. 8. See also his essay "The Velvet Hegemon," *Foreign Policy* (May–June 2003) p. 74f., which responds to my critique "Think Again: Power," *Foreign Policy* (March–April 2003).

95. Joseph S. Nye, Jr., *Paradox*, p. 141.

96. Ibid., p. 140f.

97. On Americanization, see Bell, *Americanization and Australia*. Cf. Judge, "Hegemony of the Heart."

98. Held et al., *Global Transformations*, pp. 344–63. Cf. Smith, *Talons of the Eagle*, p. 235f. Latin American cinemas are also dominated by U.S. films.

99. Shawcross, *Deliver Us from Evil*, p. 119.

100. Figures from the Evangelism and Missions Information Service, the U.S. Council of World Missions and the North American Missions Board.

101. http:bible.acu.edu/missions/page.asp?ID=174; ID=894.

102. Coker, *Conflicts*, p. 11. Cf. Stoll, *Is Latin America Turning Protestant?*

103. David van Biema, "Should Christians Convert Muslims?," *Time*, June 30, 2003.

104. See, e.g., Mandelbaum, *Ideas*, p. 1.

105. Ibid., p. 288.

106. Office of the President, "The National Security Strategy of the United States of America," September 17, 2003, http:usinfo.state.gov/topical/pol/terror/secstrat.htm.

107. See Bacevich, *American Empire*, p. 2f. But even Bacevich understates the extent of the resemblance: Andrew Bacevich, "Does Empire Pay?," *Historically Speaking, 4, 4* (April 2003), p. 33.

108. See my *Empire*, passim. Cf. Joseph S. Nye, Jr., *Paradox*, pp. 10, 144; Kurtz, "Democratic Imperialism."

109. Quoted in Morris, *Pax Britannica*, p. 517.

110. Julien, *America's Empire*, p. 13f.

111. "President Bush's Address to the Nation," *New York Times*, September 7, 2003.

112. See Jack P. Greene, "Empire and Identity," p. 223. See also Pagden, "Struggle for Legitimacy," p. 52.

113. Office of the President, "National Security Strategy," part 5: "Prevent Our Enemies from Threatening Us, Our Allies, and Our Friends with Weapons of Mass Destruction"

114. See Acemoglu et al., "African Success Story."

115. Stephen Haber, Douglass C. North and Barry R. Weingast, "If Economists Are So Smart, Why Is Africa So Poor?" *Wall Street Journal*, July 30, 2003.

116. This is something the people of Sierra Leone acknowledged when they openly welcomed British intervention in September 2000. In the space of a few days eight hundred paratroopers achieved what had hitherto eluded more than ten thousand United Nations peacekeepers: they ended the country's horribly bloody internecine conflict.

117. I first advanced this case in my book *The Cash Nexus*. For echoes of the same argument, see Cooper, "Post-

modern State" and Mallaby, "Reluctant Imperialist."

118. See my Empire. Cf. Kurtz, "Democratic Imperialism."

119. Symonds, Oxford and Empire, p. 188.

120. Louis, "Introduction," pp. 5f.

121. "Success of a free Iraq will be watched and noted throughout the region. Millions will see that freedom, equality and material progress are possible at the heart of the Middle East. Leaders in the region will face the clearest evidence that free institutions and open societies are the only path to long-term national success and dignity. . . . And a transformed Middle East would benefit the entire world by undermining the ideologies that export violence to other lands. . . . The advance of democratic institutions in Iraq is setting an example that others [in the region] would be wise to follow": New York Times, September 23, 2003.

122. Ferguson, "Hegemony or Empire," p. 154.

CHAPTER 1: THE LIMITS OF THE AMERICAN EMPIRE

1. Ibid.

2. See Smith, Civic Ideals, esp. pp. 87–89, 116.

3. Ibid., pp. 130–34. Cf. Keyssar, Right to Vote.

4. Van Alstyne, American Empire, p. 3; Hanson, American Empire, p. 55.

5. Hanson, American Empire, p. 56.

6. Williams, Empire as a Way of Life, p. 35.

7. Madison, "The Union as a Safeguard Against Domestic Faction and Insurrection," Federalist No. 10.

8. Hamilton, "General Introduction," Federalist No. 1.

9. Freeman and Nearing, Dollar Diplomacy, p. 233.

10. Van Alstyne, American Empire, p. 1.

11. Ibid., p. 9.

12. Maddison, World Economy, pp. 35, 250.

13. Milner et al. (eds.), History of the American West, p. 161.

14. Richardson et al., Texas, p. 57.

15. Milner et al. (eds.), History of the American West, p. 162.

16. Billington, Westward Expansion, pp. 5–10.

17. Figures from the University of Michigan Correlates of War database.

18. Sylla, "U.S. Financial System," p. 259ff. The United States had to pay an additional $3.8 million to cover previous claims filed by American merchants against France for ship seizures. See in general Kastor, Louisiana Purchase. On the complex constitutional implications of Jefferson's action, see Adams, Formative Years, pp. 367–69.

19. Kastor, Louisiana Purchase, p. 7f.

20. Richardson et al., Texas, p. 83f.

21. Ibid., p. 89ff.

22. Ibid., p. 98.

23. Ibid., p. 151.

24. Ibid., p. 152.

25. Ibid., p. 157.

26. Milner et al. (eds.), History of the American West, p. 166. On the subsequent use of the phrase manifest destiny, see Horlacher, "Language," p. 37.

27. Richardson et al., Texas, p. 166.

28. Grant, Memoirs, p. 41. Lincoln, Grant and others suspected that Polk was motivated by a desire to create more slave states.

29. Richardson et al., Texas, p. 167f.

30. Ibid., p. 168.

31. Hanson, American Empire, p. 51.

32. The Canadian border up until this point had been agreed in stages: in 1818 (along the top of what is now

Montana and North Dakota), 1842 (along the borders of New York, Vermont, New Hampshire, Maine and Minnesota) and 1846 (cession of what became the states of Oregon, Washington and Idaho).

33. Van Alstyne, *American Empire*, p. 8f.

34. Boot, *Savage Wars*, pp. 10–26.

35. The Supreme Court rejected the suit of the slave Dred Scott that in crossing from a slave state to a federal territory he gained his freedom.

36. Pratt, *America's Colonial Experiment*, p. 158.

37. May, *American Imperialism*, p. 205f.

38. Pratt, *America's Colonial Experiment*, p. 159f. This argument was confirmed by the judgment in *Downes v. Bidwell* a year and half later.

39. Freeman and Nearing, *Dollar Diplomacy*, p. 236f. See also Smith, "Latin America, the United States and the European Powers," p. 85.

40. The idea arguably originated with the British foreign secretary George Canning, who proposed a joint Anglo-American declaration along these lines following British recognition of the independence of the South American states. Monroe preferred to make it a unilateral declaration by the United States, but in practice it could be enforced—or overthrown—only by the Royal Navy.

41. Smith, "Latin America, the United States and the European Powers," p. 85ff.

42. Ibid., p. 83f.

43. Freeman and Nearing, *Dollar Diplomacy*, p. 248; Smith, "Latin America, the United States and the European Powers," p. 91f. Of critical importance were British incursions on Venezuelan sovereignty.

44. Boot, *Savage Wars*, p. 62.

45. Roskin, "Generational Paradigms," p. 579.

46. Freeman and Nearing, *Dollar Diplomacy*, p. 266.

47. Smith, "Latin America, the United States and the European Powers," p. 100.

48. See my *Pity of War* for the argument that Germany, with its relatively insignificant overseas presence, did not come into this category.

49. Cole, *America's Foreign Relations*, p. 182; Black, *Good Neighbor*, p. 6.

50. Black, *Good Neighbor*, p. 12.

51. Freeman and Nearing, *Dollar Diplomacy*, p. 247. See also Smith, "Latin America, the United States and the European Powers," p. 89f.

52. Freeman and Nearing, *Dollar Diplomacy*, p. 243f.

53. Merk, *Manifest Destiny*, p. 232.

54. Conrad, *Nostromo*, p. 76f.

55. Bacevich, *American Empire*, p. 55; Pratt, *America's Colonial Experiment*, p. 168. The American commitment to free trade was never unqualified; the Open Door did not apply to the United States itself. In practice, no duties were charged on American imports to American possessions (with the exception of Samoa after 1909), whereas duties were charged on imports to American possessions from other countries. The British rejected such "imperial preference" until the 1930s.

56. Freeman and Nearing, *Dollar Diplomacy*, pp. 265, 257.

57. "If I read not amiss, this powerful race will move down upon Mexico, down upon Central and South America, out upon the islands of the sea, over upon Africa and beyond. And can anyone

doubt that the result of this competition of races will be the 'survival of the fittest?'": Merk, *Manifest Destiny*, p. 238ff. See also Horlacher, "Language," pp. 35–37.

58. Hofstadter, "Cuba, the Philippines and Manifest Destiny." Cf. Black, *Good Neighbor*, p. 2ff.; May, *American Imperialism*, pp. 192–97, 207–09.

59. Morris, *Pax Britannica*, p. 28.

60. See Cain and Hopkins, *British Imperialism*, passim.

61. Merk, *Manifest Destiny*, p. 243f.; Black, *Good Neighbor*, p. 16f.

62. Freeman and Nearing, *Dollar Diplomacy*, p. 244f.; Boot, *Savage Wars*, pp. 64–66. Samoa was divided among Britain, Germany and the United States.

63. Freeman and Nearing, *Dollar Diplomacy*, p. 246. For Mahan's role in arguing for annexation, see Merk, *Manifest Destiny*, pp. 235–37; Daws, *Shoal of Time*, p. 287.

64. Which was more advantageous to American refiners than consumers: LaFeber, *New Empire*, p. 35.

65. Daws, *Shoal of Time*, p. 285.

66. Merk, *Manifest Destiny*, pp. 232–35.

67. On the complex question of trade "reciprocity" between Hawaii and the United States, the effect of which was to make the United States practically the sole customer for Hawaiian sugar, see LaFeber, *New Empire*, pp. 115–20, 142.

68. Hofstadter, "Cuba, the Philippines and Manifest Destiny," p. 169f.

69. Daws, *Shoal of Time*, p. 289f.; Merk, *Manifest Destiny*, p. 255.

70. Daws, *Shoal of Time*, p. 294f.

71. Ibid., p. 295f.

72. Ibid., p. 298f.

73. Ibid., p. 316.

74. Pratt, *America's Colonial Experiment*, p. 160ff. The cases in question were *De Lima v. Bidwell* and *Downes v. Bidwell*.

75. Boot, *Savage Wars*, p. 103f.

76. Merk, *Manifest Destiny*, p. 254; Rauchway, *Murdering McKinley*, p. 7. With unintended bathos, McKinley added the characteristic peroration "And then I went to bed, and went to sleep, and slept soundly."

77. Horlacher, "Language," pp. 40–43.

78. On the complex motivations at work, see May, *American Imperialism*, pp. 5–16.

79. Freeman and Nearing, *Dollar Diplomacy*, p. 253f.

80. See, e.g., Boot, *Savage Wars*, p. 99f., 107–09.

81. Ibid., pp. 100–02.

82. Ibid., p. 120.

83. Ibid., p. 125.

84. Horlacher, "Language," p. 44. Cf. Boot, *Savage Wars*, pp. 114–16.

85. May, *American Imperialism*, pp. 199–205.

86. Pratt, *America's Colonial Experiment*, pp. 79–82.

87. Zwick, "Twain."

88. Freeman and Nearing, *Dollar Diplomacy*, pp. 255–57.

89. Hofstadter, "Cuba, the Philippines and Manifest Destiny," p. 169.

90. Boot, *Savage Wars*, p. 122f. A Senate committee was established to begin hearings on the atrocities. Waller was acquitted of murder, after it became clear that Jake Smith had been the first to issue the order of taking no prisoners, and Smith was convicted of "conduct to the prejudice of good order and military discipline" and forced into retirement.

91. May, *American Imperialism*, pp. 210–13, 221–23.

92. Vidal, *Decline and Fall*, p. 18.

93. May, *American Imperialism*, pp. 214–22.

94. Pratt, *America's Colonial Experiment*, pp. 291–310.

95. Louis, *Imperialism at Bay,* p. 149n.

96. Pratt, *Colonial Experiment,* p. 125. See Robert Freeman Smith, "Latin America, the United States and the European Powers," p. 102.

97. Pratt, *America's Colonial Experiment,* p. 140.

98. Robert Freeman Smith, "Latin America, the United States and the European Powers," p. 106f.

99. Platt, *Finance, Trade and British Foreign Policy,* p. 326ff.

100. Horlacher, "Language," p. 42.

101. Pratt, *America's Colonial Experiment,* p. 115f.

102. Boot, *Savage Wars,* pp. 60–62.

103. Ibid., p. 133. The new Republic's first constitution was drafted in a Washington hotel room; its first flag was sewn together in Highland Falls, New York: Black, *Good Neighbor,* p. 17.

104. Edmund Morris, *Theodore Rex,* p. 290. See also Robert Freeman Smith, "Latin America, the United States and the European Powers," p. 100f.

105. Black, *Good Neighbor,* p. 19f.

106. Pratt, *America's Colonial Experiment,* p. 132. Cf. Maddison, *World Economy,* p. 63.

107. Cole, *America's Foreign Relations,* p. 325.

108. Pratt, *America's Colonial Experiment,* p. 137.

109. Robert Freeman Smith, "Latin America, the United States and the European Powers," p. 108.

110. Pratt, *America's Colonial Experiment,* p. 119.

111. Ibid., p. 121.

112. Cole, *America's Foreign Relations,* p. 313.

113. Robert Freeman Smith, "Latin America, the United States and the European Powers," p. 102.

114. Boot, *Savage Wars,* p. 137f.

115. Cole, *America's Foreign Relations,* p. 316.

116. May, *American Imperialism,* p. 214.

117. Pratt, *America's Colonial Experiment,* pp. 127–30.

118. Ibid., p. 150f.

119. Ibid., p. 151.

120. According to one account, over three thousand Haitians were killed by the Americans: Robert Freeman Smith, "Latin America, the United States and the European Powers," p. 108.

121. Pratt, *America's Colonial Experiment,* pp. 143–47.

122. Cole, *America's Foreign Relations,* p. 323f.

123. Black, *Good Neighbor,* p. 35.

124. Ibid., p. 56.

125. Boot, *Savage Wars,* pp. 231–35.

126. Ibid., p. 249.

127. Black, *Good Neighbor,* p. 46.

128. Robert Freeman Smith, "Latin America, the United States and the European Powers," pp. 112–15.

129. Black, *Good Neighbor,* p. 71.

130. Schmidt, *Maverick Marine,* p. 231.

131. Cole, *America's Foreign Relations,* pp. 326–28.

132. Boot, *Savage Wars,* pp. 182–85, 188f.

133. Ibid., pp. 193–200.

134. Ibid., p. 204.

135. Cole, *America's Foreign Relations,* p. 328.

136. Boot, *Savage Wars,* p. 203. In 1920 General Álvaro Obregon seized power; both Carranza and Villa were gunned down within a few years.

137. The Calvo Doctrine explicitly rejected the idea that foreign subjects or companies had claims to "extraterritorial" legal status. In truth, Central America was more Balkan than Bolshevik, as the journalist Frank L. Kluckhohn noted in 1937: Black, *Good Neighbor,* p. 73.

138. Robert Freeman Smith, "Latin America, the United States and the European Powers," p. 109f.

139. Julien, *America's Empire,* p. 14.

CHAPTER 2: THE IMPERIALISM
OF ANTI-IMPERIALISM

1. Vonnegut, *Slaughterhouse 5*, p. 53f.

2. Gaddis, *We Now Know*, p. 109.

3. Ambrose, *Rise to Globalism*.

4. For a good recent account, see Ramsay, *Lusitania*.

5. Roskin, "Generational Paradigms," p. 566.

6. Incredibly, the German foreign minister Arthur Zimmermann sent the fateful telegram to his ambassador in Mexico via the State Department's own cable system (as well as two other routes). The British intercepted the telegram, decoded it and passed it on to the United States, finally forcing Wilson to abandon his policy of neutrality.

7. Black, *Good Neighbor*, p. 42.

8. Louis, *Imperialism at Bay*, p. 566.

9. Though it is important not to exaggerate the magnitude of the American contribution to victory in 1918, as does Mosier, *Myth of the Great War*. See my *Pity of War*, p. 312f.; also Zieger, *America's Great War*, pp. 97–114.

10. A view substantially endorsed after Wilson's death by the Nye Committee.

11. Knock, *To End All Wars*, p. 35.

12. Ibid., p. 77.

13. Ibid., p. 113.

14. Ibid., p. 143ff.

15. Ibid., p. 152.

16. Bacevich, *Empire*, p. 225.

17. Zimmermann, *First Great Triumph*, p. 476.

18. Dallas, *1918*, pp. 371–77, 393–417.

19. Quoted in Karnow, *Vietnam*, p. 14.

20. Melosi, *Pearl Harbor*, passim. For detail on the attacks, see Clarke, *Pearl Harbor*, pp. 276–83.

21. Melosi, *Pearl Harbor*, p. ix.

22. Louis, *Imperialism at Bay*, pp. 226f., 356.

23. Kagan, *Paradise and Power*, p. 71.

24. Louis, *Imperialism at Bay*, p. 26.

25. Ibid., p. 150.

26. Anderson, *United States, Great Britain and the Cold War*, p. 4.

27. Louis, *Imperialism at Bay*, p. 198.

28. Ibid., pp. 271–73.

29. Ibid., pp. 353–56.

30. Ibid., p. 351.

31. Ibid.

32. Quoted in Hanson, *American Empire*, p. 64.

33. Lundestad, *American "Empire,"* p. 39.

34. Ibid.

35. "President Bush's Address to the Nation," *New York Times*, September 7, 2003.

36. Dower, *Embracing Defeat*, p. 79.

37. Ibid., p. 80f.

38. Ibid., p. 27.

39. Bailey, *Postwar Japan*, p. 29.

40. Dower, *Embracing Defeat*, p. 38f.; Bailey, *Postwar Japan*, p. 27f.

41. Bailey, *Postwar Japan*, pp. 24–27.

42. Ibid., p. 41f.

43. Ibid., pp. 32–34; Dower, *Embracing Defeat*, p. 223. To be precise, the Japanese Foreign Ministry established a Central Liaison Office, which mediated between MacArthur and the Japanese bureaucracy.

44. Dower, *Embracing Defeat*, p. 223.

45. Bailey, *Postwar Japan*, p. 29.

46. Dower, *Embracing Defeat*, p. 204.

47. Ibid., p. 209.

48. Bailey, *Postwar Japan*, p. 25.

49. Ibid., p. 36f.

50. It was estimated that before the war ten *zaibatsu* had controlled—via sixty-seven holding companies and over four thousand subsidiaries—three-quarters of Japan's nonagricultural economy.

51. Bailey, *Postwar Japan*, p. 30.

52. Ibid., p. 23f.

53. Dower, *Embracing Defeat*, p. 115.

54. Wolfe (ed.), *Americans as Proconsuls*, p. 104.

55. Oppen (ed.), *Documents*, p. 14.

56. Gimbel, "Governing the American Zone," p. 93f.

57. Ibid., p. 95. Cf. Clay to War Department, September 18, 1945, in Smith (ed.), *Clay Papers*, p. 82f.

58. Gimbel, "Governing the American Zone," pp. 92–97.

59. See, e.g., Jean Edward Smith (ed.), *Clay Papers*, p. 174.

60. Wolfe (ed.), *Americans as Proconsuls*, p. 112f.

61. Peterson, "Occupation."

62. See, e.g., Gimbel, *American Occupation;* Backer, *Priming the German Economy*.

63. Fullbrook, *Divided Nation*, pp. 138–50.

64. Smith (ed.), *Clay Papers*, p. 172.

65. Porch, "Occupational Hazards," p. 37.

66. Oppen (ed.), *Documents*, p. 20.

67. Ibid., pp. 16, 19.

68. Gimbel, "Governing the American Zone," p. 93.

69. Pulzer, *German Politics*, pp. 29–32.

70. James F. Byrnes, "Restatement of Policy on Germany," http:www.usembassy.de /usa/usrelations4555.htm.

71. Robert Wolfe (ed.), *Americans as Proconsuls*, p. 105f.

72. Ibid., p. 109.

73. Gimbel, "Governing the American Zone," p. 102.

74. Oppen (ed.), *Documents*, p. 375f.

75. Schlauch, "American Policy," p. 115.

76. Oppen (ed.), *Documents*, p. 21.

77. Backer, *Priming the German Economy*, p. 37. Cf. Schlauch, "American Policy," p. 115f.

78. Gimbel, *American Occupation*, p. 1.

79. Schlauch, "American Policy," p. 121.

80. Ibid., p. 123.

81. Oppen (ed.), *Documents*, p. 93.

82. Ibid., pp. 152–60

83. Ibid., pp. 195–99.

84. Jean Edward Smith (ed.), *Clay Papers*, p. 143.

85. Backer, *Priming the German Economy*, p. 188, table 6.

86. Davidson, *Death and Life of Germany*, p. 260f.

87. See Gimbel, "Governing the American Zone," pp. 92–96; Schlauch, "American Policy," p. 125.

88. The phrase was the British economist Lionel Robbins's.

89. Gaddis, *We Now Know*, p. 20.

90. President Harry S. Truman's Address Before a Joint Session of Congress, March 12, 1947, www.yale.edu/ lawweb/avalon/trudoc.htm.

91. Hoge and Zakaria, *American Encounter*, pp. 155–70.

92. Text from http:www.cnn.com/ SPECIALS/cold.war/episodes/05/ documents/nsc.report.68/.

93. Lundestad, *American "Empire*," p. 44.

94. Bell, *Americanization*, p. 3.

95. Reinstein, "Reparations," p. 146.

96. Bailey, *Postwar Japan*, p. 38.

97. Ibid., p. 60f.

98. Ibid., pp. 52–61.

99. Dower, "Occupied Japan," p. 487.

100. The average annual growth rate of West German *per capita* GDP averaged over 5 percent a year between 1950 and 1973, as against 8 percent in Japan. Greece, Spain and Portugal enjoyed even more rapid growth than Germany in the same period, according to Maddison, *World Economy*, table A1-d.

101. Backer, *Priming the German Economy*, p. 186f.

102. United States Agency for International Development, Statistics and Reports Division, November 17, 1975.

103. Backer, *Priming the German Economy*, pp. 174–78.

104. In 2001 69,200 U.S. troops were deployed in Germany and 40,200 in Japan, mostly on the island of Okinawa.

105. Oppen (ed.) *Documents,* pp. 156–60.

106. Layne, "America as European Hegemon," p. 20.

107. Maddison, *World Economy,* p. 261, table B-18.

108. Lundestad, *American "Empire,"* p. 40.

109. Schiller, *Mass Communications,* p. 50.

110. See esp. Gilpin, *Political Economy.*

111. Office of the Undersecretary of Defense (Comptroller), "National Defense Budget Estimates for FY 2004," (Green Paper), March 2003. Cf. Malkasian, *Korean War,* p. 13f, 73.

112. Gaddis, *We Now Know,* pp. 89, 102f.

113. University of Michigan, Correlates of War database.

114. Magdoff, *Age of Imperialism,* p. 42. For different figures, see Peter H. Smith, *Talons of the Eagle,* p. 119.

115. Lundestad, *American "Empire,"* p. 54.

116. Ibid., p. 65.

117. Pei, "Lessons," p. 52. Oddly, Pei ignores the case of South Korea; admittedly, its transition to democracy came a long time after the intervention.

118. Witness the vain attempts by Dean Rusk to discourage the emergence of a "Bonn–Paris axis" in 1963: Layne, "America as European Hegemon," p. 24f.

119. Stueck, *Korean War,* p. 26.

120. Gaddis, *We Now Know,* p. 71f.

121. Malkasian, *Korean War,* p. 15. Cf. Spanier, *Truman-MacArthur,* p. 257ff.

122. Malkasian, *Korean War,* pp. 11–17.

123. Mueller, *War, Presidents and Public Opinion,* table 3.2, p. 48.

124. Foot, *Wrong War,* pp. 189–94.

125. Malkasian, *Korean War,* p. 9.

126 Stueck, *Korean War,* p. 132f.

127. This consciousness of European vulnerability had already been clearly expressed in NSC 68, which warned of the danger of "surprise attack" in Europe. Text at http:www.cnn.com/ SPECIALS/cold.war/episodes/05/ documents/nsc.report.68/.

128. Gaddis, *We Now Know,* p. 103.

129. McCullough, *Truman,* p. 837.

130. Ferrell, *Truman,* p. 330.

131. Truman, *Years of Trial and Hope,* p. 467ff. MacArthur invited the Chinese commander in chief to "confer in the field" or face the risk of "an expansion of our military operations to [China's] coastal areas and interior bases."

132. Ibid., 472f. Ferrell, *Truman,* p. 332.

133. Ferrell, *Truman,* p. 334. The mood of panic in Washington was palpable. The rushed press conference happened because Truman and his advisers feared that MacArthur "was going on a world-wide broadcast network" to resign before he could be fired: McCullough, *Truman,* p. 842.

134. See Wittner (ed.), *MacArthur,* pp. 103–08.

135. McCullough, *Truman,* pp. 837–50.

136. Ibid., p. 852.

137. Truman, *Years of Trial and Hope,* p. 459.

138. Ibid., p. 464.

139. McCullough, *Truman,* p. 833f.

140. Foot, *Wrong War,* p. 23.

141. McCullough, *Truman,* p. 853ff.; Ferrell, *Truman,* p. 335.

142. McCullough, *Truman,* p. 854.

143. Spanier, *Truman-MacArthur,* p. 273.

144. For an overly sympathetic account, see Willoughby and Chamberlain, *MacArthur,* pp. 418–25.

145. Foot, *Wrong War,* p. 176. The Chinese were fearful that a large proportion of the POWs would refuse to return home voluntarily.

146. Ibid., p. 176f.

147. Ibid., p. 184.

148. Ibid., p. 25.

149. Mueller, *War, Presidents and Public Opinion*, p. 105.

150. The percentage of U.S. Army personnel killed in action fell from 13.6 percent in the second half of 1950 to just 3.6 percent in 1951 and little more than 1 percent in 1952 and 1953. See the figures in http://history.amedd. army.mil/booksdocs/korea/reister/ ch1.htm.

151. For Korean War casualty statistics, there are now excellent electronic sources. See http://www.koreanwar-educator.org/ old%20site/public_html/toc/ detail_casualty/PAGE%20FIVE.htm; http://www.centurychina.com/history/ krwarcost.html; and the invaluable http://users.erols.com/mwhite28/war- stat2.htm.

152. Kissinger, "Reflections on American Diplomacy" p. 50f.

153. Greene, *Quiet American*, p. 124.

154. Ibid., p. 96.

155. Caputo, *Rumor*, p. 16.

156. Ibid., p. 88f.

157. Baker, *Nam*, p. 133.

158. Ferguson, "Prisoner Taking."

159. Herring, *Longest War*, p. 268.

160. Ibid., p. 192f.

161. Karnow, *Vietnam*, p. 19.

162. Herring, *Longest War*, p. 268.

163. Karnow, *Vietnam*, p. 19.

164. Ravenal et al., "Was Failure Inevitable?," p. 268f.

165. Palmer, *Twenty-five Year War*, p. 204f

166. Karnow, *Vietnam*, p. 20f.

167. Coker, *Conflicts*, p. 22.

168. Palmer, *Twenty-five Year War*, p. 195.

169. Ibid., p. 192f.

170. Though of course there had been military advisers in Vietnam for some years; the first American to be killed there died as early as 1961. But the direct and overt participation of American forces in the war really dates from 1965.

171. Mueller, *War, Presidents and Public Opinion*.

172. Ravenal, *Never Again*, p. 106. Cf. Palmer, *Twenty-five Year War*, p. 190.

173. Ravenal et al., "Was Failure Inevitable?" p. 275f; Abshire, "Lessons," p. 406; Karnow, *Vietnam*, p. 17.

174. Mueller, *War, Presidents and Public Opinion*, table 3.2, p. 49.

175. Edelman, *Dear America*, p. 205.

176. Julien, *Empire*, p. 13.

177. Edelman, *Dear America*, p. 207.

178. Siracusa, "Lessons," p. 228.

179. Roskin, "Generational Paradigms," p. 569.

180. Siracusa, "Lessons," p. 228; Gaddis, *We Now Know*, p. 58.

181. Herring, *Longest War*, p. 270.

182. Siracusa, "Lessons," p. 233; Roskin, "Generational Paradigms," p. 575.

183. Kupchan, *End*, p. 200. Cf. Lundestad, "Empire," p. 92.

184. Herring, *Longest War*, p. 267.

185. Gaddis, *We Now Know*, p. 177; Lowenthal, *Partners in Conflict*, pp. 31–33.

186. Swomley, *American Empire*, p. 1.

187. Gaddis, *We Now Know*, pp. 179, 182. Cf. Lowenthal, *Partners in Conflict*, pp. 28–30.

188. Not least because, unknown to the Americans, the Russians had sent tactical nuclear missiles to Cuba, which could have been used to annihilate any invading force.

189. The best account of the crisis is Fursenko and Naftali, *One Hell of a Gamble*.

CHAPTER 3: THE
CIVILIZATION OF CLASHES

1. Statement by Osama bin Laden, October 7, 2001, http://news.bbc.co.uk/1/hi/world/south_asia/1585636.stm.

2. Woodward, *Bush at War,* p. 131.

3. Geoffrey Wheatcroft, "Two Years of Gibberish," *Prospect,* September 2003, pp. 30–33.

4. Knapp, "United States and the Middle East," pp. 11–13.

5. Reich, "United States Interests," p. 56.

6. Yergin, *Prize,* pp. 195–97, 204.

7. Ibid., p. 393.

8. Gause, "U.S.-Saudi Relationship," p. 344.

9. Yergin, *Prize,* p. 401.

10. Ibid., pp. 403f, 410–16, 427f.

11. Gause, "U.S.-Saudi Relationship," p. 345.

12. Reich, "United States Interests," p. 81.

13. Gaddis, *We Now Know,* p. 164.

14. Reich, "United States Interests," p. 72.

15. Ibid., p. 240f.

16. Rosecrance, "Objectives," p. 31.

17. Knapp, "United States and the Middle East," p. 14f.

18. Ibid., p. 15.

19. Kinzer, *All the Shah's Men,* p. 205.

20. Knapp, "United States and the Middle East," p. 25.

21. Louis and Robinson, "Imperialism of Decolonization"

22. Gaddis, *We Now Know,* p. 169.

23. Knapp, "United States and the Middle East," p. 25.

24. Gaddis, *We Now Know,* p. 175.

25. Yergin, *Prize,* p. 508f.

26. Gause, "U.S.-Saudi Relationship," p. 346.

27. Rosecrance, "Objectives," p. 32.

28. Reich, "United States Interests," p. 81.

29. Rosecrance, "Objectives," p. 34.

30. See, e.g., Reich, "United States and Israel," pp. 227, 241.

31. Ibid., p. 228.

32. Reich, "United States and Israel," p. 232.

33. Ibid., p. 234.

34. Ibid., p. 234f.

35. Ibid., p. 229f.

36. Lundestad, *"Empire,"* p. 90. Cf. Rosecrance, "Objectives," p. 36.

37. Reich, "United States Interests," p. 66; Gause, "U.S.-Saudi Relationship," p. 347.

38. Gause, "U.S.-Saudi Relationship," p. 346.

39. Priest, *Mission,* p. 84f.

40. Reich, "United States Interests," p. 64f.

41. Ibid., p. 62.

42. Ibid., p. 82.

43. Ibid., p. 69.

44. Knapp, "United States and the Middle East," p. 23f.

45. Maddison, *World Economy,* p. 151, table 3–21.

46. Lundestad, *"Empire,"* p. 97.

47. Power, *"Problem from Hell,"* p. 234.

48. Gause, "U.S.-Saudi Relationship," p. 347.

49. Ibid. See also Haass, *Intervention,* p. 28.

50. "Declaration of the World Islamic Front for Jihad Against the Jews and the Crusaders February 23, 1998," http://www.fas.org/irp/world/para/docs/980223-fatwa.htm.

51. "Conversation with Terror," *Time,* January 11, 2001.

52. See also the purported letter published on November 24, 2002, http://observer.guardian.co.uk/worldview/story/0,11581,845725,00.html, and the message broadcast on al Jazeera on February 11, 2003.

53. Huntington, *Clash of Civilizations.* Cf. Lewis, *Crisis of Islam.*

54. Lewis, *What Went Wrong?*, p. 159.

55. Burleigh, *Third Reich*.

56. See Christopher Hitchens, "Against Rationalization," *Nation,* October 8, 2001. Hitchens used the phrase "fascism with an Islamic face."

57. Marshall, *Demanding the Impossible*, p. 284.

58. Pettiford and Harding, *Terrorism*, p. 36.

59. Conrad, *Secret Agent*, pp. 65–68.

60. Knapp, "United States and the Middle East," p. 21f.

61. John Keegan, "Diary," *Spectator,* October 13, 2001. During the later stages of the Second World War, five thousand Japanese pilots killed themselves flying kamikaze ("divine wind") missions. At Okinawa nearly five thousand American sailors were killed, and such attacks sank no fewer than thirty-six vessels. Nor was this the only suicide tactic the Japanese adopted as the Pacific war turned against them. They also trained suicide divers—*fukuryu* or "crouching dragons"—whose mission was to swim out and attach mines to approaching landing craft.

62. Pettiford and Harding, *Terrorism,* p. 116.

63. United States Commission on National Security/21st Century, *New World Coming: American Security in the 21st Century—Major Themes and Implications,* September 15, 1999; http://www. nssg. gov./Reports/NWC.pdf.

64. Martin Wolf, "Frightening Flexibility of Terrorism," *Financial Times,* June 3, 2003.

65. On the basis of the 1993 Federal Budget Request: International Institute of Strategic Studies, *The Military Balance, 1992–1993,* p. 17.

66. Ibid., p. 218.

67. "September 11 Death Toll Revised," Associated Press, June 11, 2003. It is now estimated that 2,940 people died in the World Trade Center attacks, 189 in the Pentagon attack and 44 when a fourth plane crashed in Pennsylvania.

68. Looney, "Economic Costs." This proved much too pessimistic.

69. See the debate in University of Chicago, Graduate School of Business, "What's Next? The Economic Effects of September 11," http://gsbwww. uchicago.edu/news/gsbchicago/ win02/features/effects1.htm.

70. By way of comparison, the insurance losses caused by the severe flooding in Central Europe in 2002 amounted to $2.5 billion. The death toll of the earthquake in Afghanistan and Pakistan that same year was around 2,000. See the *Economist,* May 24, 2003.

71. There were nearly 1,000 terrorist incidents in Europe between 1991 and 1996, compared with just 241 in the years 1997 to 2002, a fall of 75 percent.

72. "There can be no military solution to the problem [of Palestine]," retired CENTCOM commander Anthony Zinni told a journalist in 2002. "You know, there is no military solution to terrorism either": Priest, *Mission,* p. 11f.

73. The statistics are of course controversial. I have consulted the Israeli Information Center for Human Rights in the Occupied Territories, http://www. btselem.org.

74. While there is no conclusive evidence that Saddam Hussein's regime gave assistance to al Qa'eda, it did support Abu Nidal and Hamas. Saddam also aided the Iranian group Mujahedeen-e-Khlaq and the Kurdistan Workers' Party.

75. Smith, *Talons of the Eagle*, p. 5ff.

76. Haass, *Intervention*, p. 26f.

77. Pettiford and Harding, *Terrorism*, p. 135.
78. Woodward, *Bush at War*, p. 38.
79. Schirmer, "U.S. Bases in Central America."
80. Mead, *Special Providence*, p. 31.
81. Haass, *Intervention*, p. 25f.
82. Schirmer, "U.S. Bases in Central America."
83. Priest, *Mission*, p. 95.
84. Ibid., p. 71.
85. By the mid-1990s these forces would have undertaken over two thousand operations in 167 different countries: Coker, *Conflicts*, p. 20.
86. Priest, *Mission*, p. 45f.
87. Boot, *Savage Wars*, p. 318.
88. Haass, *Intervention*, p. 30f.

CHAPTER 4: SPLENDID MULTILATERALISM

1. I am grateful to Mr. Arria for permission to quote what I hope will one day be the title of a memoir by him about his time at the Security Council.
2. Woodward, *Bush at War*, p. 333.
3. The number is controversial. The United States claimed that its "coalition of the willing" numbered forty-nine. However, one independent survey on March 28, 2003, could confirm the support of only thirty-seven countries, with a further ten countries apparently, though not explicitly, supportive. Only Britain, Australia and Poland sent fighting forces to Iraq, though another ten countries offered small numbers of noncombat forces, mostly either medical teams and specialists in decontamination: http://en.wikipedia.org/wiki/U.S.-led_coalition_against_Iraq#Invasion_coalition.
4. The phrase is usually ascribed to the Marquess of Salisbury, but his minister George Goschen seems to have used it more often. Salisbury regarded isolation as highly dangerous and preferred to embed Britain in a network of alliances and understandings.
5. By June 1998, according to the UN, the United States owed about $1.5 billion in dues and assessments. This was made up of $298 million owing for the 1998 regular budget and $271 for the regular budgets of prior years, as well as $95 million for peacekeeping operations in 1998 and $871 million for peacekeeping in previous years: Christopher S. Wren, "Unpaid Dues at the U.N. Could Cost U.S. Its Vote," *New York Times*, June 28, 1998. Under the Helms-Biden compromise of 1999 the United States agreed to pay slightly under half its arrears in return for a series of reforms of the UN and the other affiliated institutions.
6. http://www.un.int/usa/FactSheets_GA58.htm.
7. Madeleine Albright, "Think Again: United Nations," *Foreign Policy*, September–October 2003, p. 22.
8. The United States walked out of the International Court in 1984 after being sued by Nicaragua for mining its harbors.
9. Forman et al., *United States in a Global Age*, p. 10f. The principal opt-outs are from the Comprehensive Test Ban Treaty, the Antiballistic Missile Treaty, the Rome Statute of the International Criminal Court, the Biological Weapons Convention (verification protocol), a proposed UN convention on small arms and light weapons, the Ottawa Convention banning the production, trade and use of antipersonnel land mines, the conventions on the Rights of the Child and on the Elimi-

nation of Discrimination against Women, and (perhaps most famously) the Kyoto Protocol on global warming.

10. Karnow, *Vietnam*, p. 16.

11. Department of Veterans Affairs, http://www.va.gov/pressrel/amwars01.htm.

12. Priest, *Mission*, p. 69.

13. Boot, *Savage Wars*, p. 320.

14. A recurrent error of recent American policy since 1991 has been to give military enterprises names more suitable to brands of medication. "Provide Comfort," "Southern Watch," "Deliberate Force" and "Enduring Freedom" all are unwittingly reminiscent of remedies for diarrhea.

15. Haass, *Intervention*, p. 37.

16. Ibid., p. 168.

17. Gause, "U.S.-Saudi Relationship," p. 351.

18. Ibid., p. 343. In 1990 the Saudi armed forces totaled just 111,500. Iraq, with a population less than double the size, had an army five times larger.

19. Bergen, *Holy War Inc.*, p. 85f.

20. Reich, "United States and Israel," p. 235f.

21. Ibid., p. 237.

22. Ibid., p. 236.

23. Bowden, *Black Hawk Down*, p. 166.

24. Note that the aversion of American politicians and voters to military casualties has nothing to do with the attitudes of American service personnel, whose often reckless bravery Aidid's men sought to exploit.

25. Haass, *Intervention*, p. 46.

26. See Power, *Problem from Hell*.

27. The United Nations Convention of the Prevention and Punishment of the Crime of Genocide of 1948 is a widely misunderstood document. Its second article sets out a clear definition of the word that Raphael Lemkin coined four

years before. It covers "any of the following acts committed with intent to destroy, in whole or in part, a national, ethnical, racial or religious group, as such":

a. killing members of the group;

b. causing serious bodily or mental harm to members of the group;

c. deliberately inflicting on the group conditions of life calculated to bring about its physical destruction in whole or in part;

d. imposing measures intended to prevent births within the group;

e. forcibly transferring children of the group to another group.

It is not only genocide that is declared a punishable offense by the convention, but also conspiracy to commit genocide, direct and public incitement to commit genocide, attempt to commit genocide and complicity in genocide. There can be no question that according to this definition, crimes of genocide were committed in Burundi in 1972, Iraq in 1987–88, Bosnia in 1992 and 1995, Rwanda in 1994 and Kosovo in 1998 and 1999.

28. Simms, *Unfinest Hour*, p. 54.

29. Ibid., p. 56. Cf. Shawcross, *Deliver Us from Evil*, p. 83.

30. Simms, *Unfinest Hour*, p. 339f.

31. Ibid., p. 57ff.

32. Ibid., pp. 88, 95f, 120f, 130f.

33. Ibid., p. 133.

34. Shawcross, *Deliver Us from Evil*, pp. 92, 94.

35. Holbrooke, *To End a War*, pp. 231–312.

36. Ibid., pp. 318, 322.

37. The full text of the agreement can be found at http://www.mondediplomatique.fr/dossiers/kosovo/rambouillet.html.

38. See my article on the subject in the *Financial Times*, April 3, 1999. See also Bobbitt, *Shield of Achilles*, pp. 468–77.

Article 2(4) of the UN Charter states that "all Members shall refrain . . . from the threat or use of force against the territorial integrity or political independence of any state," while Article 2(7) prohibits intervention "in matters which are essentially within the domestic jurisdiction of any state." In addition, the General Assembly's 1970 Declaration on Principles of International Law denies members "the right to intervene, directly or indirectly, for any reason whatever, in the internal affairs of any other state." Under the UN Charter, force may be used only in self-defense or with the explicit authorization of the Security Council in response to an act of aggression (Chapter VII, Articles 39 to 51). Only by ignoring the UN Charter (or, in the words of Tony Blair, "qualifying . . . the principle of non-interference . . . in important respects") could the military intervention by NATO on behalf of the Albanians of Kosovo be justified. See Caplan, "Humanitarian Intervention: Which Way Forward?" p. 25f.

39. On the "'no casualties' mindset" that characterized the war, see Boot, *Savage Wars*, pp. 325–27.

40. *New York Times*, August 15, 2003.

41. Ignatieff, *Empire Lite*, p. 70f.

42. Boot, *Savage Wars*, p. 327. The war's diplomatic low point came when the Chinese Embassy in Belgrade was unintentionally hit by a guided missile. Still more damage was done to the legitimacy of the NATO intervention by the use of cluster bombs on civilian targets in Serbia.

43. Ignatieff, *Virtual War*.

44. This was the conclusion of Ferguson, *Cash Nexus*.

45. Power, *"Problem from Hell."*

46. Shawcross, *Deliver Us from Evil*, p. 118f.

47. Ibid., pp. 106, 119, 207ff.

48. Ibid., p. 211.

49. Bacevich, *American Empire*, p. 202f.

50. *New York Times*, September 24, 2003.

51. Woodward, *Bush at War*, esp. pp. 30, 150.

52. Bush's words to a group of senators on September 13, 2001, quoted by Howard Fineman in *Newsweek*, September 24, 2001.

53. Clausewitz, *On War*, ch. 1, p. 87.

54. Around ten thousand Mahdists were killed to just forty-eight British soldiers. For an account of the battle, see Ferguson, *Empire*, pp. 267–70.

55. American forces had been operating in post-Soviet Central Asia since the mid-1990s, in Kyrgyzstan, Kazakhstan, Tajikistan and Uzbekistan as well as in Pakistan. But it was still far from easy to mount even an air war from territories so recently added to the U.S. sphere of influence: Priest, *Mission*, pp. 38, 101f.

56. See the exceptionally well-informed account in Woodward, *Bush at War*.

57. Text from http://usinfo.state.gov/topical/pol/terror/secstrat.htm.

58. See, e.g., Galston, "Perils of Preemptive War."

59. Leffler, "9/11."

60. Shawcross, *Deliver Us from Evil*, p. 224f.

61. The list of transgressions was eloquently presented to the House of Commons by the prime minister, Tony Blair, on March 18, 2003.

62. Six in 1999, three in 2000, three in 2001 and five in 2002 alone.

63. Shawcross, *Deliver Us from Evil*, pp. 250, 320.

64. Stanley Hoffman, "America Goes Backward," *New York Review of Books*, June 12, 2003; James P. Rubin, "Stumbling into War," *Foreign Affairs*, September–October 2003; Madeleine K. Albright, "Bridges, Bombs or Bluster," ibid.

65. Pollack, *Threatening Storm.*

66. "The Divided West," *Financial Times* supplement, June 2003, p. 5.

67. Text at http://ods-dds-ny.un.org/doc/ UNDOC/GEN/N02/682/26/PDF/ N0268226.pdf?OpenElement.

68. It would be interesting to see how credible this document looks today.

69. See the inferences drawn by Mark Danner, "Iraq: The New War," *New York Review of Books,* September 25, 2003, p. 90.

70. "The Divided West," *Financial Times* supplement, June 2003, p. 5.

71. "It is not well brought-up behavior," snapped Chirac. "They missed a good opportunity to keep quiet." For good measure, he added: "If they wanted to diminish their chances of joining Europe, they could not have found a better way."

72. Hoffman, "America Goes Backward," p. 74. Hoffman argues that the United States is pursuing "a policy of hubris in which international domination is presented under the mask of universal benign ideals." If anyone was wearing that mask in March 2003, it was surely Jacques Chirac.

73. Mark Husband and Stephen Fidler, "No Smoking Gun," *Financial Times,* June 4, 2003.

74. *Financial Times,* June 4, 2003.

75. Testimony of John Scarlett before the Hutton Inquiry into the death of Michael Kelly, August 28, 2003: http: //www.the-hutton-inquiry.org.uk/.

76. Hansard, March 18, 2003: http://www. parliament.the-stationery-office.co.uk/pa/cm200203/cmhansrd/ cm030318/debtext/30318-06.htm and -08.htm.

77. Woodward, *Bush at War,* p. 106.

78. Rodric Braithwaite, "End of the Affair," *Prospect,* May 2003, pp. 20–23.

79. Gilbert, *Never Despair,* p. 1271.

80. Ibid.

81. Dimbleby and Reynolds, *Ocean Apart,* p. 255.

82. Ibid., p. 252.

83. Ibid., p. 288.

84. Ibid., p. 264.

85. Pew Global Attitudes Project, "Views of a Changing World," June 2003.

86. Richard Burkholder, "Ousting Saddam Hussein 'Was Worth Hardships,'" Gallup Web site: http://www.gallup.com/poll /tb/goverpubli/20030923c.asp.

87. Ibid.

88. Woodward, *Bush at War,* p. 220.

89. Ibid., pp. 231, 237.

90. Ignatieff, *Empire Lite,* p. 2.

91. Etzioni, "Implications of American Anti-Terrorism Coalition," p. 26.

92. Stewart Stogel, "Food Fight," *Time,* May 3, 2003.

CHAPTER 5: THE CASE FOR LIBERAL EMPIRE

1. Louis, *Imperialism at Bay,* p. 227.

2. Ibid., p. 14.

3. On the limits of sovereignty and the various models of partial sovereignty, including empire, see Krasner, "Troubled Societies."

4. Diamond, "Universal Democracy."

5. Townsend, *European Colonial Expansion,* p. 19.

6. Despite his repeated demands for a "timetable" for decolonization, the time frame Roosevelt had in mind was always kept vague. He spoke of some South Asian colonies as being "ready for self-government in 20 years," but Borneo he expected would need a century of trusteeship: ibid., pp. 157, 437.

7. Louis, *Imperialism at Bay,* p. 175. See Jeffery, "Second World War," p. 314.

8. Louis and Robinson, "Imperialism of Decolonization."

9. The British never tired of pointing out these inconsistencies. They lost no opportunity to remind the Americans of their *de facto* imperial position in Hawaii, Puerto Rico and the Virgin Islands. It turned out, conveniently enough, that these lay "outside the scope of the trusteeship program": Louis, *Imperialism at Bay,* p. 236. Later they referred to the preferential treatment accorded by Roosevelt to the Russian empire as the "salt water fallacy": ibid., p. 570.

10. Alesina et al., "Economic Integration and Political Disintegration," pp. 1, 23.

11. Diamond, "Promoting Real Reform in Africa."

12. Ibid., p. 11.

13. They were Lesotho, Pakistan, Egypt, Botswana, Malaysia, Malta, Barbados, Cyprus, Israel, Ireland, Singapore, Hong Kong, Canada and, of course, the United States.

14. Calculated from World Bank, *World Development Indicators* database. *Per capita* GDP is adjusted for purchasing power parity in current international dollars.

15. Ibid. Income refers to gross national income *per capita,* Atlas method (current U.S. dollars), 2002.

16. The exceptions are Bangladesh, Nepal, Laos, Cambodia, Kyrgyzia and Tajikistan: two former British colonies, two former French colonies and two former Russian colonies.

17. Diamond, "Promoting Real Reform in Africa."

18. James Wolfensohn, "A Good 'Pro-Poor' Cancún Could Help Rich as Well," *Financial Times,* September 8, 2003.

19. Tobias Buck, Guy de Jonquières and Frances Williams, "Fischler's New Era for Europe's Farmers," *Financial Times,*

June 27, 2003. Cf. Runge, "Agrivation."

20. Diamond, "Promoting Real Reform in Africa," p. 31; national income data from the World Bank.

21. Sachs and Warner, "Economic Reform," esp. p. 36. See also their "Fundamental Sources of Long-run Growth," pp. 184–88.

22. Chiswick and Hatton, "International Migration."

23. Rodrik, "Feasible Globalizations," p. 19.

24. Lucas, "Why Doesn't Capital Flow from Rich to Poor Countries?"

25. Baldwin and Martin, "Two Waves of Globalization," p. 20.

26. Schularick, "Development Finance," p. 20f, chart 2.

27. Easterly, *Elusive Quest,* p. 58f.

28. See, e.g., Sachs, "Tropical Underdevelopment."

29. See Acemoglu et al., "Colonial Origins" and the same authors' "Reversal of Fortune."

30. Landes, *Wealth and Poverty of Nations,* p. 217f.

31. Barro, "Determinants of Economic Growth." The three others were the provision of secondary and higher education, the provision of health care and the promotion of birth control.

32. North and Weingast, "Constitutions and Commitment."

33. Ferguson, *Cash Nexus.* See also Sylla, "Shaping the U.S. Financial System."

34. Lindert, "Voice and Growth."

35. "Zambia received $2 billion of aid in 1985 dollars since 1960. If all the aid had gone into investment, and investment had gone into growth, its *per capita* income would now be $20,000. In fact it is $600": Easterly, *Elusive Quest,* p. 42.

36. "Governments so often cause low growth [by creating] poor incentives for growth: high inflation, high black market premiums, high budget deficits, strongly negative real interest rates, restrictions on free trade, excessive red tape, and inadequate public services": ibid., p. 239.

37. According to one estimate, the private international assets of poor countries' residents may amount to two trillion dollars, the equivalent of almost 40 percent of poor countries' combined GDP in 2000: Schularick, "Development Finance," p. 32.

38. James K. Boyce and Léonce Ndikumana, "Africa's Odious Debts," Project Syndicate, June 2003.

39. Diamond, "Promoting Real Reform in Africa," p. 6. The number of African countries holding democratic elections has risen slightly since the nadir of the 1980s and now stands at nineteen, but only a quarter of these offer their citizens meaningful civil and political freedom. The distinction between liberal and illiberal democracy is explored at length in Zakaria, *Future of Freedom.* For an illuminating critique, see Diamond's review in *Journal of Democracy,* 14, 4 (2003), pp. 167–71.

40. Acemoglu et al., "African Success Story," p. 2f.

41. Ibid., p. 4. Acemoglu et al. give no credit whatever to the legacy of British colonial rule. Another interpretation might be that, compared with (for example) Zimbabwe, the rulers of Botswana have done relatively little to dismantle the British system of non-corrupt administration.

42. Diamond, "Promoting Real Reform in Africa," p. 9.

43. Collier and Hoeffler, "Economic Causes of Civil War." Cf. Collier, "The Market for Civil War," *Foreign Policy,* May–June 2003, pp. 38–45; "The Global Menace of Local Strife," *Economist,* May 24, 2003.

44. Gleditsch et al., "Armed Conflict."

45. For a useful introduction to the noneconomic facets of globalization, see Held et al., *Global Transformations.*

46. Though it should be emphasized that there are limits to how far a complete standardization of economic institutions could be—or for that matter needs to be—taken: Rodrik, "Feasible Globalizations." As Rodrik argues, there is more than one path to prosperity; witness the diversity of institutional arrangements in the world's largest economies. However, that is not an argument against trying to establish one or other of the successful institutional frameworks in countries that have failed to grow their own. It is not that every country needs to choose among the nation-state, democracy and global economic integration; it is just that some nation-states—usually undemocratic ones—need to have globalization forced upon them.

47. Ibid., pp. 6–10. For the evidence that the late nineteenth century was indeed the "first age of globalization," see O'Rourke and Williamson, "When Did Globalization Begin?" See also their *Globalization and History.*

48. By one measure (net customs revenue as a percentage of net import values) France was in fact more liberal from the 1820s until the mid-1870s: John Vincent Nye, "Myth of Free-Trade Britain." The real significance of British free trade is that the British retained it even after globalization began to drive down commodity prices in the 1870s.

49. Bairoch, "European Trade Policy" p. 139.

50. Edelstein, "Imperialism: Cost and Benefit," p. 205.

51. Cain and Hopkins, *British Imperialism,* p. 141.

52. Ibid., p. 432.

53. Williamson, "Land, Labor and Globalization."

54. See Cain and Hopkins, *British Imperialism,* esp. p. 212.

55. Clemens and Williamson, "A Tariff-Growth Paradox?"

56. Irwin, "Tariff-Growth Correlation of the Late Nineteenth Century."

57. Constantine, "Migrants and Settlers," p. 167.

58. Williamson, "Winners and Losers"; idem, "Land, Labor and Globalization."

59. Engerman, "Servants to Slaves," p. 272.

60. Tinker, *New System of Slavery.*

61. Cain and Hopkins, *British Imperialism,* pp. 161–63.

62. Maddison, *World Economy,* table 2-26a.

63. Davis and Huttenback, *Mammon,* p. 46.

64. Maddison, *World Economy,* table 2-26b.

65. According to Clemens and Williamson, "about two-thirds of [British capital exports] went to the labor-scarce New World where only a tenth of the world's population lived, and only about a quarter of it went to labor-abundant Asia and Africa where almost two-thirds of the world's population lived": Clemens and Williamson, "Where Did British Foreign Capital Go?"

66. Obstfeld and Taylor, "Globalization and Capital Markets," p. 60, figure 10.

67. Ibid., table 2.

68. Schularick, "Development Finance," p. 14 and table 4.

69. Drazen, "Political-Economic Theory of Domestic Debt."

70. The definitive statement is Bordo and Rockoff, "Gold Standard as a 'Good Housekeeping Seal of Approval.' "

71. Eichengreen and Flandreau, "Geography of the Gold Standard," table 2.

72. Bordo and Kydland, "Gold Standard as a Commitment Mechanism," p. 56; Bordo and Schwartz, "Monetary Policy Regimes," p. 10.

73. Bordo and Rockoff, " 'Good Housekeeping,' " pp. 327, 347f.

74. Ferguson, *Empire,* esp. ch. 4. A modern survey of forty-nine countries concluded that common-law countries offered "the strongest legal protections of investors." The fact that eighteen of the countries in the sample have the common law system is of course almost entirely due to their having been at one time or another under British rule: La Porta et al., "Law and Finance."

75. Schularick, "Development Finance," table 5.

76. For more details, see Ferguson, "City of London."

77. I am grateful to Alan M. Taylor for making these data available to me.

78. Lindert and Morton, "How Sovereign Debt Has Worked."

79. As demonstrated by Obstfeld and Taylor, "Sovereign Risk." For a contrary argument, see Bordo and Rockoff, "Adherence to the Gold Standard."

80. Cain and Hopkins, *British Imperialism,* pp. 439, 570. See for a detailed discussion, J. M. Keynes, "Foreign Investment and National Advantage," in Moggridge (ed.), *Collected Writings,* vol. 19, part I, pp. 275–84.

81. MacDonald, *Free Nation Deep in Debt,* p. 380.

82. Atkin, "Official Regulation," pp. 324–35.

83. Writing in the 1950s, the Canadian historian Harold Innis declared: "The constitution of Canada, as it appears on the statute book of the British Parliament, has been designed to secure capital for the improvement of navigation and transport": Cain and Hopkins, *British Imperialism*, p. 233.

84. Ibid., p. 584f.

85. Hale, "British Empire in Default."

86. Cain and Hopkins, *British Imperialism*, p. 439.

87. J. M. Keynes, "Advice to Trustee Investors," in Moggridge (ed.), *Collected Writings*, vol. 19, part I, p. 204f.

88. Maddison, *World Economy*, p. 264, table B-21.

89. Calculated from figures ibid., p. 112.

90. Dutt, "Origins of Uneven Development."

91. Davis, *Late Victorian Holocausts*.

92. See, e.g., Raychaudhuri, "British Rule in India," pp. 361–64.

93. See Washbrook, "South Asia, the World System, and World Capitalism," p. 480f.

94. Roy, *Economic History of India*, p. 42ff.

95. Ibid., p. 250.

96. Maddison, *World Economy*, table 2-21b. The "drain" of resources from Indonesia to Holland was substantially larger and more deserving of that appellation. It is nevertheless undeniable that Indian monetary policy was governed with managing this transfer of resources, not with maximizing Indian output, as its principal objective.

97. Roy, *Economic History*, p. 241.

98. Ibid., pp. 22, 219f., 254, 285, 294. Cf. McAlpin, *Subject to Famine*.

99. Roy, *Economic History*, pp. 32–36, 215.

100. Ibid., pp. 258–63.

101. Ibid., p. 46f.

102. Ibid., p. 257.

103. Maddison, *World Economy*, p. 110f.

104. Roy, *Economic History*, p. 226–29.

105. See Goldsmith, *Financial Development of India*.

106. Thanks to the liberalization of the 1990s, India has since managed to narrow that gap.

107. Stephen Haber, Douglass C. North and Barry R. Weingast, "If Economists Are So Smart, Why Is Africa So Poor?" *Wall Street Journal*, July 30, 2003.

CHAPTER 6: GOING HOME OR ORGANIZING HYPOCRISY

1. Fromkin, *Peace to End All Peace*, pp. 449–54.

2. Ibid., p. 509.

3. Yergin, *Prize*, pp. 186–90, 195–97, 201, 204.

4. Fromkin, *Peace to End All Peace*, p. 509.

5. *Newsday*, April 9, 2003.

6. *New York Times*, April 11, 2003.

7. "Transcript of President Bush's Remarks on the End of Major Combat in Iraq," *New York Times*, p. A16.

8. *New York Times*, February 27, 2003.

9. *Financial Times*, April 7, 2003

10. *New York Times*, July 15, 2003.

11. "Elections in Iraq a Possibility Next Year, Bremer Says," *New York Times*, July 31, 2003.

12. Steven R. Weisman, "Powell Gives Iraq 6 Months to Write New Constitution," *New York Times*, September 26, 2003.

13. "Iraqi Handover to Be Speeded Up," http://news.bbc.co.uk, November 2, 2003.

14. Fromkin, *Peace to End All Peace*, p. 449f.

15. Ibid., p. 453.

16. Ibid., p. 497, 503.

17. Ibid., p. 507f.

18. Ibid. p. 508.

19. Yergin, *Prize*, p. 195.

20. A good selection of Bell's correspondence can be found at http://www.gerty.ncl.ac.uk/letters.

21. Gertrude Bell to her father, August 28, 1921, http://www.gerty.ncl.ac.uk/letters//l1448.htm.

22. Calculated from figures in Constantine, "Migrants."

23. Maddison, World Economy, p. 110.

24. Calculated from figures in Kirk-Greene, On Crown Service.

25. Potter, India's Political Administration, pp. 68–70; Symonds, Oxford and Empire, pp. 185–93.

26. He was beaten by his future antagonist at the Treasury, Otto Niemeyer.

27. Kirk-Greene, On Crown Service.

28. Between 15 and 25 percent of all undergraduates who matriculated at Balliol, Keble, St. John's and Corpus Christi colleges ended up in some kind of imperial employment: Symonds, Oxford and Empire, p. 306.

29. Machonochie, Life in the Indian Civil Service.

30. Tony Allen-Mills, "Rumsfeld Plan for a Tight Little Army Hits Trouble on the Right," Sunday Times, September 21, 2003. Cf. Stephen Fidler and Gerard Baker, "The Best-laid Plans?," Financial Times, August 3, 2003.

31. Felicity Barringer and David E. Sanger, "U.S. Drafts Plan for U.N. to Back a Force for Iraq," New York Times, September 3, 2003.

32. Statistical Abstract of the United States 2002, table 495; Porter (ed.), Atlas of British Overseas Expansion.

33. Statistical Abstract of the United States 2001, table 494.

34. http://dbease.mconetwork.com/dbEase/cgi-bin/go_getpl.

35. Central Intelligence Agency, World Factbook.

36. International Herald Tribune, October 16–27, 2002.

37. See Kurth, "Migration."

38. Department of Defense, "Population Representation in the Military Services" (2001), table 3.3.

39. Ash, History of the Present, p. 375. This may be to overlook the growing importance of more recently arrived ethnic minorities, notably Hispanic and Asian first- and second-generation immigrants.

40. Yale University Office of the FAS Registrar; Yale University Office of Institutional Research. I have since heard that this lone student of the Near East is working in California.

41. Yale University Office of Development; Yale University Office of Institutional Research.

42. Porch, "Occupational Hazards," p. 40.

43. San Jose Mercury News, March 18, 2003.

44. Reuel Marc Gerecht, "The Counterterrorist Myth," Atlantic Monthly, July–August 2001.

45. Woodward, Bush at War, p. 201.

46. Wall Street Journal, April 4, 2003.

47. http://www.peacecorps.gov/about/index.cfm.

48. I am grateful to Bill Whelan for his help on this point.

49. "What Baghdad Really Thinks," Spectator, July 19, 2003.

50. See the astute remarks on this subject by the high representative in Bosnia, in a speech he gave in June this year: Ashdown, "Broken Communities."

51. President Bush, speech at the American Enterprise Institute, New York Times, February 26, 2003.

52. For a somewhat flawed discussion of these issues, see Pei, "Lessons of the Past." Pei also overlooks South Korea.

53. Lydia Saad, "What Form of Govern-

ment for Iraq?," Gallup Organization, http://www.gallup.com/poll/tb/ goverpubli/20030923d.asp.

54. Larry Diamond and Michael McFaul, "Rushing Elections Will Only Hurt Iraq," *San Jose Mercury News,* September 28, 2003.

55. Matthew, *Gladstone,* vol. 2, p. 24.

56. Ibid., p. 131.

57. Shannon, *Gladstone,* p. 301.

58. Ibid., p. 302f.

59. Ibid., p. 304.

60. Roberts, *Salisbury,* p. 229.

61. Ibid., p. 266.

62. Shannon, *Gladstone,* p. 306.

63. Judd, *Empire,* p. 97.

64. Shannon, *Gladstone,* p. 318.

65. Ibid., p. 305.

66. Matthew, *Gladstone,* vol. 2, p. 139.

67. Shannon, *Gladstone,* p. 318.

68. Roberts, *Salisbury,* p. 343.

69. Matthew, *Gladstone,* vol. 2, p. 135.

70. Calculated from figures in Crouchley, *Economic Development,* p. 274ff.

71. Calculated from the figures in Stone, *Global Export of Capital.*

72. Fieldhouse, "For Richer, for Poorer," p. 121.

73. Their lot was far from disagreeable; see Lawrence Durrell's intoxicating *Alexandria Quartet* of novels.

74. All statistics from Mitchell, *International Historical Statistics: Africa, Asia, Oceania.*

75. According to a briefing in February 2004: by Lorenzo Perez, head of the IMF's Iraq mission team, loans to Iraq may be possible in the second half of 2004: IMF Survey, 33, 2, February 2, 2004, p. 18.

76. See Krasner, "Troubled Societies" and his *Organized Hypocrisy.*

77. Ashdown, "Broken Communities."

CHAPTER 7: "IMPIRE": EUROPE BETWEEN BRUSSELS AND BYZANTIUM

1. Glennon, "Why the Security Council Failed."

2. Chris Patten, "The State of the Euro-Atlantic Partnership," Trilateral Commission, October 20, 2002.

3. George Parker and Daniel Dombey, "Berlusconi Eyes Bigger E.U. Role on World Stage," *Financial Times,* July 1, 2003.

4. Timothy Garton Ash, "The Peril of Too Much Power," *New York Times,* April 9, 2002.

5. "A European Armaments, Research and Military Capabilities Agency shall be established to identify operational requirements, to promote measures to satisfy those requirements, to contribute to identifying and, where appropriate, implementing any measure needed to strengthen the industrial and technological base of the defense sector, to participate in defining a European capabilities and armaments policy, and to assist the Council of Ministers in evaluating the improvement of military capabilities": European Convention, "Draft Treaty Establishing a Constitution for Europe," CONV 850/03, Brussels, July 18, 2003.

6. See, e.g., Andrew Sullivan, "The Euro Menace: The USE vs. the USA," *Sunday Times,* June 16, 2003.

7. Robert Kagan, "Power and Weakness," *Policy Review* (2002). Cf. Kagan, *Of Paradise and Power.*

8. France is, by a considerable margin, the world's most popular tourist destination, accounting for more than 10 percent of all international tourist arrivals in 2000: World Tourist Organization.

The second most popular is the United States, but the third, fourth and fifth places go to EU members: Spain, Italy and the United Kingdom.

9. Huntington, "Lonely Superpower."

10. Kupchan, *End of the American Era,* pp. 119, 132.

11. "Washington today, like Rome then, enjoys primacy, but is beginning to tire of the burdens of hegemony. . . . And Europe today, like Byzantium then, is emerging as an independent center of power, dividing a unitary realm in two": ibid., pp. 131, 153.

12. Cooper, "Postmodern State."

13. Joseph Nye, "The New Rome Meets the New Barbarians: How America Should Wield Its Power," *Economist,* March 23, 2002. See also Joseph Nye, "Lessons in Imperialism," *Financial Times,* June 16, 2002. Cf. Bergsten, "American and Europe."

14. Mearsheimer, *Tragedy,* p. 385.

15. Paul M. Kennedy, "What Hasn't Changed Since September 11th," *Los Angeles Times,* September 11, 2002.

16. Calculated from the figures in the World Bank's World Development database.

17. Depending on the measure used, EU output will rise by between 3 and 9 percent.

18. Figures from Maddison, *World Economy.*

19. According to figures for 1999 from Eurostat.

20. Danthine et al., "European Financial Markets After EMU," table 2.2.

21. Figures from the Bank for International Settlements. This was in fact predicted by the BIS: McCauley and White, "The Euro and European Financial Markets."

22. Figures from Economagic, OECD.

23. *Economist,* April 12, 2003, p. 100.

24. Al Jazeera, July 2002.

25. European Convention, "Draft Treaty Establishing a Constitution for Europe," CONV 850/03, Brussels, July 18, 2003.

26. Michael Pinto-Duchinsky, "All in the Translation," *Times Literary Supplement,* June 13, 2003.

27. "Snoring While a Superstate Emerges," *Economist,* May 10, 2003, p. 42.

28. Richard Baldwin and Mike Widgren, "Europe's Voting Reform Will Shift Power Balance," *Financial Times,* June 22, 2003.

29. Pew Global Attitudes Project, "Views of a Changing World," June 2003.

30. "America's Image Further Erodes, Europeans Want Weaker Ties," Pew Research Center, March 2003.

31. The pro-American percentages currently stand at 70 in Britain, 43 in France, 60 in Italy, 45 in Germany and 38 in Spain.

32. "Contradictions," *Economist,* April 12, 2003.

33. Statistics from various Eurobarometer surveys at http://europa.eu.int/comm/public_opinion/archives.

34. Calculated from figures in the CIA *World Factbook.*

35. Calculated from figures published by the Stockholm International Peace Research Institute.

36. Figures from the Center for Global Development.

37. David Roodman, "An Index of Donor Aid Performance," Center for Global Development, April 2003.

38. The results can be found in *Foreign Policy,* May/June 2003.

39. Coker, *Empires in Conflict,* p. 38f.

40. "Revitalising Old Europe," *Economist,* March 15, 2003, p. 91.

41. Ferguson and Kotlikoff, "Degeneration of EMU," pp. 110–21.

42. See Milward, *European Rescue.*

43. Figures from Maddison, *World Economy,* table B-22.

44. International Monetary Fund, *World Economic Outlook,* April 2003.

45. Figures from the International Monetary Fund.

46. Figures from the OECD (standardized unemployment rates).

47. "Europe's Heavyweight Weakling," *Economist,* June 7, 2003, p. 44.

48. *Economist,* March 22, 2003, p. 120. International measures of productivity are controversial, but even after one adjusts for the differences in statistical methods between the United States and the European Union, it is clear that labor productivity rose in the United States during the 1990s and declined in the EU: ibid., November 16, 2002, p. 100.

49. Evans et al., "Trends in Working Hours in OECD Countries."

50. "Revitalising Old Europe," *Economist,* March 15, 2003, p. 91.

51. *Economist,* May 3, 2003, p. 108

52. European Convention, "Draft Treaty Establishing a Constitution for Europe," CONV 850/03, Brussels, July 18, 2003.

53. The EU will stop paying production-linked subsidies to arable farmers, but member states may continue to pay subsidies up to a specified percentage of past payments—up to a quarter in the case of cereals—if they wish: Rory Watson, "E.U. Hails New Era of Healthy Food and Green Living," *Times,* June 27, 2003. The total amount spent on the CAP will continue at around $50 billion until 2013: Tobias Buck, Guy de Jonquières and Frances Williams, "Fischler's New Era for Europe's Farmers," *Financial Times,* June 27, 2003.

54. Lea Paterson, "Farm-fresh Chance for Reform in Enlargement," *Times,* July 29, 2003.

55. *Economist,* May 27, 2003.

56. Subsidies to American agriculture, most of which go to around four hundred thousand farmers, rose from $7.3 billion in 1996 to $22.9 billion in 2000. The 2002 farm bill restored the link between farm subsidies and production and will raise the total subsidy to American agriculture by around 22 percent compared with the 1996–2001 average. See in general Runge, "Agrivation," p. 86f.

57. At the time of writing, consumer price inflation in Greece was 3.8 percent per annum—the highest rate in the Eurozone—compared with just 0.7 percent in Germany, the lowest rate.

58. German interest rates were around 2.5 percent on the eve of the monetary union. Thereafter Germany had to adjust to the Eurozone-wide discount rate of 4.5 percent. Only in 2003 did rates return to their pre-1999 levels.

59. Figures from the Bundesbank.

60. "A Boom Out of Step," *Economist,* May 29, 2003. Cf. Posen, "Frog in the Pot"; Martin Feldstein, "Britain Must Avoid Germany's Mistake," *Financial Times,* April 22, 2003.

61. I am grateful to my student Michael Darcy for his work on this question.

62. Anatole Kaletsky, "How Blair Has Priced Britain Out of the Euro," *Times,* June 12, 2003.

63. Martin Wolf, "The Benefits of Euro Entry Will Be Modest," *Financial Times,* May 12, 2003.

64. Begg et al., "Sustainable Regimes of Capital Movements."

65. Figures from the International Monetary Fund, *World Economic Outlook.*

66. Milward, *European Rescue.*

67. "Giscard Plan for President Enters Most Divisive Phase," *Financial Times,* April 22, 2003.

68. Details can be found in Milward, *European Rescue.*

69. Niall Ferguson, "The Cash Fountains of Versailles," *Spectator,* August 14, 1993, pp. 14–16. Between 1958 and 1994 Germany paid 163 billion marks to the rest of Europe in form of net contributions to the European Economic Community/European Union budget, more (in nominal terms) than the total amount of reparations demanded at London in 1921.

70. Britain is the exception that proves the rule. Voters there seem not to have noticed that their country ceased to be a significant net contributor in 1984, when Margaret Thatcher secured an ongoing rebate of a substantial proportion of Britain's payments.

71. *Economist,* March 1, 2003.

72. Hitchcock, *Struggle for Europe,* p. 419.

73. Ibid., p. 412.

74. See Siedentop, *Democracy in Europe.*

75. Figures from Eurostat.

76. Rosecrance, "Croesus and Caesar," pp. 31–34.

77. Epitropoulos et al. (eds.), *American Culture,* p. 5.

78. Bobbitt, *Shield of Achilles,* pp. 677–95.

CHAPTER 8:
THE CLOSING DOOR

1. Gibbon, *Decline and Fall of the Roman Empire,* book I, ch. 17.

2. Maddison, *World Economy,* p. 241, table B-10, p. 261, table B-16.

3. Diamond, *Guns, Germs and Steel.*

4. Pomeranz, *Great Divergence.*

5. Platt, *Finance, Trade and Politics,* esp. pp. 95, 109. For an illuminating comparison of British and American approaches to informal empire, see Rauchway, "Competitive Imperialism." As Rauchway notes, the British went quite far in Anglicizing those institutions over which they gained control, notably the Imperial Maritime Customs Service. The American approach was to assume that Americanization would happen spontaneously. For a more positive assessment, see Osterhammel, "China," p. 643f.

6. See Rodrik, "Feasible Globalizations," p. 7f.

7. See, for a recent review of Chinese performance, Hale and Hale, "China Takes Off."

8. Calculated from the various GDP statistics in the World Bank's World Development database.

9. Martin Wolf, "Rivals and Partners," *Financial Times,* October 7, 2003.

10. See, e.g., Mearsheimer, *Tragedy of Great Power Politics,* p. 362. Cf. Medeiros and Fravel, "China's New Diplomacy."

11. See, e.g., Frank, *ReOrient.*

12. Chang, *Coming Collapse of China.*

13. Kennedy, *Rise and Fall of the Great Powers,* p. 689.

14. Ibid., p. 681 and note.

15. Keynes is supposed to have said: "If the facts change, I change my opinion. What do you do, sir?"

16. Paul Kennedy, "Power and Terror," *Financial Times,* September 3, 2002.

17. Ferguson and Kotlikoff, "Going Critical."

18. Medeiros and Fravel, "China's New Diplomacy."

19. According to one estimate, members of the allied coalition reimbursed the United States for $54 billion out of the total cost of $61 billion.

20. Cf. Ignatieff, *Empire Lite,* p. 95.

21. Rubin, Hamidzada and Stoddard, "Through the Fog of Peace Building."

22. Figures from *Statistical Abstract of the United States,* various issues.

23. Calleo, "Power, Wealth and Freedom," p. 10. Cf. David Wessel, "Several Signs Highlight War's Effect on Economy," *Wall Street Journal,* March 27, 2003; Rigobon and Sack, "Effects of War Risk."

24. Davis et al., "War in Iraq Versus Containment."

25. Thom Shanker, "Bush to Focus on Benefits of Rebuilding Effort in Iraq," *New York Times,* September 21, 2003. See also Donald Hepburn, "Nice War. Here's the Bill," ibid., September 3, 2003; Richard W. Stevenson, "78% of Bush's Postwar Spending Plan Is for Military," ibid., September 9, 2003.

26. "We are spending $4 billion a month to run a country which has a monthly GDP of $2.5 billion," a retired military official told the *Financial Times* this summer. "Something is wrong here": *Financial Times,* August 29, 2003. Cf. Ali Abunimah, "Iraq's Chilling Economic Statistics," March 18, 1999, http://www.globalpolicy.org/security/issues/irq3-22.htm.

27. According to the Summers and Heston "World Tables," Iraq's real GDP *per capita* in 1980 was $6,900 in 1985 international dollars, compared with an American figure of $15,101. The World Bank's *World Development* database gives figures for gross national income *per capita* in current dollars of $3,380 for Iraq and $11,850 for the United States. The Economist Intelligence Unit estimated Iraq's *per capita* GDP in 1999 to be just $247, compared with an American figure of $32,260—130 times as high.

28. Max Boot, "A War for Oil? Not This Time," *New York Times,* February 13, 2003; Peter Slevin and Vernon Loeb,

"Bremer: Iraq Effort to Cost Tens of Billions for Iraq," *Washington Post,* August 27, 2003.

29. See, for an example, Seymour Melman, "Looting Our Lives," Znet, April 22, 2003.

30. The first owner of a commercial Hummer was the bodybuilder, actor and now governor of California Arnold Schwarzenegger.

31. Kenneth N. Gilpin, "White House Foresees Deficit Reaching $455 Billion This Year," *New York Times,* July 15, 2003. Cf. Edmund L. Andrews, "Leap in Deficit Instead of Fall Is Seen for U.S.," ibid., August 26, 2003.

32. All figures from Congressional Budget Office Web site, http://www.cbo.gov.

33. Gokhale and Smetters, "Fiscal and Generational Imbalances."

34. Details in Lawson, *View from No. 11,* p. 37.

35. Gabriel Stein, "Mounting Debts: The Coming European Pension Crisis," *Politeia,* Policy Series No. 4 (1997), pp. 32–35.

36. Interestingly, the others are nearly all ex-British colonies: Australia, Canada, Ireland and New Zealand. According to international comparisons done in 1998, each of these countries could have achieved generational balance with tax increases of less than 5 percent: Auerbach et al., *Generational Accounting Around the World.* The catch is that solving the public-sector pensions problem may simply have created a comparably large private-sector pensions problem; there is alarming evidence that many company pensions schemes are woefully underfunded and are unlikely to deliver what they have promised to company employees when they retire.

37. The proposed reform effectively bribes the elderly to join Health Management

Organizations by offering them a drug benefit. But this will increase rather than reduce expenditure inasmuch as it will cost between $400 billion and $1 trillion over the next ten years. The scheme also retains the traditional and very expensive fee-for-service Medicare system and permits the elderly to switch back to it whenever they like. Unfortunately, they are likely to switch back just when they are becoming expensive to treat. Finally, the HMOs are free to shut down and ship their customers back to the traditional plan whenever they become too expensive.

38. As Laurence Kotlikoff has argued, one way to do this would be to close down the old system at the margin and enact a federal retail sales tax to pay off, through time, its accrued liabilities. What workers would otherwise have paid in payroll taxes would now be invested in special private retirement accounts, to be split evenly between spouses. The government would make matching contributions for poor workers and would contribute fully on behalf of the disabled and the unemployed. Finally, all account balances would be invested in a global, market-weighted index of stocks, bonds and real estate.

39. Alison Shelton, Laurel Beedon and Mitja Ng-Baumhackl, "The Effect of Using Price Indexation Instead of Wage Indexation in Calculating the Initial Social Security Benefit," AARP Public Policy Institute, July 2002.

40. See most recently Catão and Terrones, "Fiscal Deficits and Inflation."

41. Figures from Economagic (Federal Reserve Bank of New York). In the middle of 2003 there were some signs of a slight upward shift in investors' infla-

tionary expectations. The yield on ten-year treasuries jumped to 4.3 percent, partly in response to expectations of higher economic growth and higher share prices, but also partly in response to the government's and the CBO's revised deficit forecasts. The yield curve, which had become more or less flat by the late 1990s, was showing signs of sloping more steeply upward. At the end of 2000, the spread between ninety-day and thirty-year interest rates had been slightly negative (minus 42 basis points). By August 2003 it stood at over 400 basis points. Finally, the spread between yields on ten-year bonds and index-linked bonds with the same maturity widened slightly, from around 140 basis points in October 2002 to over 230 basis points in late August 2003. Yet this still seemed a relatively modest reaction, given the size of the fiscal crisis facing the United States. Figures from Bondsonline.com, Economagic.

42. See Shiller, *Irrational Exuberance*.

43. See Robert J. Shiller, "Will the Bond Bubble Burst?," Project Syndicate (June 2003).

44. For a popular introduction to the subject, see Mark Buchanan, *Ubiquity*.

45. In Germany in May 1921—to give an extreme example—it was the announcement of a staggering postwar reparations burden of 132 billion marks that convinced investors the government's fiscal position was incompatible with currency stability. The assassination of the liberal Foreign Minister Walther Rathenau in July of the following year delivered the coup de grâce, sending both interest rates and exchange rates skyrocketing: Webb, "Fiscal News."

46. Chet Currier, "Deflation-Defense Strategy Uses Treasuries, Cash," www.bloomberg.com, April 26, 2003.

47. David Leonhardt, "Greenspan, Broadly Positive, Spells Out Deflation Worries," *New York Times*, May 22, 2003.

48. *Statistical Abstract of the United States, 2001*, table 552.

49. Bonney, "France, 1494–1815," pp. 131ff., 152f. Cf. Bosher, *French Finances*.

50. Maddison, *World Economy*, table 2-26a.

51. Calleo, "Power, Wealth and Wisdom," p. 9. The Bank for International Settlements estimates that the U.S. current account deficit is equivalent to almost 10 percent of the rest of the world's savings: John Plender, "On a Wing and a Prayer," *Financial Times*, July 3, 2003.

52. Hugo Dixon, "Is the U.S. Hooked on Foreign Capital?," *Wall Street Journal*, March 6, 2003.

53. Päivi Munter, "Foreign Holdings of U.S. Treasuries Hit Record 46%," *Financial Times*, September 11, 2003.

54. International Monetary Fund, "Transcript of the World Economic Outlook Press Conference," April 9, 2003.

55. That is the only way to explain the fact that the United States consistently receives higher investment income from its investments abroad than it pays out to foreigners who have put their money into American assets, even though the capital value of American-owned assets abroad is significantly smaller. I am grateful to Alan M. Taylor for this point.

56. David Hale, "The Manchurian Candidate," *Financial Times*, August 29, 2003.

57. I am very grateful to Deirdre McCloskey for her comments on this point. For two differing views, see Brad DeLong, "The Endgame for the U.S.

Current-Account Deficit," September 16, 2003: http://www.j-bradford-delong.net/movable_type/2003_archives/002242.htm.

58. Ronald McKinnon, "The Dollar Standard and Its Crisis-Prone Periphery: New Rules for the Game," unpublished paper, Stanford University, September 9, 2002.

59. See the discussion by Hali Edison, "Are Foreign Exchange Reserves in Asia Too High?," in International Monetary Fund, *World Economic Outlook*, October 2003, pp. 78–92.

60. See Edward Alden, Jeremy Grant and Victor Mallet, "Opportunity or Threat? The U.S. Struggles to Solve the Puzzle of Its Trade with China," *Financial Times*, November 4, 2003.

61. McKinnon and Schnabl, "China: A Stabilizing or Deflationary Influence?" and "Return to Exchange Rate Stability in East Asia?" See also Ronald McKinnon, "China and Japan, Déjà Vu?," Stanford University, March 2, 2003.

62. See Martin Wolf, "A Very Dangerous Game," *Financial Times*, September 30, 2003.

CONCLUSION: LOOKING HOMEWARD

1. Thomas Wolfe, *Look Homeward, Angel*, p. 5.

2. See Johnson, "America's New Empire for Liberty."

3. For a different account of the differences, see O'Brien, "Governance of Globalization."

4. For a skeptical answer, see Jowitt, "Rage, Hubris and Regime Change." See also Simes, "Reluctant Empire."

5. "The Price of Profligacy," *Economist*, September 20, 2003.

6. At the time of writing, foreign central

banks' holdings of U.S. Treasury and "quasi-governmental agency" bonds for the first time exceeded $1 trillion: Päivi Munter and Jenny Wiggins, "Treasury Holdings Top $1,000bn," *Financial Times,* November 11, 2003.

7. The interest rate on a fixed-rate fifteen-year mortgage rose from 4.5 percent to 6.4 percent between the spring and summer of 2003: "Stormy Summer," *Economist,* August 9, 2003.

8. "Flying on One Engine," *Economist,* September 20, 2003.

9. In the words of Nouriel Roubini, "Either you want the dollar to depreciate against Asian currencies or you want to maintain low interest rates. You can't have it both ways. It just doesn't add up": quoted in "Gambling with the Dollar," *Washington Post,* September 24, 2003. See also Graham Turner, "The Fed Has Not Avoided Danger," *Financial Times,* June 30, 2003; John Plender, "On a Wing and a Prayer," *Financial Times,* July 3, 2003.

10. James, *End of Globalization.*

11. Stephen Cecchetti, "America's Job Gap Difficult to Close," *Financial Times,* October 1, 2003.

12. Robert Longley, "U.S. Prison Population Tops 2 Million," http://usgovinfo.about.com/cs/censusstatistic/a/aaprisonpop.htm. One in twenty American men has now spent some time behind bars; for black men the ratio is one in six. If penal policy continues unchanged, more than one in ten of boys born in 2001 will go to jail at some point in their lives: "In the Can," *Economist,* August 23, 2003.

13. Andrew and Kanya-Forstner, *France Overseas,* p. 13.

14. In the very apt words of Tom Friedman, "America is in an imperial role here, now. Our security and standing in the world ride on our getting Iraq right. If the Bush team has something more important to do, I'd like to know about it. Iraq can still go wrong for a hundred Iraqi reasons, but let's make sure it's not because America got bored, tired or distracted:" "Bored with Baghdad Already," *New York Times,* May 18, 2003.

15. Priest, *Mission,* p. 117.

16. Forman et al, *United States in a Global Age,* p. 16f.

17. Ignatieff, *Empire Lite,* p. 115. In Ignatieff's words (p. 90): "Effective imperial power also requires controlling the subject people's sense of time, convincing them that they will be ruled forever. The illusion of permanence was one secret of the British Empire's long survival. Empires cannot be maintained and national interests cannot be secured over the long term by a people always looking for the exit." This is precisely right. See also ibid., p. 113f.

18. See, e.g., Pierre Hassner, *The United States: The Empire of Force or the Force of Empire,* Institute for Security Studies of the European Union Chaillot Paper, 54, September 2002.

19. Quoted in Bacevich, *American Empire,* p. 243.

20. Matthews, "Hard Part," p. 51.

21. Priest, *Mission,* p. 57.

22. BMI is defined as weight in kilograms divided by height in meters, squared. Anyone with a BMI index of 30 or over is defined as obsese; anyone with a BMI over 25 is overweight.

23. *Statistical Abstract of the United States, 2002,* table 190.

24. Figures are available from the World Health Organization for twenty countries.

25. Though the black woman's burden tends to be even larger in this respect. A

third of African-American females are classified as obese.

26. Ranke, "Great Powers."

27. Ikenberry, *After Victory.*

28. Ferguson, *Cash Nexus,* p. 37.

29. Ibid., p. 412 (emphasis added).

30. Ibid., p. 388.

31. Ibid., p. 417.

32. Ibid., p. 418.

33. Fischer, "Globalization and Its Challenges."

34. "Prime Minister Tony Blair's Address to a Joint Session of Congress," *New York Times,* July 17, 2003.

BIBLIOGRAPHY

Abshire, David M., "Lessons of Vietnam: Proportionality and Credibility," in Anthony Lake (ed.), *The Legacy of Vietnam: The War, American Society and Future American Foreign Policy* (New York, 1976), pp. 392–410.

Acemoglu, Daron; Simon Johnson and James A. Robinson, "Colonial Origins of Comparative Development: An Empirical Investigation," *NBER Working Paper,* 7771 (2000).

———; ——— and ———, "An African Success Story: Botswana," unpublished paper (July 11, 2001).

———; ——— and ———, "Reversal of Fortune: Geography and Institutions in the Making of the Modern World Income Distribution," *NBER Working Paper,* 8460 (September 2001).

Adams, Henry, *History of the United States of America During the Administrations of Thomas Jefferson* (New York/Cambridge, 1986).

Alesina, Alberto; Enrico Spolaore and Romain Wacziarg, "Economic Integration and Political Disintegration," *NBER Working Paper,* 6163 (1997).

———; Rafael di Tella and Robert MacCulloch, "Inequality and Happiness: Are Europeans and Americans Different?," *NBER Working Paper,* 8198 (April 2001).

Alstyne, Richard W. Van, *The American Empire: Its Historical Pattern and Evolution* (London, 1960).

Ambrose, Stephen E., *Rise to Globalism: American Foreign Policy 1938–1970* (Baltimore, 1970).

Anderson, Terry H., *The United States, Great Britain and the Cold War, 1944–1947* (Columbia, Mo., 1981).

Andrew, Christopher M., and A. S. Kanya-Forstner, *France Overseas: The Great War and the Climax of French Imperial Expansion* (London, 1981).

Arnold-Baker, Charles, *The Companion to British History* (Tunbridge Wells, 1996).

Aron, Raymond, *The Imperial Republic: The United States and the World, 1945–1973,* transl. Frank Jellinek (London, 1975).

Arria, Diego, "The Changing Nature of Sovereignty and Intervention: A Latin American Perspective," *International Institute for Strategic Studies Global Strategic Review* (September 12–14, 2003).

Ash, Timothy Garton, *History of the Present: Essays, Sketches and Despatches from Europe in the 1990s* (London, 1999).

————, *Free World: Why a Crisis of the West Reveals the Opportunity of Our Time.* (London, 2004).

Ashdown, Paddy, "Broken Communities, Shattered Lives: Winning the Savage War of Peace," Speech by the Rt. Hon. Lord Ashdown, High Representative in Bosnia and Herzegovina, to the International Rescue Committee, London (June 19, 2003).

Atkin, John, "Official Regulation of British Overseas Investment, 1914–1931," *Economic History Review,* 2nd Series, 23, 2 (August 1970), pp. 324–35.

Auerbach, Alan J.; Laurence J. Kotlikoff and Willi Leibfritz (eds.), *Generational Accounting Around the World* (Chicago, 1999).

Bacevich, Andrew J., *American Empire: The Realities and Consequences of U.S. Diplomacy* (Cambridge, Mass./London, 2002).

Backer, John H., *Priming the German Economy: American Occupational Policies, 1945–1948* (Durham, N.C., 1971).

Bailey, Paul J., *Postwar Japan 1945 to the Present* (Oxford, 1996).

Bairoch, Paul, "European Trade Policy 1815–1914," in Peter Mathias and Sidney Pollard (eds.), *The Cambridge Economic History of Europe,* vol. 8: *The Industrial Economies: The Development of Economic and Social Policies* (Cambridge, 1989), pp. 1–160.

Baker, Mark, *Nam: The Vietnam War in the Words of the Men and Women Who Fought There* (London, 1982).

Baldwin, Richard E., and Philippe Martin, "Two Waves of Globalisation: Superficial Similarities, Fundamental Differences," *NBER Working Paper,* 6904 (January 1999).

Barro, Robert J., "Determinants of Economic Growth: A Cross-Country Empirical Study," *NBER Working Paper,* 5698 (August 1996).

Begg, D.; B. Eichengreen; L. Halpern; J. von Hagen and C. Wyplosz, "Sustainable Regimes of Capital Movements in Accession Countries," *Centre for Economic Policy Research, Policy Paper,* 10 (April 2003).

Bell, Philip, *Americanization and Australia* (Sydney, 1998).

Bergen, Peter, *Holy War Inc. Inside the Secret World of Osama bin Laden* (London, 2001).

Bergsten, C. Fred, "America and Europe: Clash of the Titans?," *Foreign Affairs,* 78, 2 (March–April 1999), pp. 20–32.

Billington, Ray Allen, *Westward Expansion: A History of the American Frontier* (New York, 1967).

Black, George, *The Good Neighbor: How the United States Wrote the History of Central America and the Caribbean* (New York, 1988).

Blum, William, *Rogue State: A Guide to the World's Only Superpower* (New York, 2003).

Bobbitt, Philip, *The Shield of Achilles: War, Peace, and the Course of History* (New York, 2002).

Bonney, Richard, "France, 1494–1815," in Richard Bonney (ed.), *The Rise of the Fiscal State in Europe, c. 1200–1815* (Oxford, 1999), pp. 123–76.

Boot, Max, *The Savage Wars of Peace: Small Wars and the Rise of American Power* (New York, 2002).

Bordo, Michael, and Hugh Rockoff, "The Gold Standard as a 'Good Housekeeping Seal of Approval,'" *Journal of Economic History,* 56, 2 (June 1996), pp. 389–428.

———, and Marc Flandreau, "Core, Periphery, Exchange Rate Regimes and Globalization," in Michael Bordo, Alan Taylor and Jeffrey Williamson (eds.), *Globalization in Historical Perspective* (Chicago, 2002), pp. 417–68.

———, and Anna J. Schwartz, "Monetary Policy Regimes and Economic Performance: The Historical Record," *NBER Working Paper,* 6201 (September 1997).

Bordo, Michael D., and Hugh Rockoff, "Was Adherence to the Gold Standard a 'Good Housekeeping Seal of Approval' During the Interwar Period?," *NBER Working Paper,* 7186 (June 1999).

———, and Finn E. Kydland, "The Gold Standard as a Commitment Mechanism," in Tamim Bayoumi, Barry Eichengreen and Mark P. Taylor (eds.), *Modern Perspectives on the Gold Standard* (Cambridge, 1996), pp. 55–100.

———; Barry Eichengreen and Douglas A. Irwin, "Is Globalization Today Really Different Than Globalisation a Hundred Years Ago," *NBER Working Paper,* 7195 (June 1999).

Bosher, J. F., *French Finances, 1770–1795* (Cambridge, UK, 1970).

Bowden, Mark, *Black Hawk Down* (London, 2000).

Brands, H. W., *Inside the Cold War: Loy Henderson and the Rise of the American Empire, 1918–1961* (Oxford, 1991).

Buchanan, Keith, "The Geography of Empire," *Bulletin of Concerned Asian Scholars,* 4, 2 (1972), pp. 40–54.

Buchanan, Mark, *Ubiquity: The Science of History . . . Or Why the World Is Simpler Than We Think* (London, 2000).

Buchanan, Patrick J., *A Republic Not an Empire* (Washington, D.C., 1999).

Burleigh, Michael, *The Third Reich: A New History* (London, 2000).

Byman, Daniel, "Scoring the War on Terrorism," *National Interest,* 72 (Summer 2003), pp. 75–85.

Cain, P. J., and A. G. Hopkins, *British Imperialism, 1688–2000,* 2nd ed. (Harlow, 2001).

Calleo, David, "Reflections on American Hegemony in the Postwar Era," in Patrick Karl O'Brien and Armand Clesse (eds.), *Two Hegemonies: Britain 1846–1914 and the United States 1941–2001* (Aldershot/Burlington, Vt., 2002), pp. 248–57.

———, "Power, Wealth and Wisdom: The United States and Europe After Iraq," *National Interest,* 72 (Summer 2003), pp. 5–17.

Caputo, Philip, *A Rumor of War* (London, 1999 [1977]).

Carnegie Endowment for International Peace, "From Victory to Success: Afterwar Policy in Iraq," *Foreign Policy* (July 2003), pp. 50–72.

Catão, Luis, and Marco E. Terrones, "Fiscal Deficits and Inflation," *International Monetary Fund Working Paper,* 03/65 (2003).

Chang, Gordon G., *The Coming Collapse of China* (London, 2002).

Chiswick, Barry, and Timothy Hatton, "International Migration and the Integration of Labor Markets," in Michael Bordo, Alan Taylor and Jeffrey Williamson (eds.), *Globalization in Historical Perspective* (Chicago, 2003), pp. 65–117.

Clarke, Thurston, *Pearl Harbor Ghosts: A Journey to Hawaii Then and Now* (New York, 1991).

Clausewitz, Carl von, *On War,* ed. and transl. by Michael Howard and Peter Paret (Princeton, 1989 [1832]).

Clemens, Michael A., and Jeffrey G. Williamson, "Where Did British Capital Go? Fundamentals, Failures and the Lucas Paradox: 1870–1913," *NBER Working Paper,* 8028 (December 2000).

——— and ———, "A Tariff-Growth Paradox? Protection's Impact the World Around 1875–1997," *NBER Working Paper,* 8459 (September 2001).

Coatsworth, John, *Central America and the United States: The Clients and the Colossus* (New York/Oxford, 1994).

Coker, Christopher, "Empires in Conflict: The Growing Rift Between Europe and the United States," *Whitehall Paper*, 58 (London, 2003).

Cole, Wayne S., *An Interpretative History of American Foreign Relations* (Homewood, Ill., 1968).

Collier, Paul, and Anke Hoeffler, "On Economic Causes of Civil War," *Oxford Economic Papers*, 50 (1998), pp. 563–73.

Conrad, Joseph, *Nostromo: A Tale of the Seaboard* (Oxford/New York, 1984 [1904]).

——, *The Secret Agent* (London, 1984 [1907]).

Constantine, Stephen, "Migrants and Settlers," in Judith M. Brown and Wm. Roger Louis (eds.), *Oxford History of the British Empire: The Twentieth Century*, vol. 4 (Oxford, 1999), pp. 163–87.

Cooper, Robert, "The Postmodern State," in Foreign Policy Centre (ed.), *Reordering the World: The Long-term Implications of September 11* (London, 2002).

Crafts, Nicholas, "Globalisation and Growth in the Twentieth Century," *International Monetary Fund Working Paper*, 00/44 (March 2000).

Crouchley, A. E., *The Economic Development of Modern Egypt* (London, 1938).

Dallas, Gregor, *1918: War and Peace* (London, 2000).

Danthine, Jean-Pierre; Francesco Giavazzi and Ernst-Ludwig von Thadden, "European Financial Markets after EMU: A First Assessment," *NBER Working Paper*, 8044 (December 2000).

Davidson, Eugene, *The Death and Life of Germany: An Account of the American Occupation* (London, 1959).

Davies, R. R., *The First English Empire: Power and Identities in the British Isles, 1093–1343* (Oxford, 2000).

Davis, Lance E., and R. A. Huttenback, *Mammon and the Pursuit of Empire: The Political Economy of British Imperialism, 1860–1912* (Cambridge, 1986).

Davis, Mike, *Late Victorian Holocausts: El Niño Famines and the Making of the Third World* (London, 2001).

Davis, Steven J.; Kevin M. Murphy and Robert H. Topel, "War in Iraq Versus Containment: Weighing the Costs," unpublished paper, University of Chicago Graduate School of Business (March 2003).

Daws, Gavan, *Shoal of Time: A History of the Hawaiian Islands* (New York, 1968).

Diamond, Jared M., *Guns, Germs and Steel: The Fates of Human Societies* (London, 1997).

Diamond, Larry, "Universal Democracy," *Policy Review,* 119 (June and July 2003), pp. 3–27.

———, "Promoting Real Reform in Africa," unpublished draft chapter, Hoover Institution, Stanford Unversity (2003).

Dimbleby, David, and David Reynolds, *An Ocean Apart: The Relationship Between Britain and America in the Twentieth Century* (London, 1988).

Dollar, David, and Aaart Kraay, "Trade, Growth, and Poverty," Development Research Group, World Bank, unpublished paper (March 2001).

Dower, John, "Occupied Japan as History and Occupation History as Politics," *Journal of Asian Studies* (February 1975), pp. 485–504.

———, *Embracing Defeat: Japan in the Aftermath of World War II* (London, 1999).

Drazen, Allan, "Towards a Political-Economic Theory of Domestic Debt," in G. Calvo and M. King (eds.), *The Debt Burden and Its Consequences for Monetary Policy* (London, 1998), pp. 159–76.

Dutt, Amitava Krishna, "The Origins of Uneven Development: The Indian Subcontinent," *American Economic Review,* 82, 2 (May 1992), pp. 146–50.

Easterly, William, *The Elusive Quest for Growth: Economists' Adventures and Misadventures in the Tropics* (Cambridge, Mass., 2002).

Edelman, Bernard, *Dear America: Letters Home from Vietnam* (New York, 2002).

Edelstein, Michael, "Imperialism: Cost and Benefit," in Roderick Floud and Deirdre McCloskey (eds.), *The Economic History of Britain Since 1700, vol. 2, 1860–1939* (Cambridge, 1994), pp. 197–216.

Eichengreen, Barry, and Marc Flandreau, "The Geography of the Gold Standard," *Centre for Economic Policy Research Discussion Paper,* 1050 (October 1994).

Engerman, Stanley L., "Servants to Slaves to Servants: Contract Labor and European Expansion," in P. C. Emmer (ed.), *Colonialism and Migration: Indentured Servants Before and After Slavery* (Dordrecht, 1986), pp. 263–94.

Epitropoulos, Mike-Frank G., and Victor Roudometof (eds.), *American Culture in Europe: Interdisciplinary Perspectives* (Westport, Conn., 1998).

Etzioni, Amitai, "Implications of the American Anti-Terrorism Coalition for Global Architectures," *European Journal of Political Theory,* 1,1 (July 2002), pp. 9–30.

Evans, John M.; Douglas C. Lippoldt and Pascal Marianna, "Trends in Working Hours in OECD Countries," *Labour Market and Social Policy—Occasional Papers,* 45 (March 30, 2001).

Feis, Herbert, *Europe, the World's Banker, 1870–1914* (New York, 1930).

Ferguson, Niall, *The Pity of War: Explaining World War One* (New York, 1998).

————, *The Cash Nexus: Money and Power in the Modern World* (London, 2001).

————, "Hegemony or Empire?," *Foreign Affairs*, 82, 5 (September–October 2003), pp. 154–61.

————, *Empire: The Rise and Demise of the British World Order and the Lessons for Global Power* (New York, 2003).

————, "Prisoner Taking and Prisoner Killing in the Age of Total War: Towards a Political Economy of Military Defeat," *War in History* (forthcoming).

————, "The City of London and British Imperialism: New Light on an Old Question," in Youssef Cassis (ed.), *London and Paris as Financial Centers* (Cambridge, forthcoming).

————, and Brigitte Granville, "'Weimar on the Volga': Causes and Consequences of Inflation in 1990s Russia Compared with 1920s Germany," *Journal of Economic History*, 60, 4 (December 2000), pp. 1061–87.

————, and Laurence J. Kotlikoff, "The Degeneration of EMU," *Foreign Affairs* (March–April 2000), pp. 110–21.

————, and ————, "Going Critical: American Power and the Consequences of Fiscal Overstretch," *National Interest*, 73 (Fall 2003), pp. 22–32.

Ferrell, Robert H., *Harry S. Truman: A Life* (Columbia, Mo., 1994).

Fieldhouse, David, "For Richer, For Poorer," in P. J. Marshall (ed.), *The Cambridge Illustrated History of the British Empire* (Cambridge, 1996), pp. 108–46.

Fischer, Stanley, "Globalization and Its Challenges," *American Economic Review*, 93, 2 (May 2003).

Foot, Rosemary, *The Wrong War: American Policy and the Dimensions of the Korean Conflict, 1950–1953* (Ithaca, N.Y., 1985).

Forman, Shepard; Princeton Lyman and Stewart Patrick, *The United States in a Global Age: The Case for Multilateral Engagement* (New York, 2002).

Frank, Andre Gunder, *ReOrient: Global Economy in the Asian Age* (Berkeley/London, 1998).

Freeman, Joseph, and Scott Nearing, *Dollar Diplomacy: A Study in American Imperialism* (New York, 1928).

Fromkin, David, *A Peace to End All Peace: Creating the Modern Middle East, 1914–1922* (London, 1991).

Fukuyama, Francis, *State Building: Governance and World Order in the Twenty-First Century* (London, 2004).

Fulbrook, Mary, *The Divided Nation: A History of Germany, 1918–1990* (Oxford, 1991).

Fursenko, Aleksandr, and Timothy Naftali, *One Hell of a Gamble: Khrushchev, Castro, Kennedy and the Cuban Missile Crisis, 1958–1964* (London, 1997).

Gaddis, John Lewis, *We Now Know: Rethinking Cold War History* (Oxford, 1997).

———, *Surprise, Security, and the American Experience* (London, 2004).

Gallagher, John, and Robinson, Ronald, "The Imperialism of Free Trade," *Economic History Review*, 2nd Series, 6 (1953), pp. 1–15.

Galston, William, "Perils of Preemptive War," *American Prospect*, 13, 17 (September 23, 2002), pp. 22–25.

Gause, F. Gregory, III, "From 'Over the Horizon' to 'Into the Backyard': The U.S.-Saudi Relationship and the Gulf War," in David W. Lesch (ed.), *The Middle East and the United States: A Historical and Political Reassessment*, 2nd ed. (Oxford, 1999), pp. 341–54.

Geiss, Immanuel (ed.), *July 1914: The Outbreak of the First World War—Selected Documents* (London, 1967).

Giddens, Anthony, *Runaway World: How Globalisation Is Reshaping Our Lives* (London, 1999).

Gilbar, Gad G., "The Economics of Interdependence: The United States and the Arab World, 1973–1977," in Haim Shaked and Itamar Rabinovich (eds.), *The Middle East and the United States: Perceptions and Policies* (New Brunswick, N.J., 1980), pp. 209–41.

Gilbert, Martin, *Never Despair: Winston S. Churchill 1945–1965* (London, 1988).

Gilmour, David, *The Long Recessional: The Imperial Life of Rudyard Kipling* (London, 2002).

Gilpin, Robert, *War and Change in World Politics* (Cambridge, 1983).

———, *The Political Economy of International Relations* (Princeton, 1987).

Gimbel, John, *The American Occupation of Germany* (Stanford, Calif., 1968).

———, "Governing the American Zone of Germany," in Robert Wolfe (ed.), *Americans as Proconsuls: United States Military Government in Germany and Japan, 1944–1952* (Carbondale, Ill., 1984), pp. 92–103.

Gleditsch, Nils Petter; Peter Wallensteen; Mikael Eriksson; Margareta Sollenberg and Håvard Strand, "Armed Conflict 1946–2001: A New Dataset," 39, 5, *Journal of Peace Research* (September 2002), pp. 615–37.

Glennon, Michael J., "Why the Security Council Failed," *Foreign Affairs*, 82, 3 (May/June 2003), pp. 16–36.

Gokhale, Jagadeesh, and Kent Smetters, "Fiscal and Generational Imbalances: New Budget Measures for New Budget Priorities," *Federal Reserve Bank of Cleveland, Policy Discussion Paper* (March 2002).

Goldsmith, Raymond W., *The Financial Development of India, 1860–1977* (New Haven/London, 1983).

Grant, Ulysses S., *Memoirs and Selected Letters: Personal Memoirs of U. S. Grant, Selected Letters, 1839–1865* (New York, 1990).

Greene, Graham, *The Quiet American* (London, 2001 [1955]).

Greene, Jack P., "Empire and Identity from the Glorious Revolution to the American Revolution," in Peter Marshall (ed.), *The Oxford History of the British Empire*, vol. II: *The Eighteenth Century* (Oxford, 1998), pp. 208–230.

Grossman, Herschel I., and Juan Mendoza, "Annexation or Conquest? The Economics of Empire Building," *NBER Working Paper*, 8109 (February 2001).

Haass, Richard N., *Intervention: The Use of American Military Force in the Post-Cold War World* (Washington, D.C., 1999).

Hale, David, "The British Empire in Default: Should Newfoundland Be a Role Model for Argentina?," unpublished paper (January 28, 2003).

———, and Lyric Hughes Hale, "China Takes Off," *Foreign Affairs*, 82, 6 (November–December 2003), pp. 36–53.

Hanson, Jim, *The Decline of the American Empire* (Westport, Conn., 1993).

Hassner, Pierre, "The United States: The Empire of Force of the Force of Empire," *Institute for Security Studies of the European Union Chaillot Paper*, 54 (September 2002).

Held, David, *Global Covenant: The Social Democratic Alternative to the Washington Consensus* (Cambridge/Malden, Mass., 2004).

Held, David; Anthony McGrew; David Goldblatt and Jonathan Perraton, *Global Transformations: Politics, Economics and Culture* (Cambridge, 1999).

Herring, George C., *America's Longest War: The United States and Vietnam, 1950–1975* (New York, 1979).

Hitchcock, William I., *The Struggle for Europe: A History of Europe Since 1945* (London, 2003).

Hofstadter, Richard, "Cuba, the Philippines and Manifest Destiny," *The Paranoid Style in American Politics and Other Essays* (New York, 1965), pp. 145–87.

Hoge, Ed. James F., Jr.; and Fareed Zakaria, *The American Encounter: The United States and the Making of the Modern World* (New York, 1997).

Holbrooke, Richard, *To End a War* (New York, 1998).

Horlacher, Friedrich W., "The Language of Late Nineteenth-Century American Expansionism," in Serge Ricard (ed.), *An American Empire: Expansionist Cultures and Policies, 1881–1917* (Aix-en-Provence, 1990), pp. 31–51.

Hudson, Michael, *Super Imperialism: The Origin and Fundamentals of U.S. World Dominance* (New York, 2003).

Huntington, Samuel, *The Clash of Civilizations and the Remaking of World Order* (London, 1999).

———, "The Lonely Superpower," *Foreign Affairs,* 78, 2 (March–April 1999), pp. 35–50.

Ignatieff, Michael, *Virtual War: Kosovo and Beyond* (London, 2000).

———, *Empire Lite: Nation-building in Bosnia, Kosovo and Afghanistan* (London, 2003).

Ikenberry, G. John, *After Victory: Institutions, Strategic Restraint, and the Rebuilding of Order After Major Wars* (Princeton, 2001).

Irwin, Douglas A., "Interpreting the Tariff-Growth Correlation of the Late Nineteenth Century," *NBER Working Paper,* 8739 (January 2002).

James, Harold, *The End of Globalization: Lessons from the Great Depression* (Cambridge, Mass./London, 2001).

Jeffery, Keith, "The Second World War," in Judith Brown and Wm. Roger Louis (eds.), *The Oxford History of the British Empire,* vol. 4: *The Twentieth Century* (Oxford/New York, 1999), pp. 306–28.

Johansson, S. Ryan, "National Size and International Power: A Demographic Perspective on 'Hegemony,'" in Patrick Karl O'Brien and Armand Clesse, (eds.), *Two Hegemonies: Britain 1846–1914 and the United States 1941–2001* (Aldershot/Burlington, Vt., 2002), pp. 336–56.

Johnson, Chalmers, *Blowback: The Costs and Consequences of American Empire* (London, 2000).

Johnson, Paul, "America's New Empire for Liberty," *Hoover Digest,* 4 (2003), pp. 8–13.

Jowitt, Ken, "Rage, Hubris and Regime Change," *Policy Review,* 118 (April and May 2003), pp. 33–43.

Judd, Dennis, *Empire: The British Imperial Experience from 1765 to the Present* (London, 1996).

Judge, Clark S., "Hegemony of the Heart: American Cultural Power and Its Enemies," *Policy Review,* 110 (December 2001–January 2002), pp. 3–15.

Julien, Claude, *America's Empire,* transl. Renaud Bruce (New York, 1971).

Kagan, Robert, *Of Paradise and Power: America and Europe in the New World Order* (New York, 2003).

Kaplan, Amy, and Donald E. Pease, *Cultures of United States Imperialism* (London/ Durham, N.C.,1993).

Kaplan, Lawrence, and William Kristol, *The War over Iraq: Saddam's Tyranny and America's Mission* (San Francisco, 2003).

Kaplan, Robert, *Warrior Politics: Why Leadership Demands a Pagan Ethos* (New York, 2001).

Karnow, Stanley, *Vietnam: A History* (London, 1994).

Kastor, Peter J. (ed.), *The Louisiana Purchase: The Emergence of an American Nation* (Washington, D.C., 2002).

Kedourie, Elie, "The Transition from a British to an American Era in the Middle East," in Haim Shaked and Itamar Rabinovich (eds.), *The Middle East and the United States: Perceptions and Policies* (New Brunswick, N.J., 1980), pp. 3–11.

Kennedy, Paul, *The Rise and Fall of the Great Powers: Economic Change and Military Conflict from 1500 to 2000* (New York, 1989).

Keyssar, Alexander, *The Right to Vote: The Contested History of Democracy in the United States* (New York, 2000).

Kindleberger, Charles, *The World in Depression, 1929–1939* (Berkeley, Calif., 1973).

Kinzer, Stephen, *All the Shah's Men: An American Coup and the Roots of Middle East Terror* (New York, 2003).

Kirk-Greene, Anthony, *On Crown Service: A History of H.M. Colonial and Overseas Civil Services, 1837–1997* (London, 1999).

Kissinger, Henry, "Reflections on American Diplomacy," *Foreign Affairs,* 35, 1 (October 1956), pp. 37–57.

Klein, Michael, "Ways out of Poverty: Diffusing Best Practices and Creating Capabilities," *World Bank, Perspectives on Policies for Poverty Reduction* (January 2003).

Knapp, Wilfrid, "The United States and the Middle East: How Many Special Relationships?," in Haim Shaked and Itamar Rabinovich (eds.), *The Middle East and the United States: Perceptions and Policies* (New Brunswick, N.J., 1980), pp. 11–31.

Knock, Thomas J., *To End All Wars: Woodrow Wilson and the Quest for a New World Order* (New York/Oxford, 1992).

Kolko, Gabriel, *The Roots of American Foreign Policy: An Analysis of Power and Purpose* (Boston, 1969).

———, *The Politics of War: Allied Diplomacy and the World Crisis of 1943–1945* (New York, 1969).

———, *Anatomy of a War: Vietnam, the United States, and the Modern Historical Experience* (New York, 1985).

———, and Joyce Kolko, *The Limits of Power: The World and United States Foreign Policy, 1945–1954* (New York, 1972).

Krasner, Stephen D., *Sovereignty: Organized Hypocrisy* (Princeton, 1999).

———, "Troubled Societies, Outlaw States and Gradations of Sovereignty," unpublished paper, Stanford University Department of Political Science (July 20, 2002).

Krugman, Paul, *The Great Unraveling: Losing Our Way in the New Century* (New York, 2003).

Kupchan, Charles A., *The End of the American Era: U.S. Foreign Policy and the Geopolitics of the Twenty-first Century* (New York, 2002).

Kurth, James, "Migration and the Dynamics of Empire," *National Interest*, 71 (Spring 2003), pp. 5–16.

Kurtz, Stanley, "Democratic Imperialism: A Blueprint," *Policy Review Online*, 118 (April 2003).

La Porta, Rafael; Florencio Lopez-de-Silanes; Andrei Shleifer and Robert W. Vishny, "Law and Finance," *Journal of Political Economy*, 106, 6 (December 1998), pp. 1113–55.

LaFeber, Walter, *The New Empire: An Interpretation of American Expansion, 1860–1898* (Ithaca, N.Y., 1963).

Lal, Deepak, "EMU and Globalisation," *Politeia* (1999).

Landes, David S., *The Wealth and Poverty of Nations* (London, 1998).

Lawson, Nigel, *The View from No. 11: Memoirs of a Tory Radical* (London, 1992).

Layne, Christopher, "America as European Hegemon," *National Interest*, 72 (Summer 2003), pp. 17–31.

Leffler, Melvyn P., "9/11 and the Past and the Future of American Foreign Policy," Harmsworth Inaugural Lecture, Oxford (May 20, 2003).

Lerner, Max, *America as a Civilization* (New York, 1957).

Lewis, Bernard, *What Went Wrong? The Clash Between Islam and Modernity in the Middle East* (New York, 2001).

———, *The Crisis of Islam: Holy War and Unholy Terror* (New York, 2003).

Lieven, Dominic, *Empire: The Russian Empire and Its Rivals* (London, 2000).

Linden, Ian, *A New Map of the World* (London, 2003).

Lindert, Peter, "Voice and Growth: Was Churchill Right?," *Journal of Economic History*, 63, 2 (June 2003), pp. 315–50.

———, and Peter J. Morton, "How Sovereign Debt Has Worked," *University of California—Davis Institute of Governmental Affairs Working Paper* (August 1997).

Liska, George, *Imperial America: The International Politics of Primacy* (Baltimore, 1967).

London, Josh, "The Unlikely Imperialists," *Policy Review Online*, 114 (August-September 2002).

Looney, Robert, "Economic Costs to the United States Stemming from the 9/11 Attacks," Center for Contemporary Conflict, Strategic Insight (August 5, 2002).

Louis, Wm. Roger, *Imperialism at Bay: The United States and the Decolonisation of the British Empire 1941–1945* (New York, 1978).

———, "Introduction," in Robin W. Winks (ed.), *The Oxford History of the British Empire*, vol. 5: *Historiography* (Oxford, 1999), pp. 1–42.

———, and Ronald Robinson, "The Imperialism of Decolonization," *Journal of Imperial and Commonwealth History*, 22, 3 (1994), pp. 462–511.

Lowenthal, Abraham F., *Partners in Conflict: The United States and Latin America* (Baltimore, 1987).

Lucas, Robert, "Why Doesn't Capital Flow from Rich to Poor Countries?," *American Economic Review*, 80 (1990), pp. 93–96.

Lundestad, Geir, *The American "Empire" and Other Studies of US Foreign Policy in a Comparative Perspective* (Oxford, 1990).

McAlpin, Michelle Burge, *Subject to Famine: Food Crises and Economic Change in Western India, 1860–1920* (Princeton, 1983).

McArthur, John W., and Jeffrey D. Sachs, "Institutions and Geography: Comment on Acemoglu, Johnson and Robinson," *NBER Working Paper*, 8114 (February 2001).

McCauley, Robert N., and William R. White, "The Euro and European Financial Markets," *B.I.S. Working Paper* (May 1997).

McCormick, John, *Understanding the European Union: A Concise Introduction* (London, 1999).

McCullough, David, *Truman* (New York, 1992).

MacDonald, James, *A Free Nation Deep in Debt: The Financial Roots of Democracy* (New York, 2003).

Machonochie, Sir Evan, *Life in the Indian Civil Service* (London, 1926).

McKinnon, Ronald, and Gunther Schnabl, "China: A Stabilizing or Deflationary Influence in East Asia? The Problem of Conflicted Virtue?," *Stanford University Economics Department Working Paper* (August 2003).

————, and ————, "A Return to Exchange Rate Stability in East Asia? Mitigating Conflicted Virtue," *Stanford University Economics Department Working Paper* (October 13, 2003).

McMahon, Robert J., *The Limits of Empire: The United States and Southeast Asia Since World War II* (New York, 1999).

Maddison, Angus, *The World Economy: A Millennial Perspective* (Paris, 2001).

Magdoff, Harry, *The Age of Imperialism: The Economics of United States Foreign Policy* (New York, 1969).

Maier, Charles S., "An American Empire? Implications for Democracy, Order and Disorder in World Politics," unpublished paper, Harvard University (March 2003).

————, *Among Empires: American Ascendancy and Its Predecessors* (forthcoming).

Malkasian, Carter, *The Korean War 1950–1953* (Chicago, 2001).

Mallaby, Sebastian, "The Reluctant Imperialist: Terrorism, Failed States, and the Case for American Empire," *Foreign Affairs,* 81, 2 (March–April 2002), pp. 2–8.

Mandelbaum, Michael, *The Ideas That Conquered the World: Peace, Democracy, and Free Markets in the Twenty-first Century* (New York, 2002).

Marshall, Peter, *Demanding the Impossible: A History of Anarchism* (London, 1992).

Matthew, H. C. G., *Gladstone,* vol. 2: *1875–1898* (Oxford, 1995).

Matthews, Jessica Tuchman, "Now for the Hard Part," *Foreign Policy* (July 2003), p. 51.

May, Ernest R., *American Imperialism: A Speculative Essay* (Chicago, 1991 [1968]).

Mead, Walter Russell, *Special Providence: American Foreign Policy and How It Changed the World* (New York, 2001).

Mearsheimer, John J., *The Tragedy of Great Power Politics* (New York/London, 2001).

Medeiros, Evan S., and M. Taylor Fravel, "China's New Diplomacy," *Foreign Affairs,* 82, 6 (November–December 2003), pp. 22–35.

Melosi, Martin V., *The Shadow of Pearl Harbor: Political Controversy over the Surprise Attack, 1941–1946* (London, 1977).

Melville, Herman, *Moby Dick* (London, 1900).

Merk, Frederick, *Manifest Destiny and the Mission in American History: A Reinterpretation* (New York, 1963).

Micklethwait, John, and Adrian Wooldridge, *A Future Perfect: The Challenge and Hidden Promise of Globalisation* (London, 2000).

Milner, Clyde A.; Carol A. O'Connor and Martha A. Sandweiss (eds.), *The Oxford History of the American West* (Oxford, 1994).

Milward, Alan S., *The European Rescue of the Nation-State,* 2nd ed. (London, 2000).

Mitchell, B. R., *International Historical Statistics: The Americas, 1750–1993* (London, 1998).

———, *International Historical Statistics: Africa, Asia, Oceania, 1750–1993* (London, 1998).

Moggridge, Donald (ed.), *The Collected Writings of John Maynard Keynes,* vol. 19, *Part 1: Activities 1922–1929, The Return to Gold and Industrial Policy* (London, 1981).

Morris, Edmund, *Theodore Rex* (London, 2001).

Morris, James, *Pax Britannica: The Climax of an Empire* (London, 1992 [1968]).

Morris, Richard B., *Encyclopedia of American History,* 6th ed. (New York, 1982).

Mosier, John, *The Myth of the Great War: A New Military History of World War One* (London, 2001).

Moskin, J. Robert, *The U.S. Marine Corps Story* (New York, 1977).

Mueller, John E., *War, Presidents and Public Opinion* (New York, 1973).

Nearing, Scott, *The American Empire* (New York, 1921).

Nordhaus, William D., "Iraq: The Economic Consequences of War," *New York Review of Books,* 49, 19 (December 5, 2002).

North, Douglass C., and Barry R. Weingast, "Constitutions and Commitment: The Evolution of Institutions Governing Public Choice in Seventeenth-Century England," *Journal of Economic History,* 64, 4 (1989), pp. 803–32.

Nye, John Vincent, "The Myth of Free-Trade Britain and Fortress France: Tariffs and Trade in the Nineteenth Century," *Journal of Economic History,* 51, 1 (March 1991), pp. 23–46.

Nye, Joseph S., Jr., *The Paradox of American Power: Why the World's Only Superpower Can't Go It Alone* (Oxford/New York, 2002).

O'Brien, Patrick Karl, "The Pax Britannica and American Hegemony: Precedent, Antecedent or Just Another History?," in idem and Armand Clesse (ed.), *Two Hegemonies: Britain 1846–1914 and the United States 1941–2001* (Aldershot/Burlington Vt., 2002), pp. 3–64.

———, "The Governance of Globalization: The Political Economy of Anglo-American Hegemony," *CESifo Working Paper,* 1023 (September 2003).

———, and Armand Clesse (eds.), *Two Hegemonies: Britain 1846–1914 and the United States 1941–2001* (Aldershot/Burlington Vt., 2002).

O'Hanlon, Michael, "Come Partly Home, America: How to Downsize U.S. Deployments Abroad," *Foreign Affairs,* 80, 2 (March–April 2001), pp. 2–9.

O'Rourke, Kevin H., and Jeffrey G. Williamson, *Globalization and History: The Evolution of a Nineteenth-Century Atlantic Economy* (Cambridge, Mass./London, 1999).

———, and ———, "When Did Globalization Begin?," *NBER Working Paper,* 7632 (April 2000).

Obstfeld, Maurice, and Alan M. Taylor, "Globalization and Capital Markets," *NBER Working Paper,* 8846 (March 2002).

———, and ———, "Sovereign Risk, Credibility and the Gold Standard: 1870–1913 versus 1925–31," *NBER Working Paper,* 9345 (November 2002).

———, and ———, "Globalization and Capital Markets," in Michael D. Bordo, Alan M. Taylor and Jeffrey G. Williamson (eds.), *Globalization in Historical Perspective* (Chicago, 2003), pp. 121–83.

Oppen, Beate Ruhm von (ed.), *Documents on Germany Under Occupation, 1945–1954* (London, 1955).

Osterhammel, Jürgen, "Britain and China, 1842–1914," in Andrew Porter (ed.), *The Oxford History of the British Empire,* vol. 3: *The Nineteenth Century* (Oxford/New York, 1999), pp. 146–69.

———, "China," in Judith Brown and Wm. Roger Louis (eds.), *The Oxford History of the British Empire,* vol. 4: *The Twentieth Century* (Oxford/New York, 1999), pp. 643–66.

Pagden, Anthony, "The Struggle for Legitimacy and the Image of the Empire in the Atlantic to c. 1700," in Nicholas Canny (ed.), *The Oxford History of the British Empire,* vol. 1: *British Overseas Enterprise to the Close of the Seventeenth Century* (Oxford, 1998), pp. 34–54.

Palmer, General Bruce, Jr., *The Twenty-five Year War: America's Military Role in Vietnam* (Lexington, Ky., 1984).

Pei, Minxin, "Lessons of the Past," *Foreign Policy* (July 2003), pp. 52–55.

Peterson, Edward N., "The Occupation as Perceived by the Public, Scholars, and Policy Makers," in Robert Wolfe (ed.), *Americans as Proconsuls: United States*

Military Government in Germany and Japan, 1944–1952 (Carbondale, Ill., 1984), pp. 416–25.

Peterson Peter G., *Running on Empty: How the Democratic and Republican Parties Are Bankrupting Our Future and What Americans Can Do About It* (New York, 2004).

Pettiford, Lloyd, and David Harding, *Terrorism: The New World War* (London, 2003).

Pfaff, William, "A New Colonialism?," *Foreign Affairs*, 74, 1 (1995), pp. 2–6.

Pigman, Geoffrey Allen, "Hegemony Theory, Unilateral Trade Liberalisation and the 1996 US Farm Bill," in Patrick Karl O'Brien and Armand Clesse (eds.), *Two Hegemonies: Britain 1846–1914 and the United States 1941–2001* (Aldershot/Burlington Vt., 2002), pp. 258–83.

Platt, D. C. M., *Finance, Trade, and Politics in British Foreign Policy 1815–1914* (Oxford, 1968).

Pollack, Kenneth, *The Threatening Storm* (New York, 2002).

Pomeranz, Kenneth, *The Great Divergence: China, Europe and the Making of the Modern World Economy* (Princeton/Oxford, 2000).

Porch, Douglas, "Occupational Hazards: Myths of 1945 and U.S. Iraq Policy," *National Interest*, 71 (Summer 2003), pp. 35–48.

Porter A. N. (ed.), *Atlas of British Overseas Expansion* (London, 1991).

Posen, Adam, "Frog in the Pot," *National Interest*, 71 (Spring 2003) pp. 105–17.

Potter, David C., *India's Political Administrators, 1919–1983* (Oxford, 1986).

Power, Samantha, *"A Problem from Hell": America and the Age of Genocide* (London, 2003).

Pratt, Julius W., *America's Colonial Experiment: How the U.S. Gained, Governed and in Part Gave Away a Colonial Empire* (New York, 1950).

Prestowitz, Clyde, *Rogue Nation* (New York, 2003).

Priest, Dana, *The Mission: Waging War and Keeping Peace with America's Military* (New York, 2003).

Pritchett, Lant, "Divergence, Big Time," *Journal of Economic Perspectives*, 11, 3 (Summer 1997), pp. 3–17.

Pulzer, Peter, *German Politics, 1945–1995* (Oxford, 1995).

Purvis, Thomas L., *A Dictionary of American History* (Oxford, 1995).

Ramsay, David, *Lusitania: Saga and Myth* (London, 2001).

Ranke, Leopold von, "The Great Powers," in T. H. von Laue (ed.), *Leopold Ranke* (Princeton, 1950), pp. 181–228.

Rauchway, Eric, *Murdering McKinley: The Making of Theodore Roosevelt's America* (New York, 2003).

————, "Competitive Imperialism: British and American Tutelage and the Open Door," panel contribution, "Empire as Education: British and American Teaching in the World," American Historical Association Annual Meeting (January 9, 1998).

Ravenal, Earl C., "The Strategic Lessons of Vietnam," in Anthony Lake (ed.), *The Legacy of Vietnam: The War, American Society and Future American Foreign Policy* (New York, 1976), pp. 256–77.

————, *Never Again: Learning from America's Foreign Policy Failures* (Philadelphia, 1978).

————, Robert Komer; Ithiel Pool and Robert Pfaltzgraff, "Was Failure Inevitable? Some Concluding Perspectives," in W. Scott Thompson and Donald D. Frizzell (eds.), *The Lessons of Vietnam* (London, 1977), pp. 263–81.

Raychaudhuri, Tapan, "British Rule in India: An Assessment," in P. J. Marshall (ed.), *The Cambridge Illustrated History of the British Empire* (Cambridge, 1996), pp. 357–69.

Reich, Bernard, "United States Interests in the Middle East," in Haim Shaked and Itamar Rabinovich (eds.), *The Middle East and the United States: Perceptions and Policies* (New Brunswick, N.J., 1980), pp. 53–93.

————, "The United States and Israel: The Nature of the Special Relationship," in David W Lesch (ed.), *The Middle East and the United States: A Historial and Political Reassessment* (Oxford, 1999), pp. 227–44.

Reinstein, Jacques J., "Reparations, Economic Reform, and Reconstruction," in Robert Wolfe (ed.), *Americans as Proconsuls: United States Military Government in Germany and Japan, 1944–1952* (London, 1984), pp. 135–55.

Richardson, Rupert Norval; Ernest Wallace and Adrian N. Anderson, *Texas: The Lone Star State* (Englewood Cliffs, N.J., 1981).

Rigobon, Roberto, and Brian Sack, "The Effects of War Risk on US Financial Markets," *NBER Working Paper,* 9609 (April 2003).

Robert D. Craig, *Historical Dictionary of Honolulu and Hawaii* (Lanham, Md., 1998).

Roberts, Andrew, *Salisbury: Victorian Titan* (London, 1999).

Robinson, Joan, *Economic Philosophy* (London, 1962).

Rodrik, Dani, "Feasible Globalizations," unpublished paper, Harvard University (2003).

Rosecrance, Richard, "Objectives of U.S. Middle East Policy," in Haim Shaked and Itamar Rabinovich (eds.), *The Middle East and the United States: Perceptions and Policies* (New Brunswick, N.J., 1980), pp. 31–53.

———, "Croesus and Caesar: The Essential Transatlantic Symbiosis," *National Interest,* 72 (Summer 2003), pp. 31–35.

Rosen, Stephen Peter, "An Empire, If You Can Keep It," *National Interest,* 71 (Spring 2003), pp. 51–61.

Roskin, Michael, "From Pearl Harbor to Vietnam: Shifting Generational Paradigms and Foreign Policy," *Political Science Quarterly,* 89 (1974), pp. 563–88.

Roy, Tirthankar, *The Economic History of India, 1857–1947* (Delhi, 2000).

Rubin, Barnett R.; Humayun Hamidzada and Abby Stoddard, "Through the Fog of Peace Building: Evaluating the Reconstruction of Afghanistan," *Center on International Cooperation Policy Paper* (June 2003).

Runge, C. Ford, "Agrivation: The Farm Bill from Hell," *National Interest,* 72 (Summer 2003), pp. 85–94.

Russ, William Adam, Jr., *The Hawaii Republic (1894–1898) and Its Struggle to Win Annexation* (London, 1992).

Sachs, Jeffrey D., "Tropical Underdevelopment," *NBER Working Paper,* 8119 (2001).

———, and Andrew M. Warner, "Economic Reform and the Process of Global Integration," *Brookings Papers on Economic Activity,* 1 (1995), pp. 1–118.

———, and ———, "Fundamental Sources of Long-Run Growth," *American Economic Review,* 87, 2 (1997), pp. 184–88.

Schiller, Herbert, *Mass Communications and the American Empire* (Oxford, 1992).

Schirmer, Daniel B., "U.S. Bases in Central America and the Opposition to Them," unpublished paper presented at "Crossroads 1991," an international conference on U.S. bases, Manila, Philippines (May 14, 1990).

Schlauch, Wolfgang, "American Policy Towards Germany, 1945," *Journal of Contemporary History,* 5, 4 (1970), pp. 113–28.

Schlesinger, Stephen C., *Act of Creation: The Founding of the United Nations: A Story of Superpowers, Secret Agents, Wartime Allies and Enemies, and Their Quest for a Peaceful World* (Boulder, Colo., 2003).

Schmidt, Hans, *Maverick Marine: General Smedley D. Butler and the Contradictions of American Military History* (Lexington, Ky., 1987).

Schularick, Moritz, "Development Finance in Two Eras of Financial Globalization, (1890–1914 vs. 1990–2000)," draft chapter, Free University, Berlin (2003).

Schwabe, Klaus, "The Global Role of the United States and Its Imperial Consequences, 1898–1973," in Wolfgang J. Mommsen and Jürgen Osterhammel (eds.), *Imperialism and After: Continuities and Discontinuities* (London, 1986), pp. 13–33.

Seeley, J. R., *The Expansion of England: Two Courses of Lectures* (London, 1899 [1883]).

Shannon, Richard, *Gladstone: Heroic Minister, 1865–1898* (London, 1999).

Shawcross, William, *Deliver Us from Evil: Warlords and Peacekeepers in a World of Endless Conflict* (London, 2000).

Shiller, Robert J., *Irrational Exuberance* (Princeton, 2000).

Siedentop, Larry, *Democracy in Europe* (London, 2000).

Simes, Dimitri K., "America's Imperial Dilemma," *Foreign Affairs,* 82, 6 (November–December 2003), pp. 91–102.

Simms, Brendan, *Unfinest Hour: Britain and the Destruction of Bosnia* (London, 2001).

Siracusa, Joseph, "Lessons of Vietnam and the Future of American Foreign Policy," *Australian Outlook,* 30 (August 1976), pp. 227–37.

Smith, Jean Edward (ed.), *The Papers of General Lucius D. Clay: Germany, 1945–1949* (Bloomington, Ind., 1974).

Smith, Neil, *American Empire: Roosevelt's Geographer and the Prelude to Globalization* (Berkeley, Calif., 2003).

Smith, Peter H., *Talons of the Eagle: Dynamics of U.S.–Latin American Relations* (Oxford, 2000).

Smith, Robert Freeman, "Latin America, the United States and the European Powers, 1830–1930," in Leslie Bethell (ed.), *The Cambridge History of Latin America,* vol. 4 (Cambridge, 1986), pp. 83–121.

Smith, Rogers M., *Civic Ideals: Conflicting Visions of Citizenship in U.S. History* (New Haven, 1997).

Snyder, Jack, "Imperial Temptations," *National Interest,* 71 (Spring 2003), pp. 29–40.

Spanier, John W., *The Truman-MacArthur Controversy and the Korean War* (Cambridge, Mass., 1959).

Steel, Ronald, *Pax Americana* (New York, 1967).

Stoll, David, *Is Latin America Turning Protestant? Studies in the Politics of Evangelical Growth* (Berkeley, Calif., 1990).

Stone, Irving, *The Global Export of Capital from Great Britain, 1865–1914* (London, 1999).

Stueck, William, *The Korean War: An International History* (Princeton, 1995).

Summers, Colonel Harry G., *On Strategy: A Critical Analysis of the Vietnam War* (Novato, Calif., 1982).

Suskind, Ron, *The Price of Loyalty: George W. Bush, the White House, and the Education of Paul O'Neill* (New York, 2004).

Swomley, John M., Jr., *American Empire: The Political Ethics of Twentieth Century Conquest* (New York, 1970).

Sylla, Richard, "Shaping the US Financial System, 1690–1913: The Dominant Role of Public Finance," in idem, Richard Tilly and Gabriel Tortella (eds.), *The States, the Financial System and Economic Modernization* (Cambridge, 1999), pp. 249–70.

Symonds, Richard, *Oxford and Empire* (Oxford, 1986).

Taylor, Alan M., "Globalization, Trade and Development: Some Lessons from History," *NBER Working Paper,* 9326 (November 2002).

Tesar, Linda, and Ingrid Werner, "The Internationalization of Securities Markets Since the 1987 Crash," in R. Litan and A. Santomero (eds.), *Brookings-Wharton Papers on Financial Services* (Washington, D.C., 1998).

Tinker, Hugh, *A New System of Slavery: The Export of Indian Labour Overseas, 1830–1920* (London/New York/Bombay, 1974).

Todd, Emmanuel, *Après l'Empire: Essai sur la décomposition du système américain* (Paris, 2002).

Tower, John G., "Foreign Policy for the Seventies," in Anthony Lake, *The Legacy of Vietnam: The War, American Society and Future American Foreign Policy* (New York, 1976), pp. 242–55.

Townsend, Mary Evelyn, *European Colonial Expansion Since 1871* (Chicago, 1941).

Trefler, Daniel, "The Case of the Missing Trade and Other Mysteries," *American Economic Review,* 85, 5 (December 1995), pp. 1029–46.

Truman, Harry S., *Years of Trial and Hope, 1940–1953* (New York, 1956).

Tucker, Robert W., and David C. Hendrickson, *The Imperial Temptation: The New World Order and America's Purpose* (New York City, 1992).

United States Bureau of the Census, *Historical Statistics of the United States: Colonial Times to 1970* (Washington, D.C, 1975).

Vidal, Gore, *The Decline and Fall of the American Empire* (Berkeley, Calif., 1992).

Vonnegut, Kurt, *Slaughterhouse 5* (London, 2000 [1969]).

Wallerstein, Immanuel, "Three Hegemonies," in Patrick Karl O'Brien and Armand Clesse (eds.), *Two Hegemonies: Britain 1846–1914 and the United States 1941–2001* (Aldershot/Burlington, Vt., 2002), pp. 357–61.

Washbrook, David, "South Asia, the World System, and World Capitalism," *Journal of Asian Studies,* 49, 3 (August 1990), pp. 479–508.

Webb, Stephen B., "Fiscal News and Inflationary Expectations in Germany After World War I," *Journal of Economic History,* 46, 3 (1986), pp. 769–94.

Williams, William Appleman, *The Tragedy of American Diplomacy* (Cleveland, 1959).

———, *Empire as a Way of Life: An Essay on the Causes and Character of America's Present Predicament Along with a Few Thoughts About an Alternative* (New York, 1980).

Williamson, Jeffrey G., "Globalization, Convergence and History," *Journal of Economic History,* 56, 2 (1996), pp. 277–310.

———, "Land, Labor and Globalization in the Pre-Industrial Third World," *NBER Working Paper,* 7784 (July 2000).

———, "Winners and Losers over Two Centuries of Globalization," *NBER Working Paper,* 9161 (September 2002).

Willoughby, Major General Charles A., and John Chamberlain, *MacArthur, 1941–1951* (New York, 1954).

Windschuttle, Keith, "Lengthened Shadows, 1: The Burdens of Empire," *New Criterion,* 22, 1 (September 2003), pp. 4–15.

Wittner, Lawrence S. (ed.), *MacArthur* (Englewood Cliffs, N.J., 1971).

Wolfe, Robert, *Americans as Proconsuls: United States Military Government in Germany and Japan, 1944–1952* (Carbondale, Ill., 1984).

Wolfe, Thomas, *Look Homeward, Angel: A Story of the Buried Life* (New York, 1970 [1929]).

Woodward, Bob, *Bush at War* (New York/London, 2002).

———, *Plan of Attack* (New York/London).

Yergin, Daniel, *The Prize: The Epic Quest for Oil, Money and Power* (New York/London, 1991).

Zakaria, Fareed, *The Future of Freedom: Illiberal Democracy at Home and Abroad* (New York, 2003).

Zelikow, Philip, "The Transformation of National Security: Five Redefinitions," *National Interest,* 71 (Spring 2003), pp. 17–28.

Zieger, Robert H., *America's Great War: World War I and the American Experience* (Lanham, Md./Boulder, Colo./New York/Oxford, 2000).

Zimmermann, Warren, *First Great Triumph: How Five Americans Made Their Country a World Power* (New York, 2003).

Zwick, Jim, "Mark Twain's Anti-Imperialist Writings in the 'American Century,'" in Angel Velasco Shaw and Luis H. Francia (eds.), *Vestiges of War: The Philippine-American War and the Aftermath of an Imperial Dream, 1899–1999* (New York, 2002), pp. 38–56.

INDEX